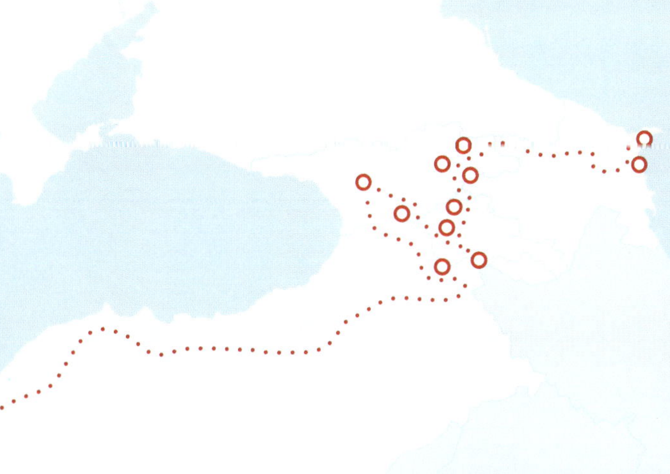

SURPRISING
EUROPE

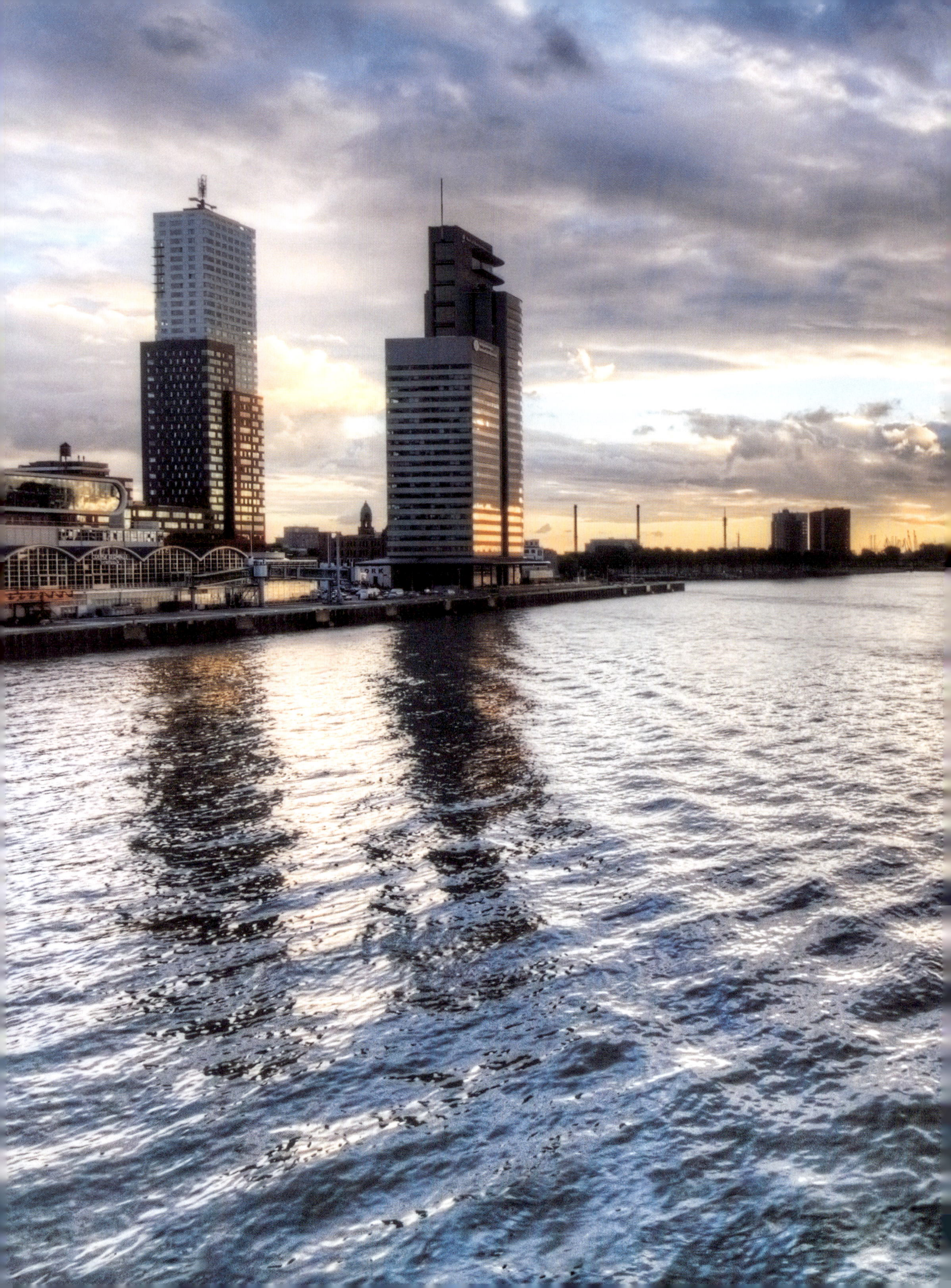

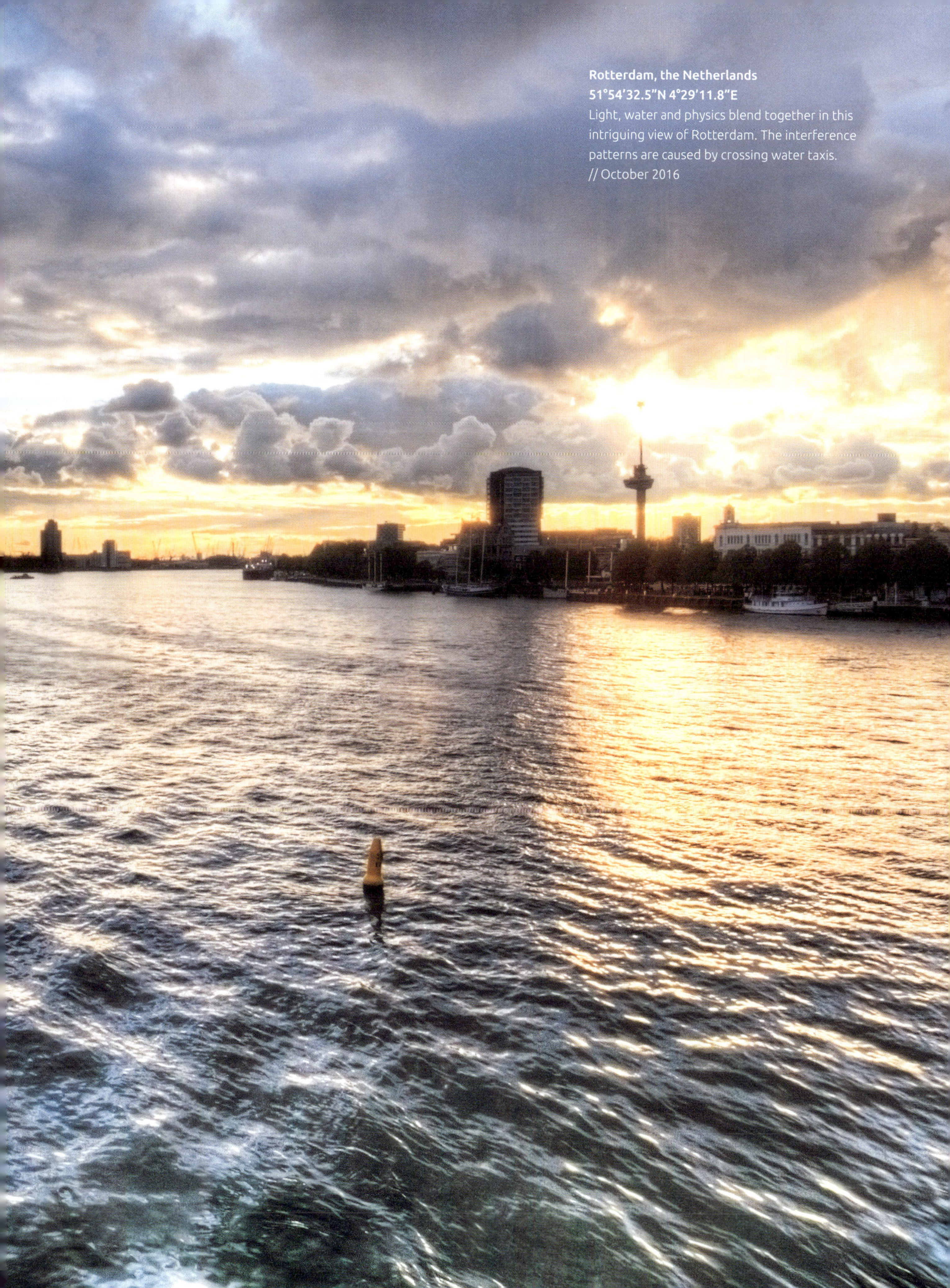

Rotterdam, the Netherlands
51°54'32.5"N 4°29'11.8"E
Light, water and physics blend together in this
intriguing view of Rotterdam. The interference
patterns are caused by crossing water taxis.
// October 2016

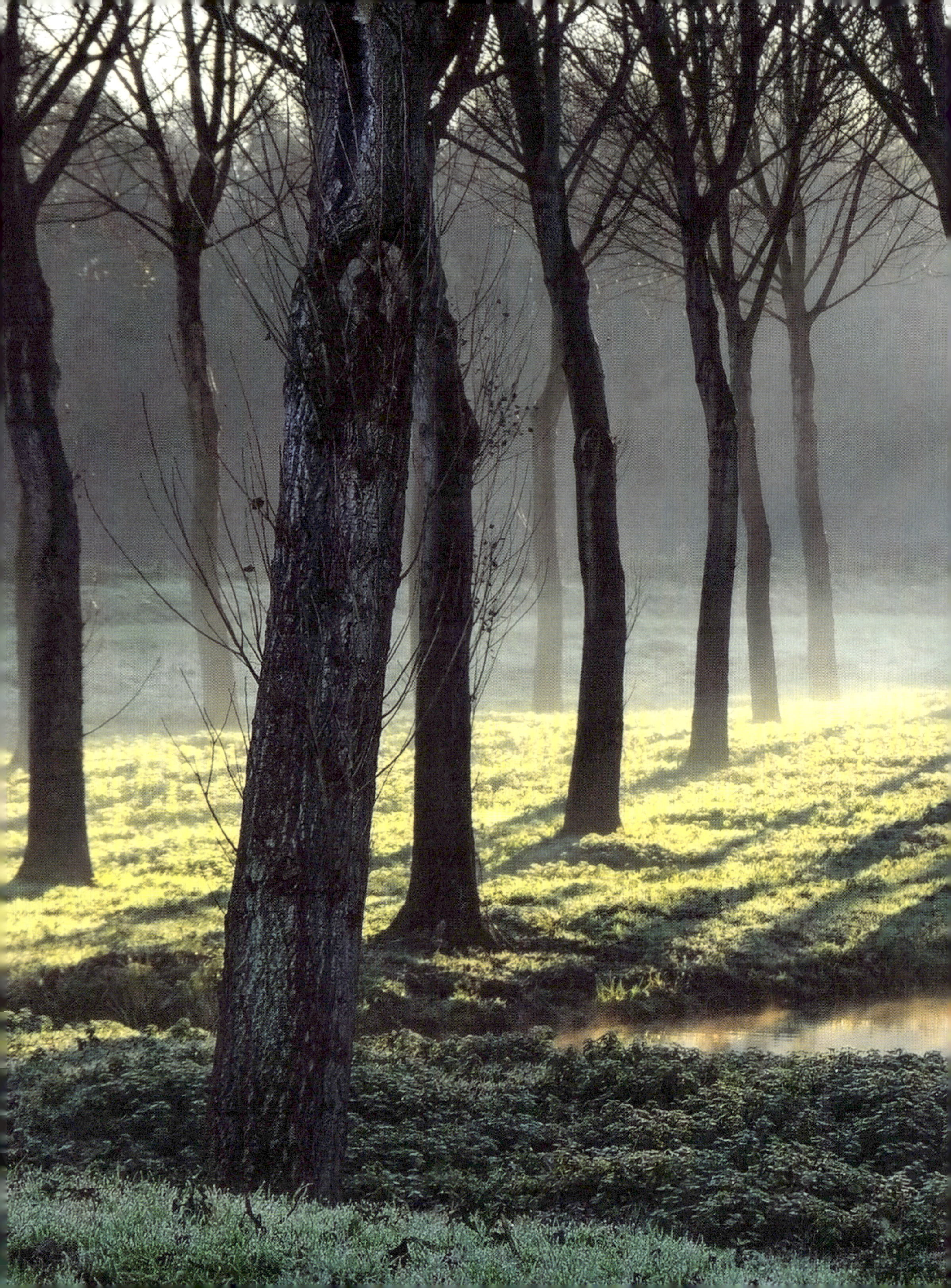

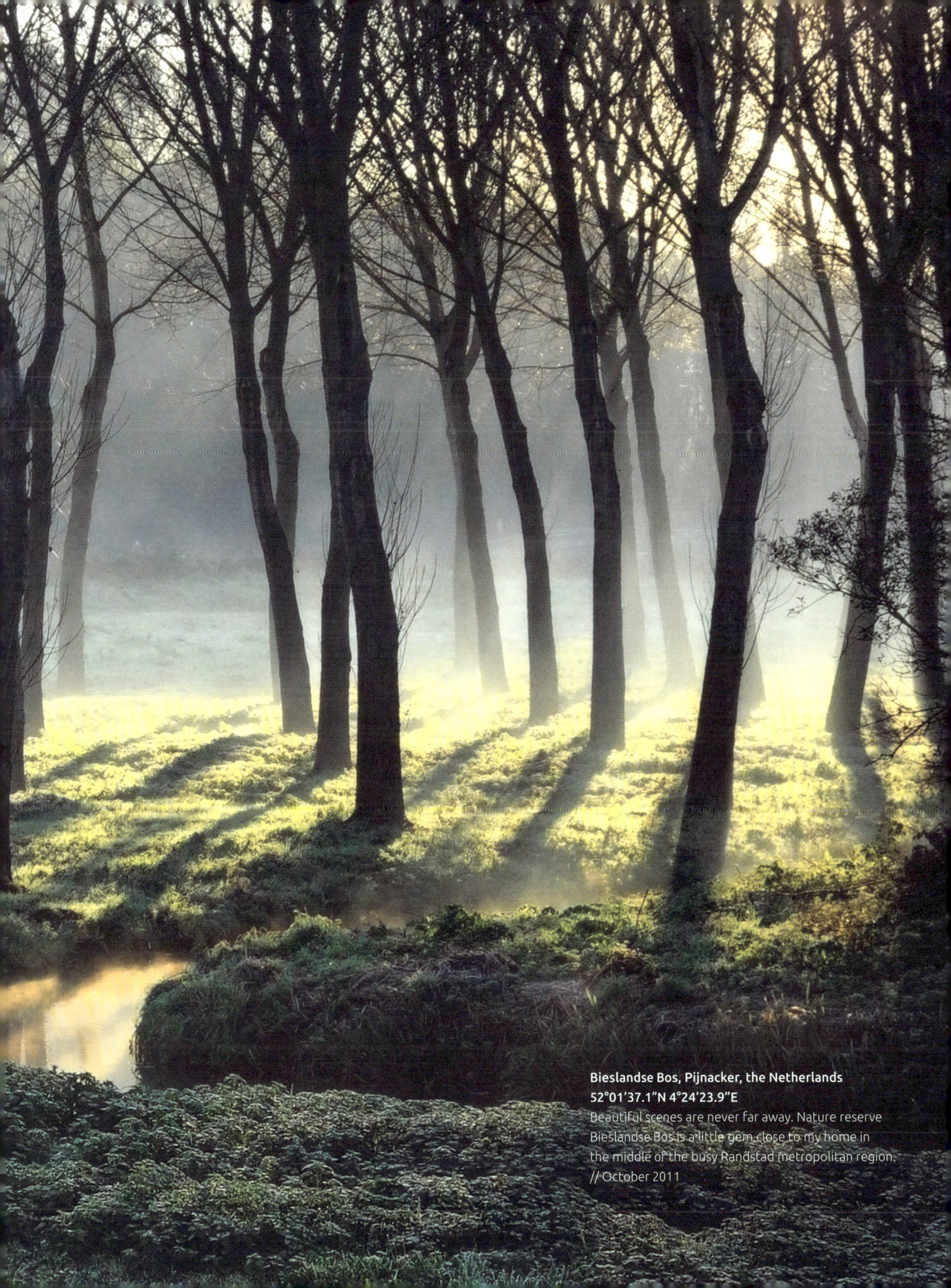

Bieslandse Bos, Pijnacker, the Netherlands
52°01'37.1"N 4°24'23.9"E
Beautiful scenes are never far away. Nature reserve
Bieslandse Bos is a little gem close to my home in
the middle of the busy Randstad metropolitan region.
// October 2011

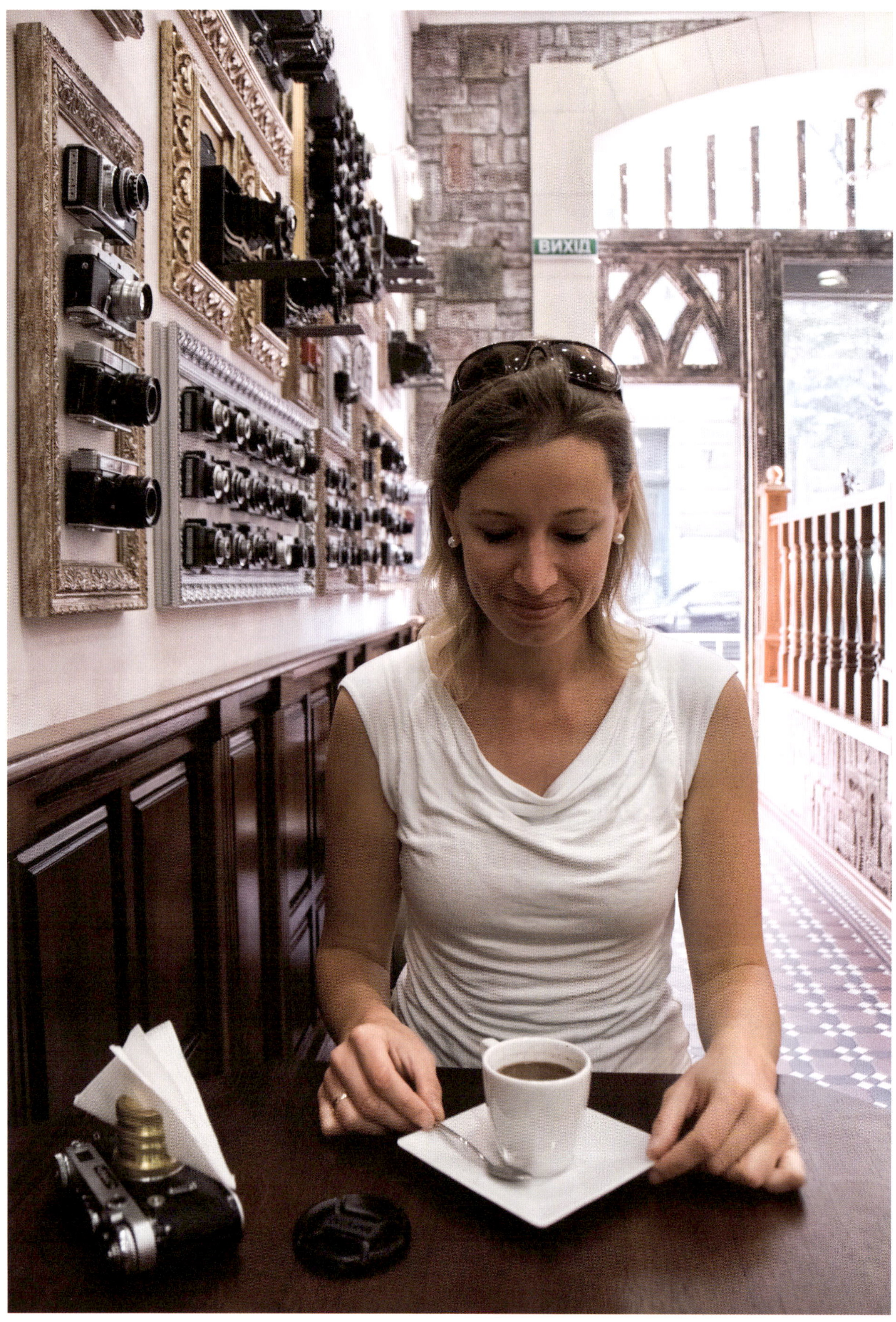
ВИХІД

Sabine de Milliano

SURPRISING
EUROPE

A Photographic Journey

TERRA

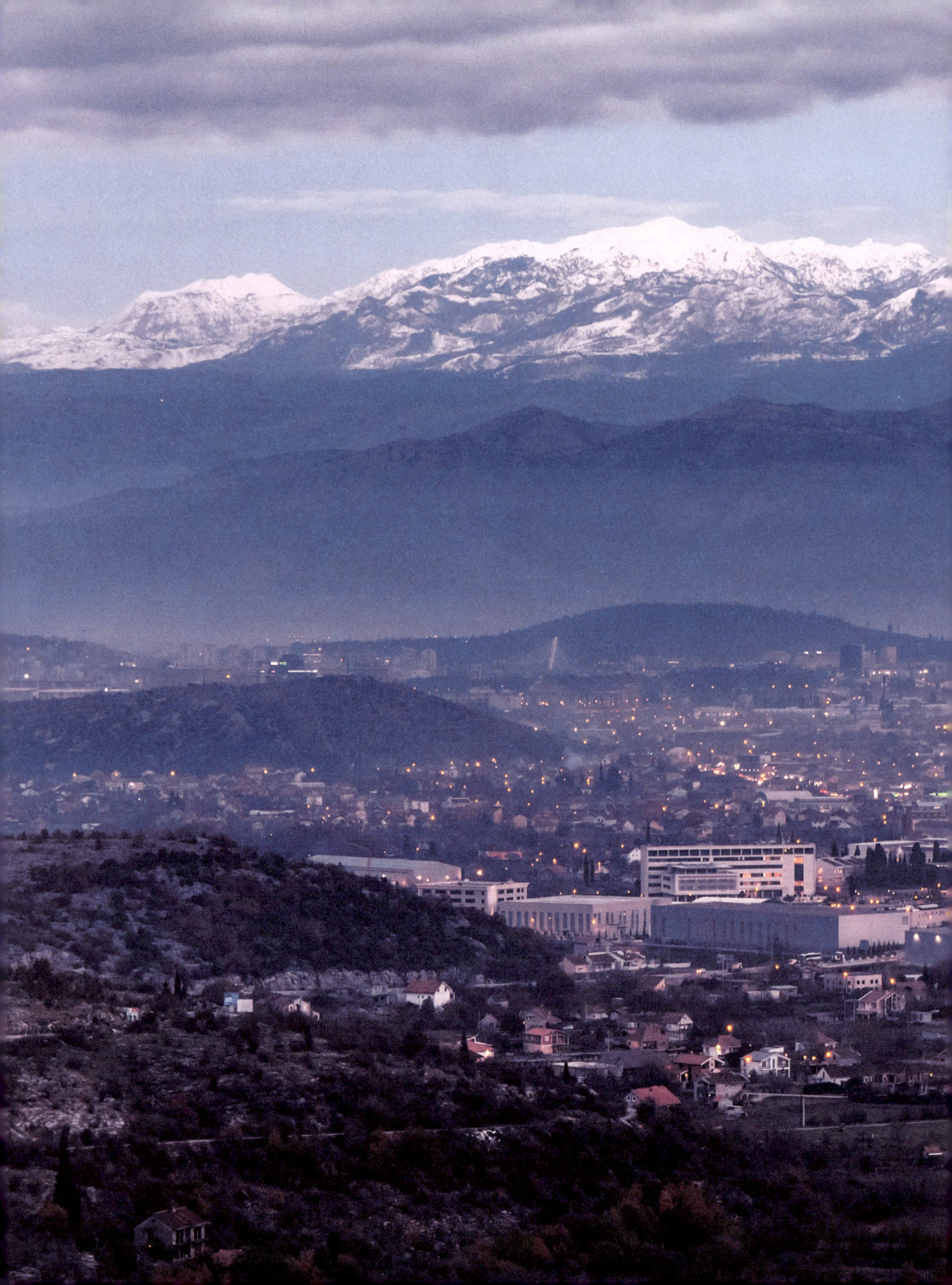

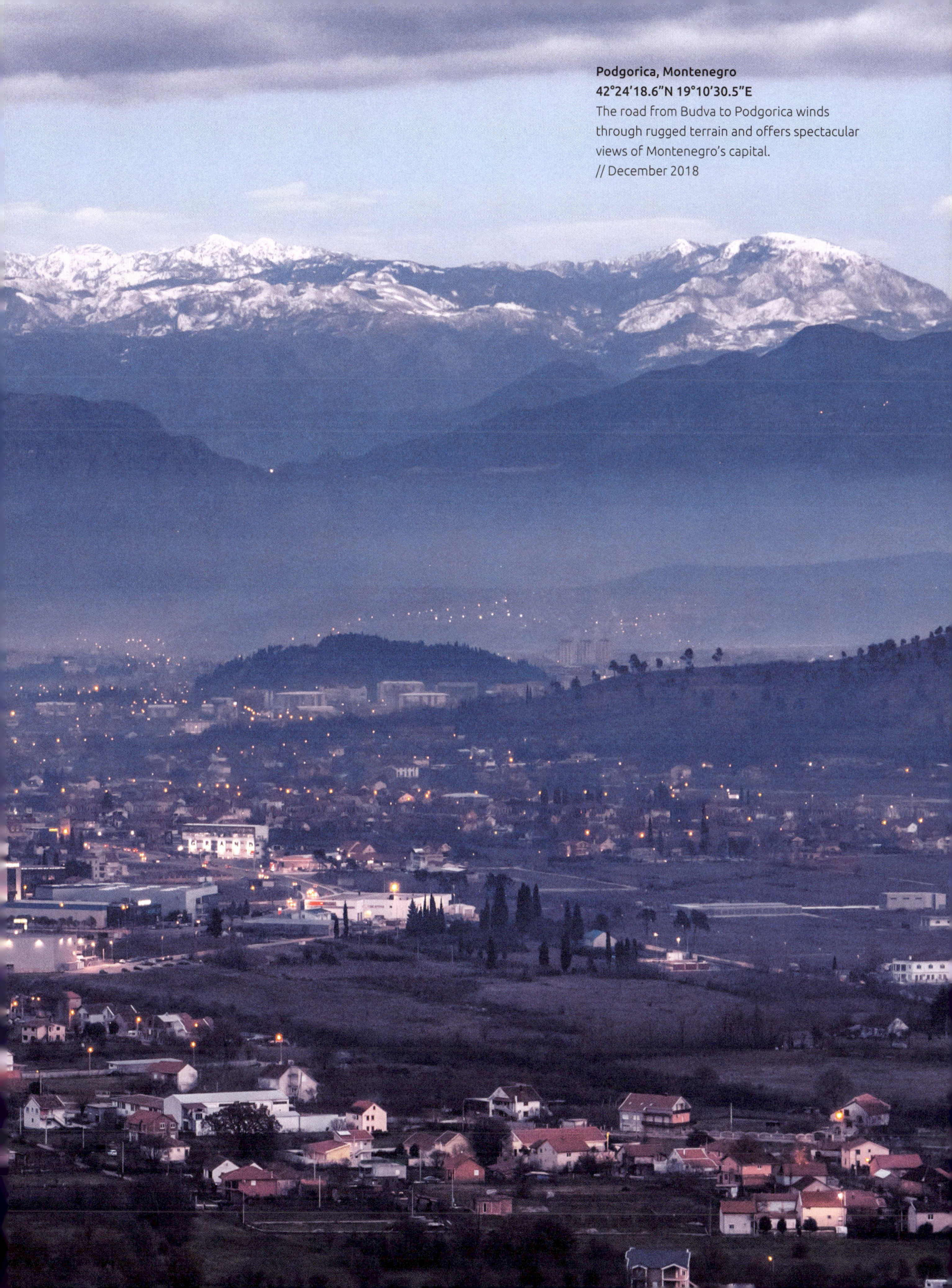

Podgorica, Montenegro
42°24'18.6"N 19°10'30.5"E
The road from Budva to Podgorica winds
through rugged terrain and offers spectacular
views of Montenegro's capital.
// December 2018

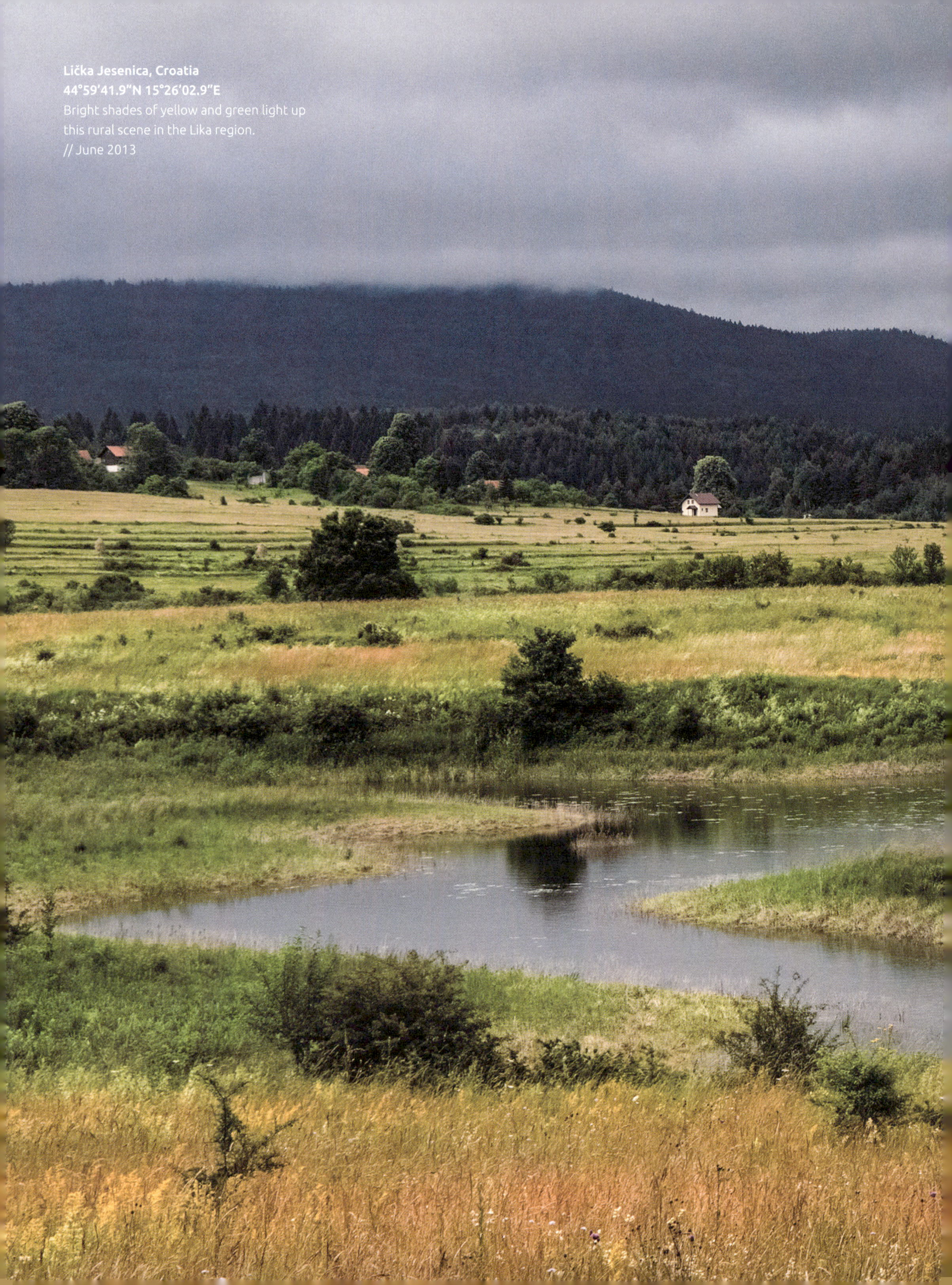

Lička Jesenica, Croatia
44°59'41.9"N 15°26'02.9"E
Bright shades of yellow and green light up
this rural scene in the Lika region.
// June 2013

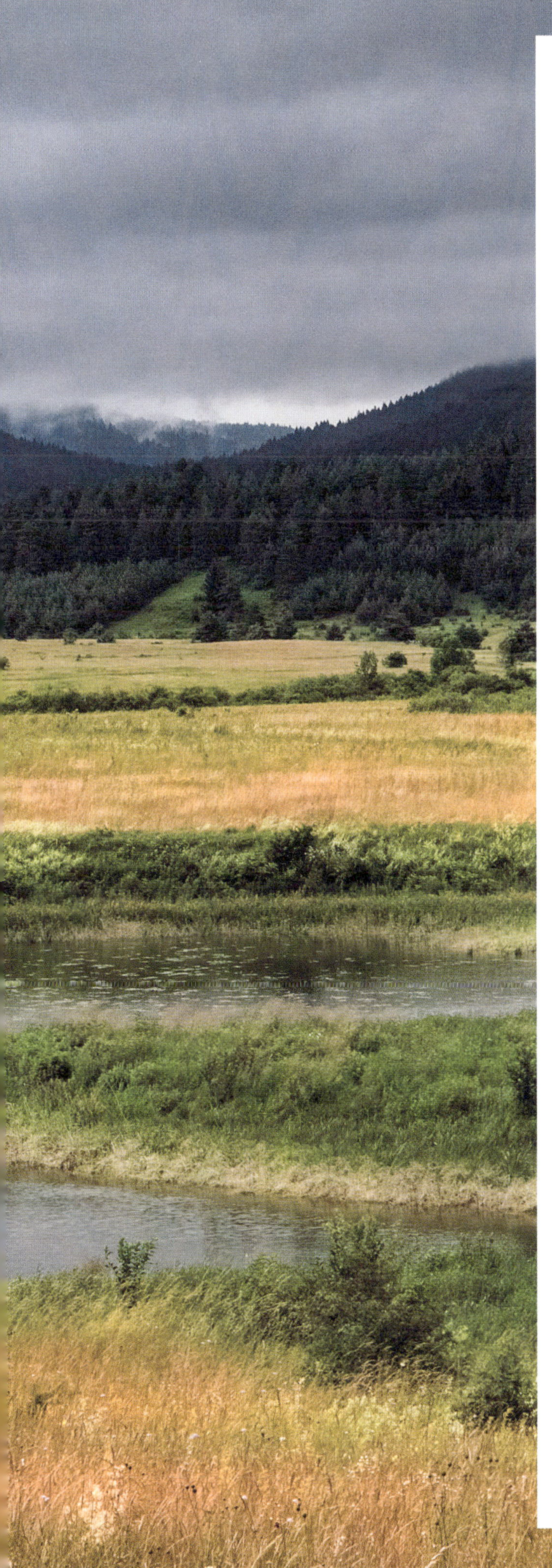

Contents

Foreword
Bart Heirweg

ALMOST A CENTURY AGO, the famous French author Marcel Proust wrote: "The real voyage of discovery consists not in seeking new landscapes, but in having new eyes." A thought which comes to you almost spontaneously when you look at Sabine de Milliano's work. Nowadays, it seems everyone is a photographer, but only a true photographer will make you look at the world differently.

In order to achieve that, the photographer needs to show you that world in a way the average reader only seldom sees it. *Surprising Europe* encompasses a broad spectrum of locations, both well-known and little-known. An impressive variety of nature and culture, landscapes and city environments. With hardly ever a human being in sight. A decision that I also consciously make as a landscape photographer. Almost as if we both subconsciously believe that our planet is even more glorious without our human presence.

Contrary to my fascination with morning's first light, Sabine often shows her destinations in the evening. In a game of light and colour, that transforms every picture into a fascinating story. A moment in time, captured on film.

'Every image confirms the astounding beauty of this old continent and shows how resplendent it is, in spite of the dense population in many areas.'

But the viewer is also instantly aware of the time that has led to these images: the meticulous scouting, preparation and above all, the long wait for that one, perfect moment when all elements come together.

With success, because this book shows Europe at its best: from the Netherlands to Albania or Azerbaijan. Every image confirms the astounding beauty of this old continent and shows how resplendent it is, in spite of the dense population in many areas. The wide-angle lens with which Sabine captures the landscape, increases that spacious effect. The fact that the human being is almost invisible in her work, almost seems a logical result of her approach.

In the end, you should read this work as an invitation – an invitation to travel even more yourself and to embrace the unknown. Not as a passive consumer, but as a driven discoverer. Throughout the seasons and in good and bad weather, Sabine exposes a Europe without borders. A Europe that is a delight to the eyes. Go ahead, take a look.

Bart Heirweg is a landscape photographer from Belgium. He is author of the book *Silent Fields: Memorial Sites of the Great War* and *De heuvels van de Ronde.*

Carpathian Mountains, Romania
45°36'19.8"N 24°36'58.2"E
Traversing Romania's wild Făgăraş Mountains
with my old faithful Subaru.
Photo by Martijn de Milliano.
// October 2015

14

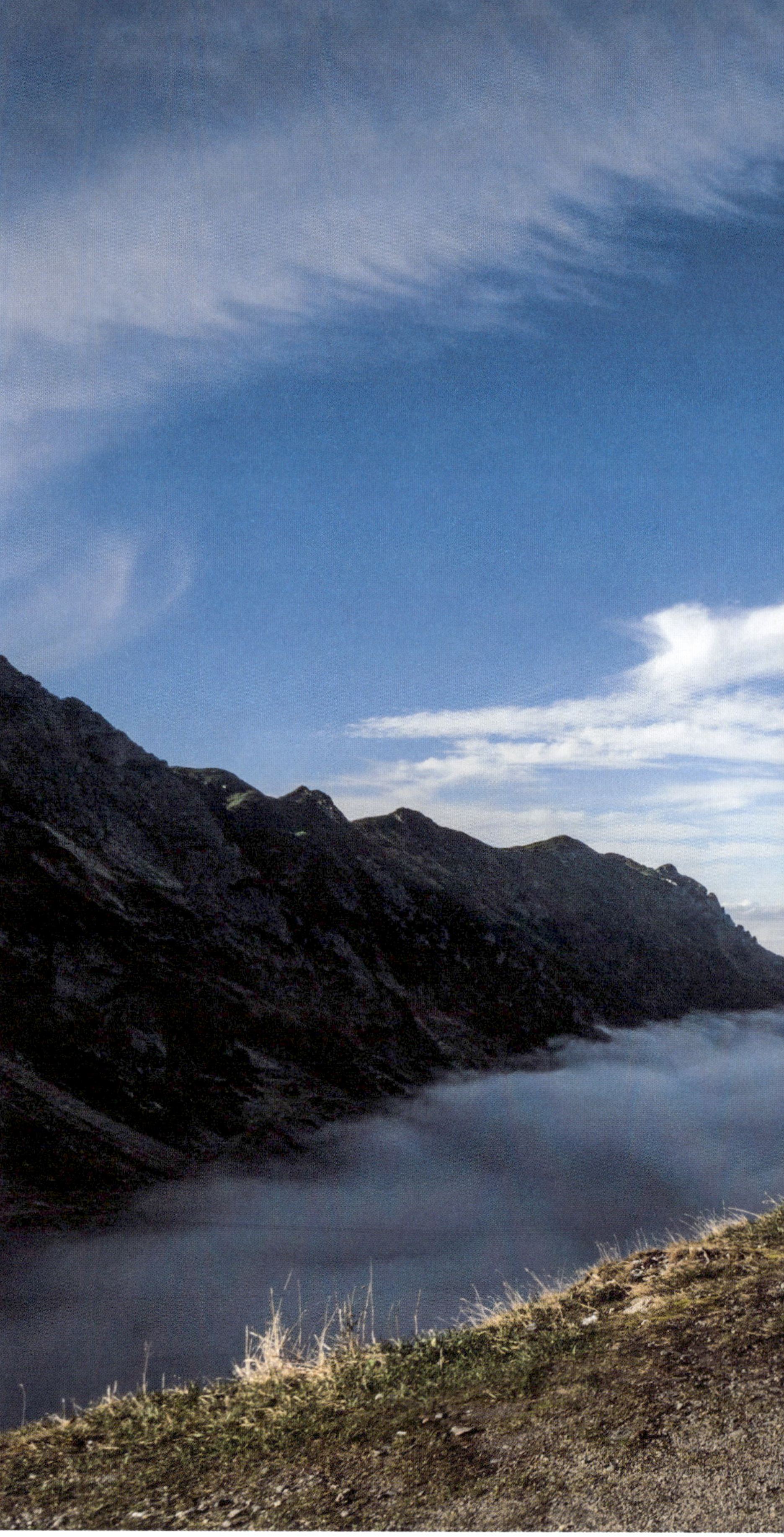

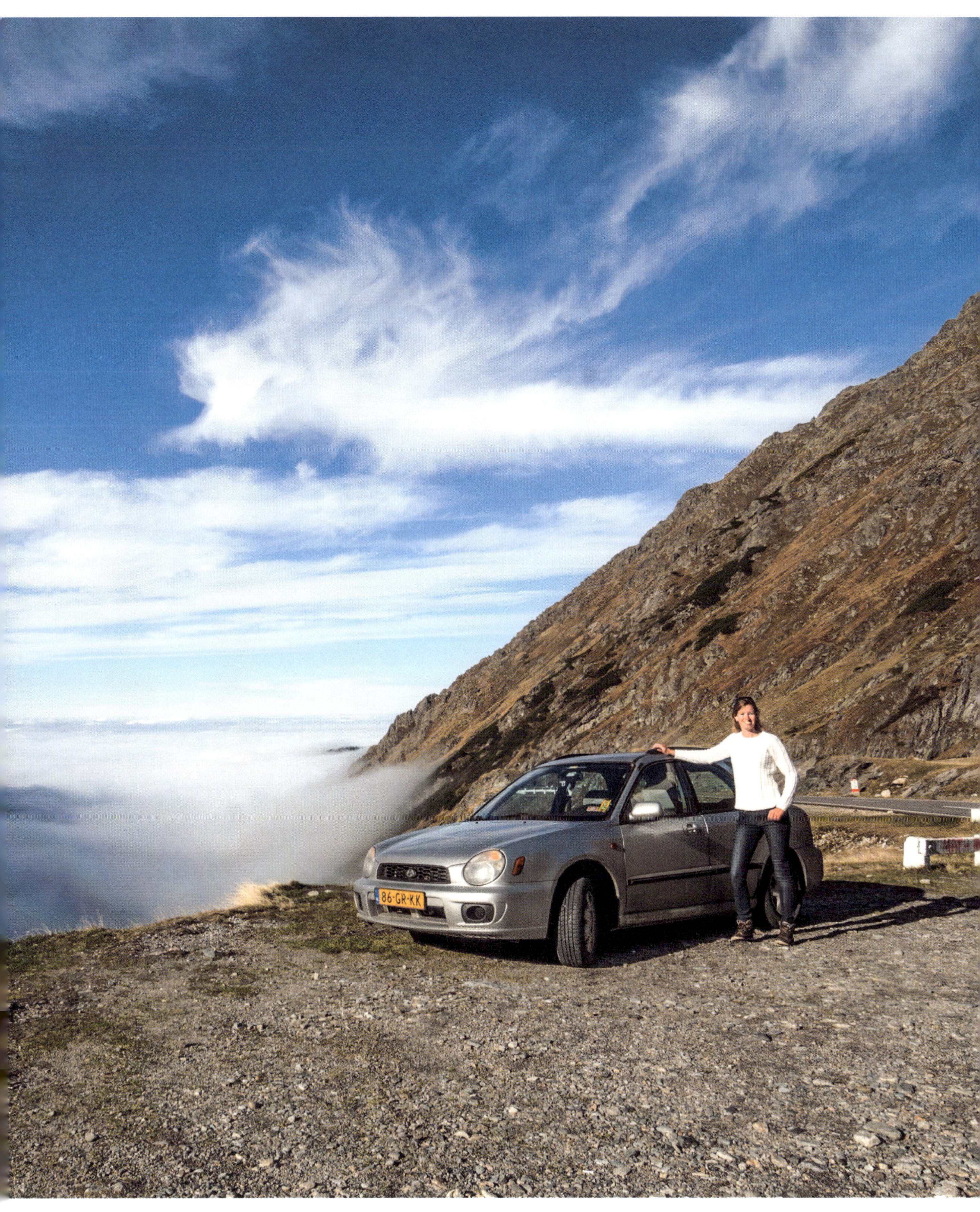
86-GR-KK

Introduction

Sabine de Milliano

After more than 100,000 km of road trip adventures, it is time to tell a story – the photographic story of Europe's stunning scenes, charming cities and surprising horizons.

A DENSE NETWORK of over seven million kilometres of roads connects Europe. It connects the Carpathian Mountains in Romania with capitals like Podgorica and Vilnius. It connects famous landmarks in St. Petersburg and Paris to remote nature reserves in Southern Spain and Italy. It connects the North Cape to the Peloponnese and Gibraltar to Baku.

All these long roads are full of surprises. The key lesson learned while driving 100,000 kilometres through more than 50 countries in 10 years is that you do not have to fly to other continents to see breathtaking landscapes and experience extraordinary cultures. Europe has so much to offer – enough for a lifetime of travel adventures.

Picture a stunning landscape on the other side of a mountain pass, a charming alley somewhere off the beaten track where you least expect it, or a mysterious cave where you and your guide are the only guests. Surprises can be found everywhere. And after all those hours on the road, it is now time to share some of those surprises and highlights with you. I want to show you how beautiful Europe really is.

The eight road trips in this book take you on a visual journey through our continent. They are created based on my experiences during one or more visits to each region. The selected routes take you past famous landmarks and hidden gems, natural and cultural heritage, known and lesser-known destinations. Whether you are a mountain lover, wildlife enthusiast or culture addict, there are inspiring places for every single one of us to enjoy.

Transfăgărășan, Romania
45°36′29.4″N 24°37′02.1″E
After waiting for two days for the weather to improve, the sky finally cleared up sufficiently to drive the spectacular Transfăgărășan.
// October 2015

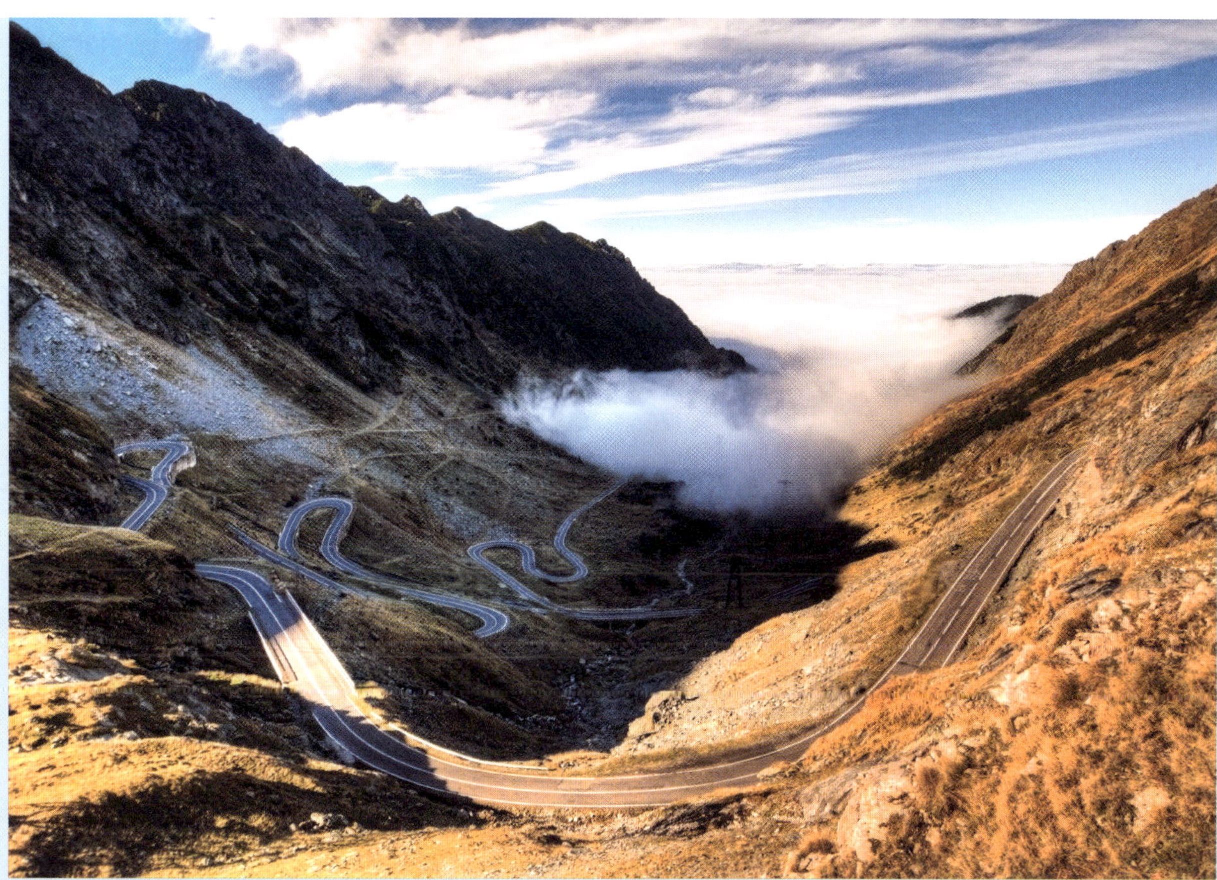

Each country is covered at least once in this book, but some regions are featured more often than others. The photographs have been selected based on their stories and aesthetics, influenced by time and weather. It goes without saying that there are many more wonderful places in Europe than can be covered in the pages of this book. Nevertheless, the list and map with travel recommendations at the end of each chapter are a starting point to help you plan your next travel adventure in Europe. These lists contain my favourite highlights, scenic routes and most dramatic destinations.

Photography plays a major role in my journeys. Without photography, I would travel less. Without travelling, I would photograph less. These two passions of mine have been entwined for a long time and form the foundation of *Surprising Europe*. Every photograph in this book tells its own story.

Some were taken following meticulous planning and a fair amount of patience. Others were shot off the cuff during straining hikes in rough environments or while rock climbing. The captions that accompany the photographs take you with me on my journey through Europe.

Being Dutch and having lived near Rotterdam for the past 13 years, I decided to dedicate the first pages of *Surprising Europe* to the place I call home. Even the densely-populated Netherlands offers many stunning views and nature scenes, proving that you do not have to travel far to experience a beautiful place.

May this book inspire you to explore more of Europe the next time you go travelling. Until that time, sit back, relax and enjoy the visual ride.

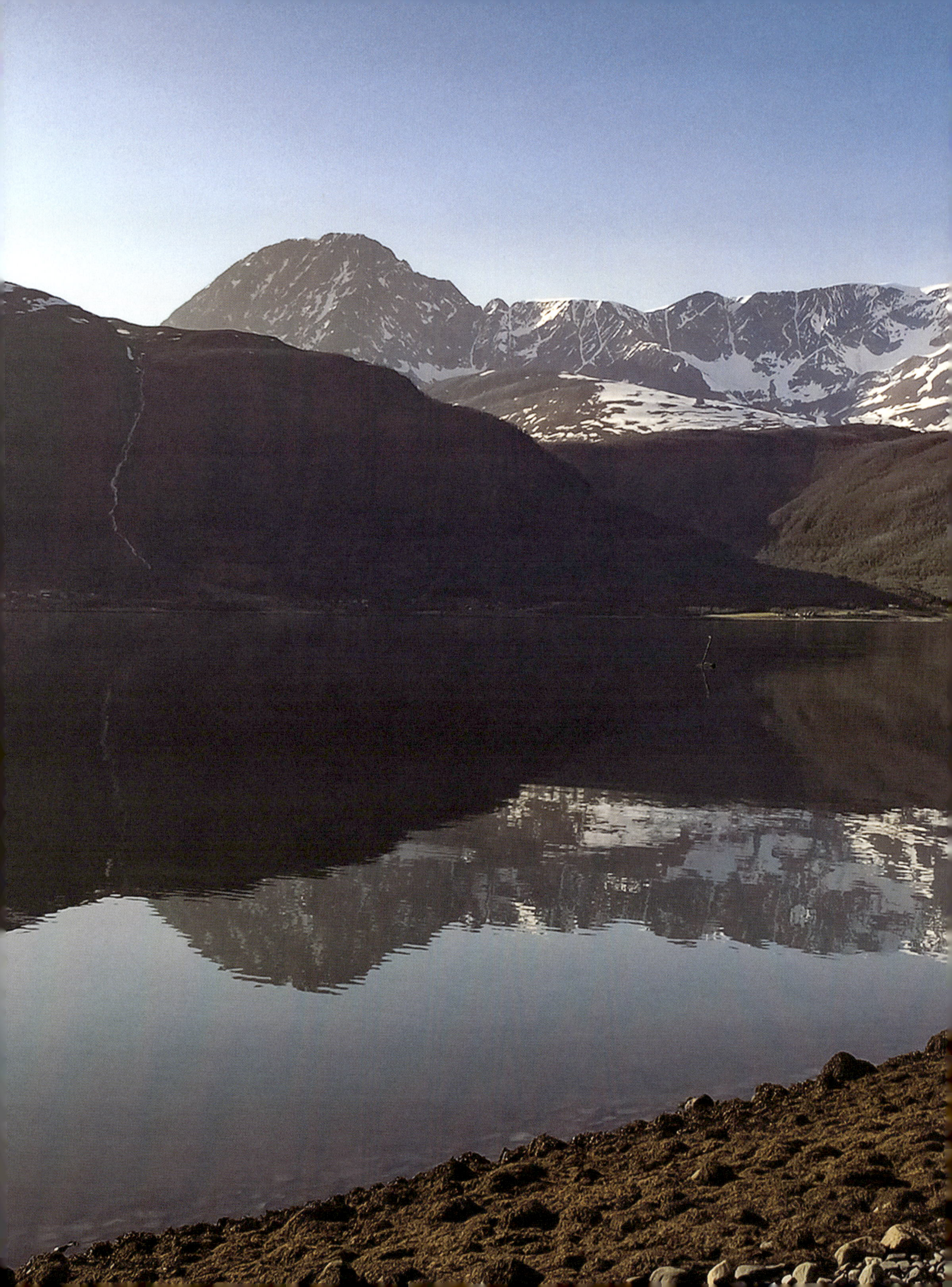

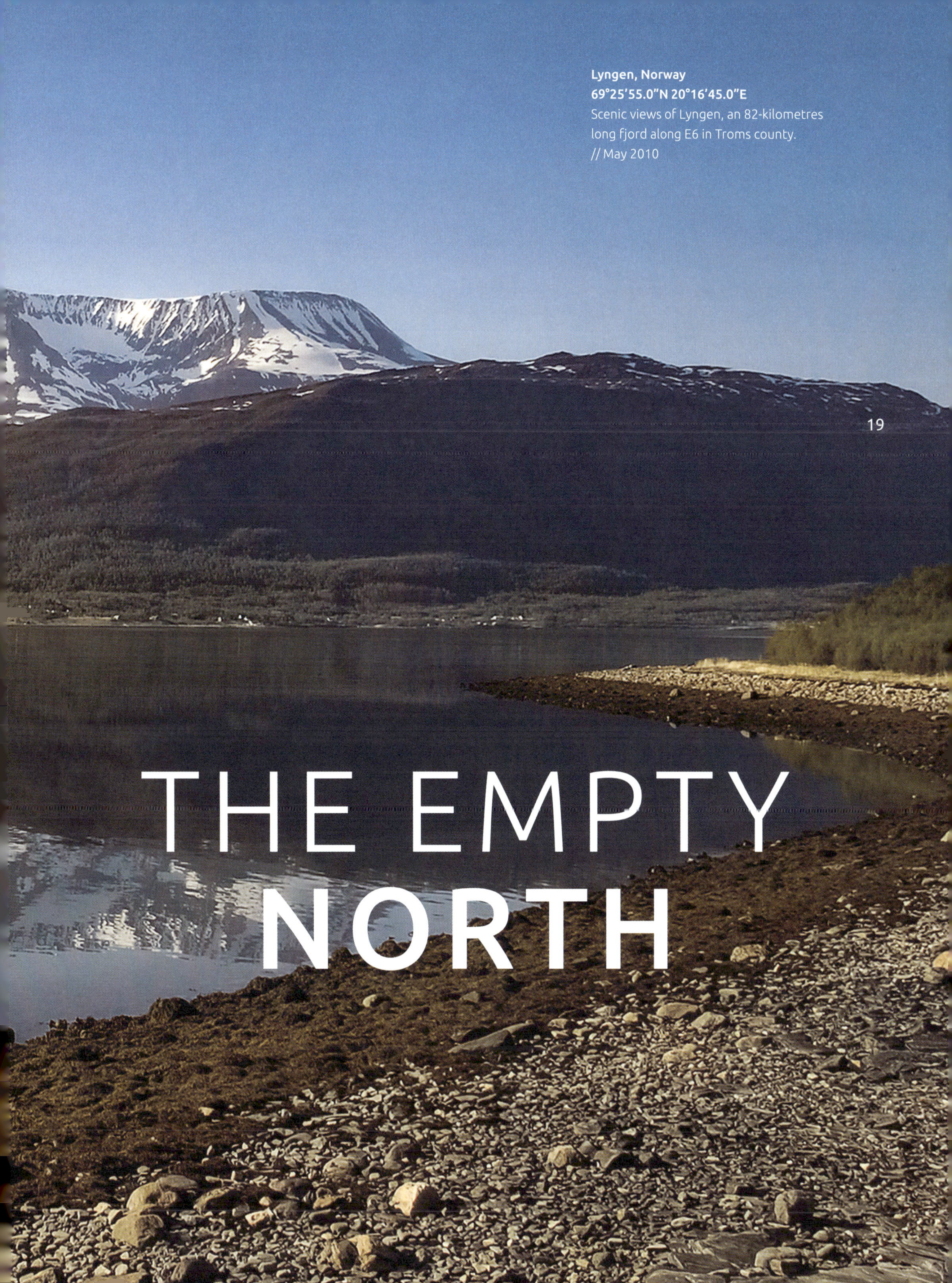

THE EMPTY NORTH

'Whether moving north or south on either
side of the Gulf of Bothnia, this is a long
but rewarding road trip for nature lovers.'

THE NORTH AND NORTHEAST

of Europe are wonderful, wild and empty.
Seemingly endless forests, uninhabited
mountain ranges and many thousands of
lakes and bogs. Reindeer are the true rulers
of the roads up north. Golden chanterelles
cover the forests in the northeast in autumn.
Bison inhabit the last part of the primeval
forest in the east. Nature clearly holds sway
in this part of Europe.

One of the things you will notice on a road
trip to the north and northeast is how the
landscape gradually changes. Between
the few scattered cities and towns, green
fields and deciduous forests slowly become
more mixed until there are only pines and
shrub-sized birches left in the landscape.
Then, if you travel beyond the Arctic Circle,
the landscape increasingly empties. At some
point, deep inside Sápmi, you no longer see
any trees. Covering the northernmost parts
of Norway, Sweden, Finland and Russia,
Sápmi (also known as Lapland) is the region
of spectacular landscapes, rough climate
and sunny summer nights.

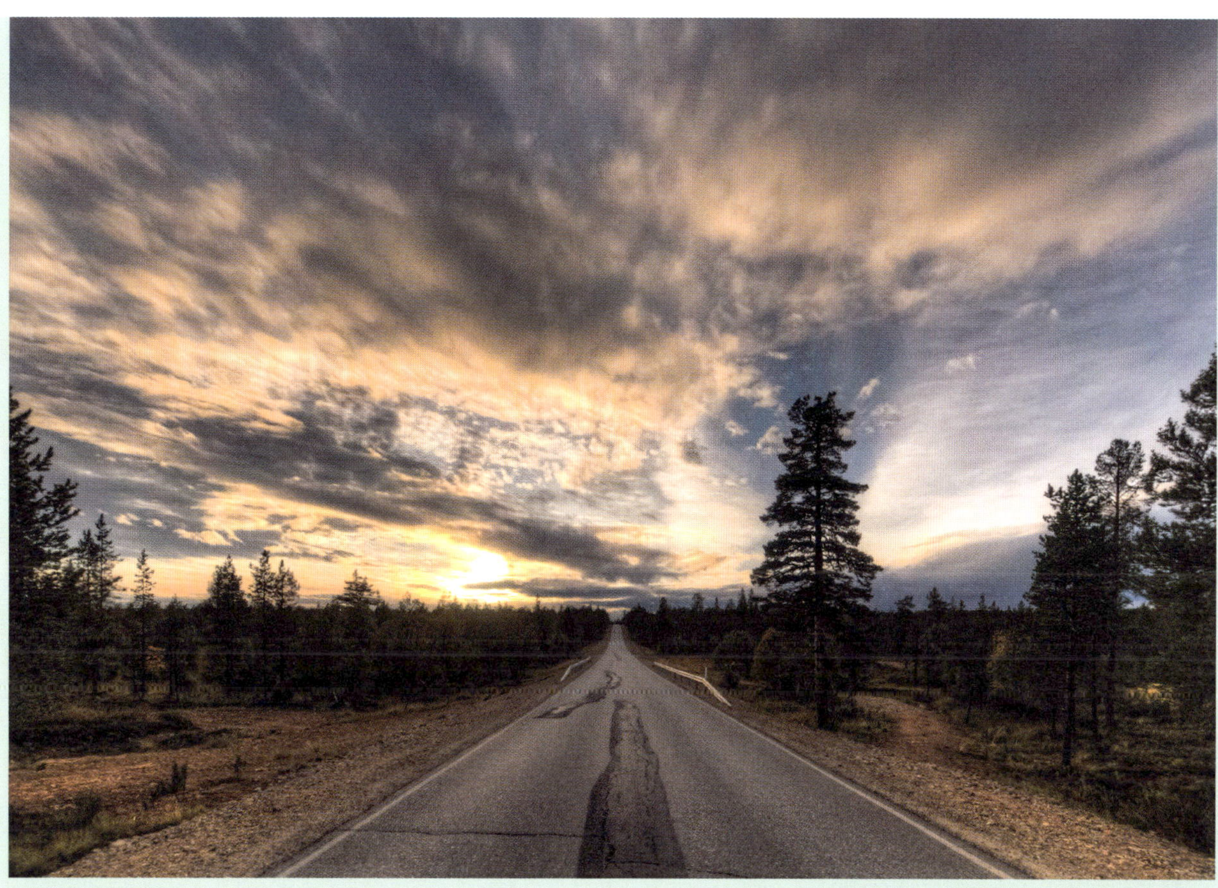

Every country has its own scenic highlights, but Lofoten is my overall favourite destination in this part of Europe. Few places show such dramatic landscapes as this archipelago in the Arctic part of Norway. It is photogenic in every weather, in every season.

Whether moving north or south on either side of the Gulf of Bothnia, this is a long but rewarding road trip for nature lovers. And, maybe surprisingly, for those who love Renaissance and Baroque style, because some of Europe's finest cities are located in the northeast. Personally, I would recommend visiting St. Petersburg, Vilnius and Lviv because of their impressive architecture and rich culture.

A stroll through the State Hermitage Museum, the view from Gediminas' Tower and tasting Lviv-style coffee are just a few examples of the great experiences the northeastern part of Europe has to offer.

E75 near Ivalo, Finland
68°29'57.0"N 27°28'41.7"E
Countless trees fill the landscape along the E75 to Ivalo.
// September 2014

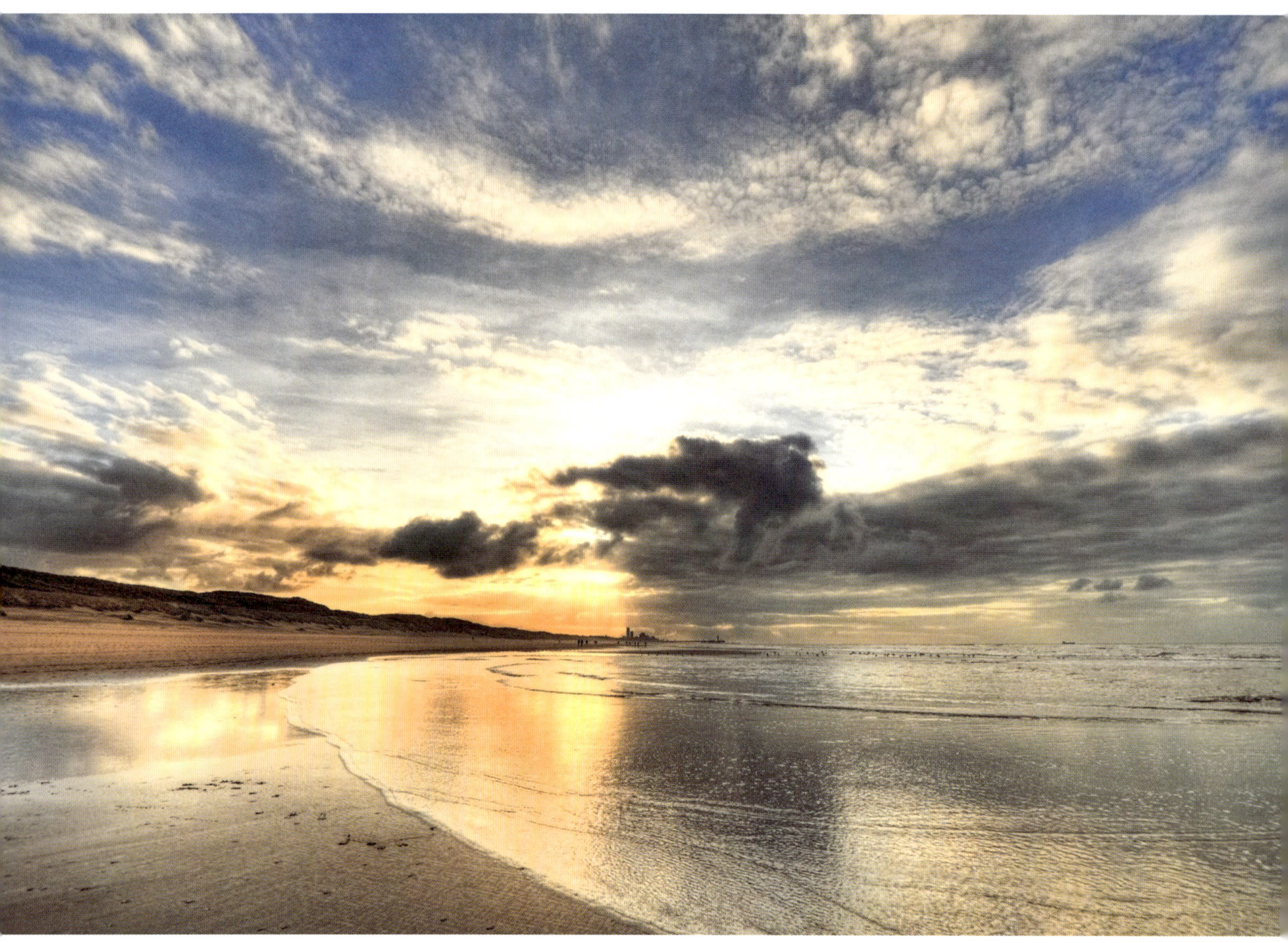

Wassenaar, the Netherlands
52°08'36.5"N 4°19'23.3"E
It was extraordinary mild weather on this January
day in Wassenaar, South Holland. Ideal conditions
for a winter walk along the Dutch coast.
// January 2012

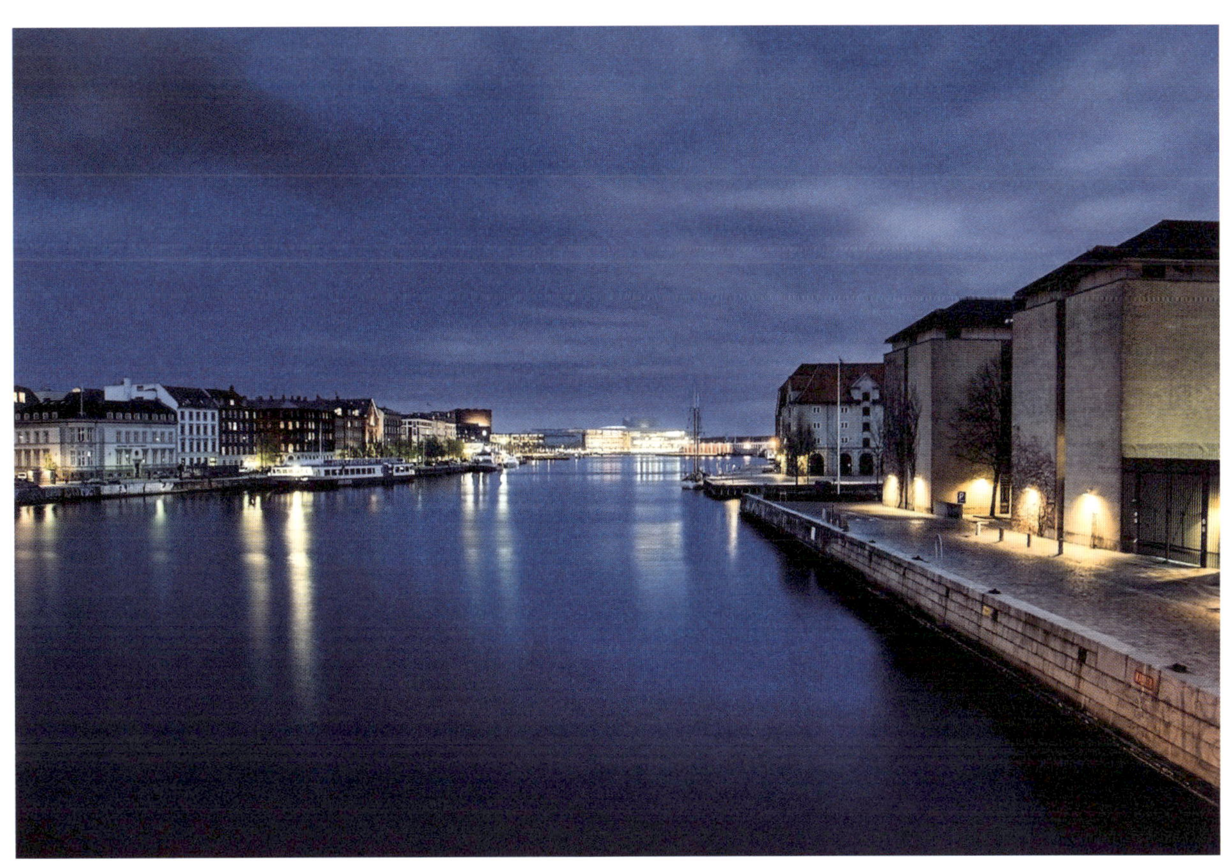

Copenhagen, Denmark
55°40'29.1"N 12°35'13.5"E
After a long day of driving I arrived in Copenhagen,
the first stop of my road trip in 2010 to the North
Cape. A very short dry spell made it possible
to take this image.
// May 2010

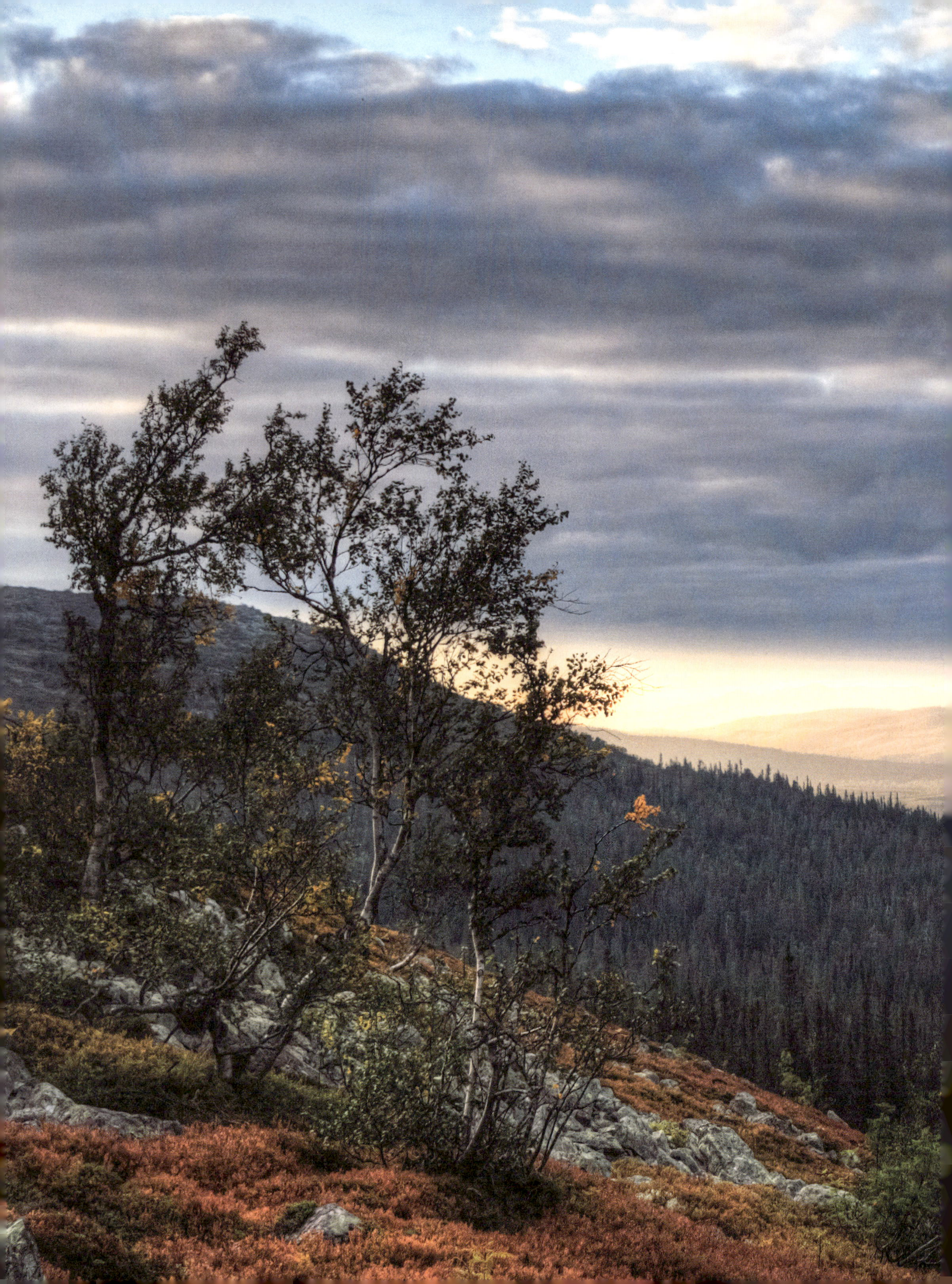

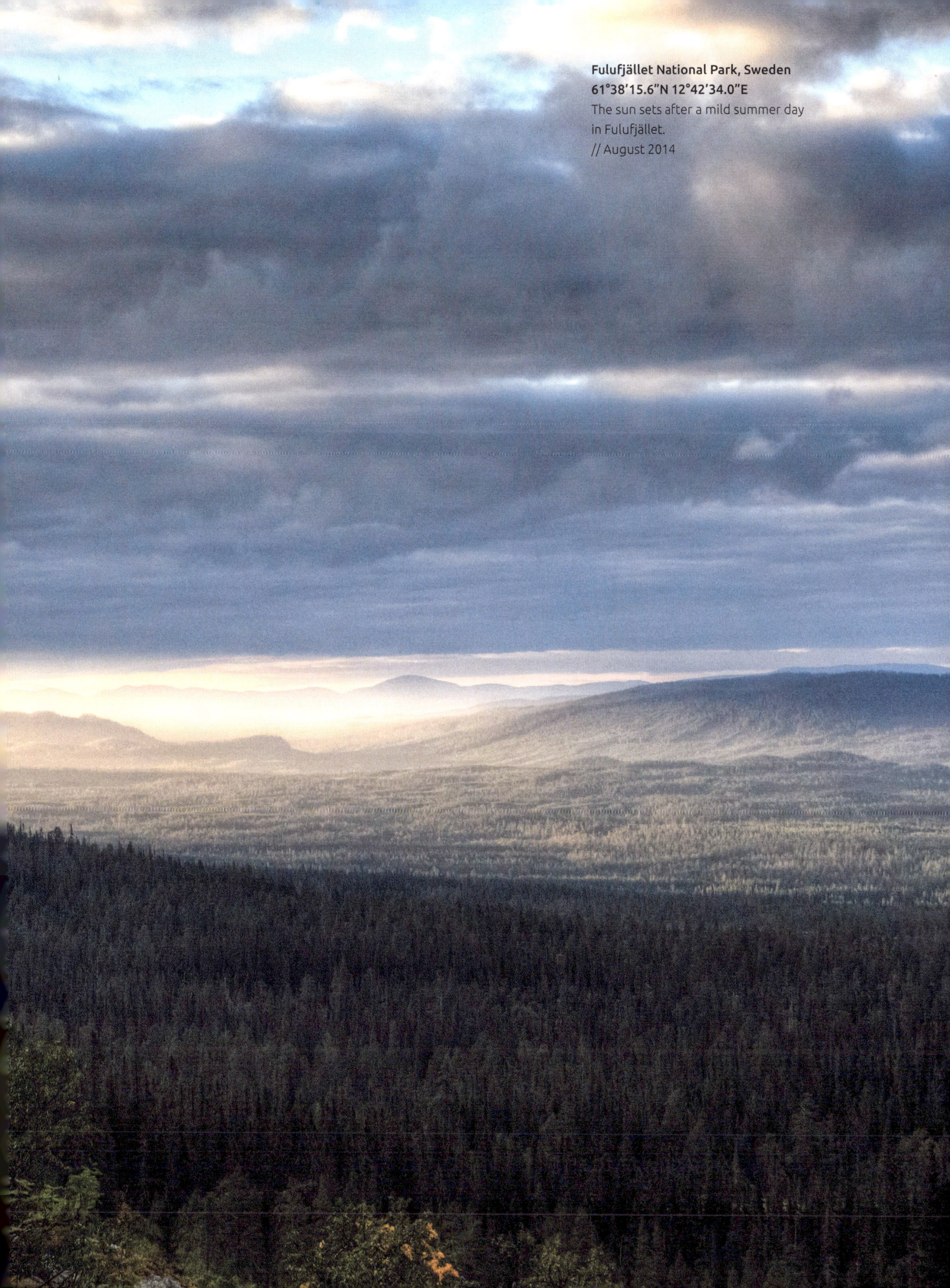

Fulufjället National Park, Sweden
61°38'15.6"N 12°42'34.0"E
The sun sets after a mild summer day
in Fulufjället.
// August 2014

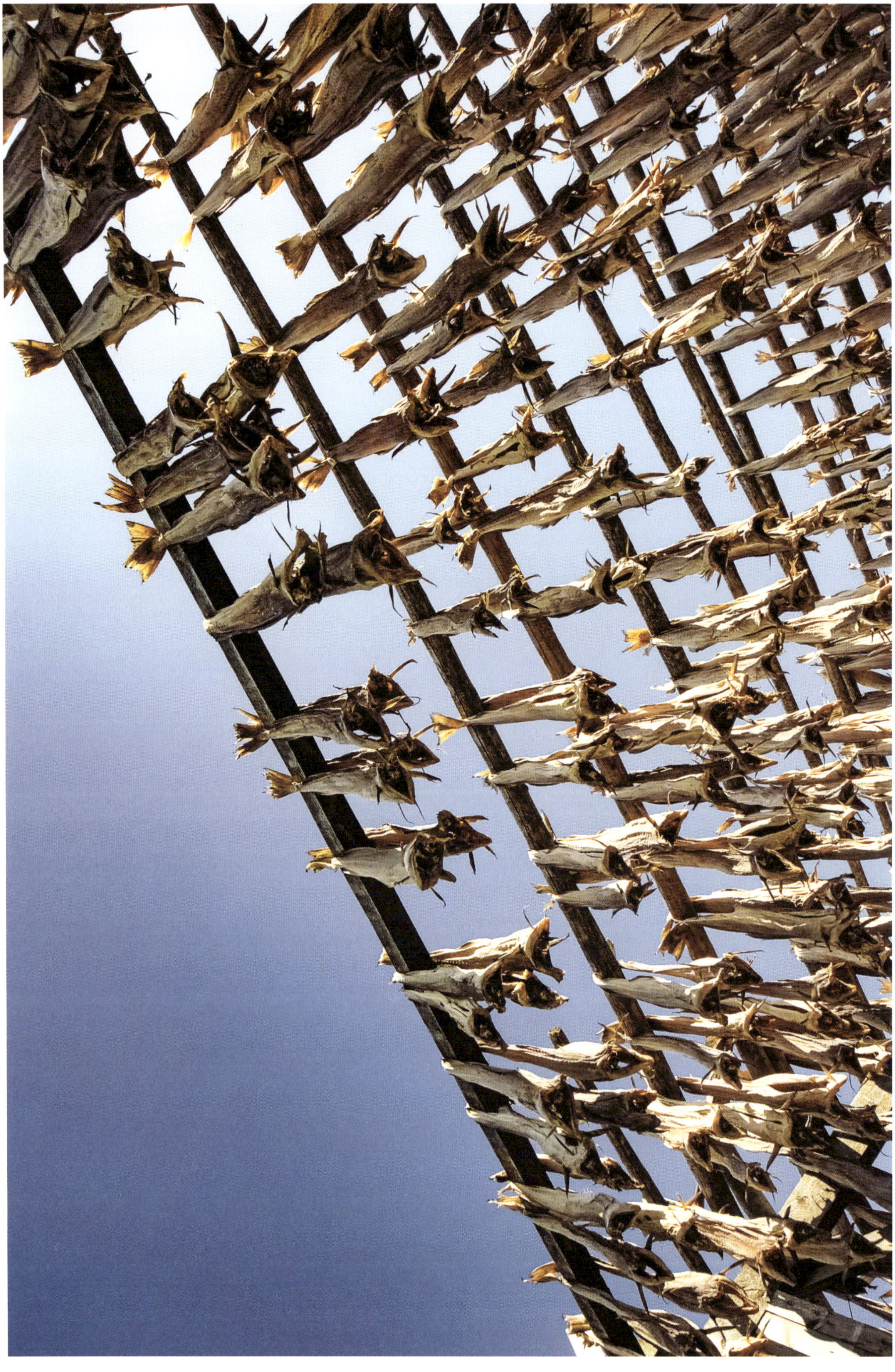

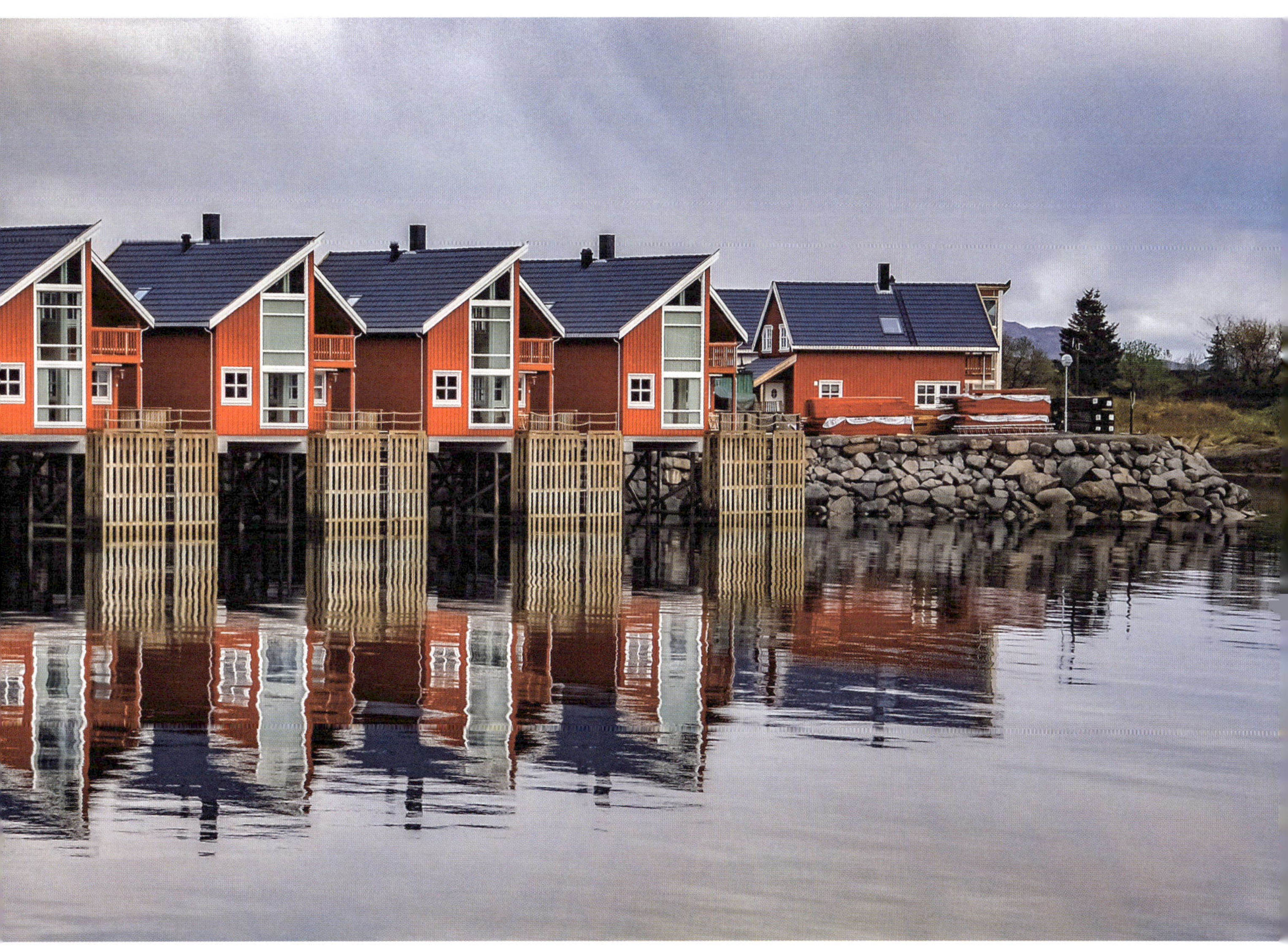

Henningsvær, Lofoten, Norway
68°09'04.9"N 14°11'50.2"E

Drying stockfish, a ubiquitous sight on Lofoten.
// May 2010

Svolvær, Lofoten, Norway
68°14'03.7"N 14°34'23.9"E

Houses in Norway's national colours.
// May 2010

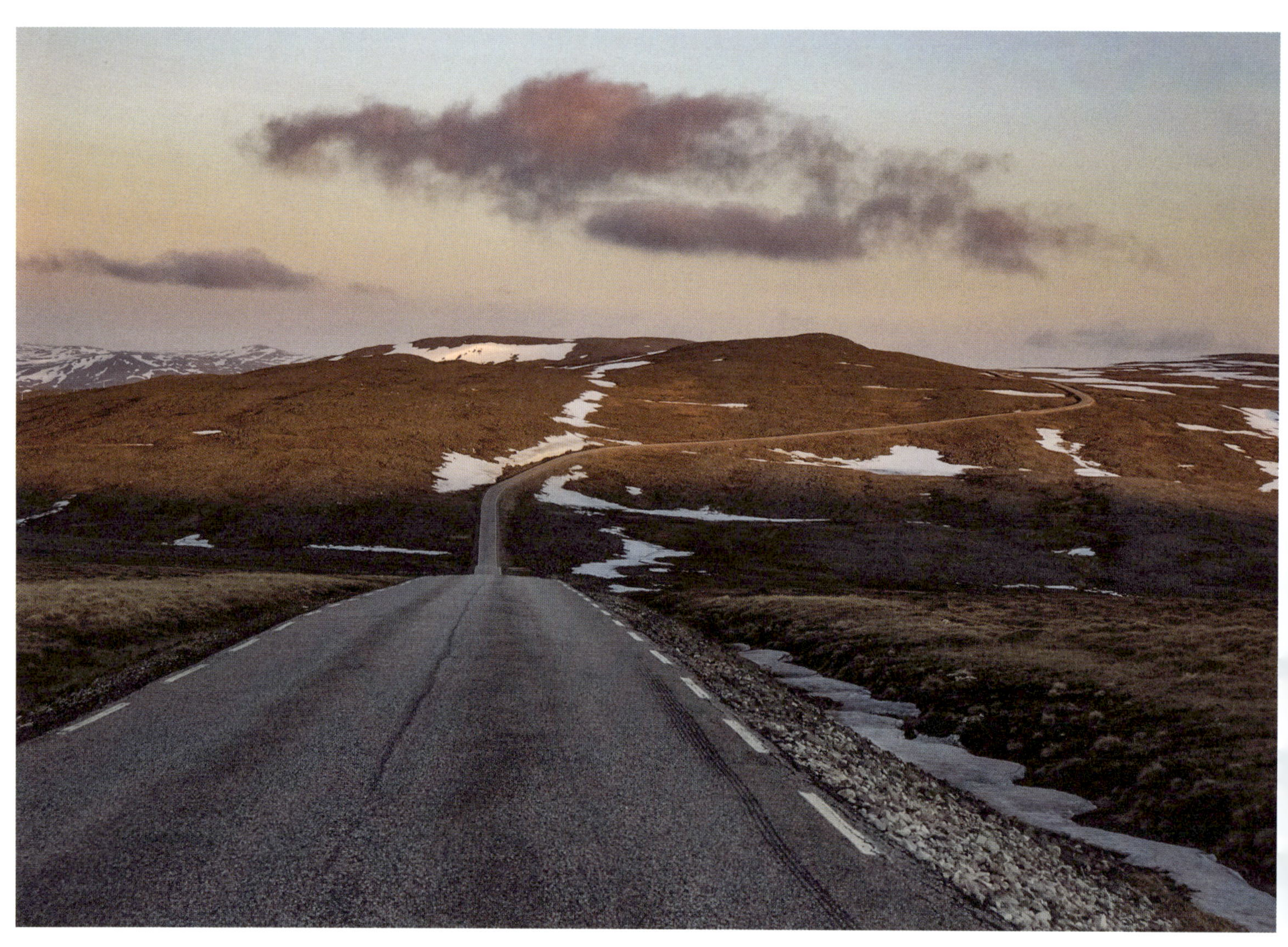

E69, Magerøya, Norway
71°02'10.9"N 25°49'32.8"E
On the way close to the most northerly
connected point of mainland Europe.
// May 2010

North Cape, Magerøya, Norway
71°08'36.9"N 25°44'39.2"E
Time seems to stand still during the season
of the Midnight Sun. This reindeer on the island
of Magerøya enjoys the sun, shining from
the north in the middle of the night.
// May 2010

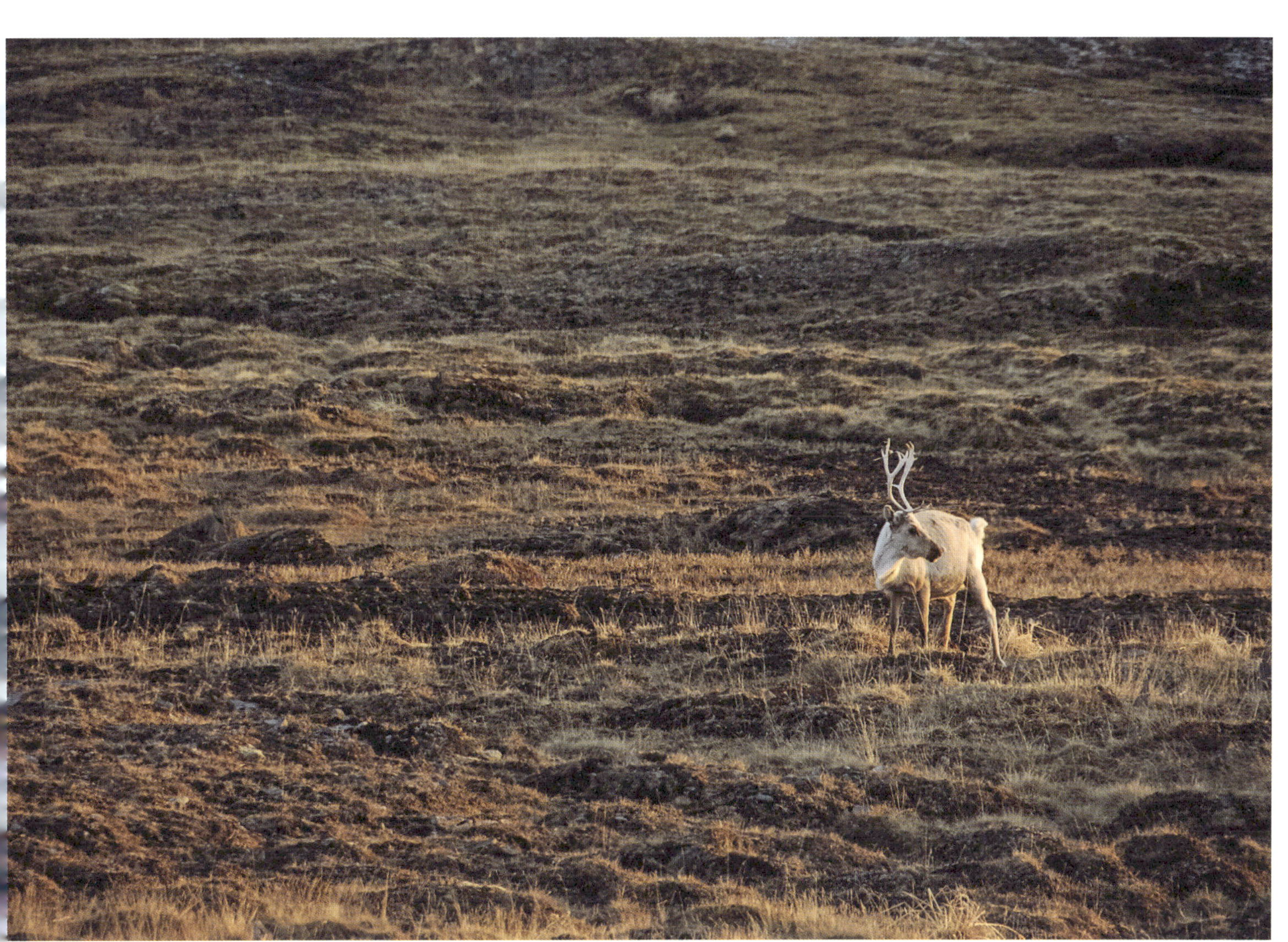

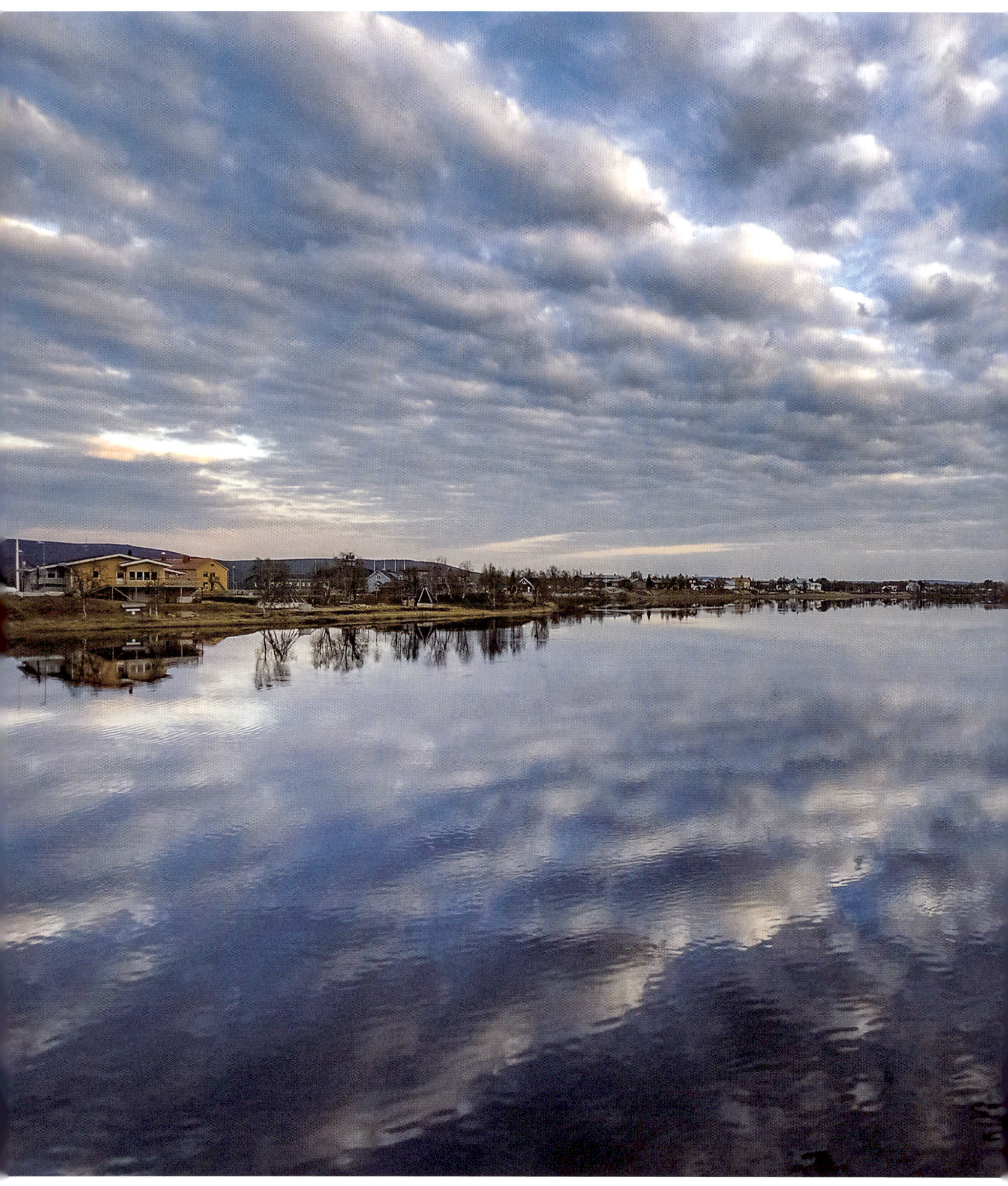

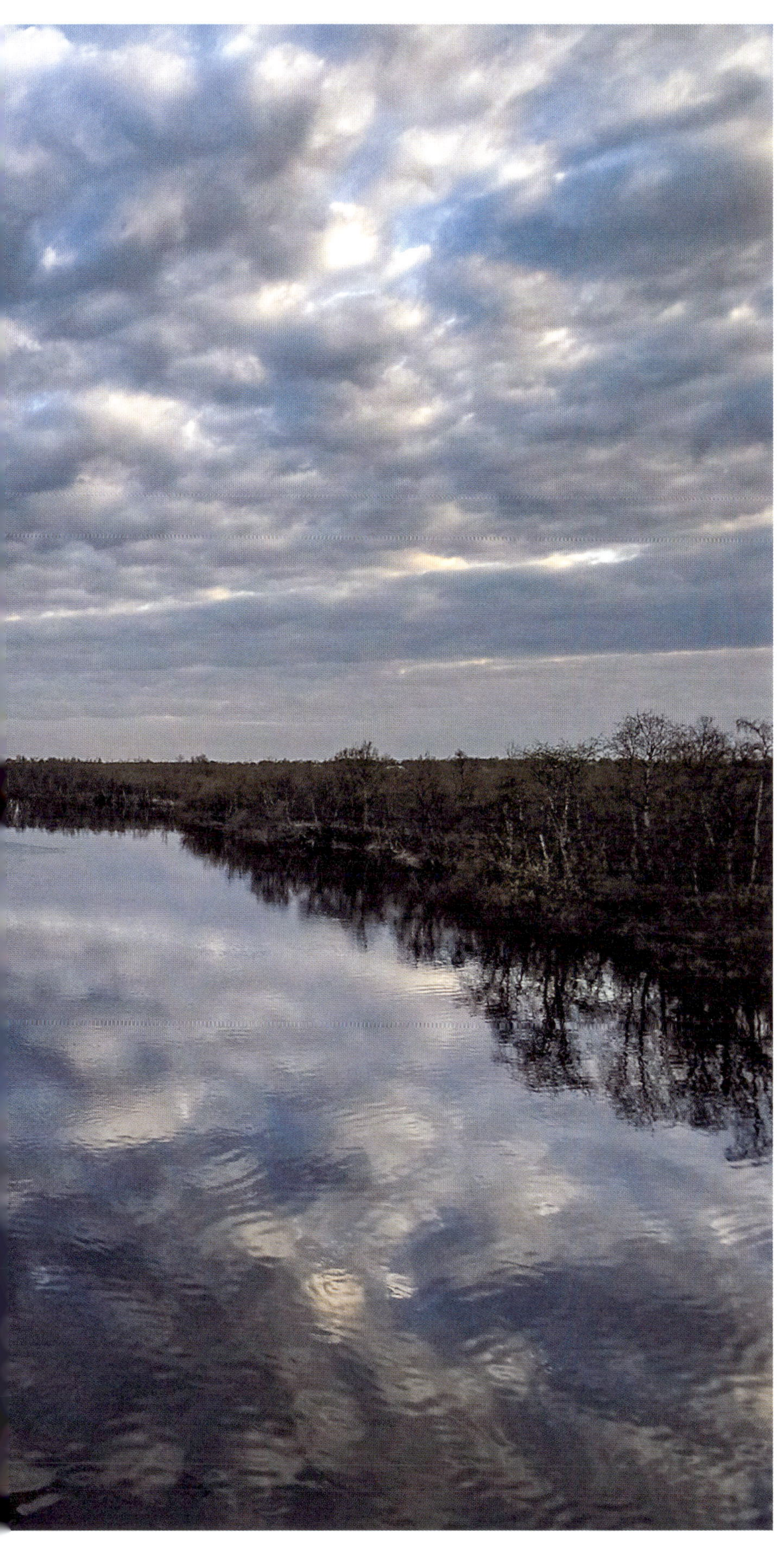

Karesuando/Karesuvanto, Sweden & Finland
68°26'34.3"N 22°28'38.1"E
On the border between Finland and Sweden,
where the long E45 road to Sicily starts and ends.
// May 2010

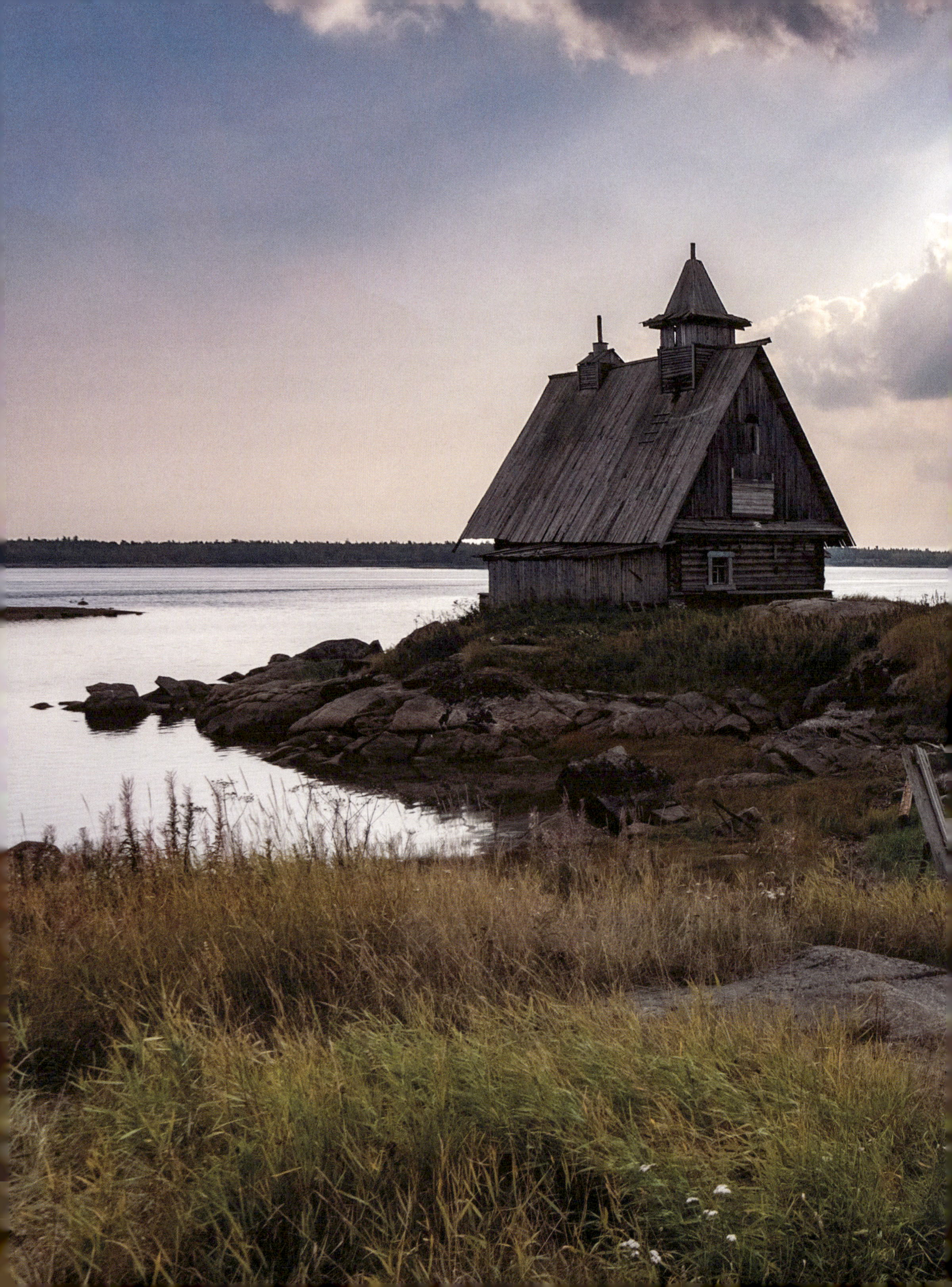

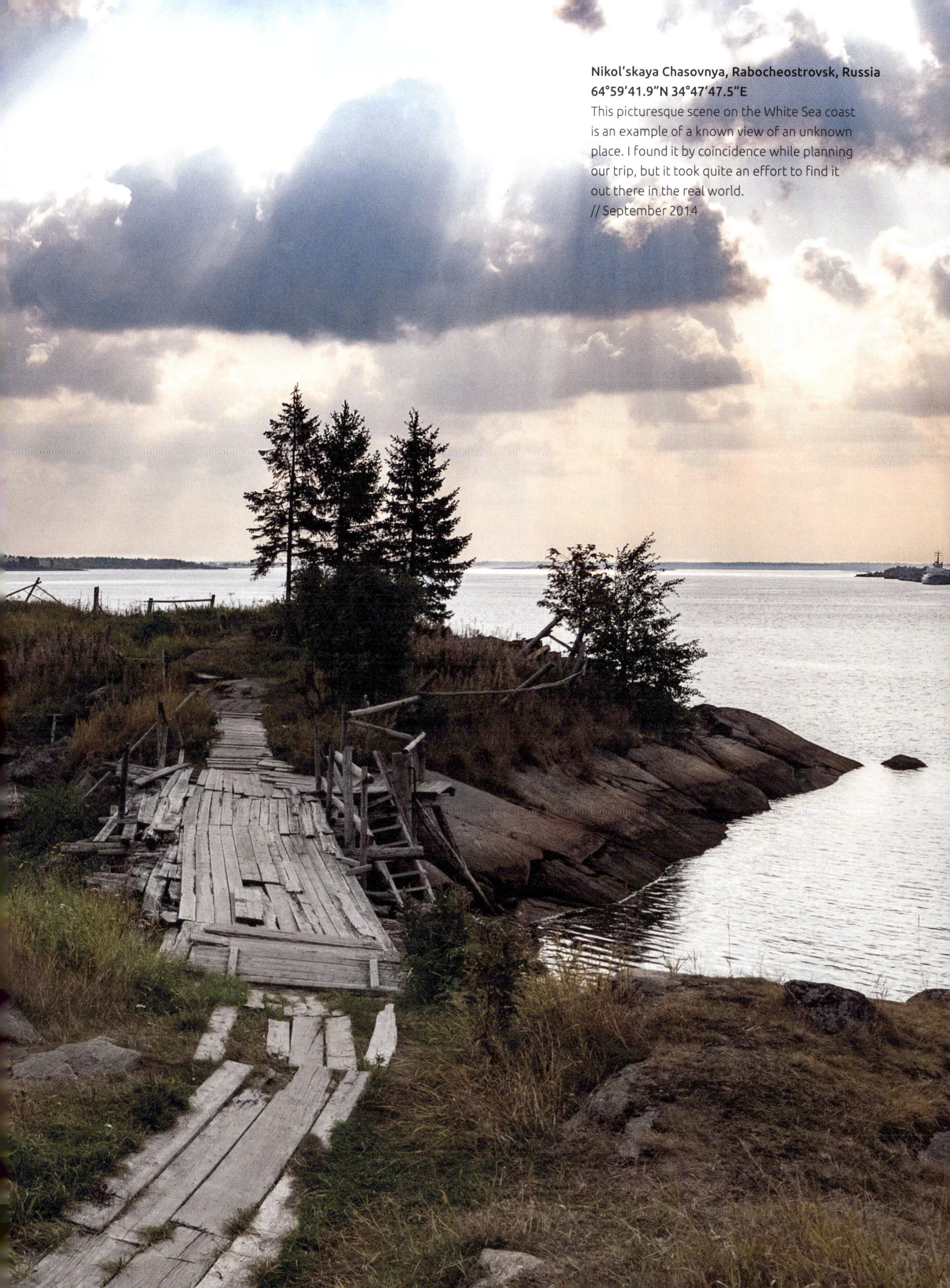

Nikol'skaya Chasovnya, Rabocheostrovsk, Russia
64°59'41.9"N 34°47'47.5"E
This picturesque scene on the White Sea coast
is an example of a known view of an unknown
place. I found it by coincidence while planning
our trip, but it took quite an effort to find it
out there in the real world.
// September 2014

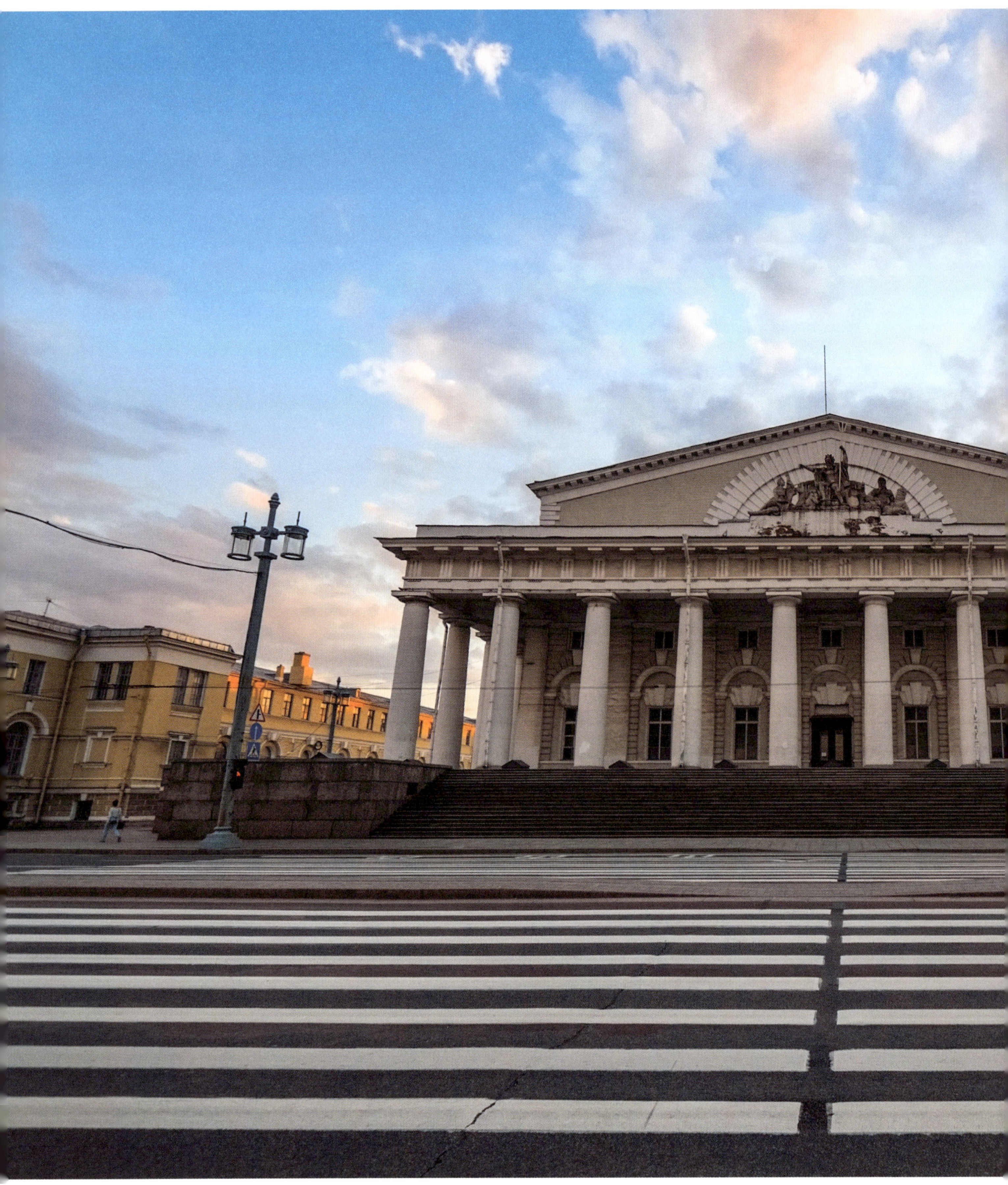

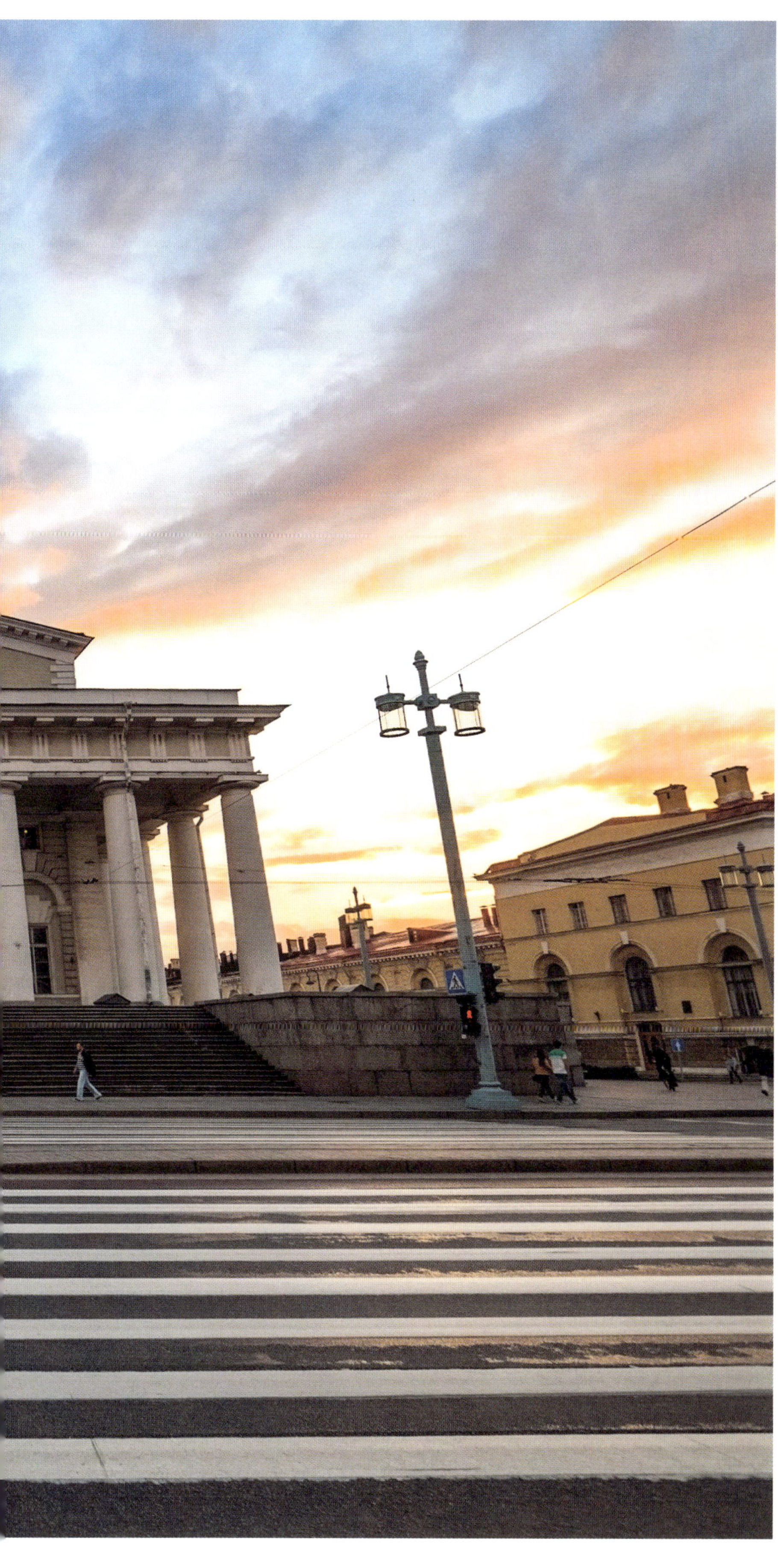

St. Petersburg, Russia
59°56'37.9"N 30°18'20.9"E
Seconds before the next batch of cars would pass,
this pedestrian crossing was completely empty
so I could capture the building on the other side
of the road. St. Petersburg is full of these views,
making it one of Europe's most photogenic cities.
// September 2014

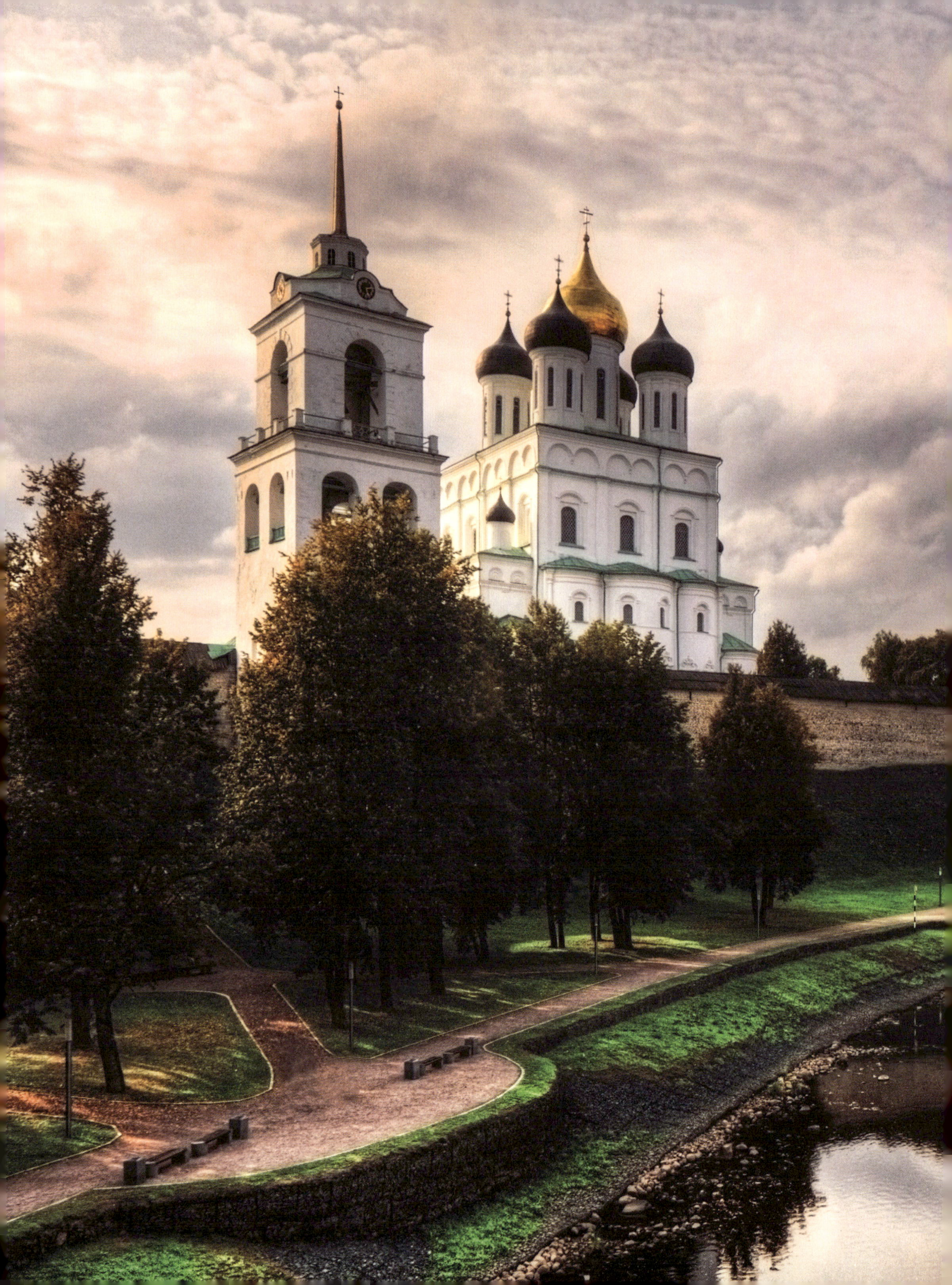

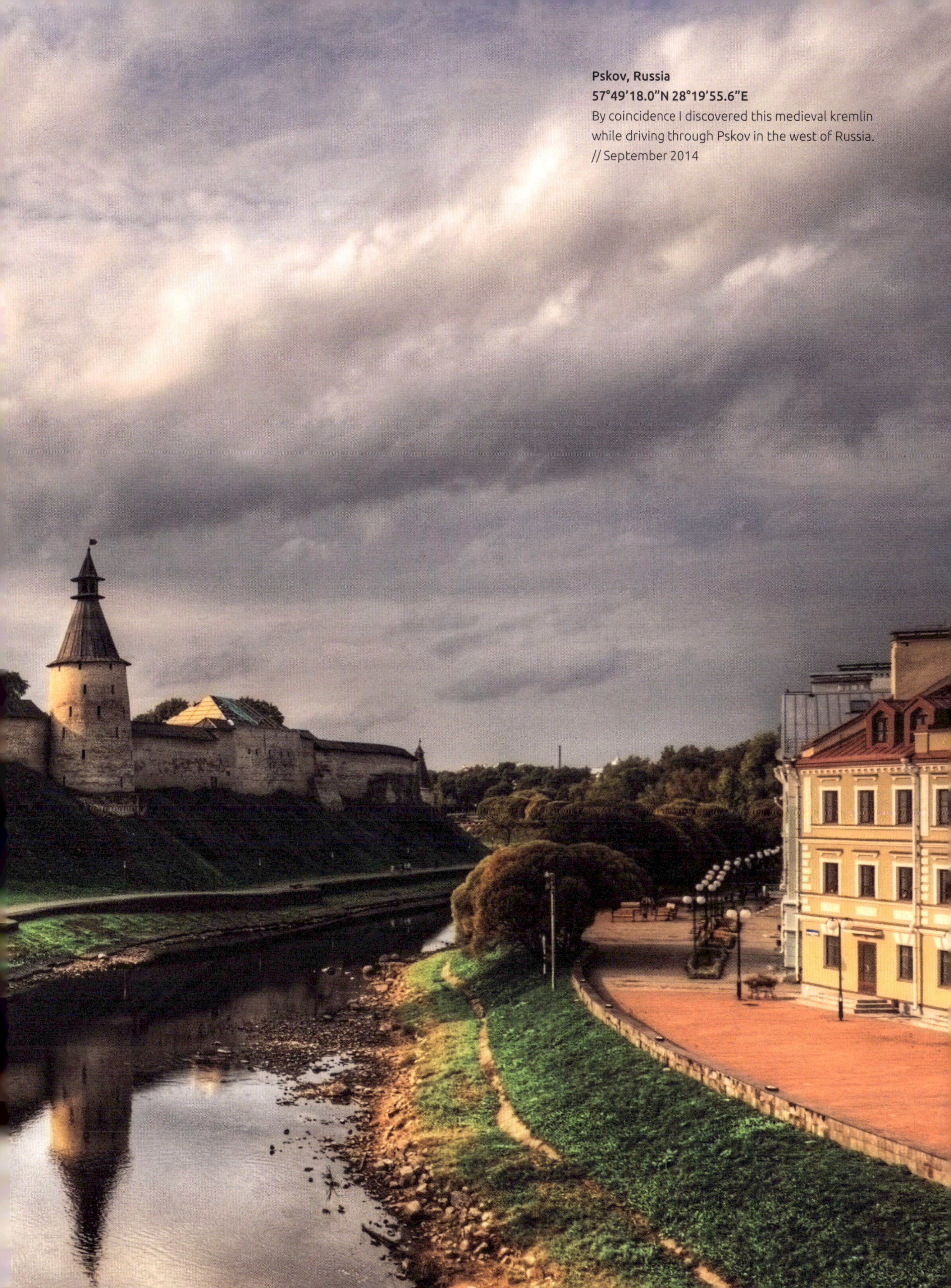

Pskov, Russia
57°49'18.0"N 28°19'55.6"E
By coincidence I discovered this medieval kremlin
while driving through Pskov in the west of Russia.
// September 2014

Soomaa, Estonia
58°27'41.5"N 25°02'09.3"E
A wooden trail disappears into the vast wetlands
of Soomaa, Estonian for 'Land of Bogs'.
// September 2014

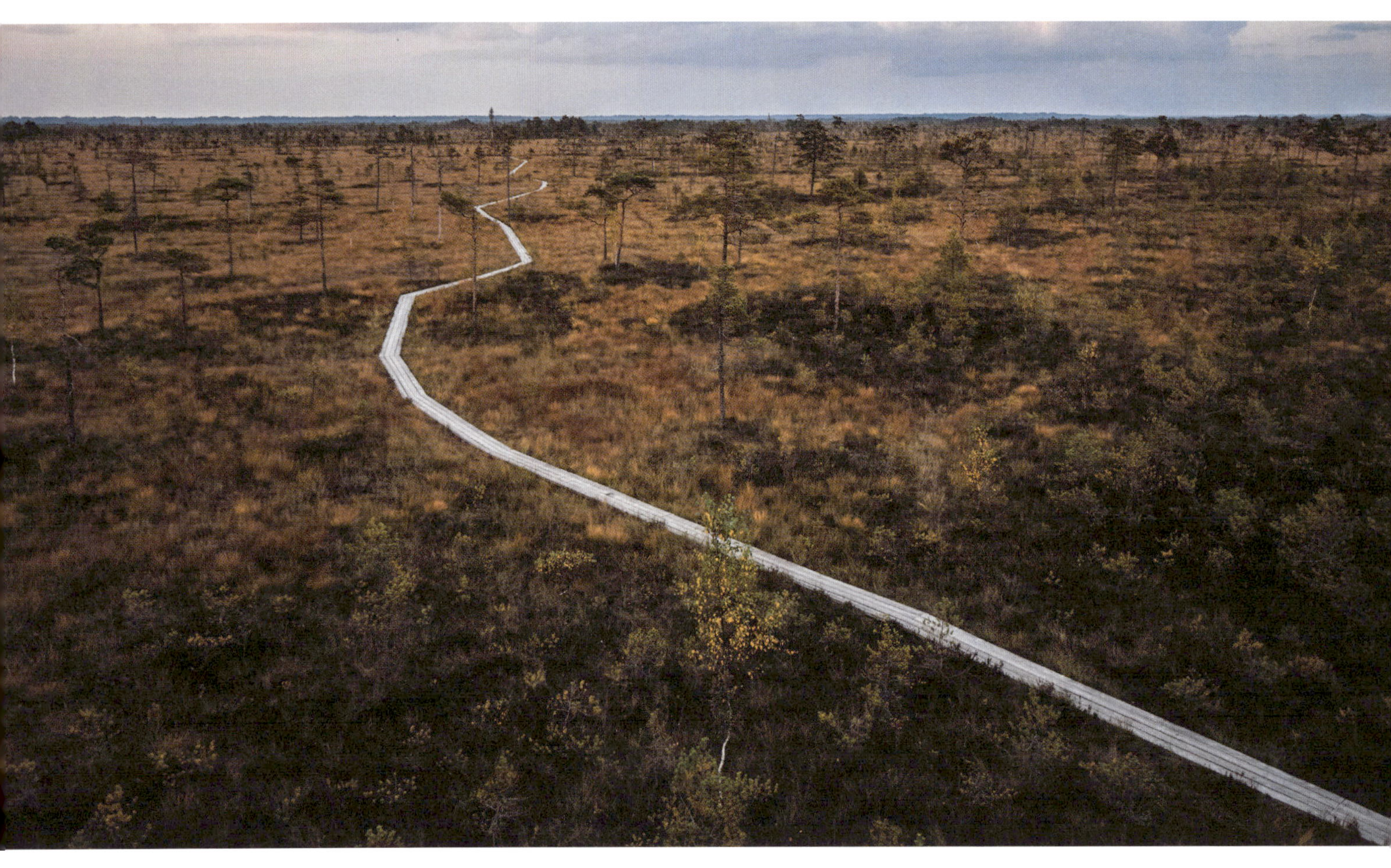

Gauja National Park, Latvia
57°16'36.8"N 25°10'52.5"E
The 20-metres tall Kvēpenes oak tree is considered
to be one of the most beautiful trees in Latvia.
// September 2014

Vilnius, Lithuania
54°41'12.8"N 25°17'26.7"E
Old meets new in Vilnius.
// September 2014

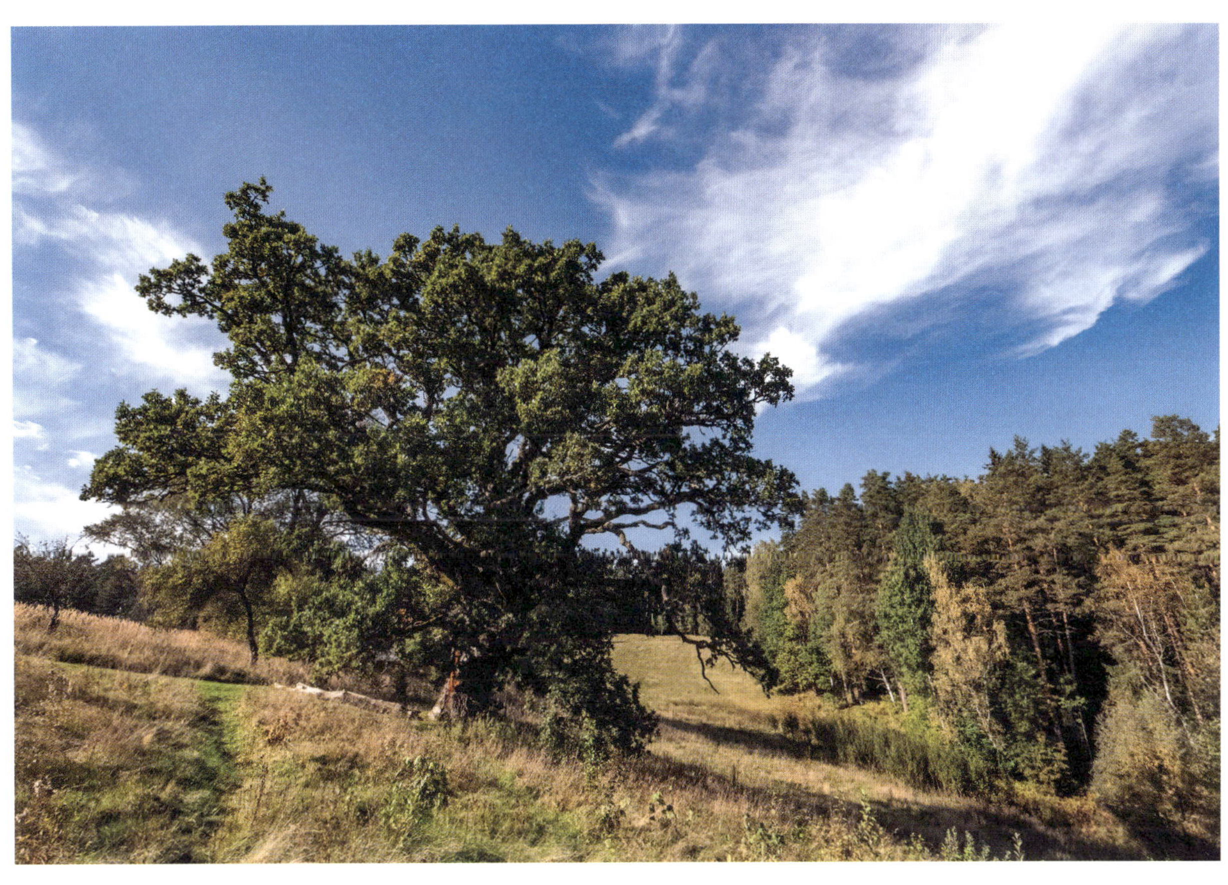

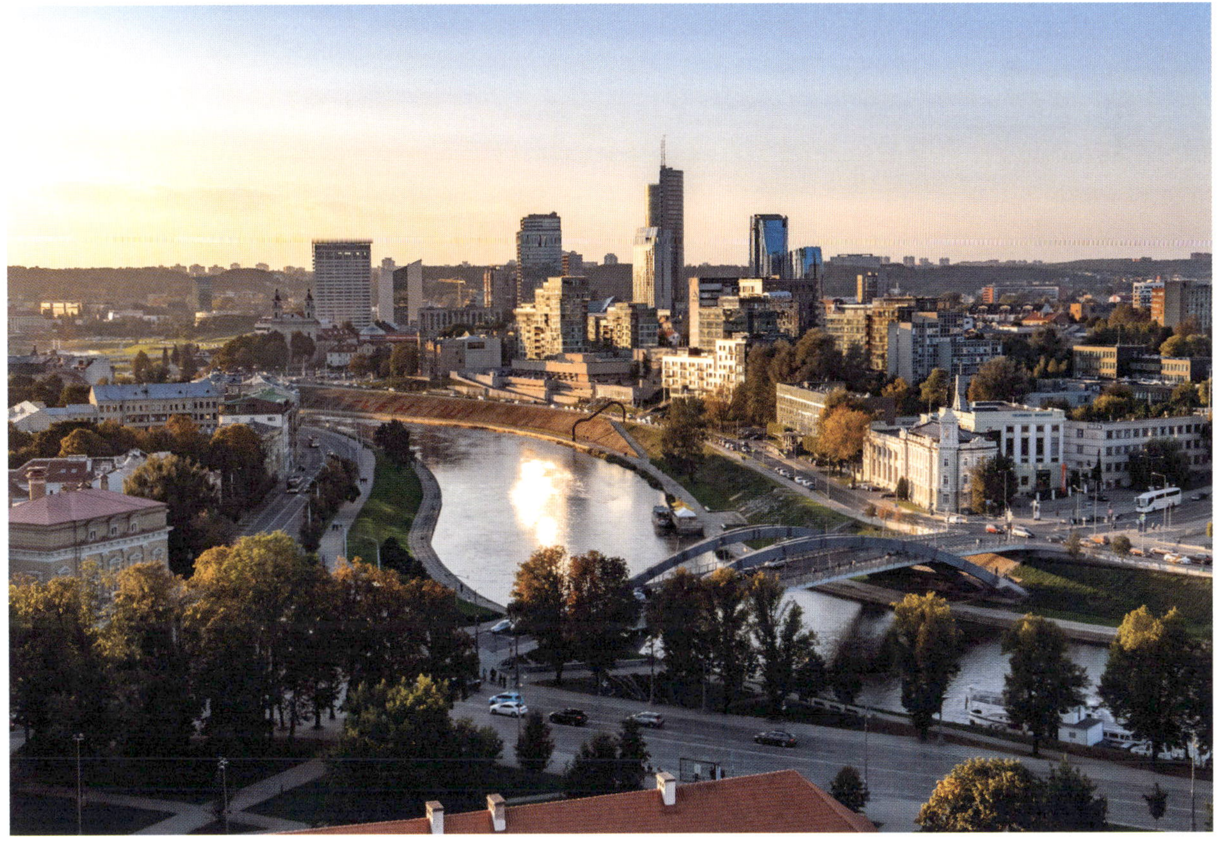

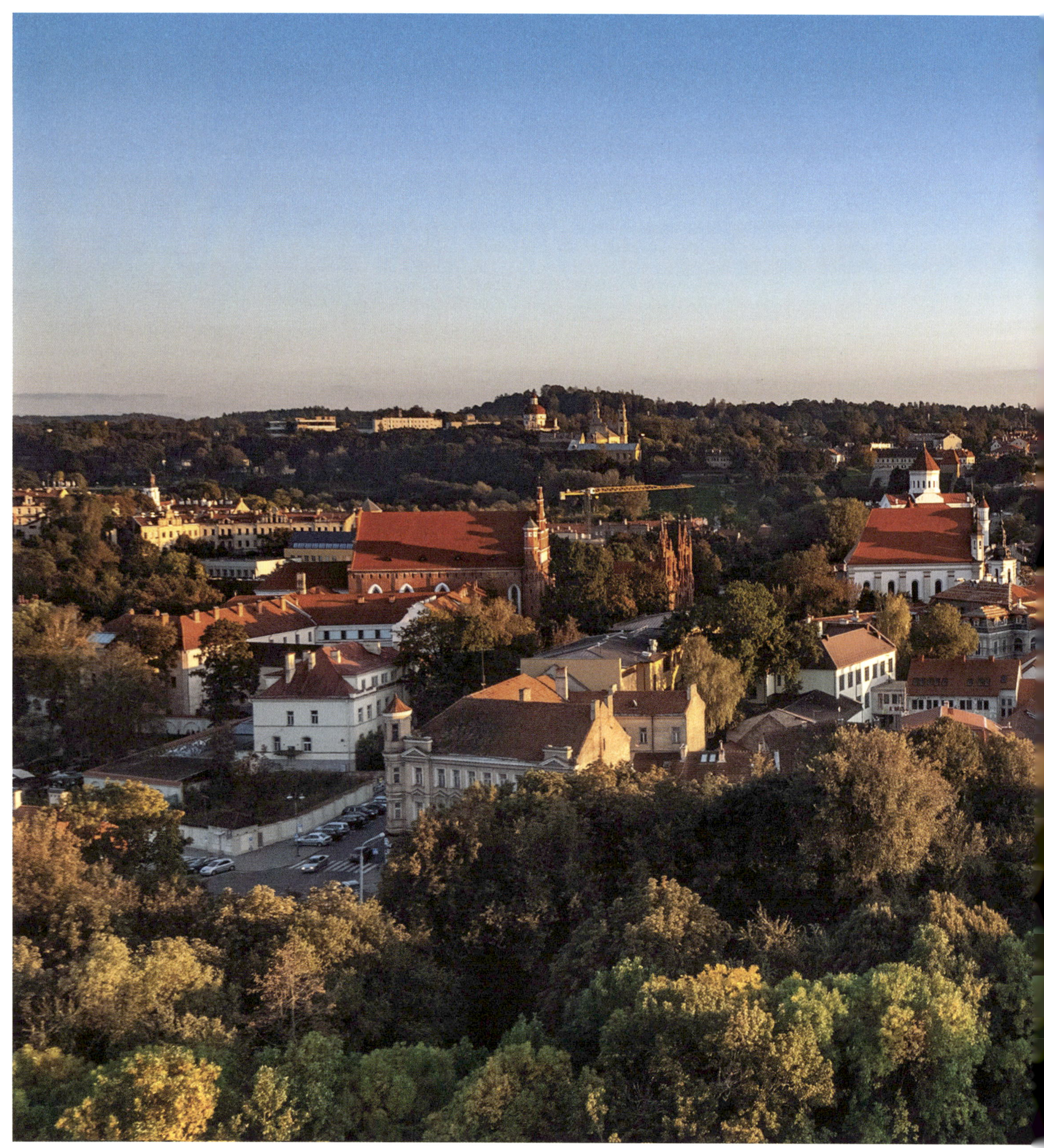

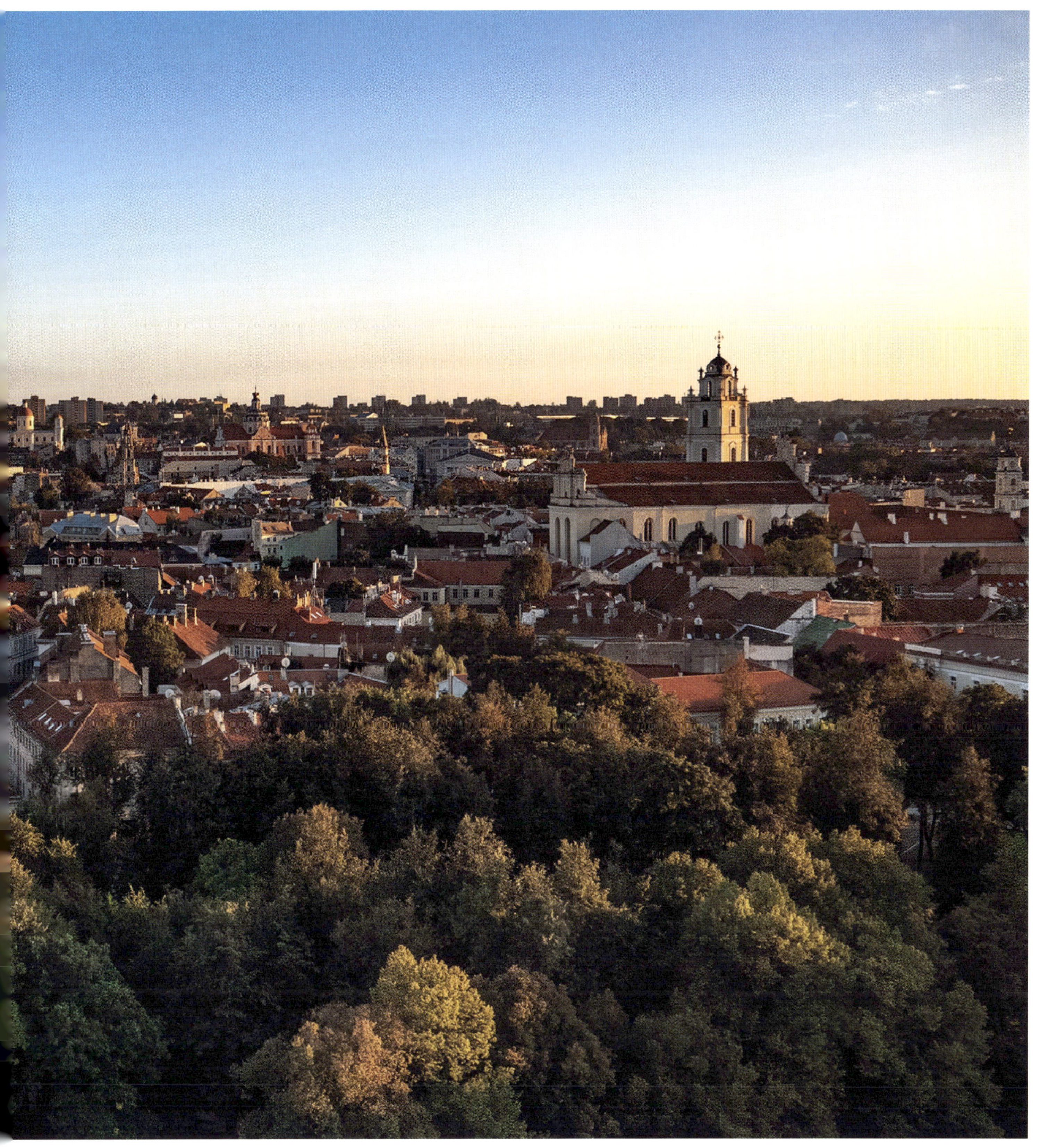

Vilnius, Lithuania
54°41'12.5"N 25°17'25.9"E
Overlooking the old town of Vilnius.
// September 2014

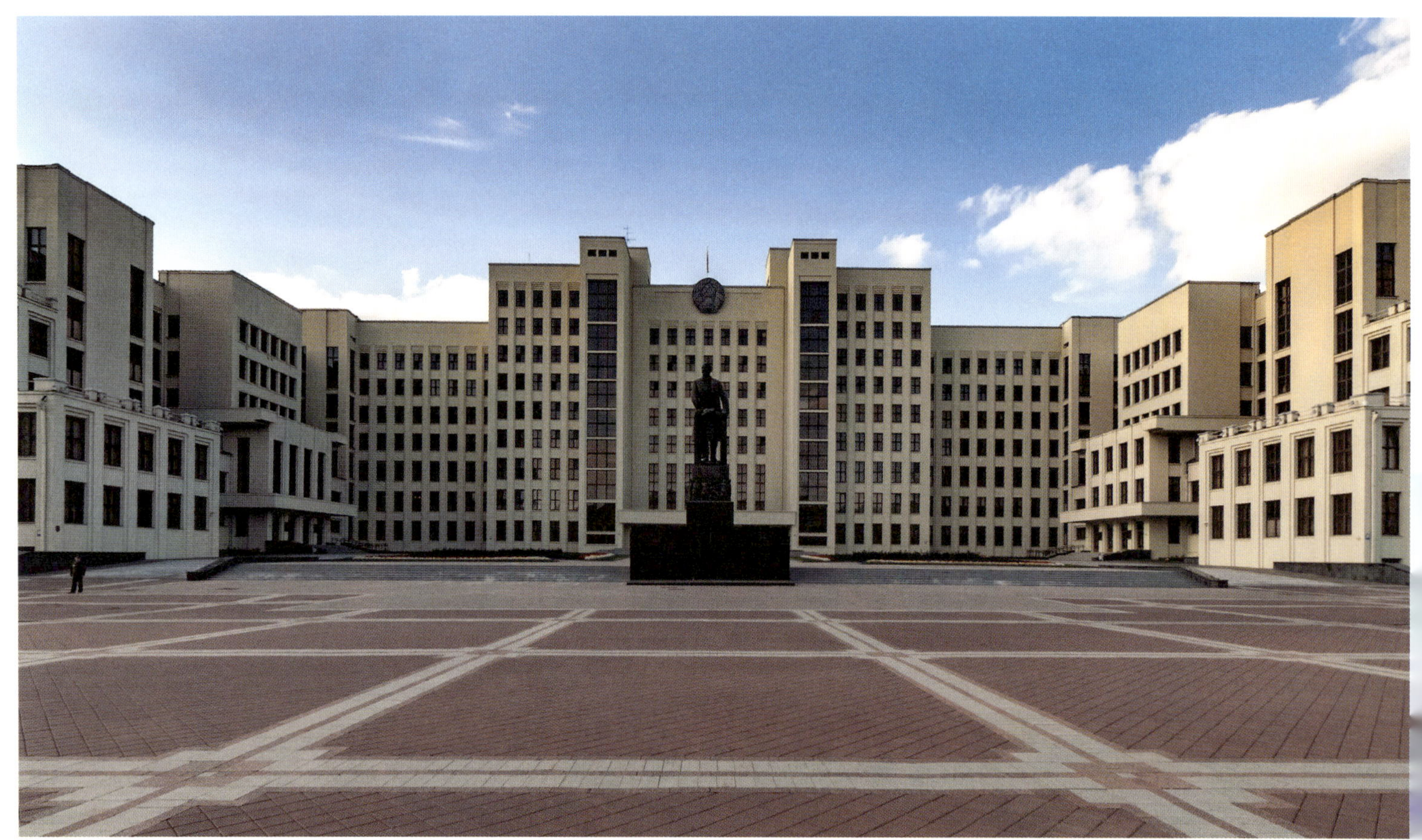

Minsk, Belarus
53°53'45.1"N 27°32'42.8"E
The Belarusian State Government Building
is just one of many imposing buildings in
the capital of Belarus.
// September 2014

Minsk, Belarus
53°54'30.8"N 27°34'29.5"E
A large granite column on Minsk's Victory Square
was erected in 1954 to honour soldiers of
the Great Patriotic War. Hidden underneath the
square lies Memorial Hall, an equally impressive
monument in the pedestrian underpass.
// September 2014

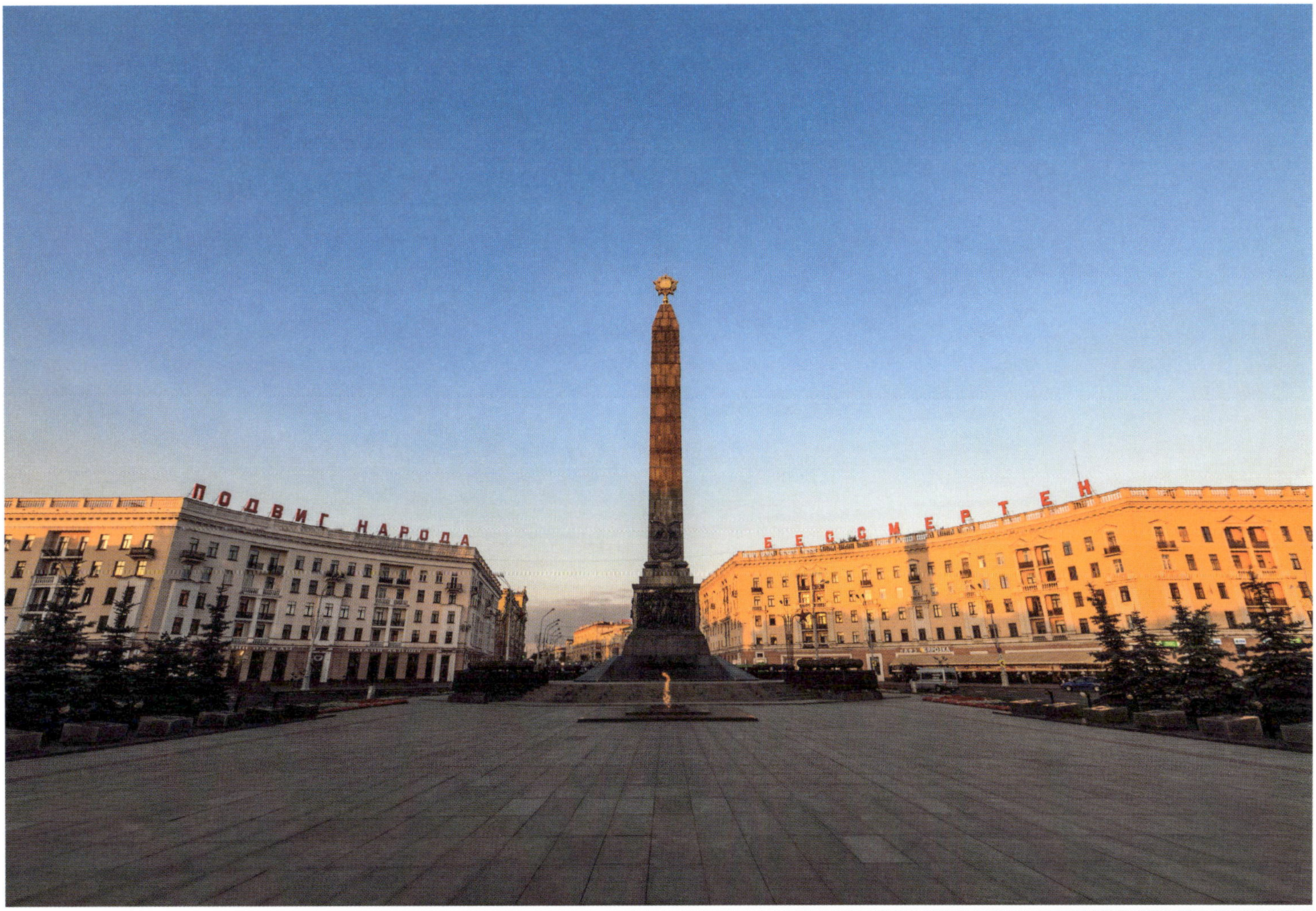

ПОДВИГ НАРОДА
БЕССМЕРТЕН

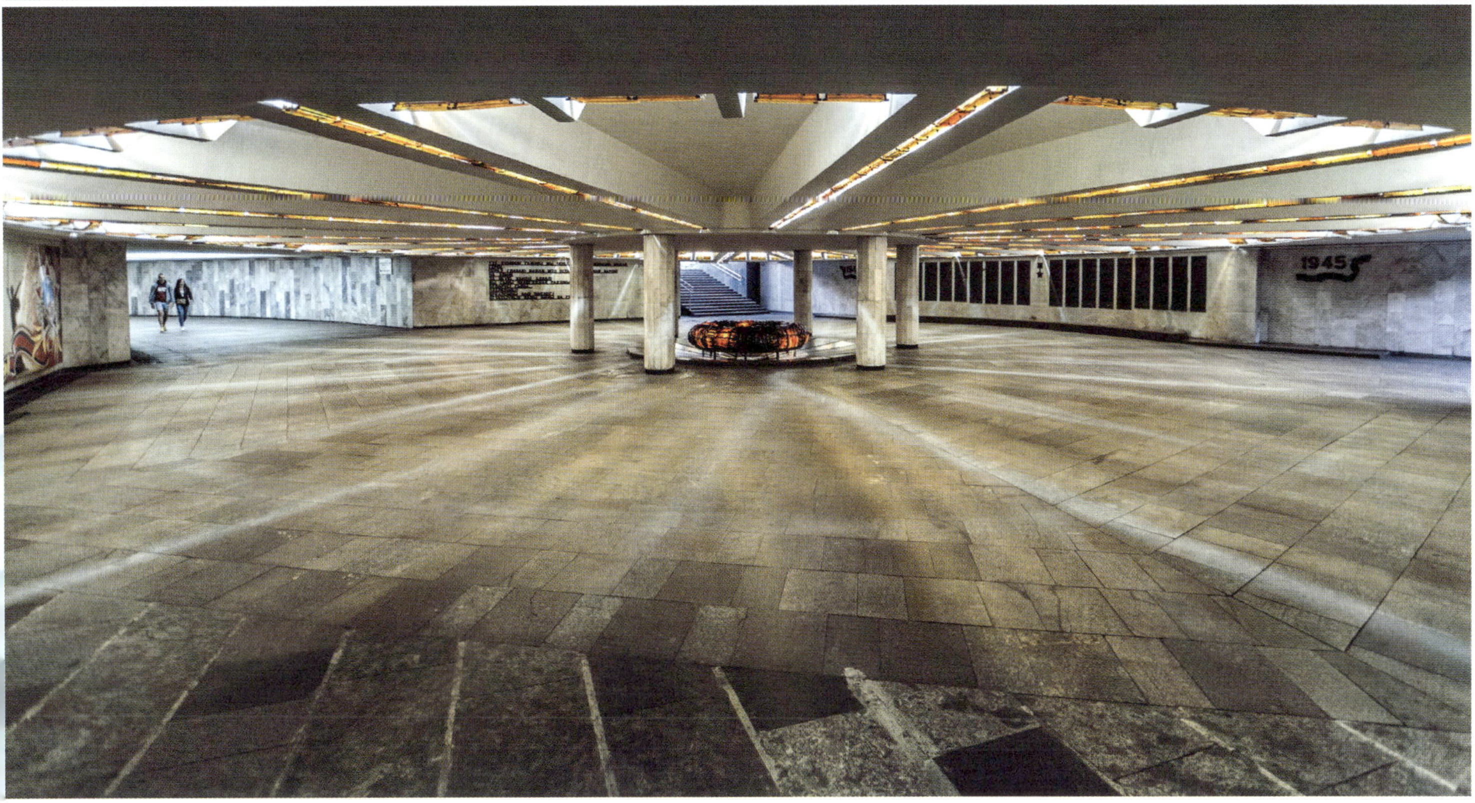

1945

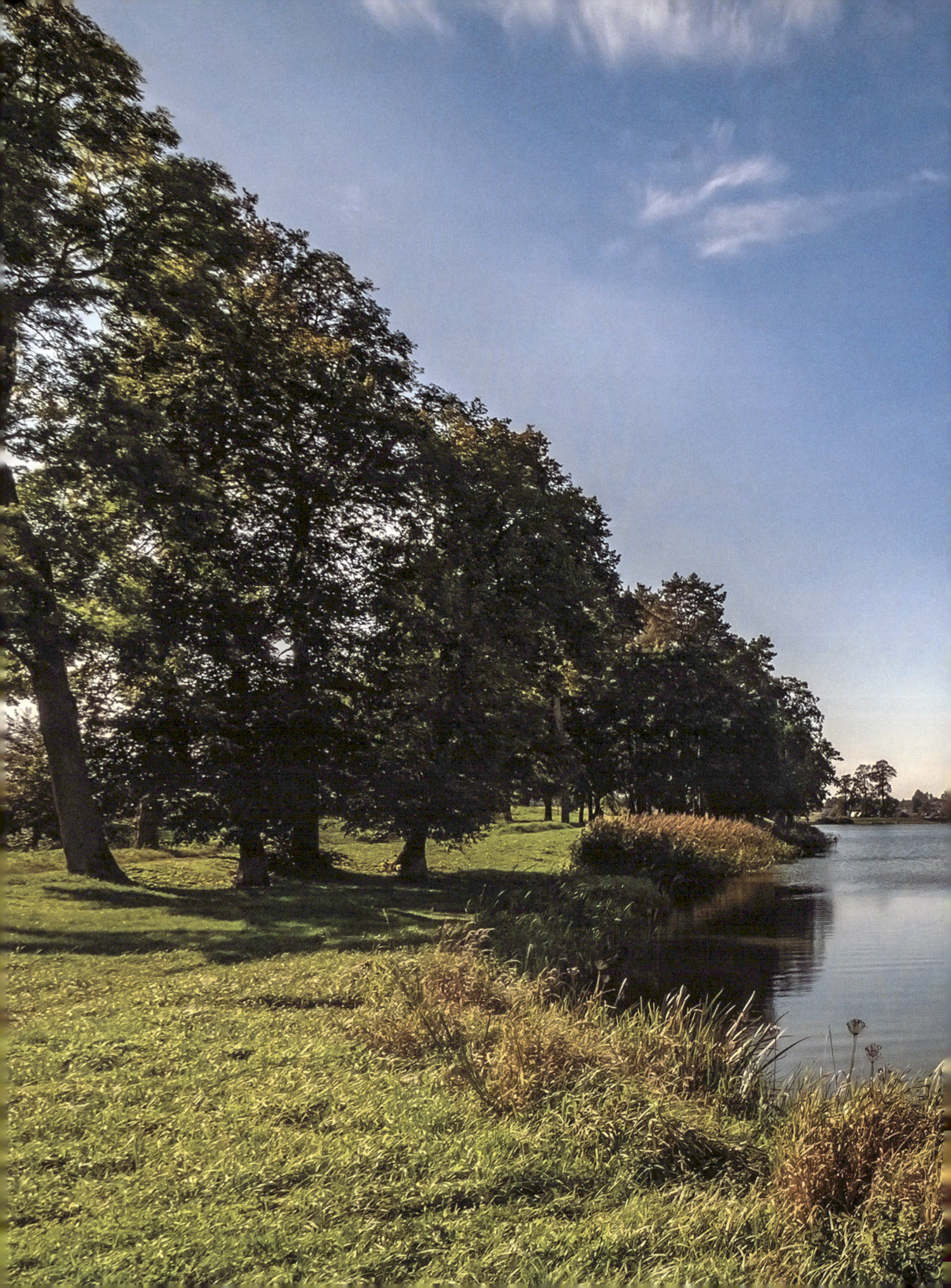

Mir, Belarus
53°26′59.2″N 26°28′42.0″E
The Mir Castle Complex seen from a distance.
// September 2014

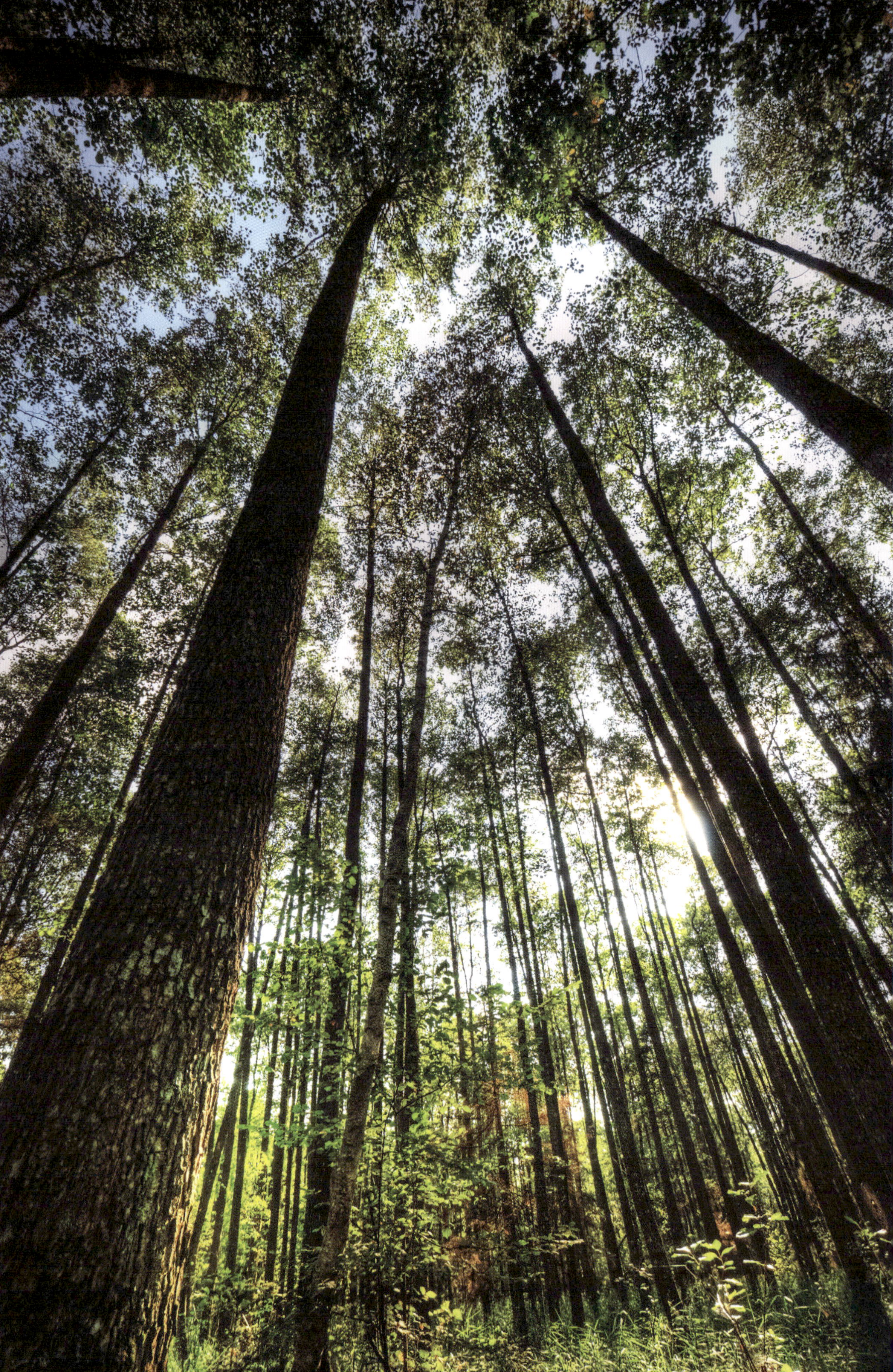

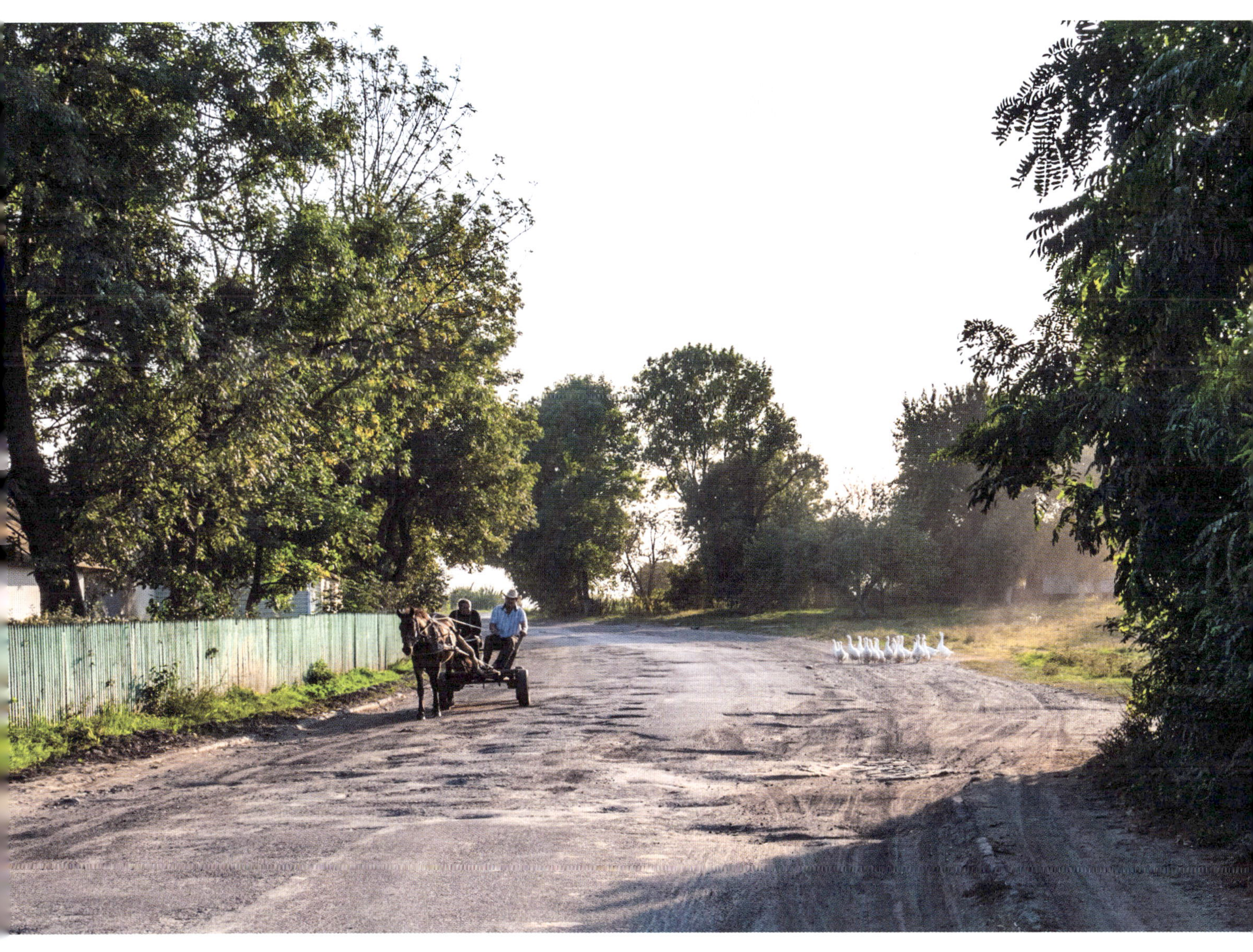

Belavezhskaya Pushcha National Park, Belarus
52°34'09.8"N 23°48'50.3"E
On the border between Belarus and Poland lies
Belavezhskaya Pushcha National Park, the largest
remaining primeval forest in Europe. This green
haven is home to the European bison, wild boar,
elk, konik horse and many impressive trees.
// September 2014

Lviv Oblast, Ukraine
50°23'47.1"N 24°02'53.0"E
The road from Brest in Belarus to Lviv in Ukraine
took many, many hours due to the poor road
conditions at that time. Fortunately, this route
also treats you to many picturesque rural scenes
that seem to be lost in time.
// September 2014

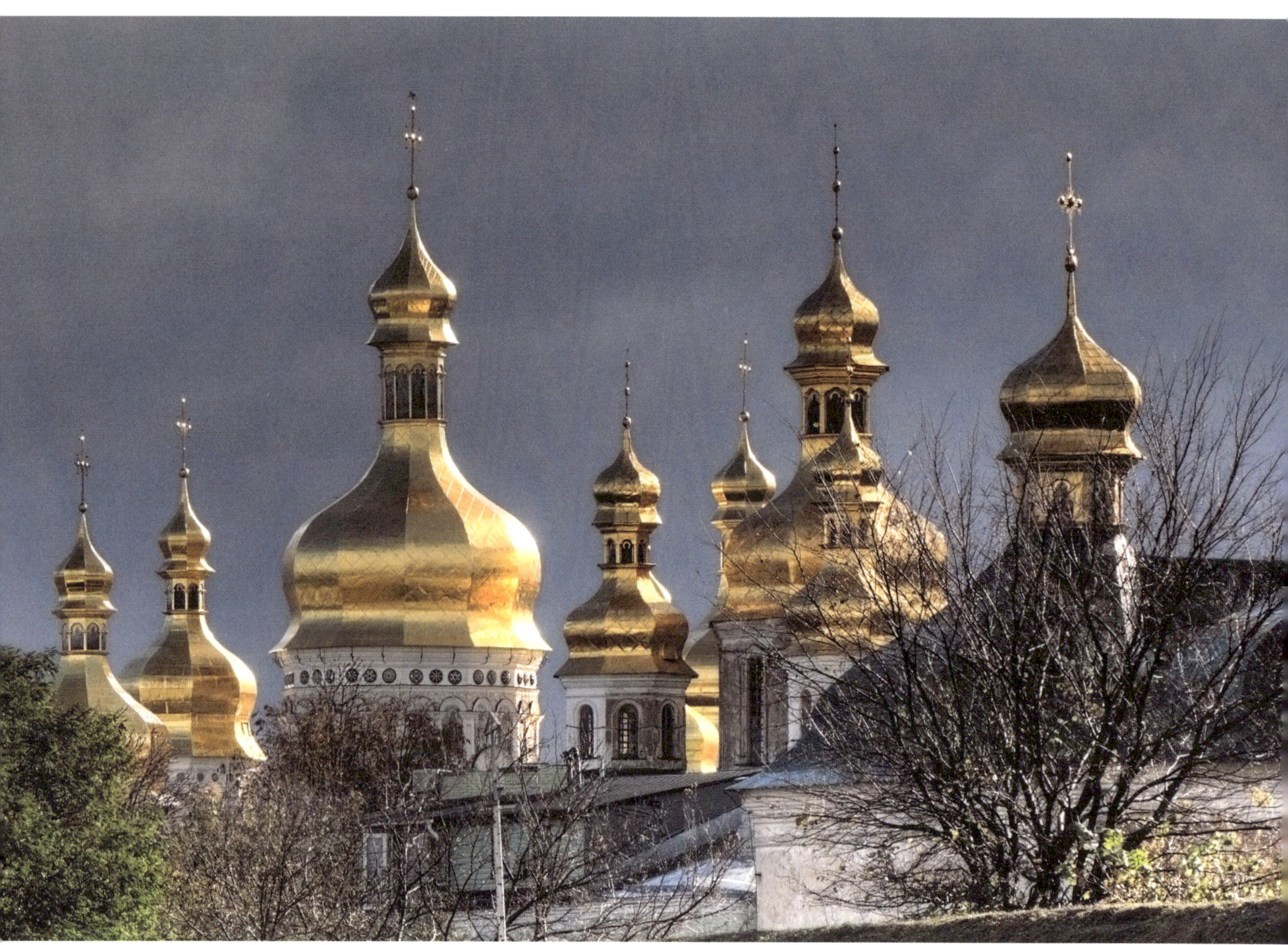

Kiev, Ukraine
50°26'17.9"N 30°33'15.2"E
In between some heavy autumn showers, rays
of sunlight illuminate the golden roofs of Kiev
Pechersk Lavra, an Orthodox Christian monastery.
// October 2016

Kiev, Ukraine
50°26'58.6"N 30°31'33.8"E
Maidan Nezalezhnosti ('Independence Square'),
carefully restored after the violent Euromaidan
Revolution of 2013-2014.
// October 2016

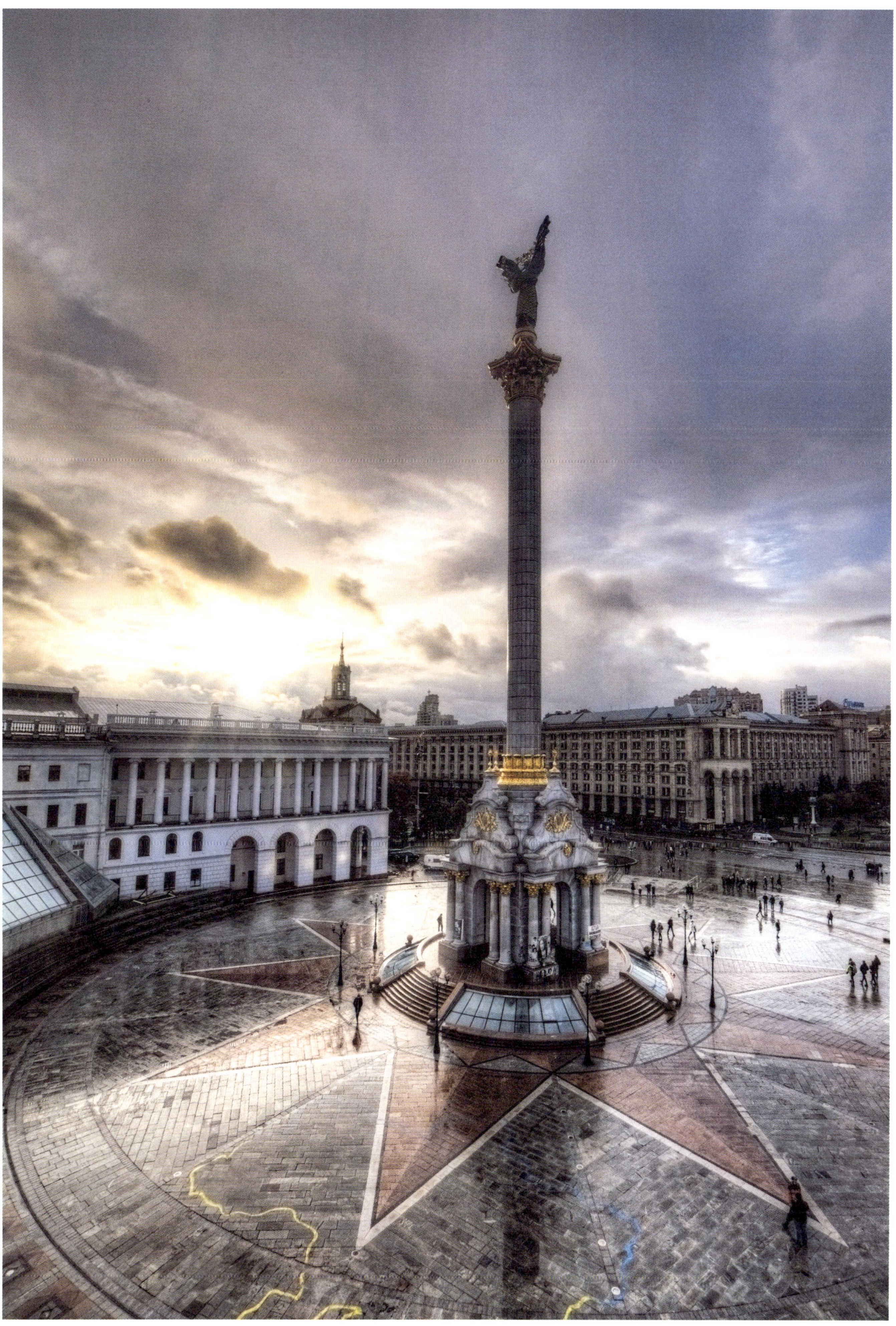

The Empty North
Route and travel suggestions

50

Scenic regions and nature reserves

1 Belavezhskaya Pushcha // **Belarus & Poland**
2 Höga Kusten // **Sweden**
3 Lofoten // **Norway**
4 Lyngen // **Norway**
5 Soomaa // **Estonia**
6 Tiveden // **Sweden**
7 Torneträsk, Abisko & Laponia // **Sweden**
8 Urho Kekkonen National Park // **Finland**

Cities and towns

9   Copenhagen // **Denmark**
10 Kamianets-Podilskyi // **Ukraine**
11 Lviv // **Ukraine**
12 Minsk // **Belarus**
13 Örebro // **Sweden**
14 St. Petersburg // **Russia**
15 Tallinn // **Estonia**
16 Tartu // **Estonia**
17 Vilnius // **Lithuania**

Cultural experiences

18 Brest Fortress // **Belarus**
19 Coffee houses in Lviv // **Ukraine**
20 Gammelstad Church Town, Luleå // **Sweden**
21 Kiev Pechersk Lavra // **Ukraine**
22 Kiruna Mine // **Sweden**
23 Lenin (1957 Icebreaker), Murmansk // **Russia**
24 Mir Castle Complex // **Belarus**
25 Rock art of Alta // **Norway**
26 State Hermitage Museum, St. Petersburg // **Russia**

Spectacular roads and scenic routes

27 E6 between Skibotn and Alta // **Norway**
28 E10 between Kiruna and Å // **Sweden & Norway**
29 E69 to Magerøya // **Norway**

○ Photo location

● Travel suggestion

123 Photo page number

123 Travel suggestion number

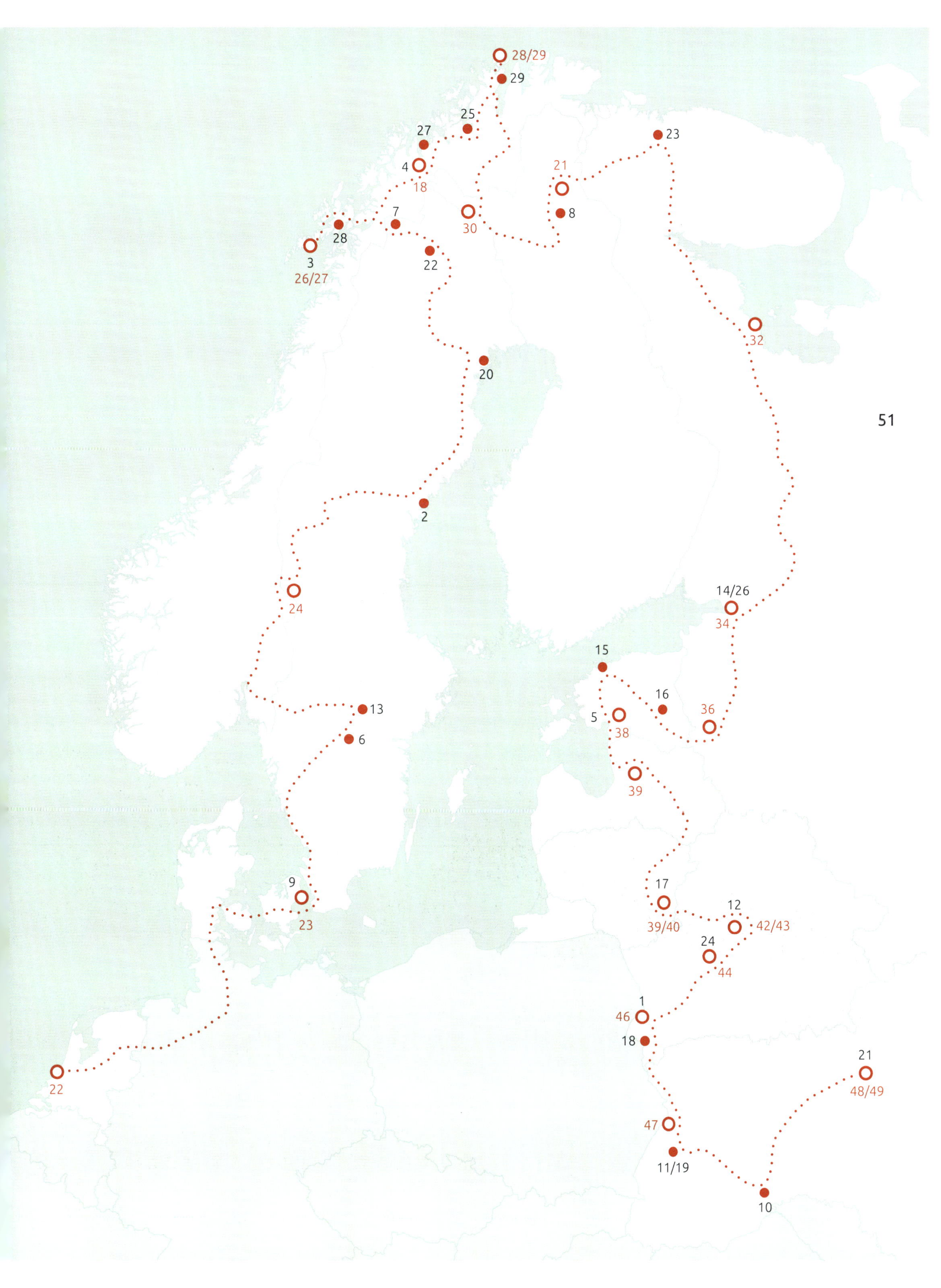

28/29
29
25
27
4
18
23
21
7
28
30
8
3
26/27
22
32
20
51
2
24
14/26
34
15
13
16
5
6
38
36
39
9
23
17
12
39/40
42/43
24
44
1
46
18
21
22
48/49
47
11/19
10

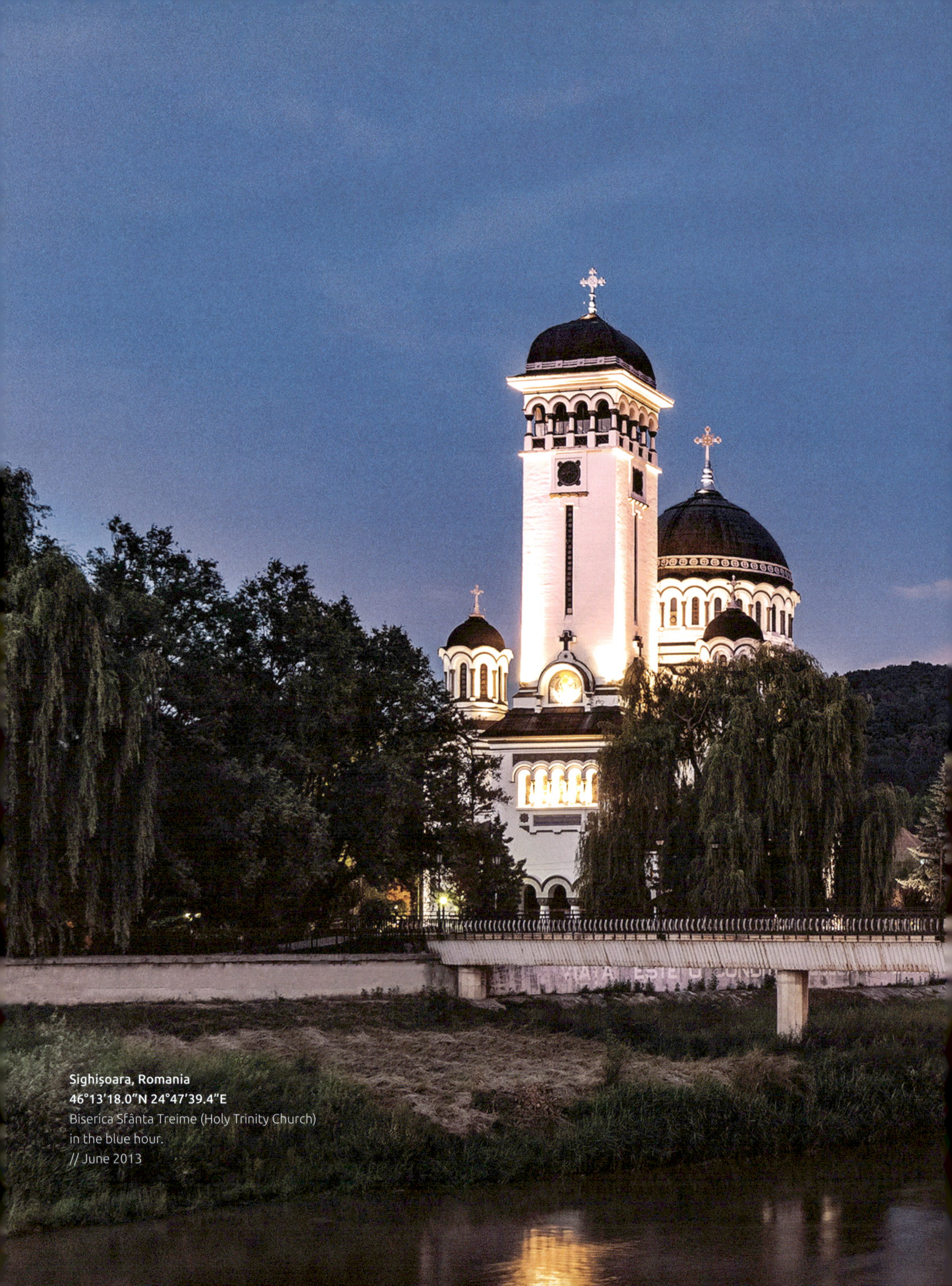

Sighișoara, Romania
46°13'18.0"N 24°47'39.4"E
Biserica Sfânta Treime (Holy Trinity Church)
in the blue hour.
// June 2013

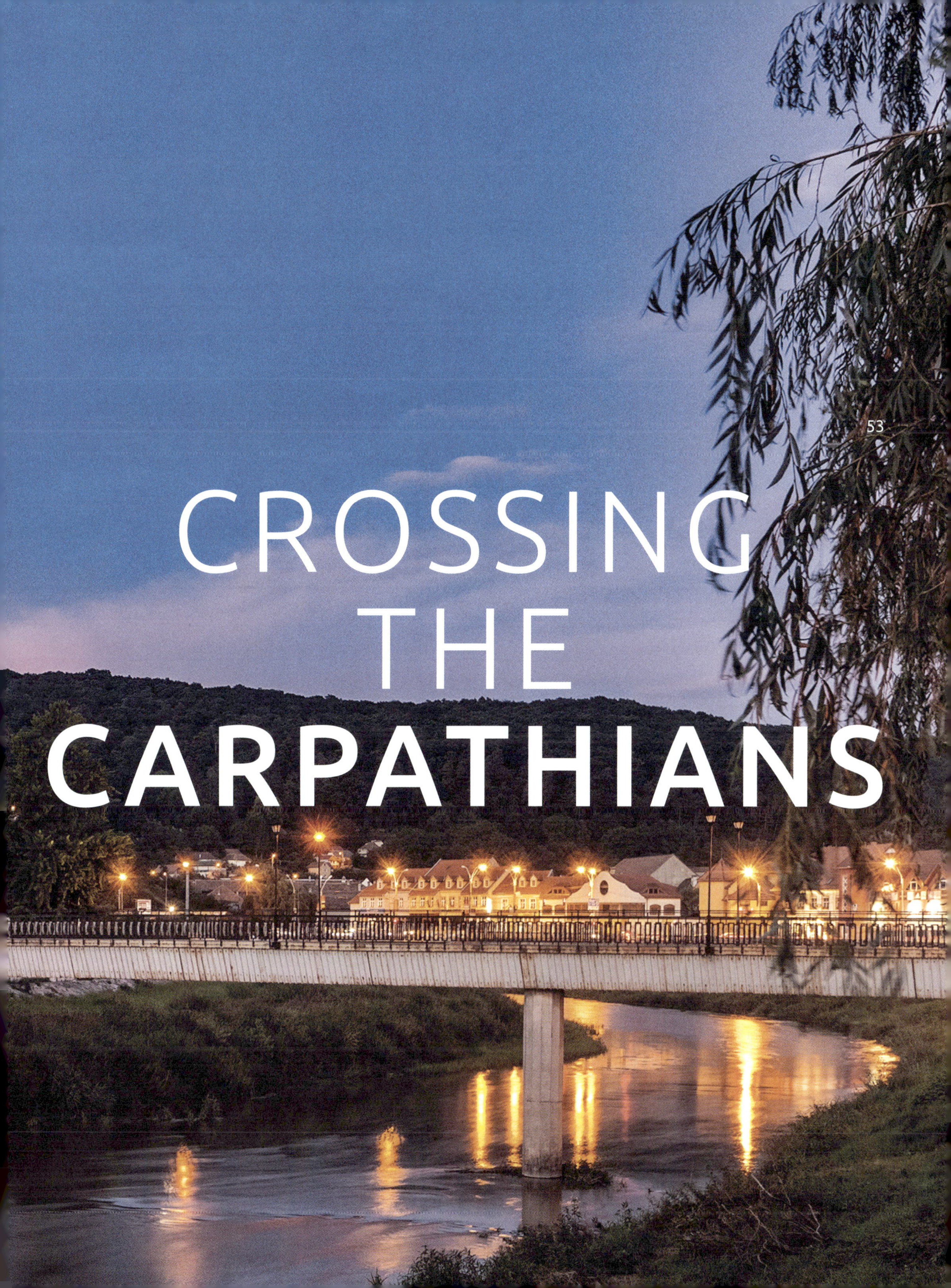

CROSSING THE CARPATHIANS

'The trip from the Netherlands to the Black
Sea is one of countless mountains in various
shapes and colours that seamlessly form
a whole.'

THE 1,500-KILOMETRES-LONG
Carpathian Mountains define a large part
of the landscape in Central and Eastern
Europe. A journey to the Carpathians starts
in Germany, with picturesque towns in
regions like the Moselle valley and fascinating cities like Bamberg and Dresden.
Bohemian Switzerland, a scenic part of the
Elbe Sandstone Mountains, is only an hour
away from Dresden. These mountains
connect to the Sudetes, which cover a large
part of the Czech Republic and the southwest of Poland. These in turn merge with
the Carpathians, making the trip from
the Netherlands to the Black Sea one of
countless mountains in various shapes and
colours that seamlessly form a whole.

The High Tatras in Slovakia and the south
of Poland, together with the Southern
Carpathians in Romania, are the highest
parts of the Carpathians. They form a fantastic backdrop while driving from west to east,
with medieval towns like Banská Štiavnica
as photogenic cultural stops along the way.
The Kriváň, voted by many as the most
beautiful mountain of Slovakia, offers a
fantastic panoramic view that is definitely
worth the hike to the summit at an altitude
of nearly 2,500 metres.

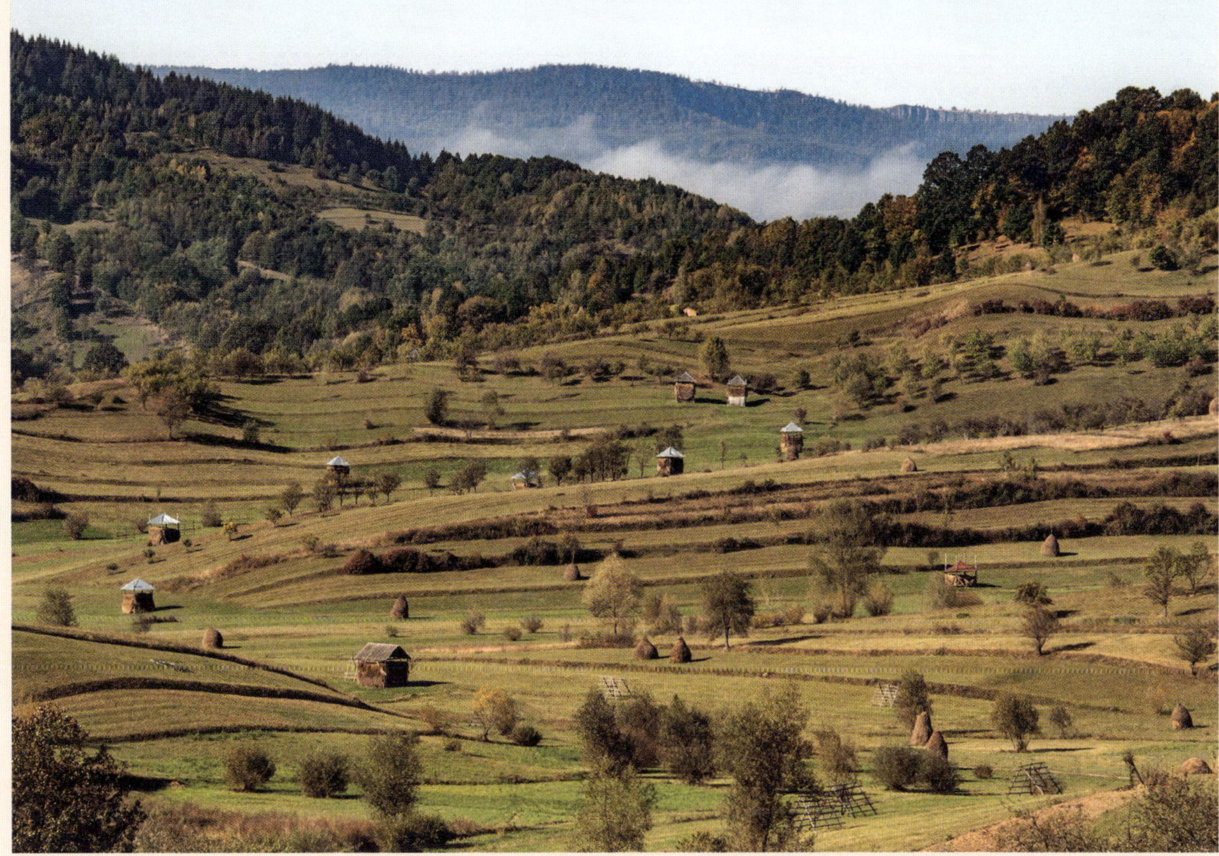

Then, further east, the Carpathians extend deep into Romania. Few regions have left such a lasting impression on me as Maramureș. This charming historic area in the north of Romania seems to have been lost in time. Horse carts occupy the street scene, mountain slopes are covered with round haystacks and the villagers have a largely self-supporting lifestyle. Although the villages and towns are full of life, there is no rush in Maramureș.

Looking at Romania as a whole, it is a country of wild landscapes, friendly people, good food and great wines – although the biggest wine surprise in Europe is to be found in its eastern neighbour, Moldova.

The underground cellars of Mileștii Mici and Cricova store the world's largest and second-largest wine collections (together over three million bottles) in two cave road complexes that are 200 and 120 kilometres long, respectively. In the world of wines, it does not get any more impressive than a visit to one of these bizarre underground wine cities.

Last but not least, Romania is home to some of the most exciting mountain roads in Europe. It just never gets boring in Romania.

Maramureș, Romania
47°56'16.7"N 24°00'34.9"E
Going to Maramureș in the far north of Romania is like going back in time. Horse carts and neat haystacks are everywhere, and many people still work the land with their bare hands.
// September 2014

Dresden, Germany
51°03′18.8″N 13°44′28.6″E
The photogenic skyline of the centre of Dresden.
Extensive reconstruction activities in recent
decades have finally restored the friendly,
culture-rich atmosphere of this city.
// May 2017

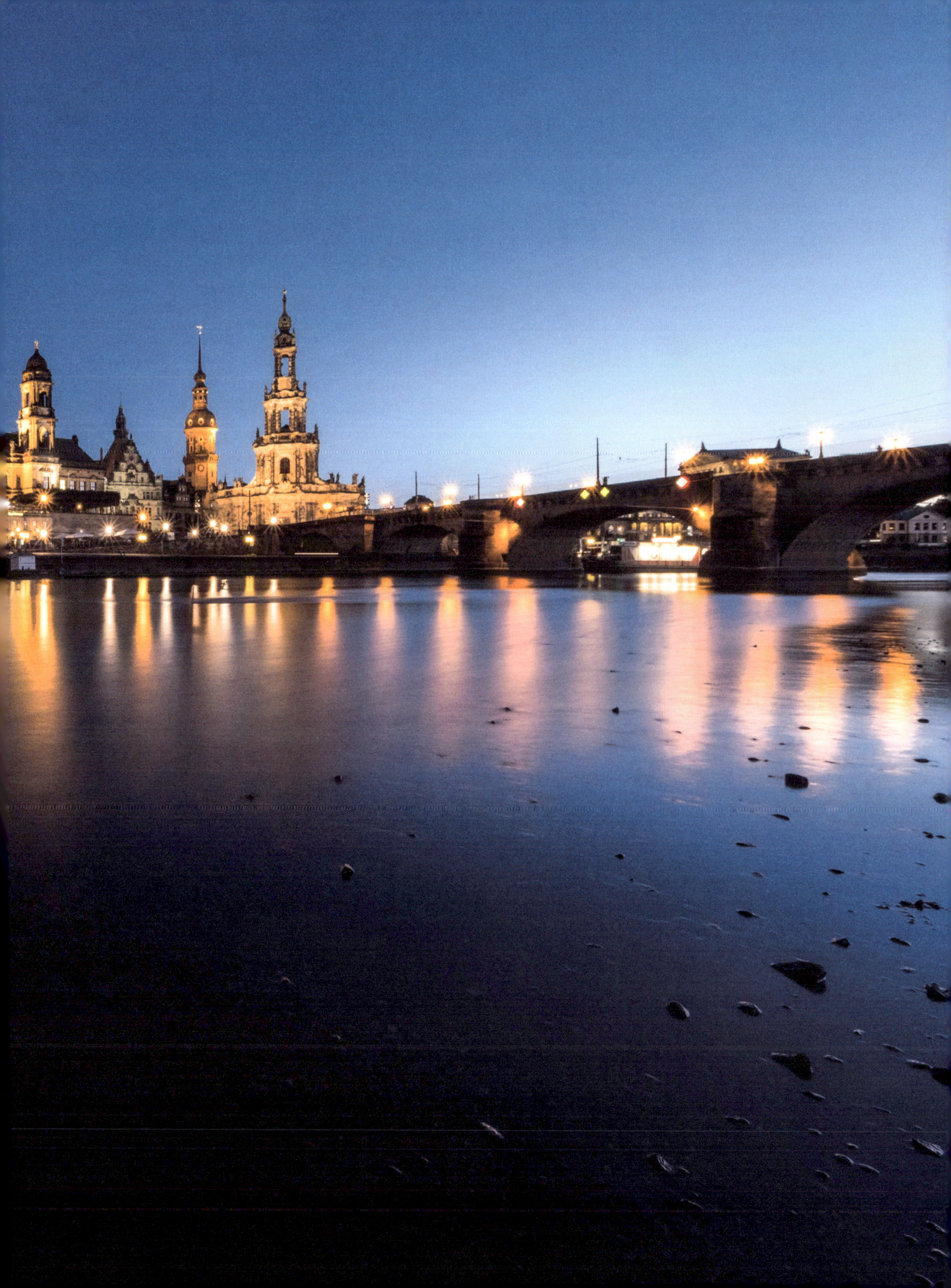

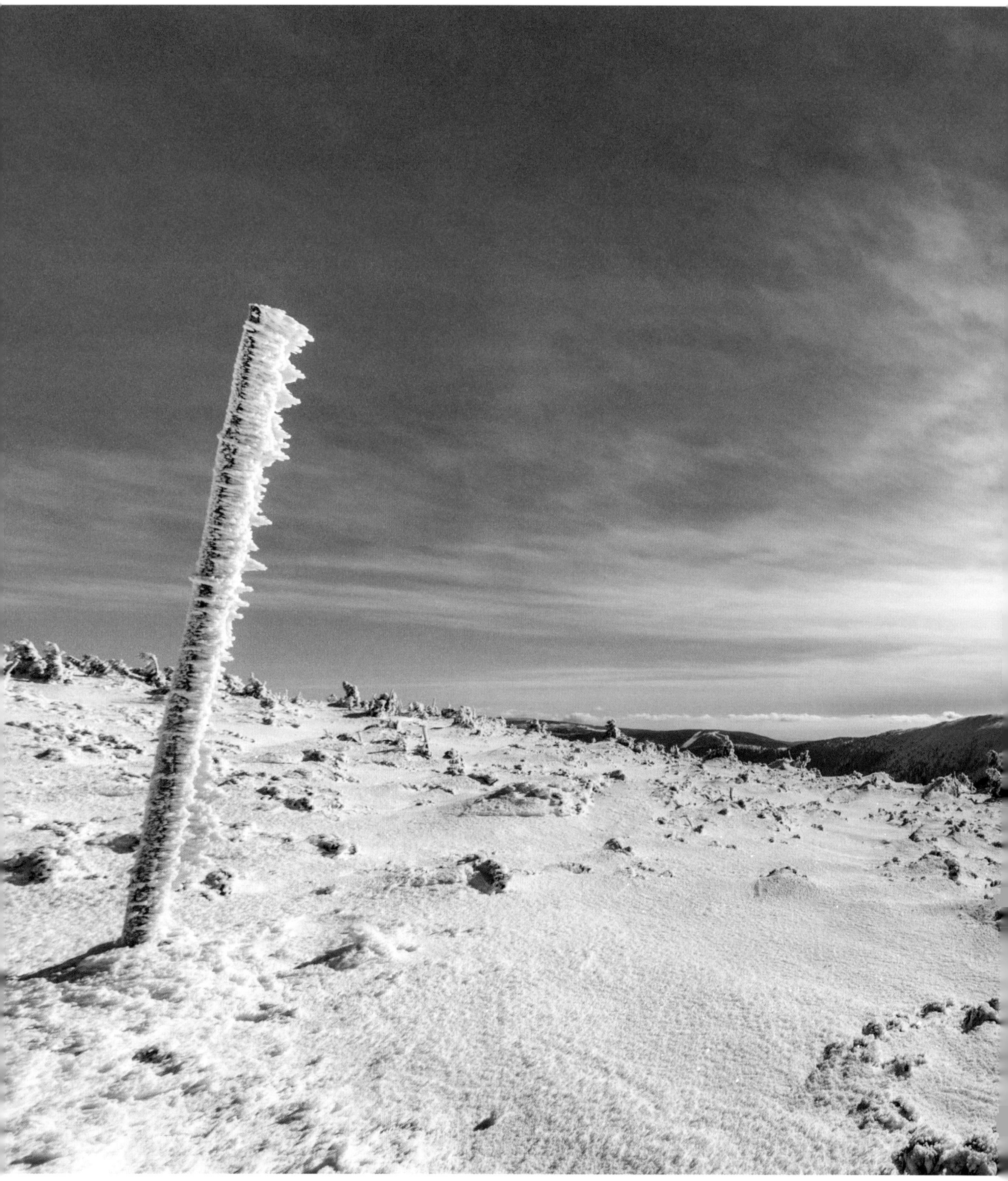

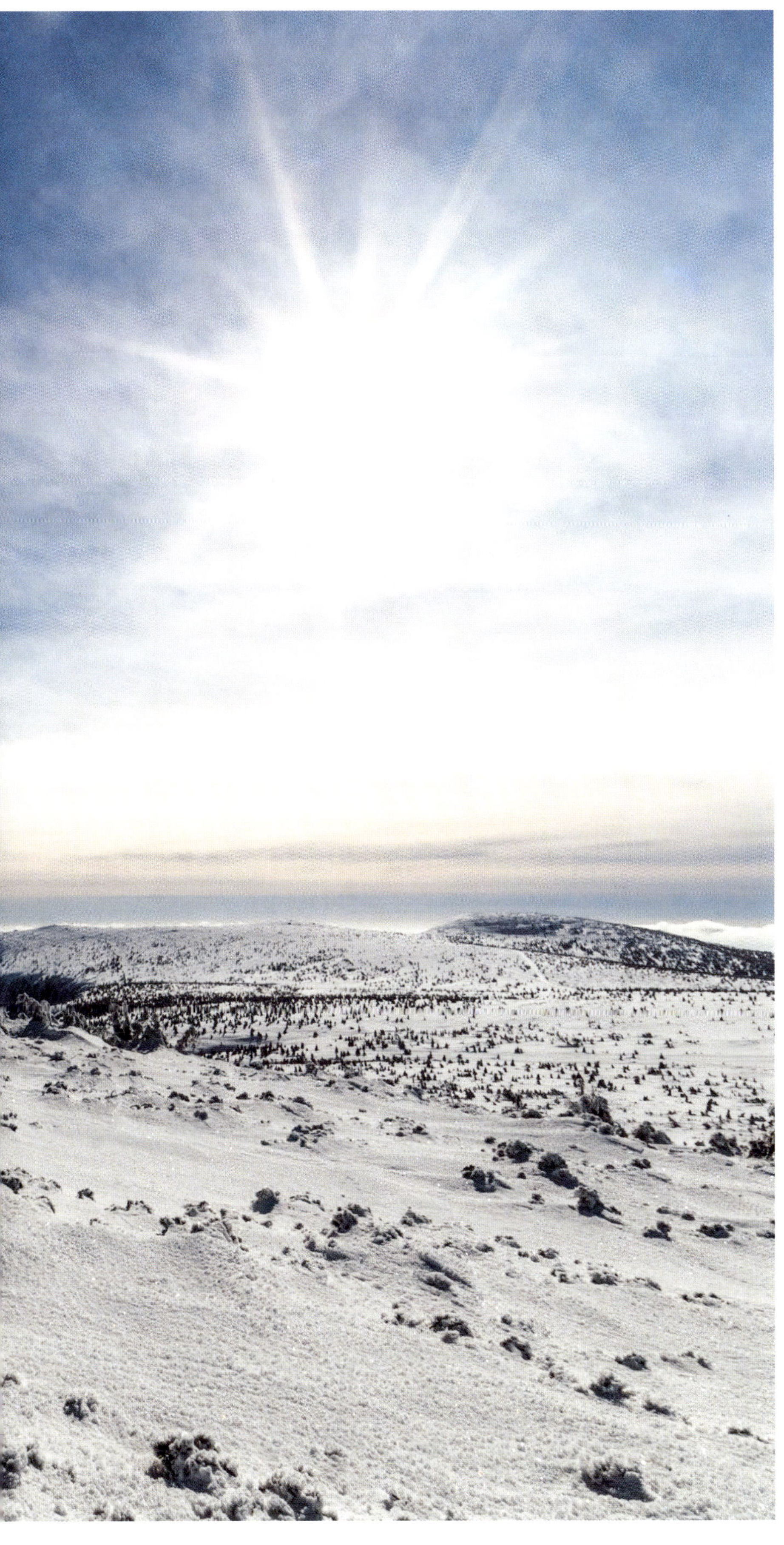

Szrenica, Polish-Czech border
50°46'48.6"N 15°32'26.5"E
Harsh winds have formed ice crystals on
the wooden poles on top of the Szrenica.
// February 2014

60

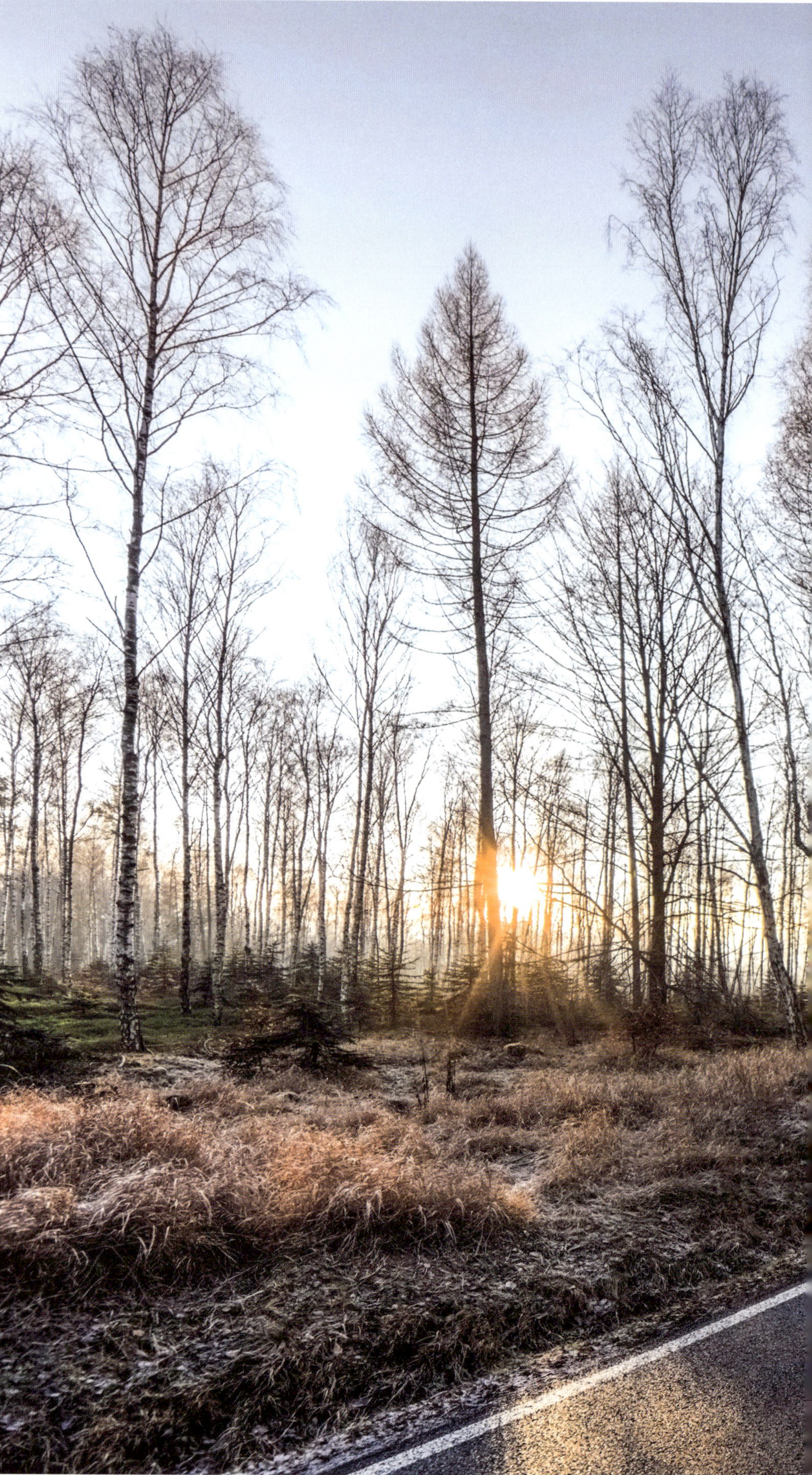

Sněžník, Czech Republic
50°48'22.8"N 14°06'15.9"E
The afternoon sun illuminates the frosty
forest on the road to the Tisa Rocks
in Bohemian Switzerland.
// January 2020

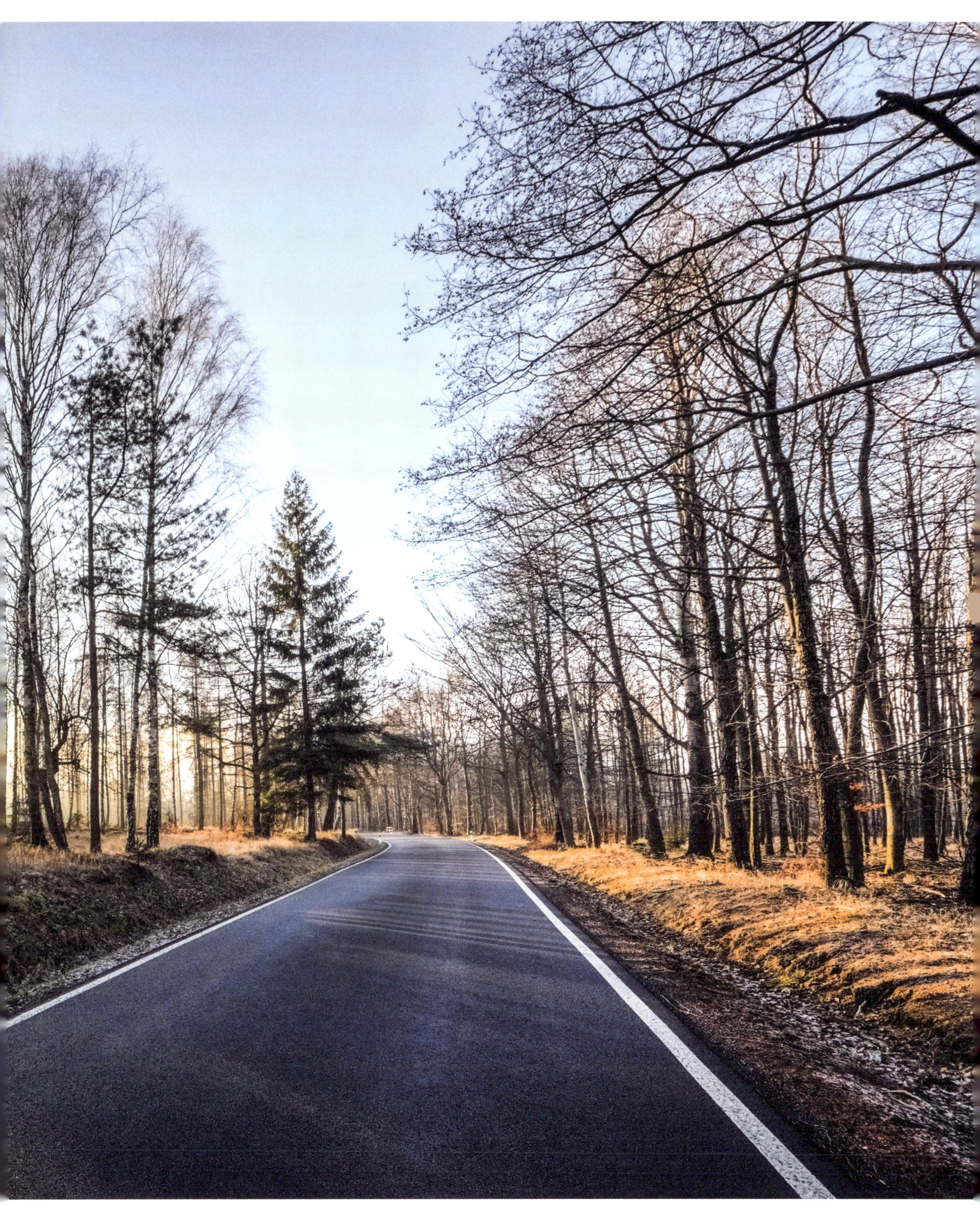

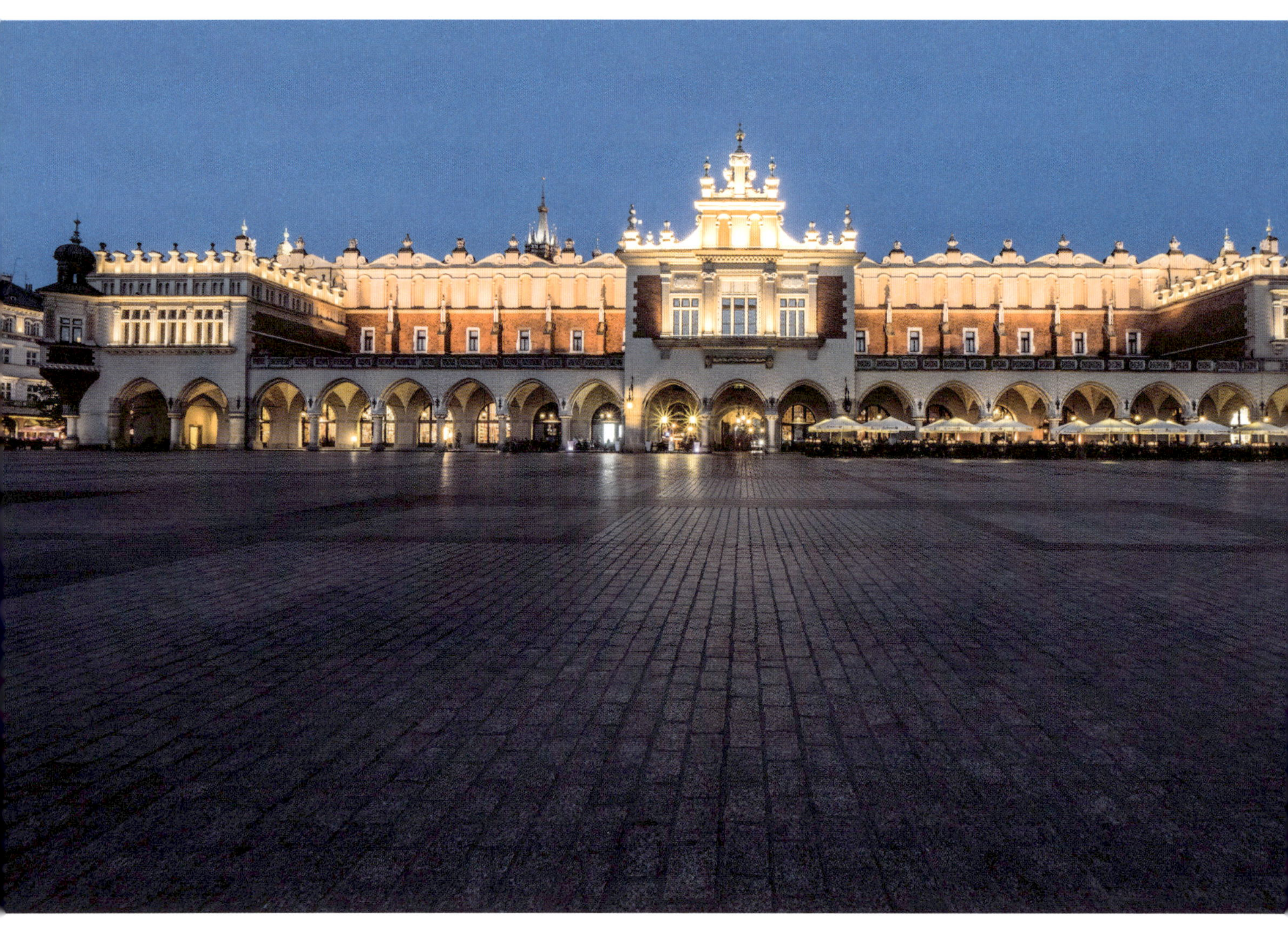

Kraków, Poland
50°03'43.2"N 19°56'10.9"E
The heavy rain just stopped in time for me to take
this image of the Kraków Cloth Hall.
// May 2017

Kraków, Poland
50°03'42.1"N 19°56'22.0"E
The spectactular ceiling of Saint Mary's Basilica.
// May 2017

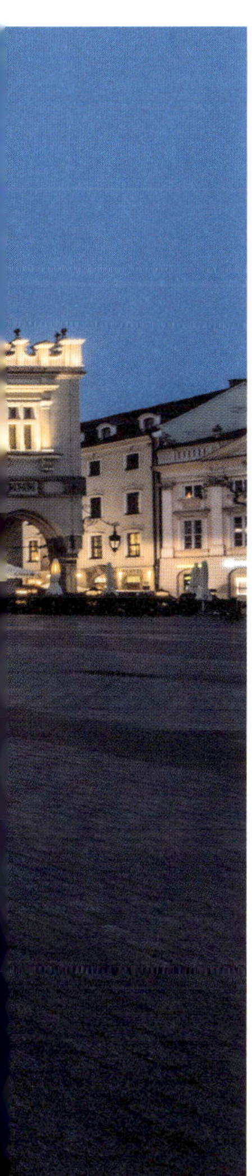

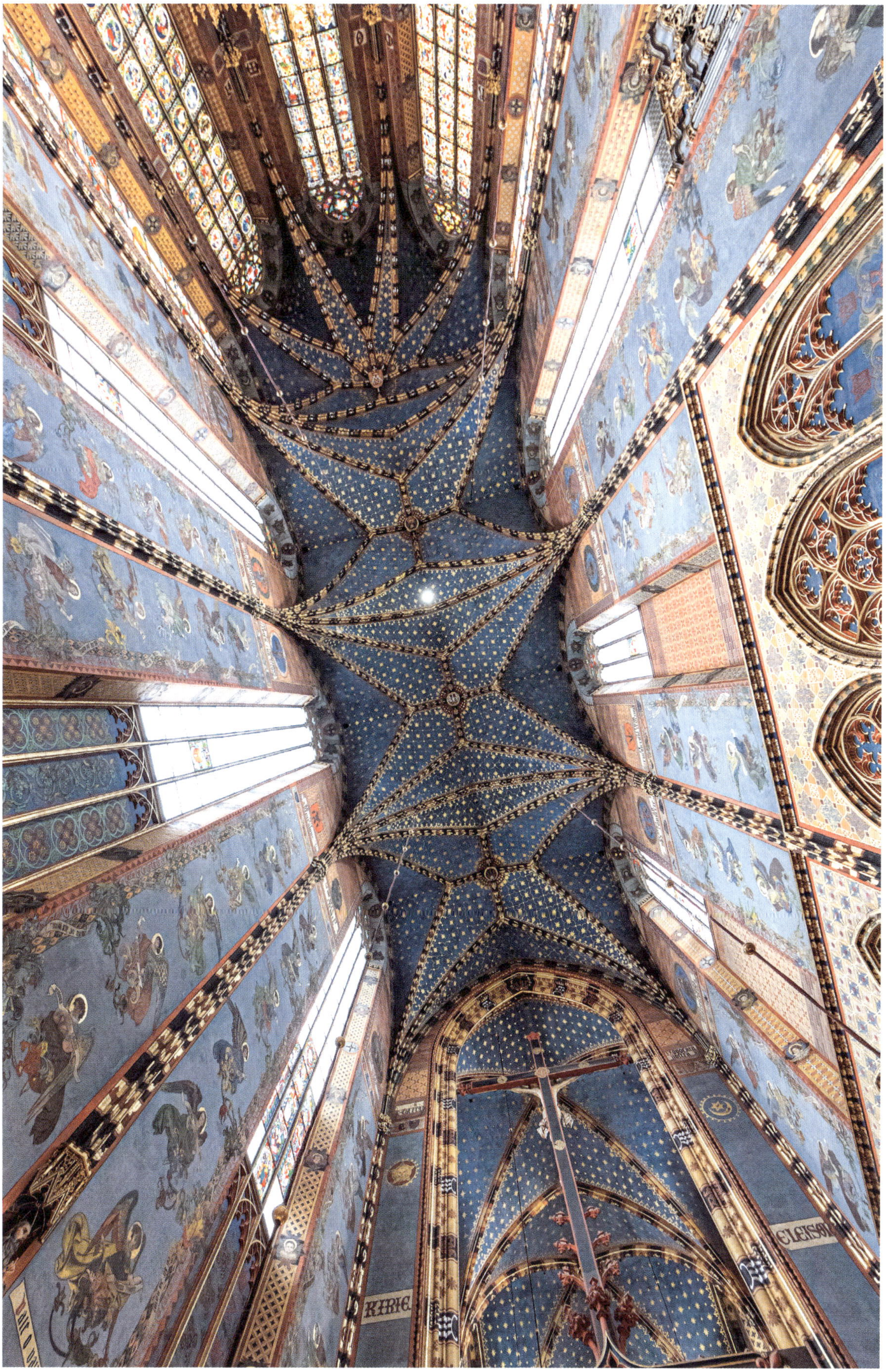

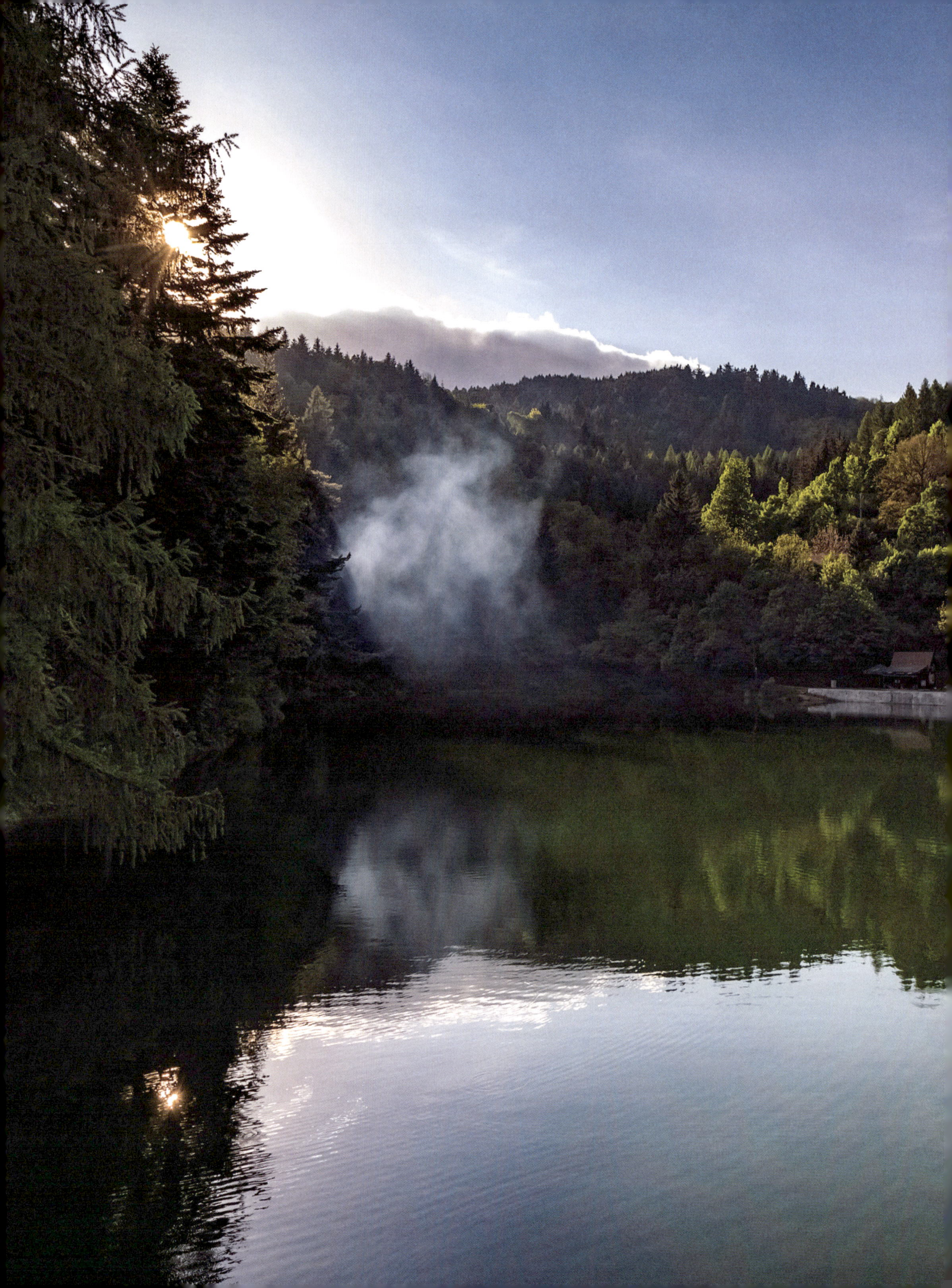

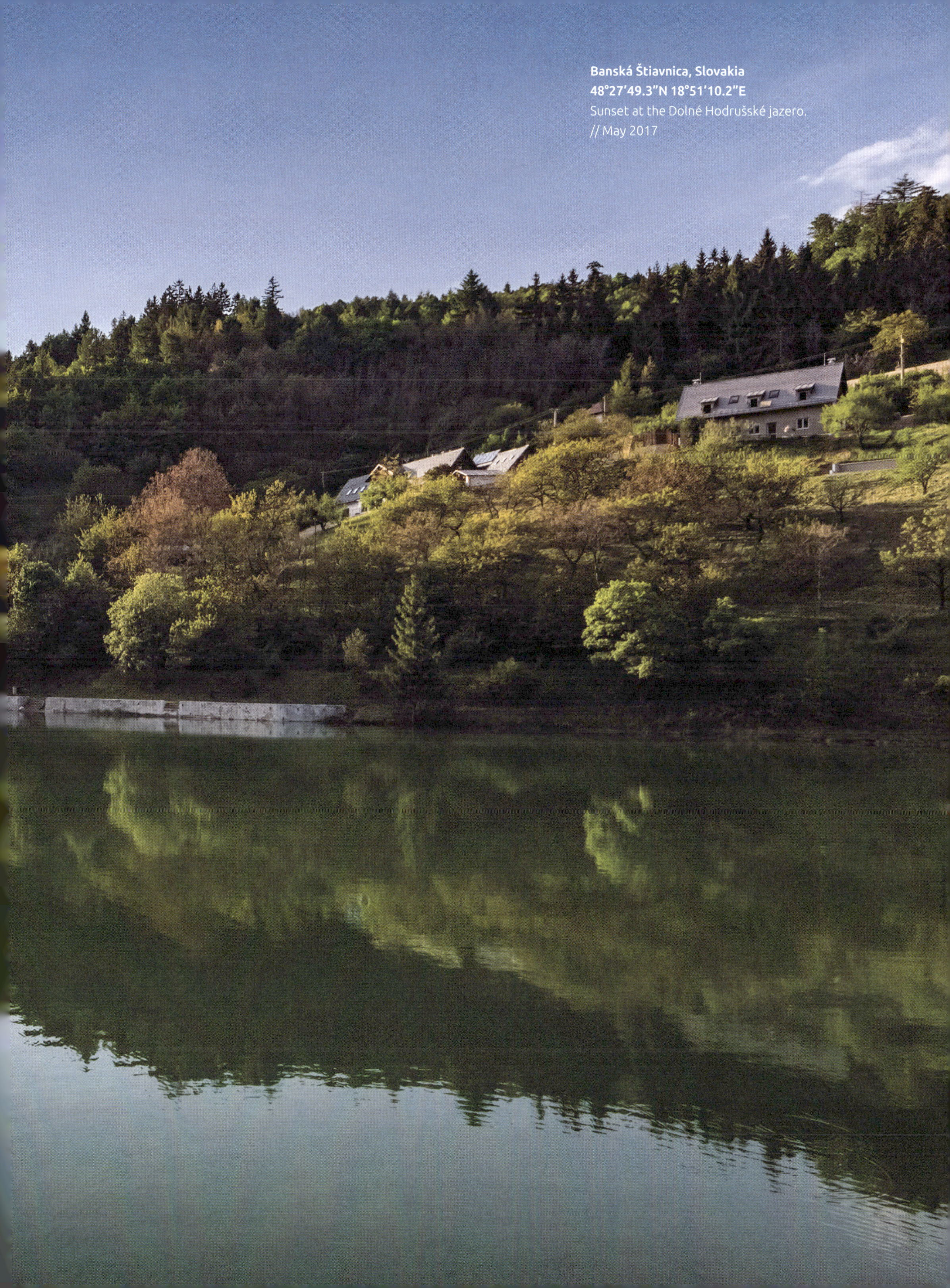

Banská Štiavnica, Slovakia
48°27'49.3"N 18°51'10.2"E
Sunset at the Dolné Hodrušské jazero.
// May 2017

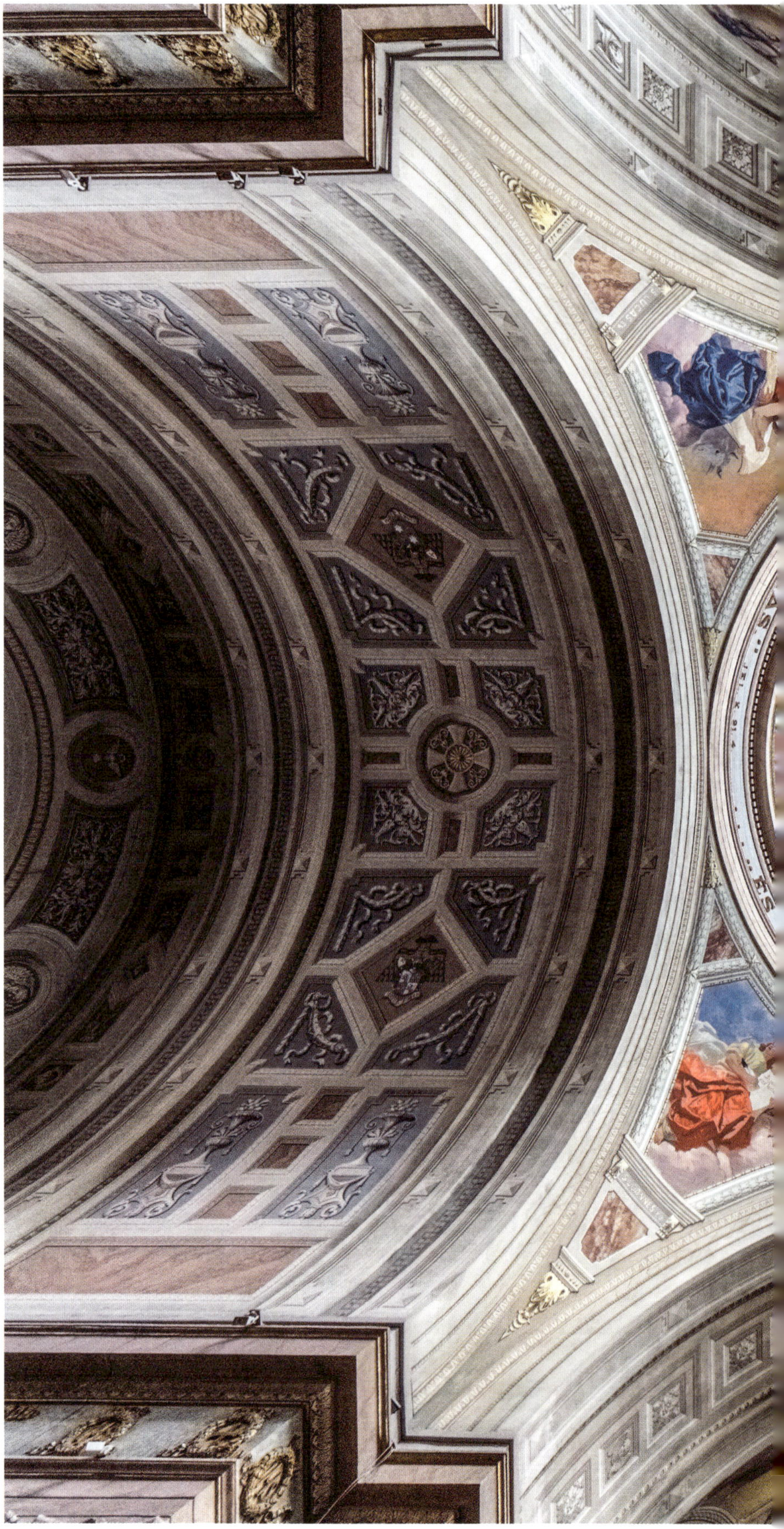

66

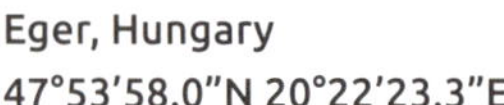

Eger, Hungary
47°53′58.0″N 20°22′23.3″E
The impressive ceiling of the Cathedral Basilica
of St. John the Apostle in Eger.
// May 2017

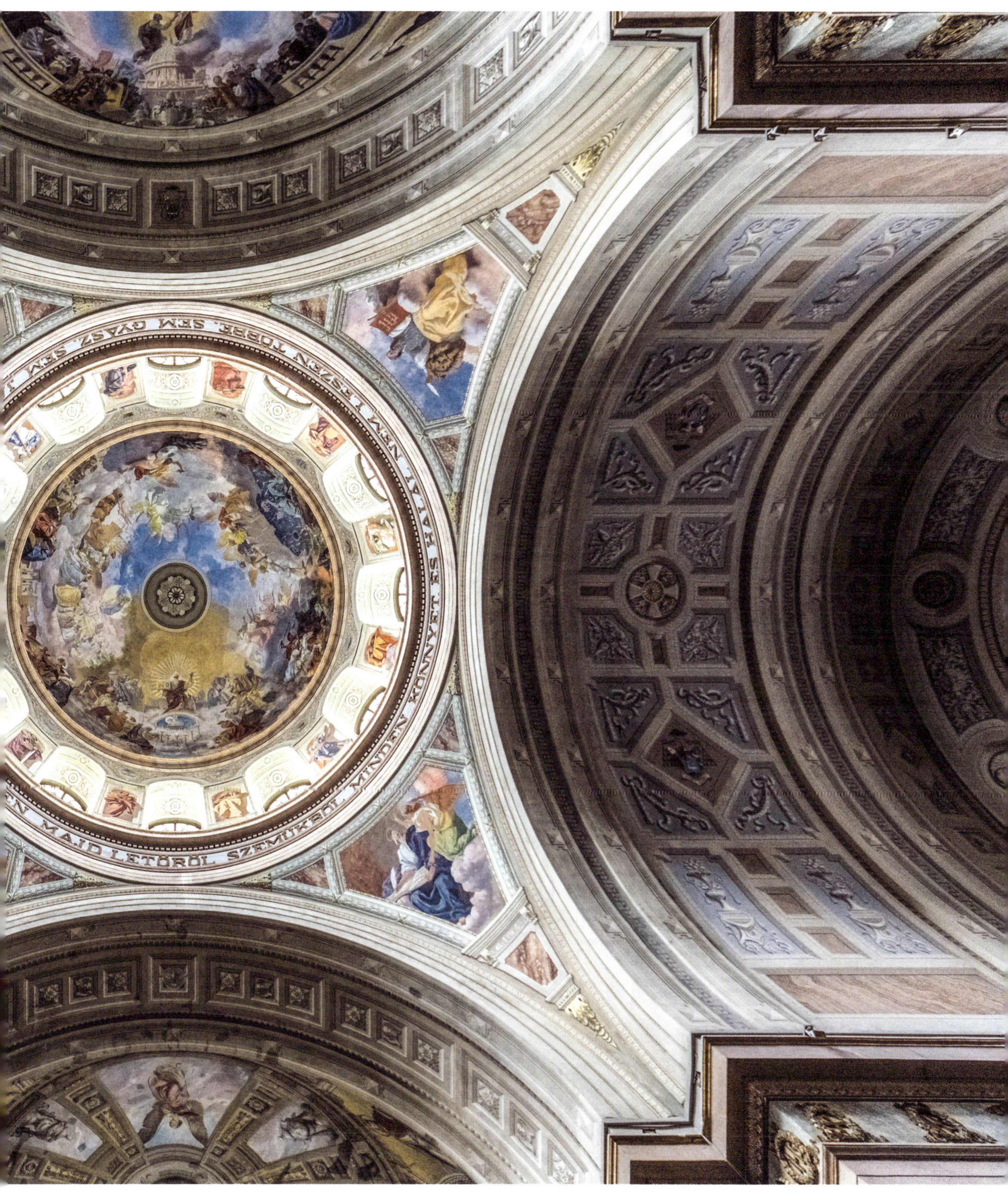

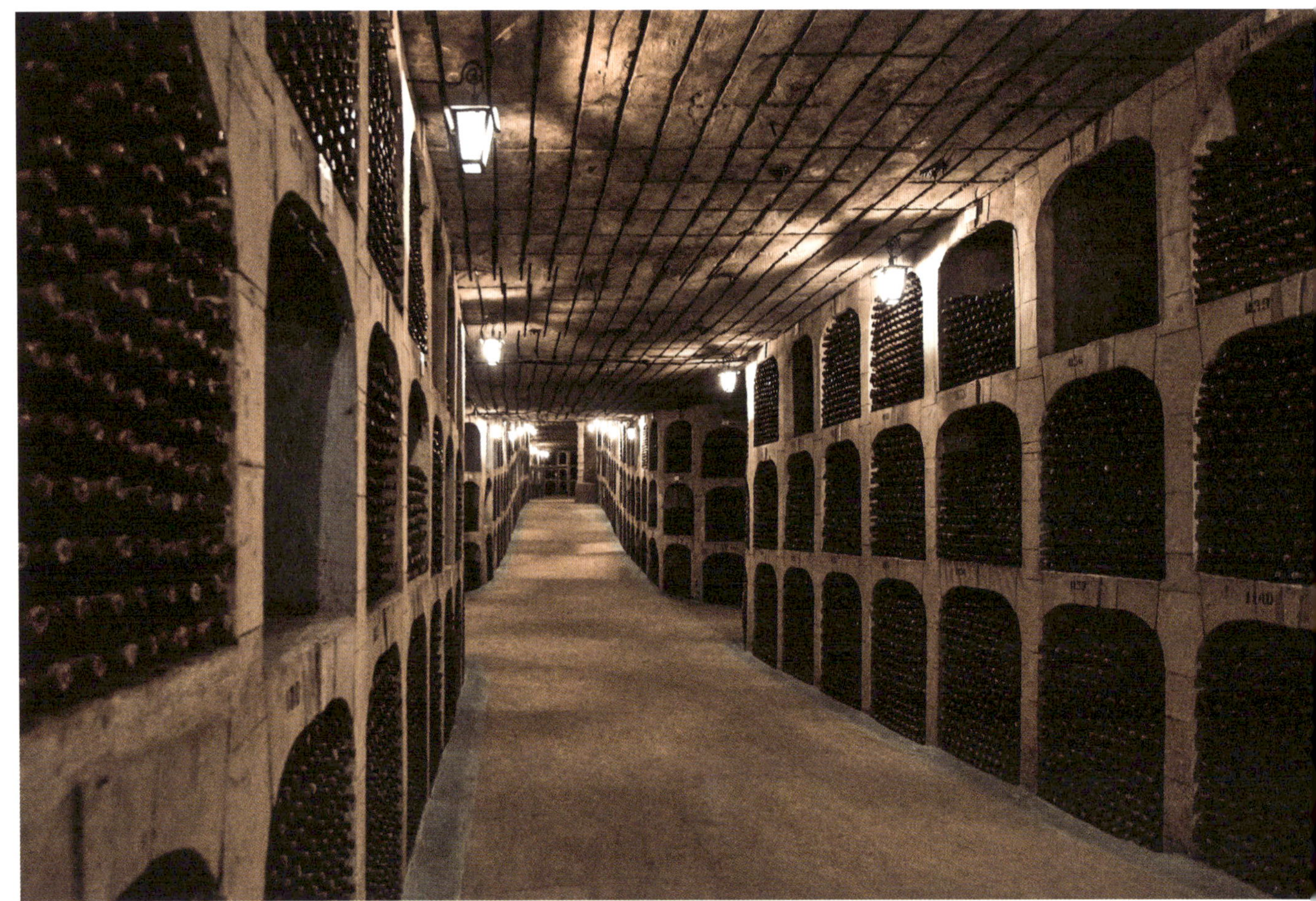

Mileştii Mici, Ialoveni, Moldova
46°55'16.4"N 28°49'12.2"E
Just a few of the 2 million wine bottles inside
the largest wine cellar in the world, hidden deep
underground.
// September 2014

Cricova, Moldova
47°08'17.6"N 28°51'19.4"E
The underground wine city of Cricova is one of
the most remarkable places in Europe. A network
of over 120 kilometres of underground roads
takes you to various impressive underground
tasting rooms, such as this Presidential Hall.
// June 2013

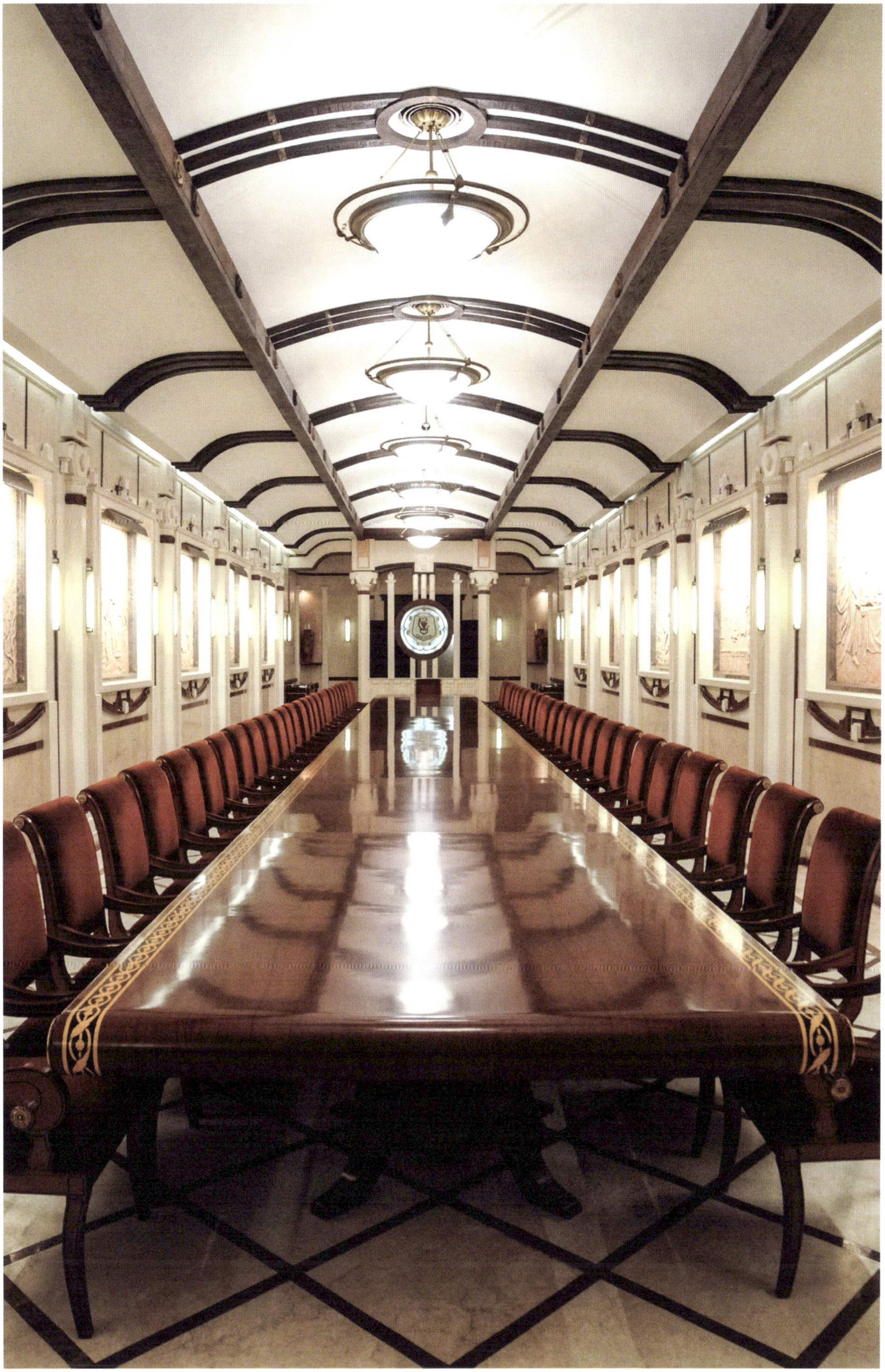

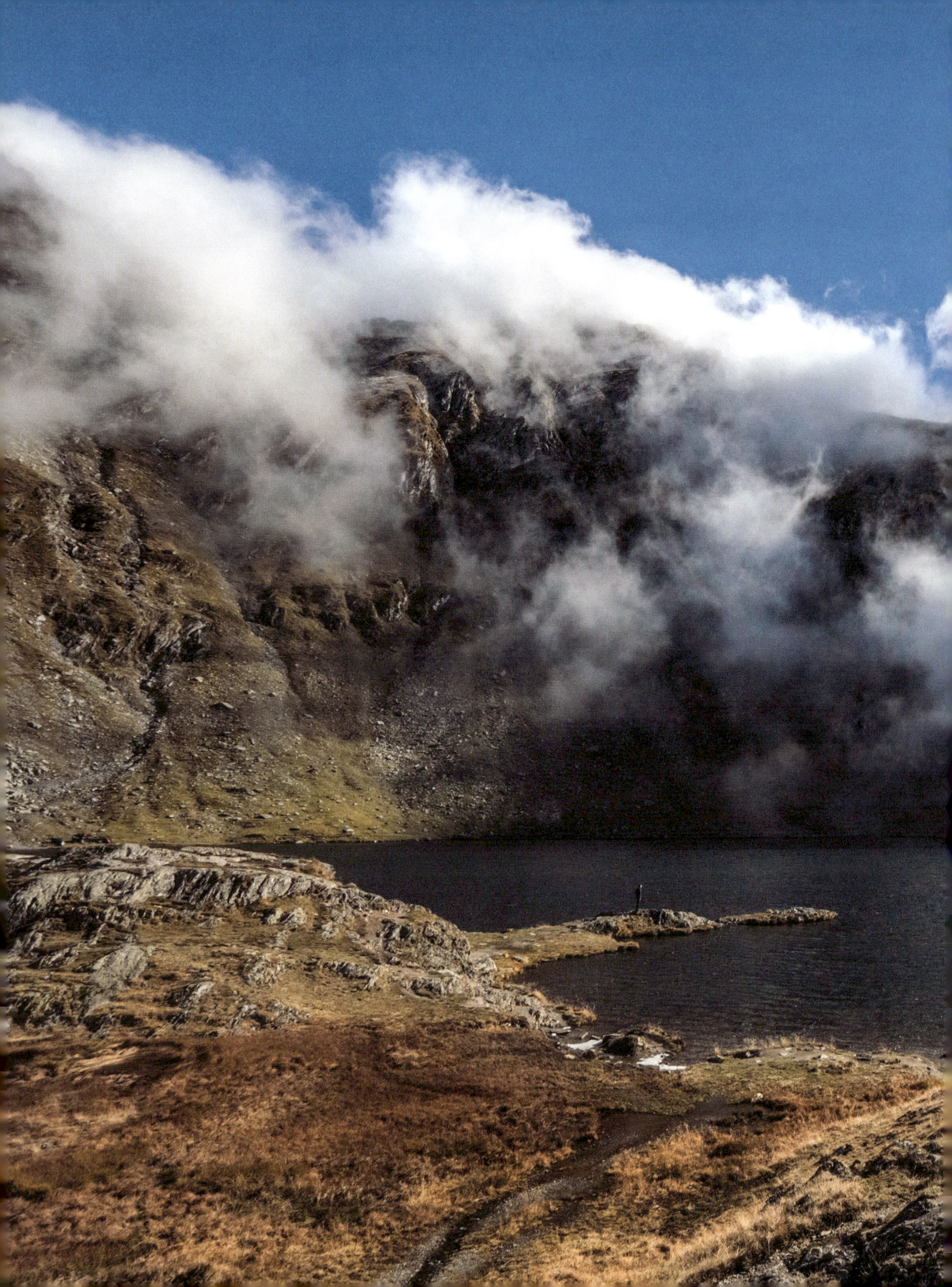

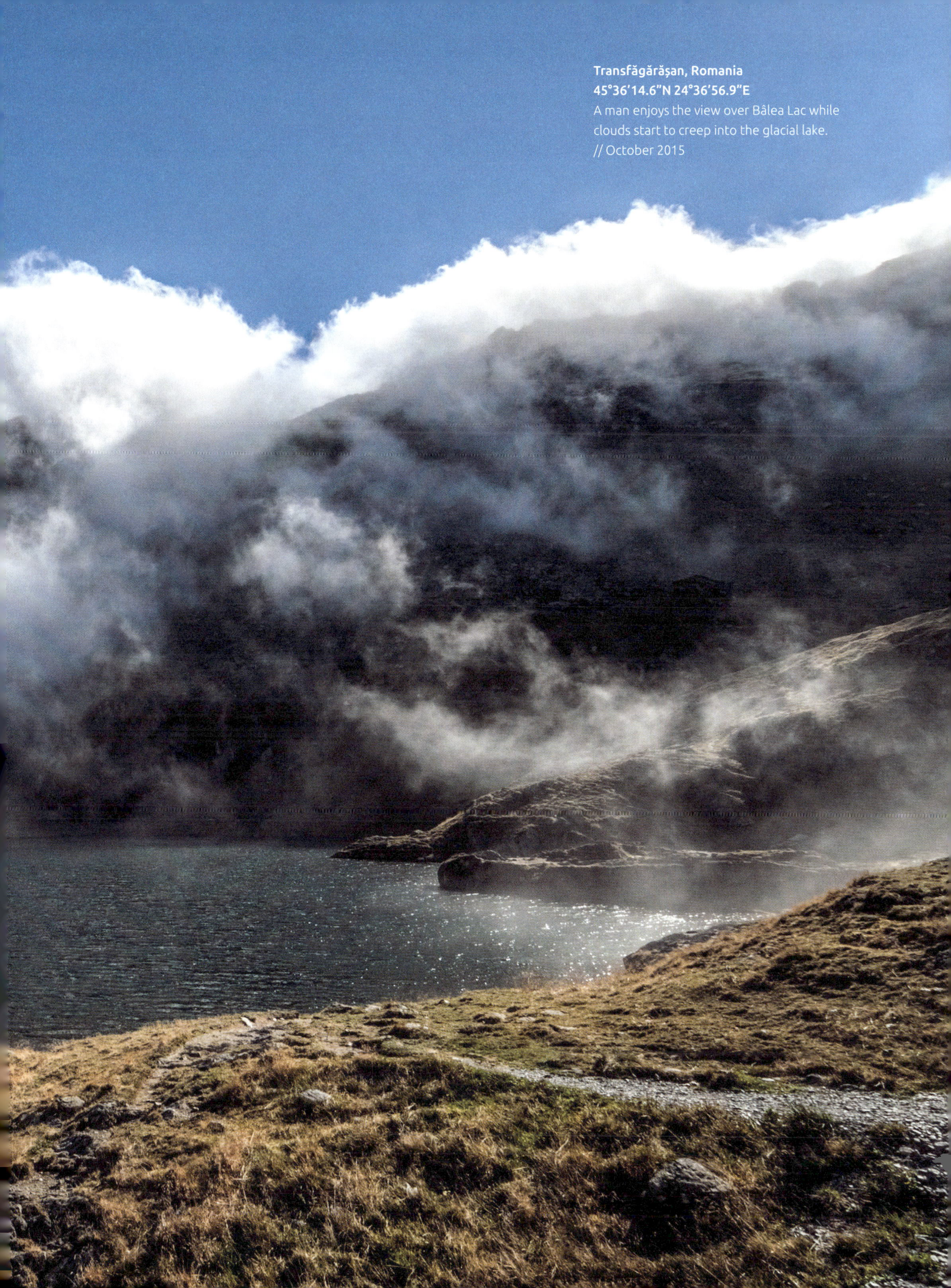
Transfăgărășan, Romania
45°36'14.6"N 24°36'56.9"E
A man enjoys the view over Bâlea Lac while
clouds start to creep into the glacial lake.
// October 2015

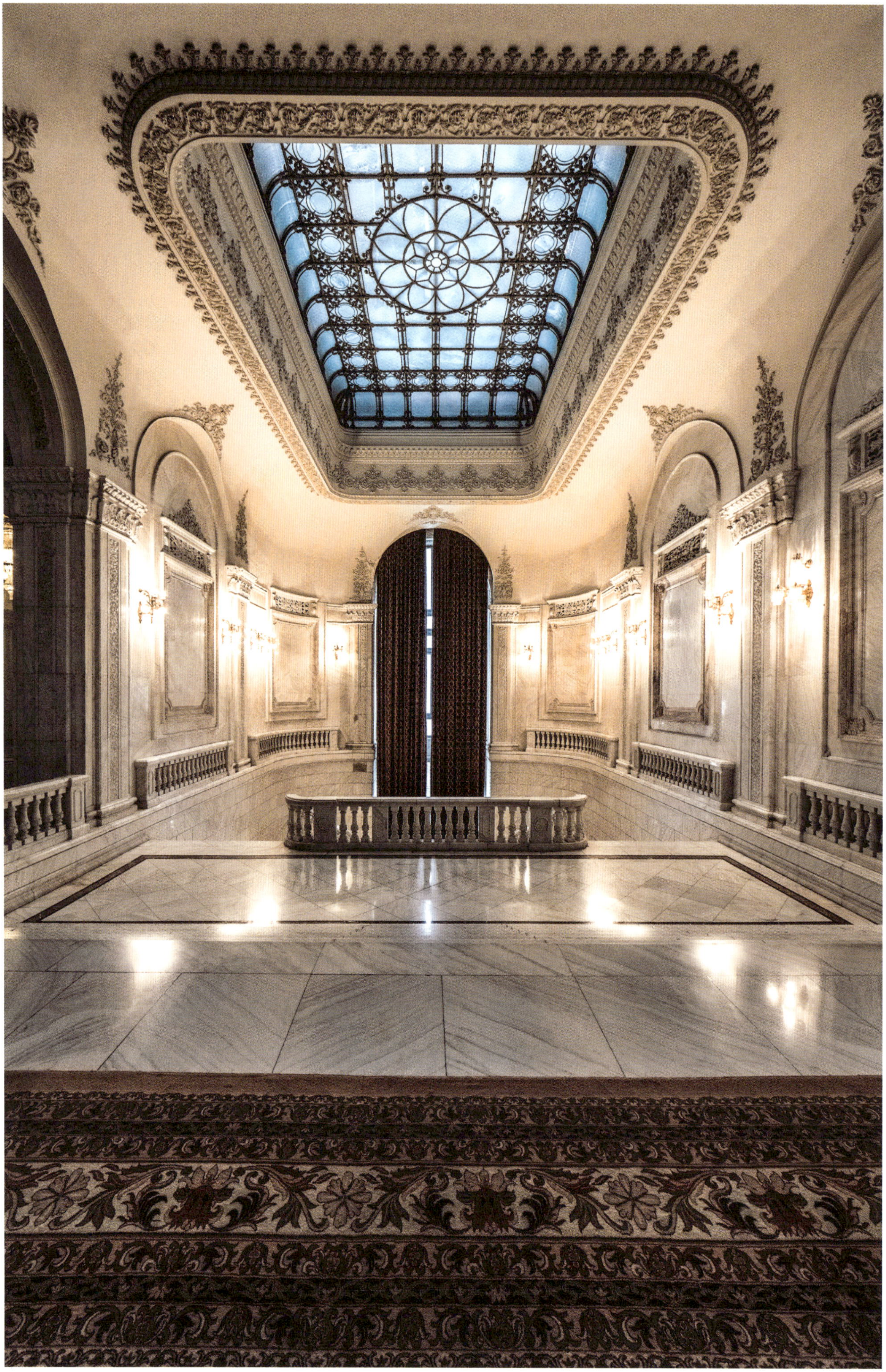

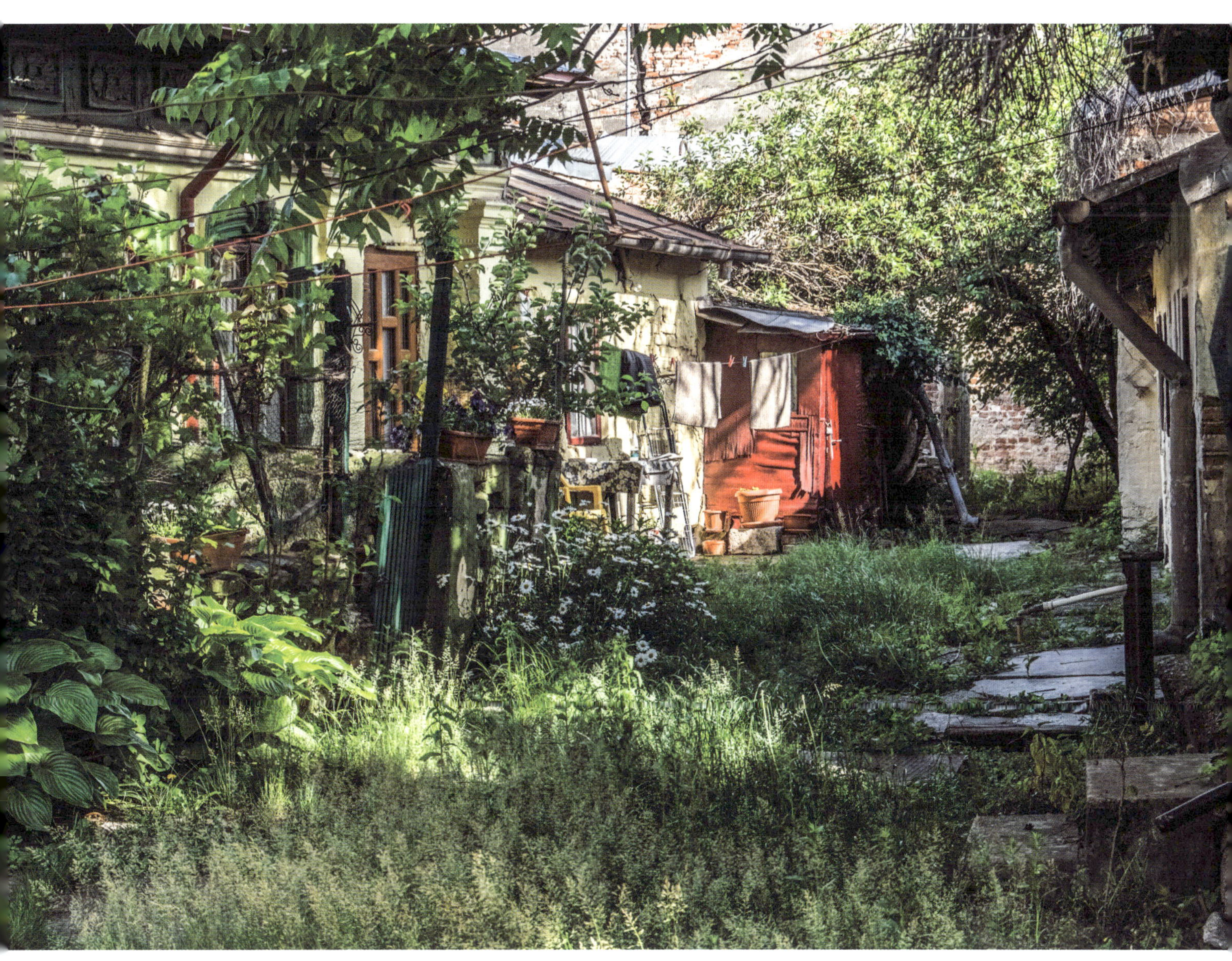

Palace of the Parliament, Bucharest, Romania
44°25'39.0"N 26°05'14.6"E
Heavy curtains 18 metres tall decorate the majestic
staircase inside the world's heaviest building.
An impressive place of superlatives.
// May 2017

Bucharest, Romania
44°25'10.3"N 26°05'56.3"E
A surprisingly rural scene is hidden in the middle
of Romania's busy capital. A rare sight to see,
that immediately grabbed my attention as I was
passing by.
// May 2017

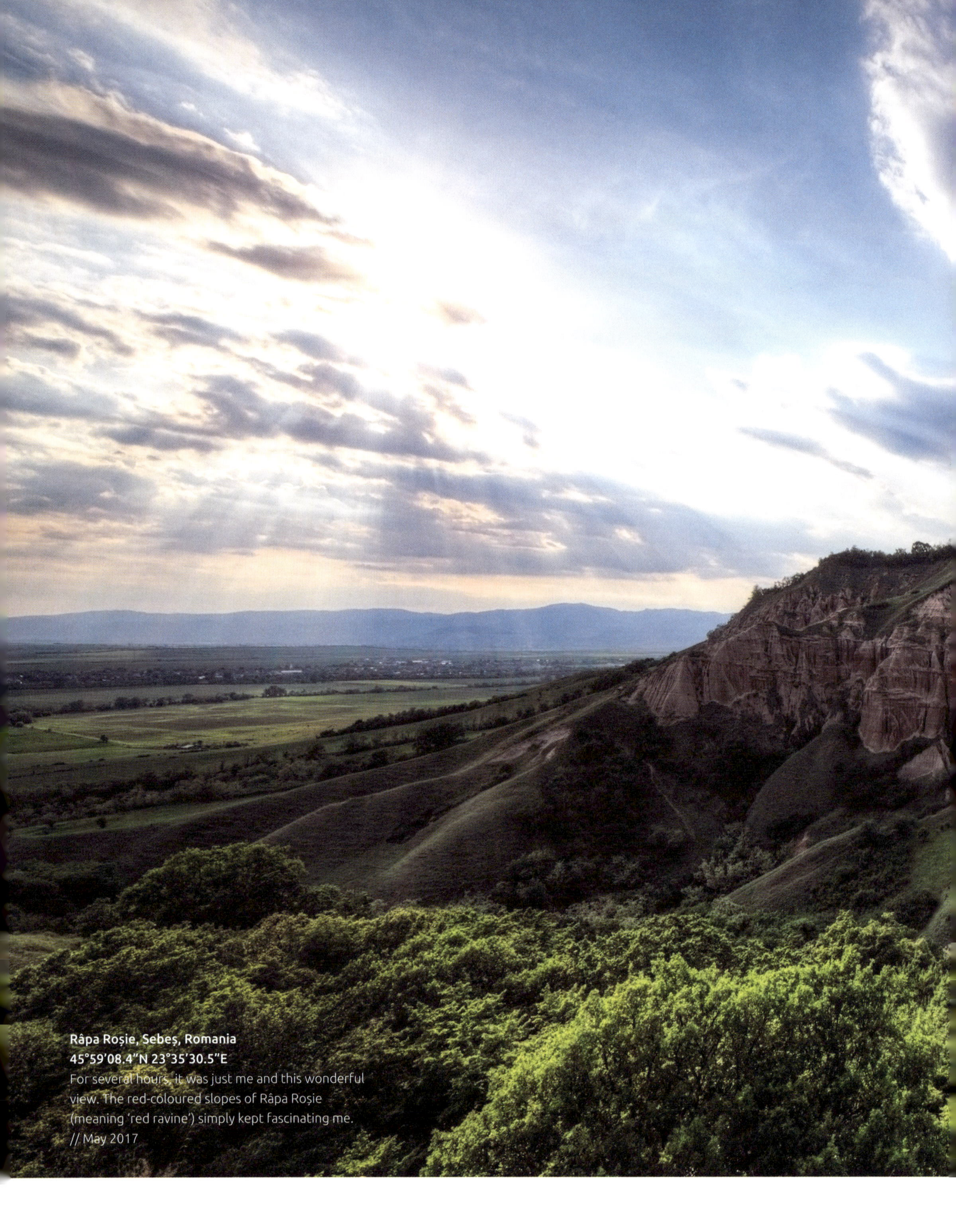

Râpa Roşie, Sebeş, Romania
45°59'08.4"N 23°35'30.5"E
For several hours, it was just me and this wonderful
view. The red-coloured slopes of Râpa Roşie
(meaning 'red ravine') simply kept fascinating me.
// May 2017

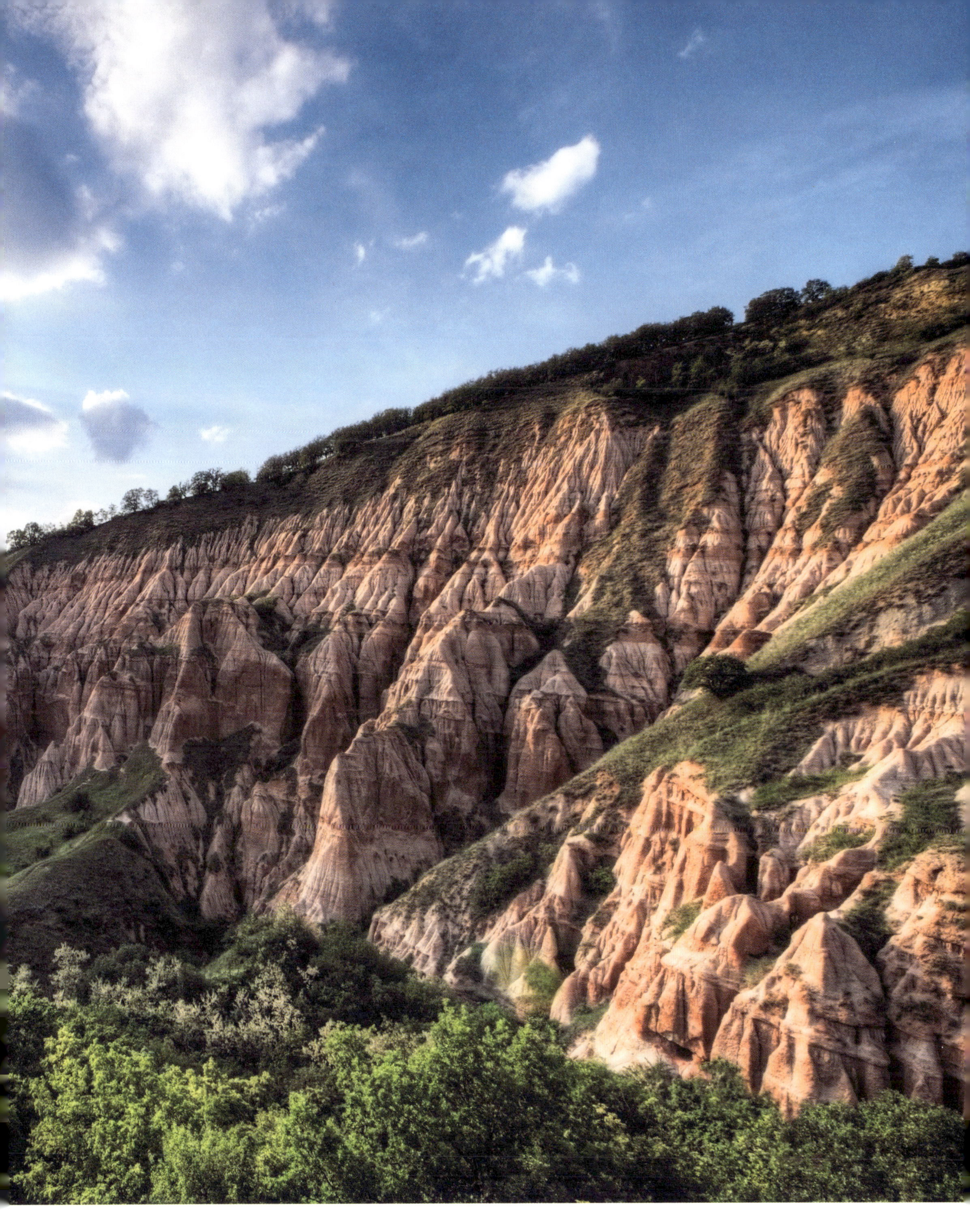

Sighişoara, Romania
46°13'08.3"N 24°47'32.4"E
Colourful houses along the cosy streets
of Sighişoara.
// June 2013

Sighişoara, Romania
46°13'12.6"N 24°47'34.3"E
An enthusiastic dog greets every passerby
in the centre of the city.
// June 2013

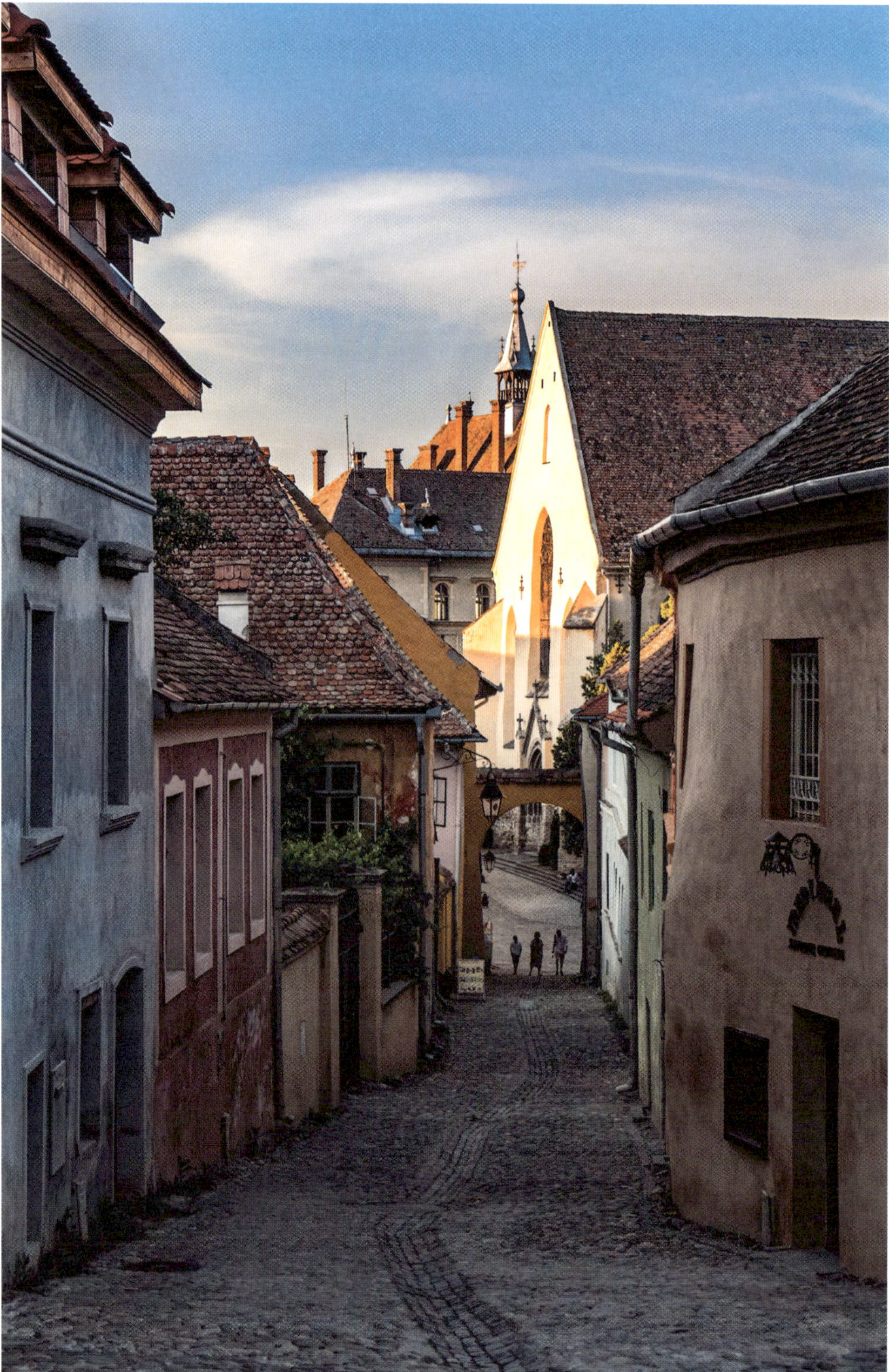

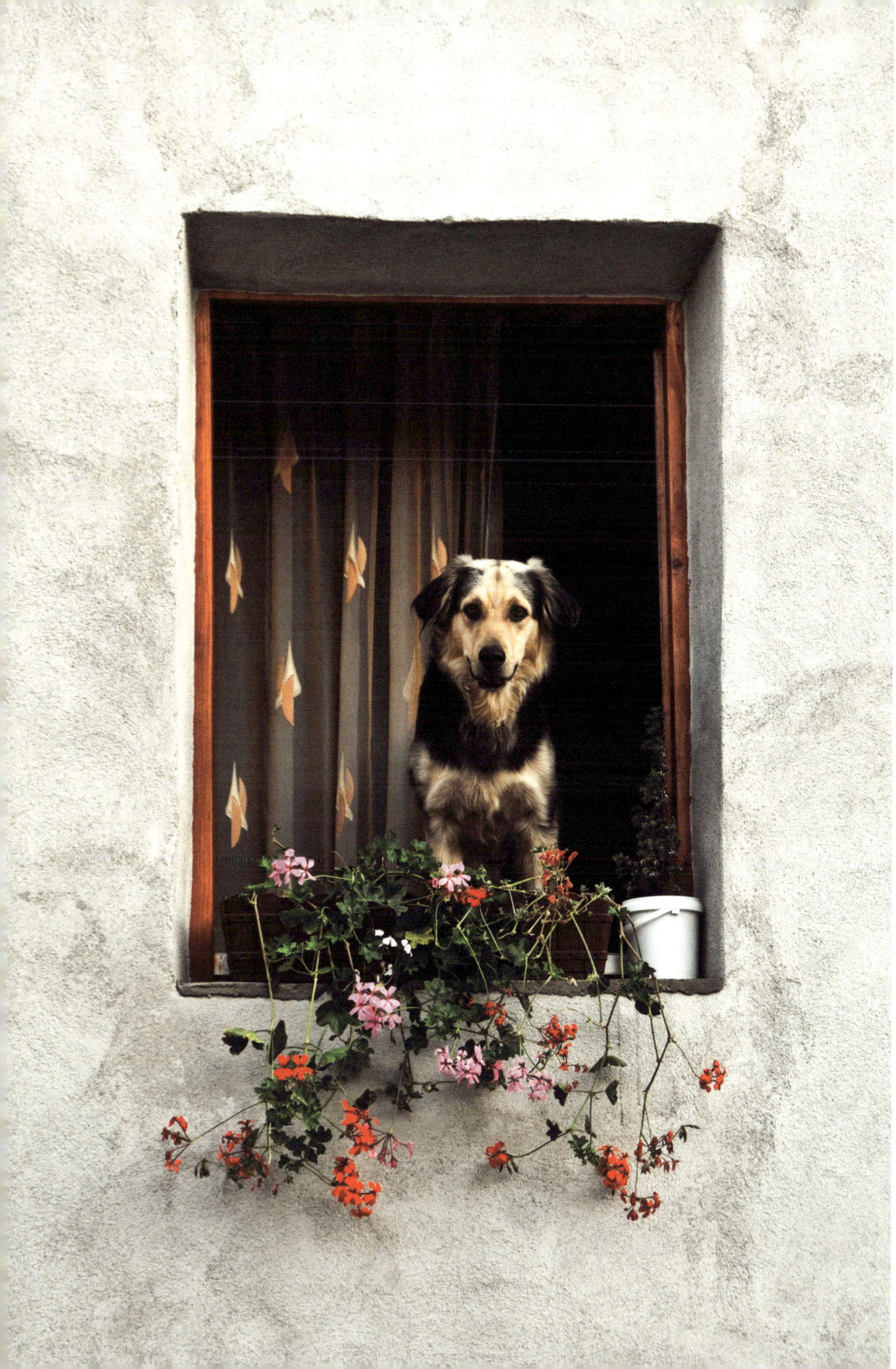

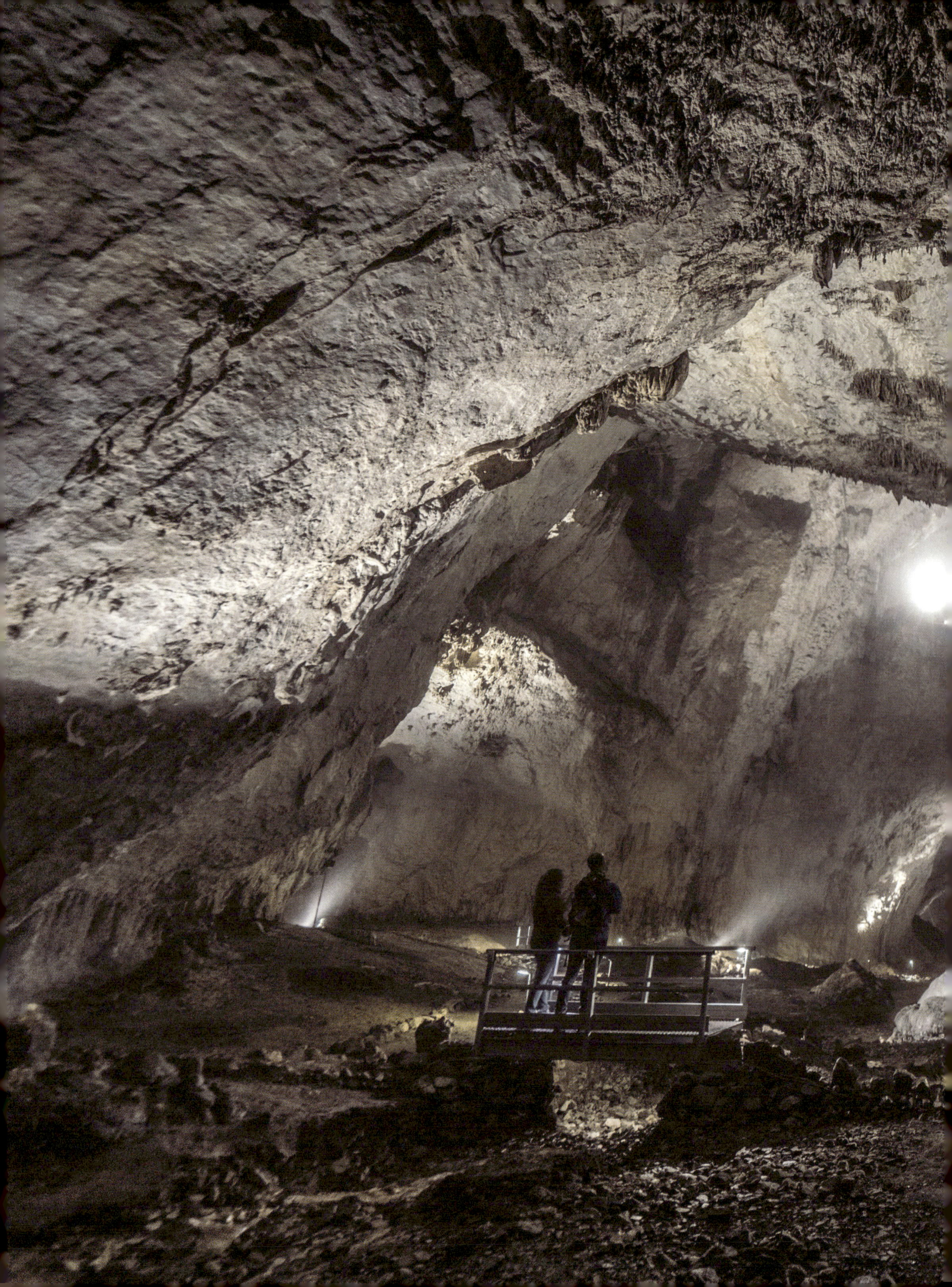

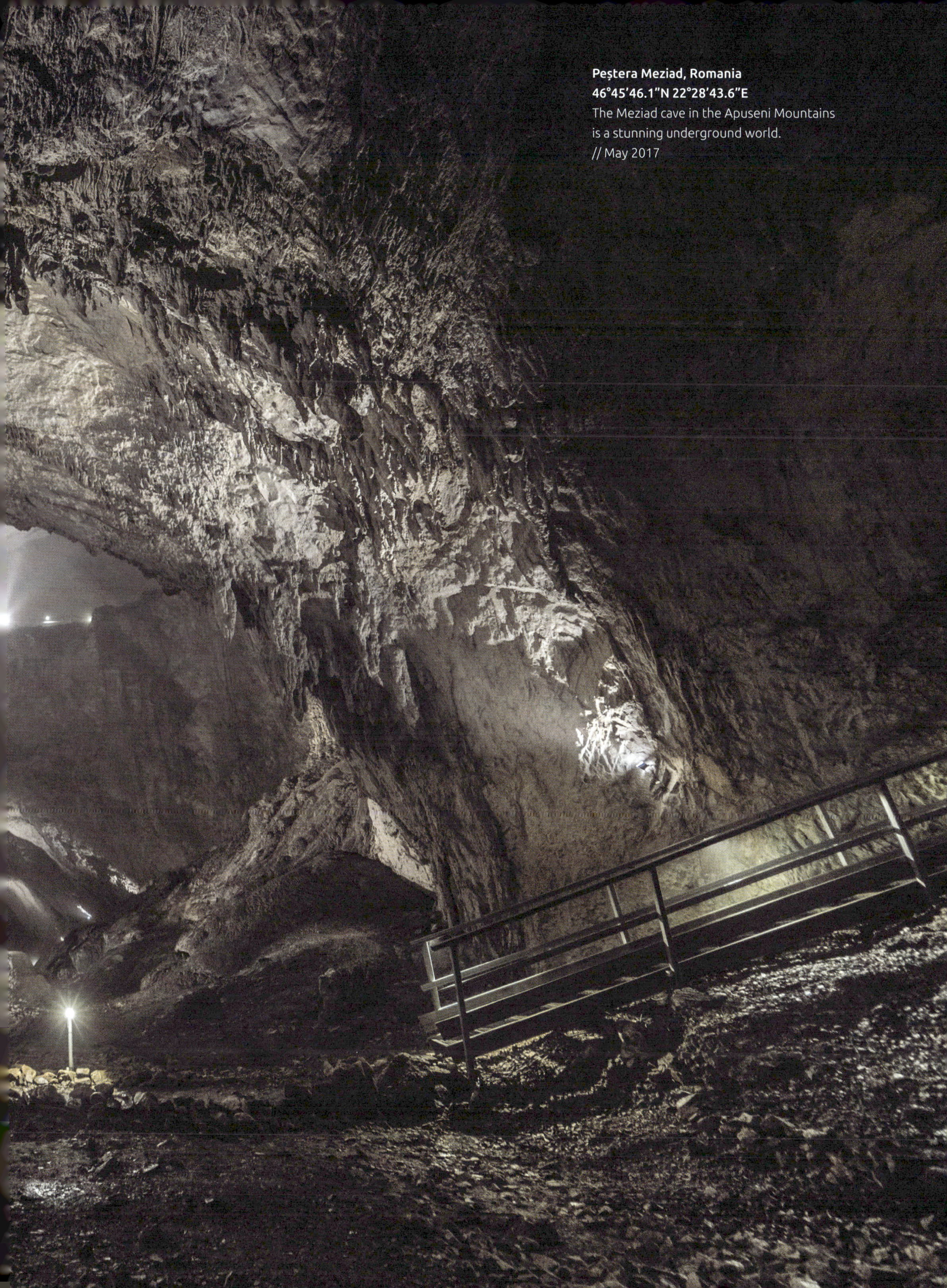

Peștera Meziad, Romania
46°45'46.1"N 22°28'43.6"E
The Meziad cave in the Apuseni Mountains
is a stunning underground world.
// May 2017

Crossing the Carpathians
Route and travel suggestions

Scenic regions and nature reserves

1 Apuseni // **Romania**
2 Bohemian Switzerland // **Czech Republic & Germany**
3 Ceahlău // **Romania**
4 Făgăraş Mountains // **Romania**
5 Maramureş // **Romania**
6 Râpa Roşie // **Romania**
7 Retezat // **Romania**
8 Slovenský Raj // **Slovakia**
9 Vysoké Tatry (High Tatras) // **Slovakia & Poland**

Cities and towns

10 Bamberg // **Germany**
11 Banská Štiavnica // **Slovakia**
12 Chochołów // **Poland**
13 Debrecen // **Hungary**
14 Dresden // **Germany**
15 Kraków // **Poland**
16 Sibiu // **Romania**
17 Sighişoara // **Romania**

Cultural experiences

18 Churches of Moldavia // **Bucovina, Romania**
19 Cricova // **Moldova**
20 Mileştii Mici // **Moldova**
21 Palace of the Parliament // **Bucharest, Romania**
22 Sighet Prison, Sighetu Marmaţiei // **Romania**
23 Spišský Hrad, Žehra // **Slovakia**
24 Tokaj wine region // **Hungary**
25 Wooden Churches of Maramureş // **Romania**

Spectacular roads and scenic routes

26 DN18 between Şesuri and Borşa // **Romania**
27 DN57 along the Iron Gates // **Romania**
28 Transalpina (DN67C) // **Romania**
29 Transfăgărăşan (DN7C) // **Romania**

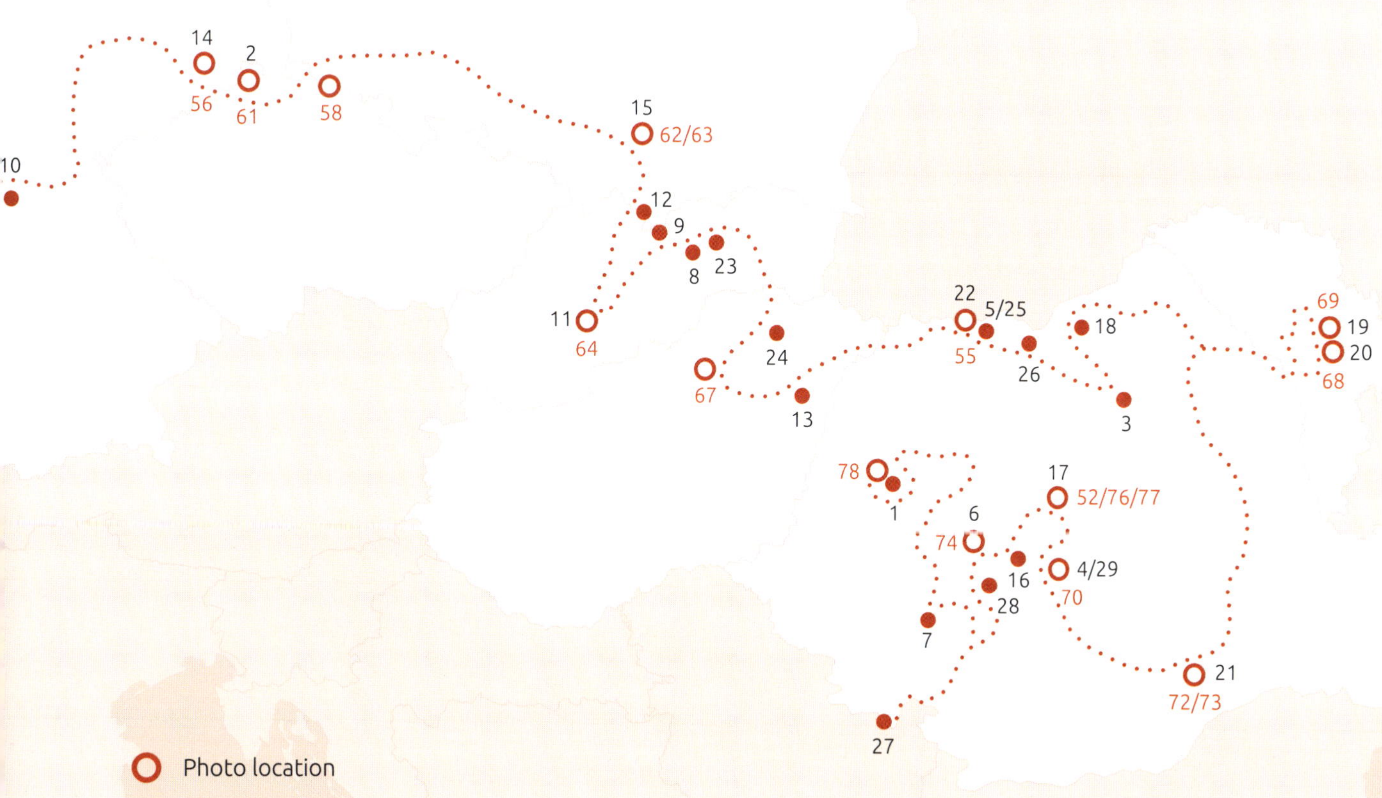

Photo location

Travel suggestion

123 Photo page number

123 Travel suggestion number

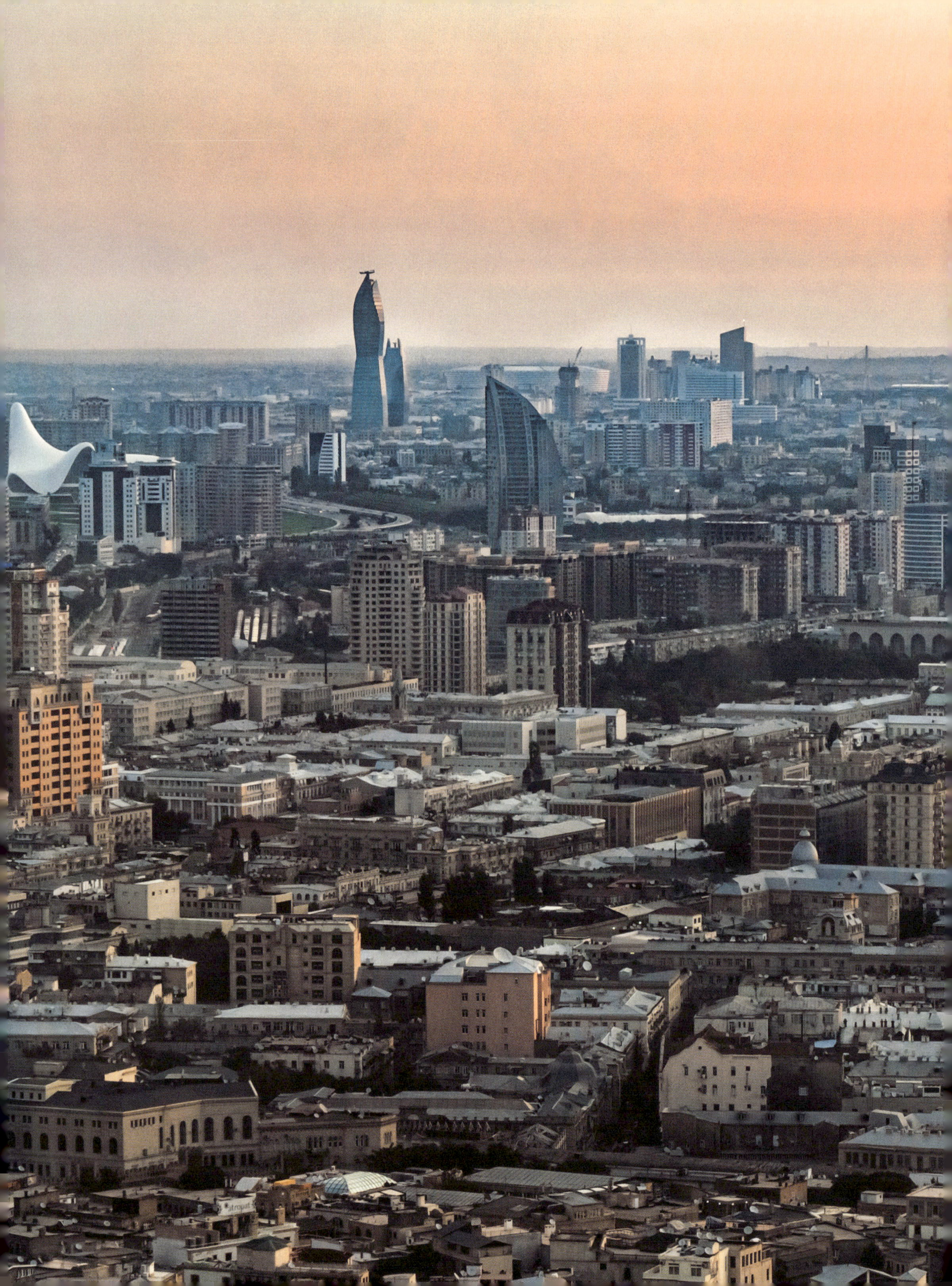

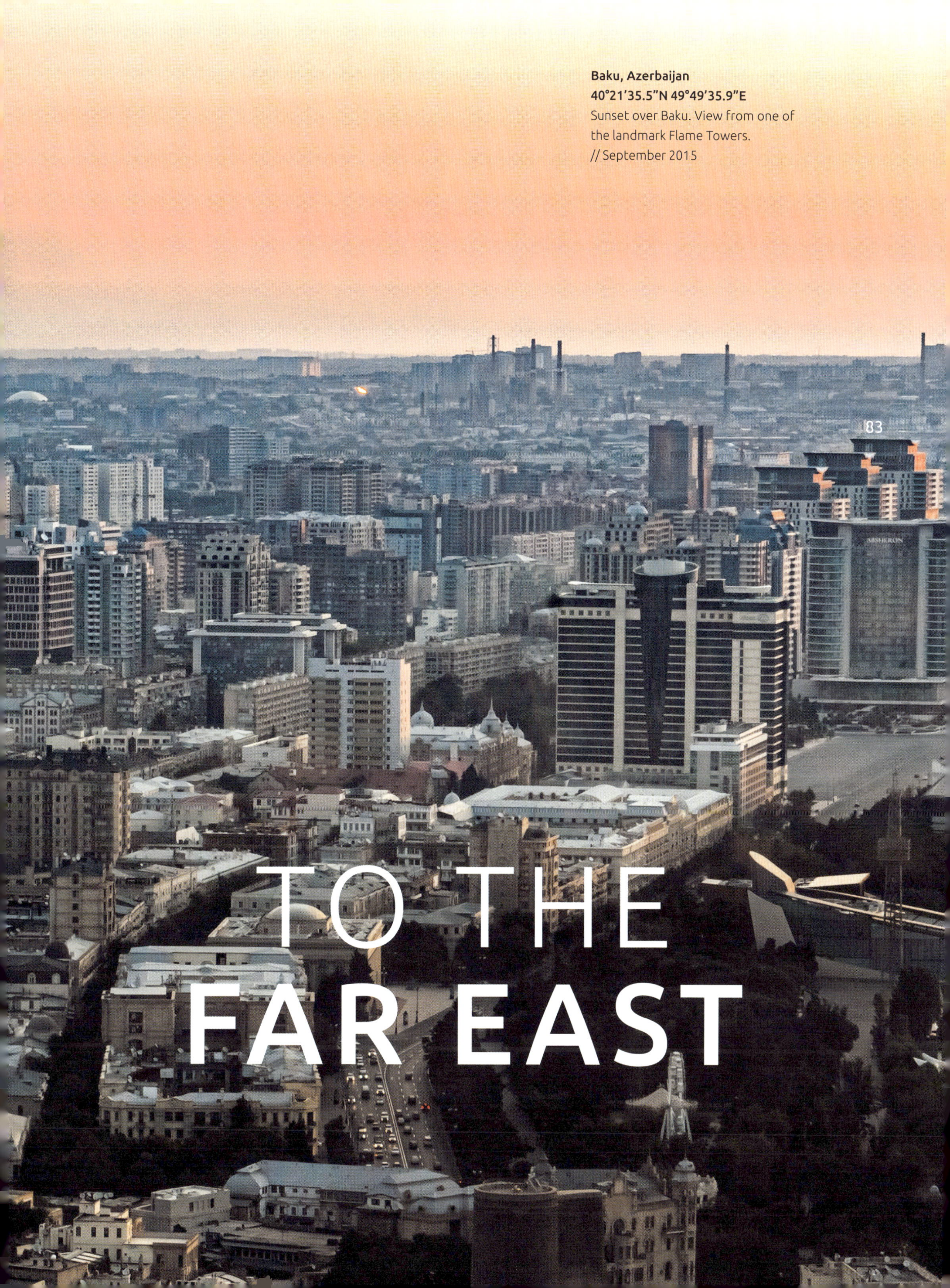

TO THE
FAR EAST

To the Far East

THE LONG EUROPEAN route E80 in Serbia takes us through the heart of Bulgaria and Anatolia, all the way to Doğubayazıt near the border with Iran. From there we drive north to reach the Caucasus, on the edge of our continent. This 'Far East' of Europe is influenced by European, Central Asian and Middle Eastern cultures. Few places in Europe show such great diversity in culture and nature in a relatively small area as the Caucasian region.

From the Greater Caucasus with its majestic 5000ers to tea fields in Georgia and the northeast of Anatolia. From mud volcanoes in the desert near the Caspian Sea to long lanes of walnut trees in the northwest of Azerbaijan. From medieval monasteries in the north of Armenia to the futuristic sky-scrapers of Baku – the capital of 'The Land of Fire', as the Azerbaijanis call their own country. Adding to the diversity are the various scripts in use (Georgian, Armenian, Cyrillic and Latin), different religions, and the region's long and turbulent history. The Caucasus just seems to have it all.

David Gareja, border Georgia and Azerbaijan
41°26'36.3"N 45°22'29.4"E
Straddling the border between Georgia and Azerbaijan, this toad-headed agama carefully follows any movement.
// September 2015

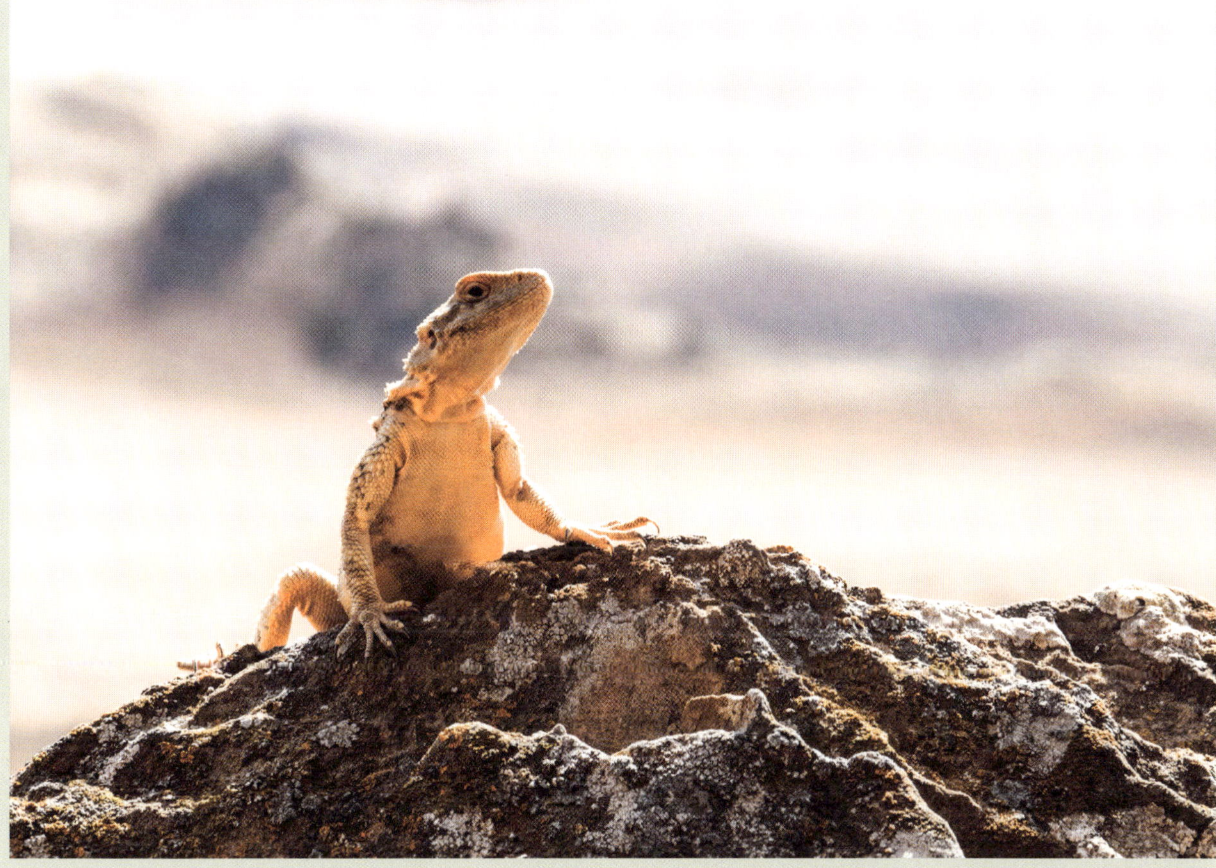

Of the 170-hour drive to Baku and back, two parts of the route will stay in my memory forever. The first one being the path from Udabno in Georgia to the Monastery of David Gareja on the border between Georgia and Azerbaijan. On a sunny afternoon in autumn, the ridge on the border overlooking the desert of Azerbaijan, the endless golden fields of grass and the white-blue Jikurebi salt lake provide almost unearthly views.

The second part of the road trip that made a deep impression on me is the drive from Akhaltsikhe in Georgia to Doğubayazıt in Turkey. The views without any sign of civilisation, high mountain passes and Martian landscapes make this one of the most empty and impressive routes imaginable. In short, the road to Baku is long and a little rough at times, but very rewarding with magnificent scenic routes and unexpected encounters.

'Few places in Europe show such great diversity in culture and nature in a relatively small area as the Caucasian region.'

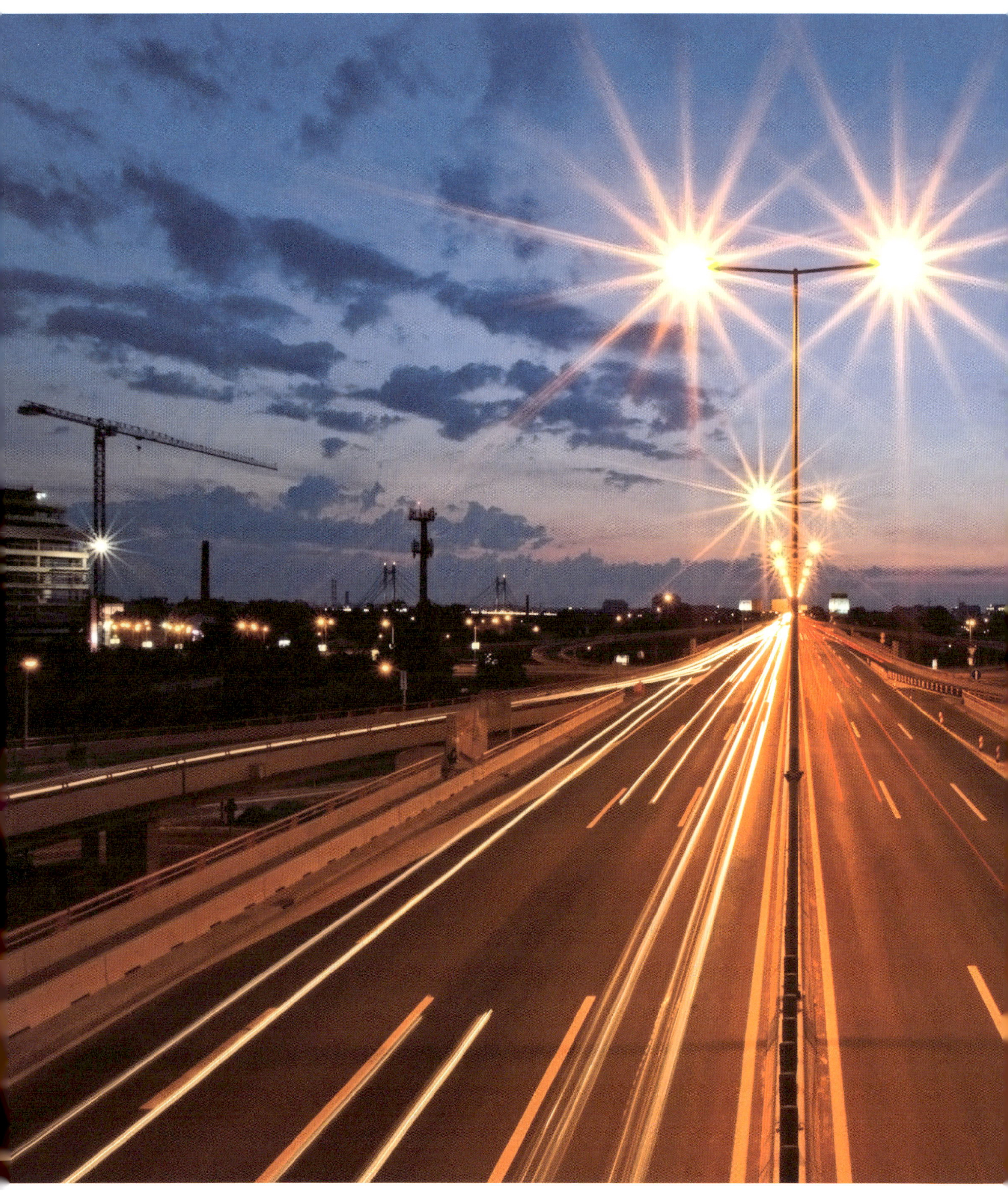

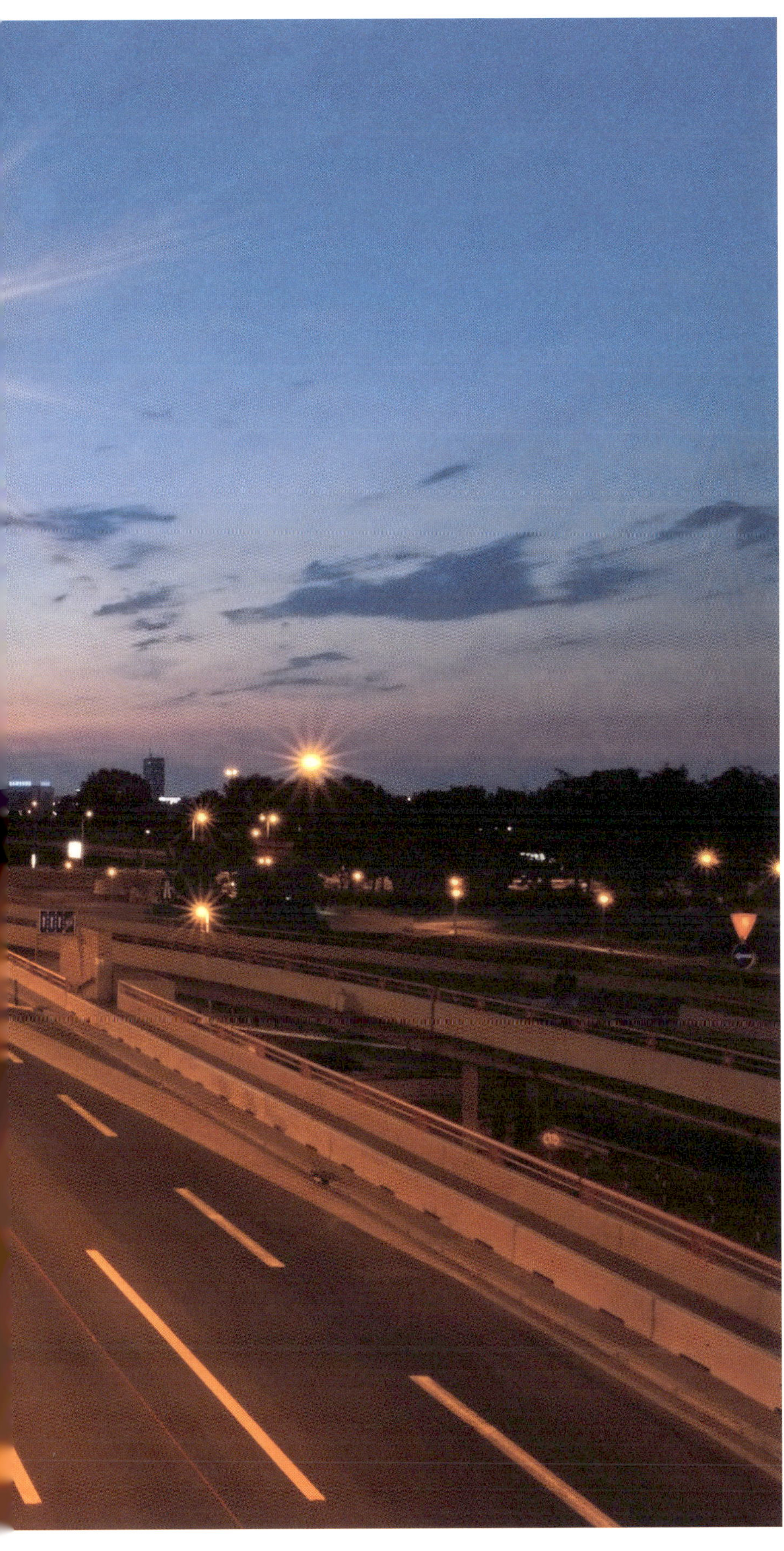

Belgrade, Serbia
44°47'52.2"N 20°27'01.0"E
Trails of car headlights give away the intensity
of traffic in both directions on this highway
transcending Belgrade. I remember it had been
a very, very hot day with temperatures reaching
almost 40°C.
// June 2013

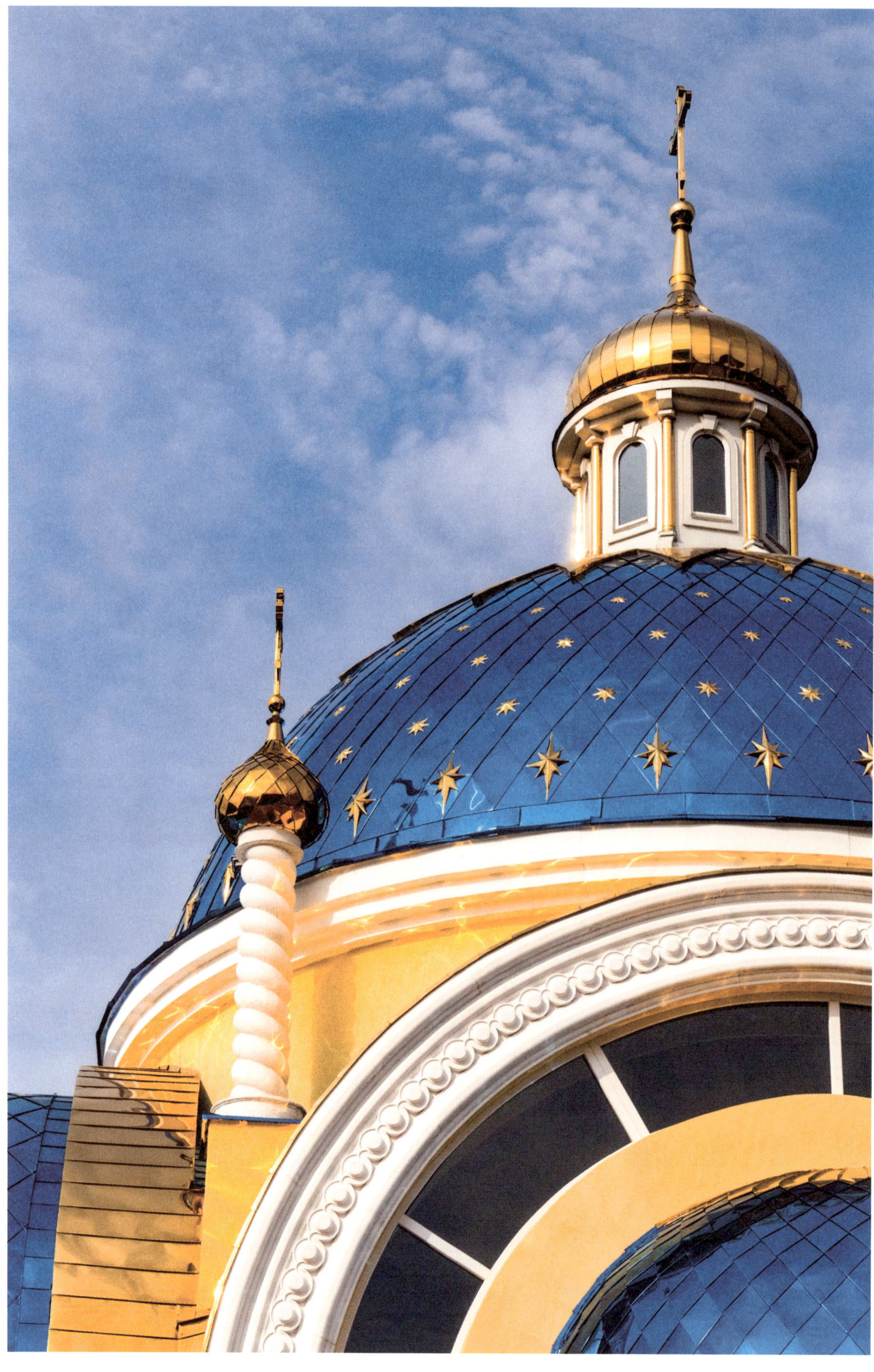

Plovdiv, Bulgaria
42°08'29.7"N 24°43'34.5"E
The St. Nicholas is a newly-built church opened
in 2015. The bright roof and use of glass give
this building a sunny character all-year round.
// September 2015

89

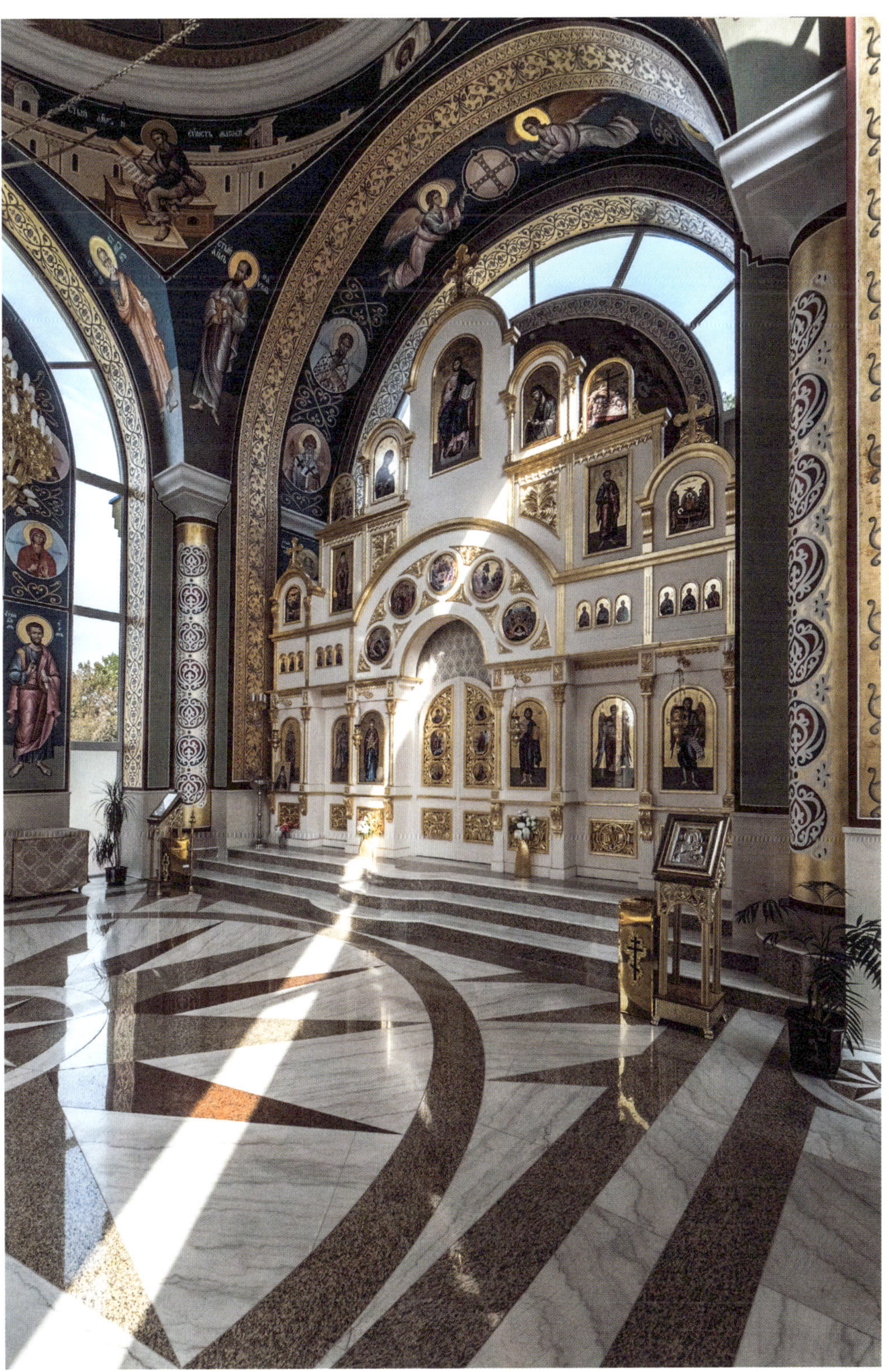

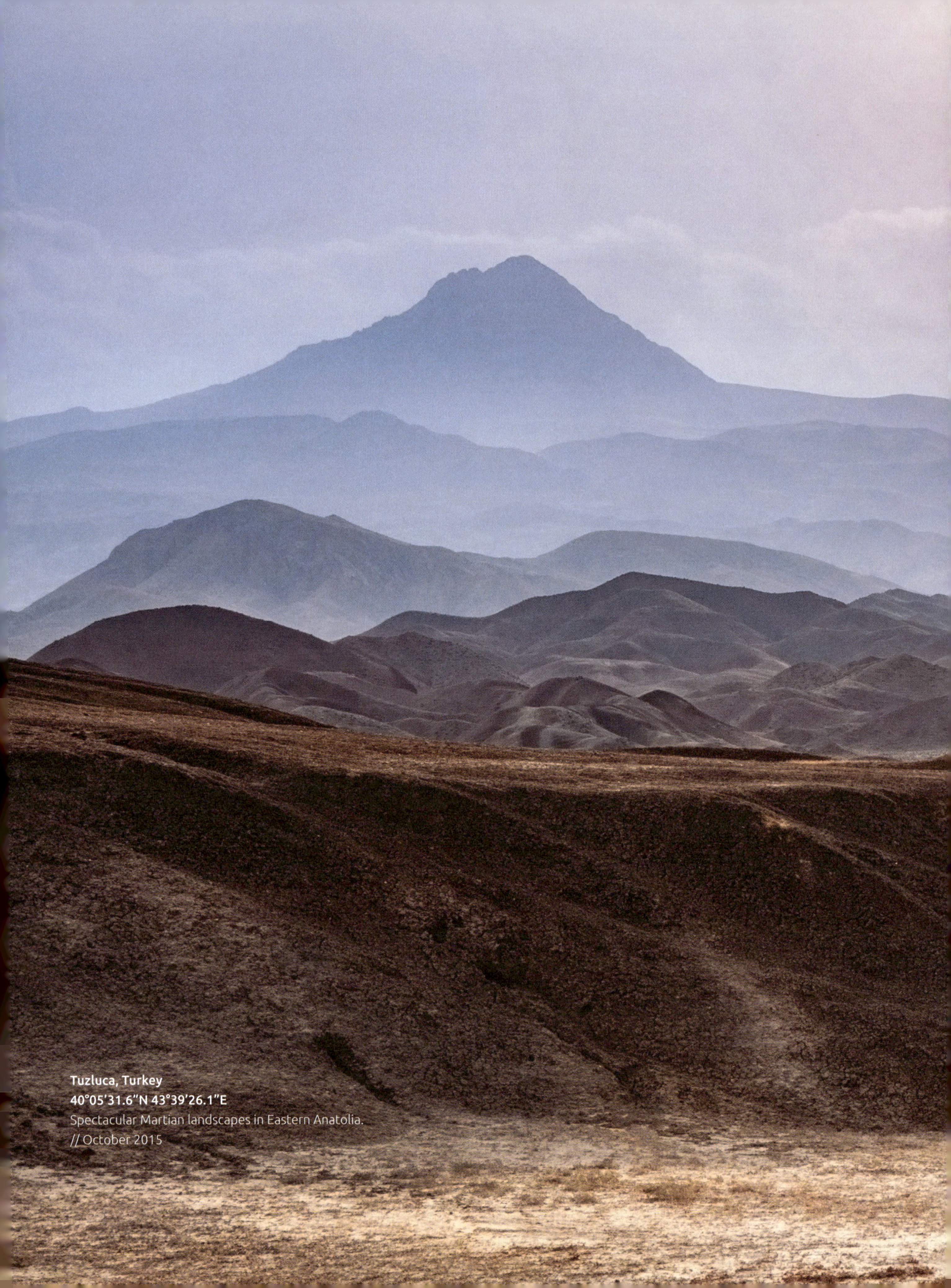

Tuzluca, Turkey
40°05'31.6"N 43°39'26.1"E
Spectacular Martian landscapes in Eastern Anatolia.
// October 2015

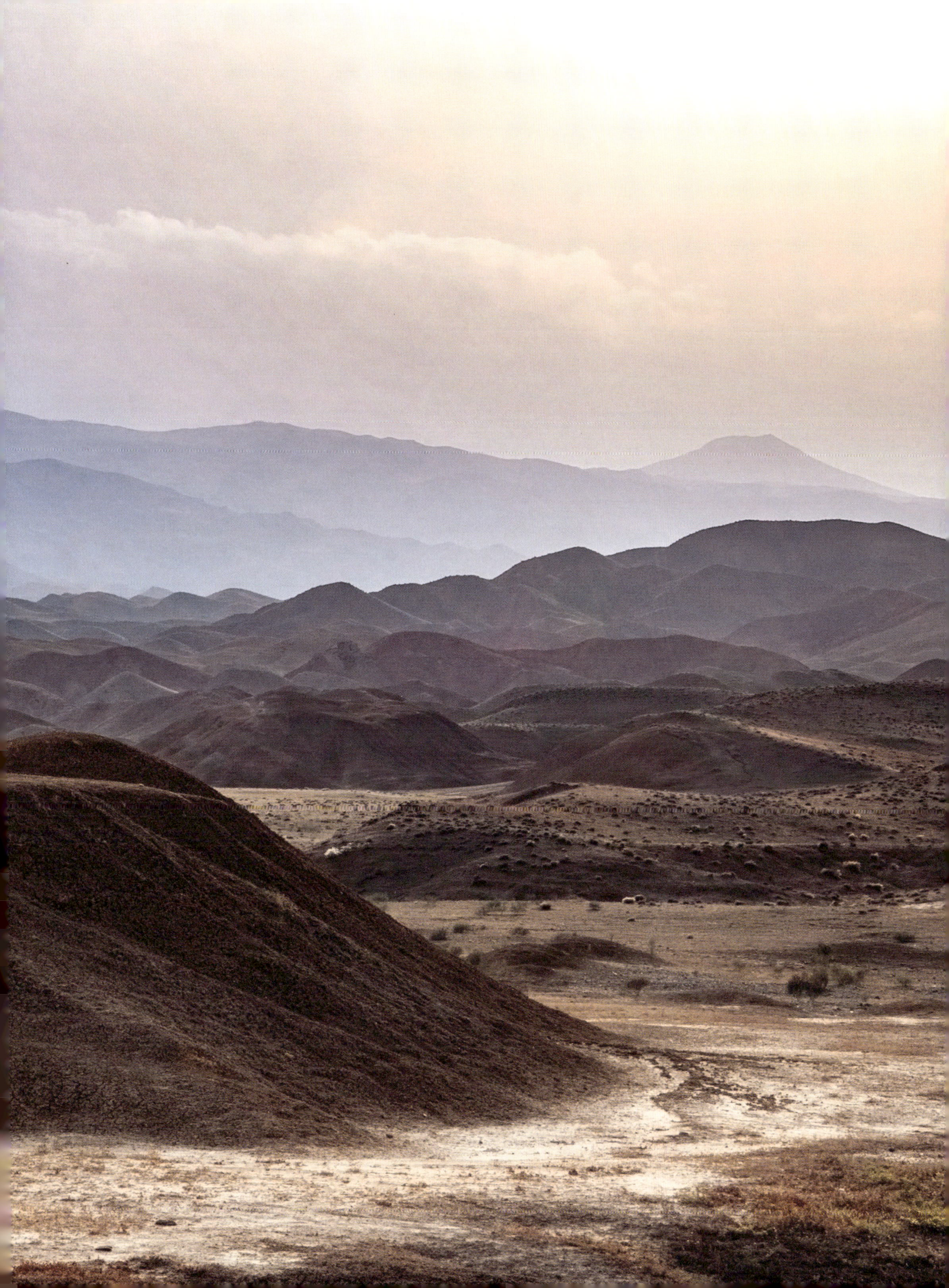

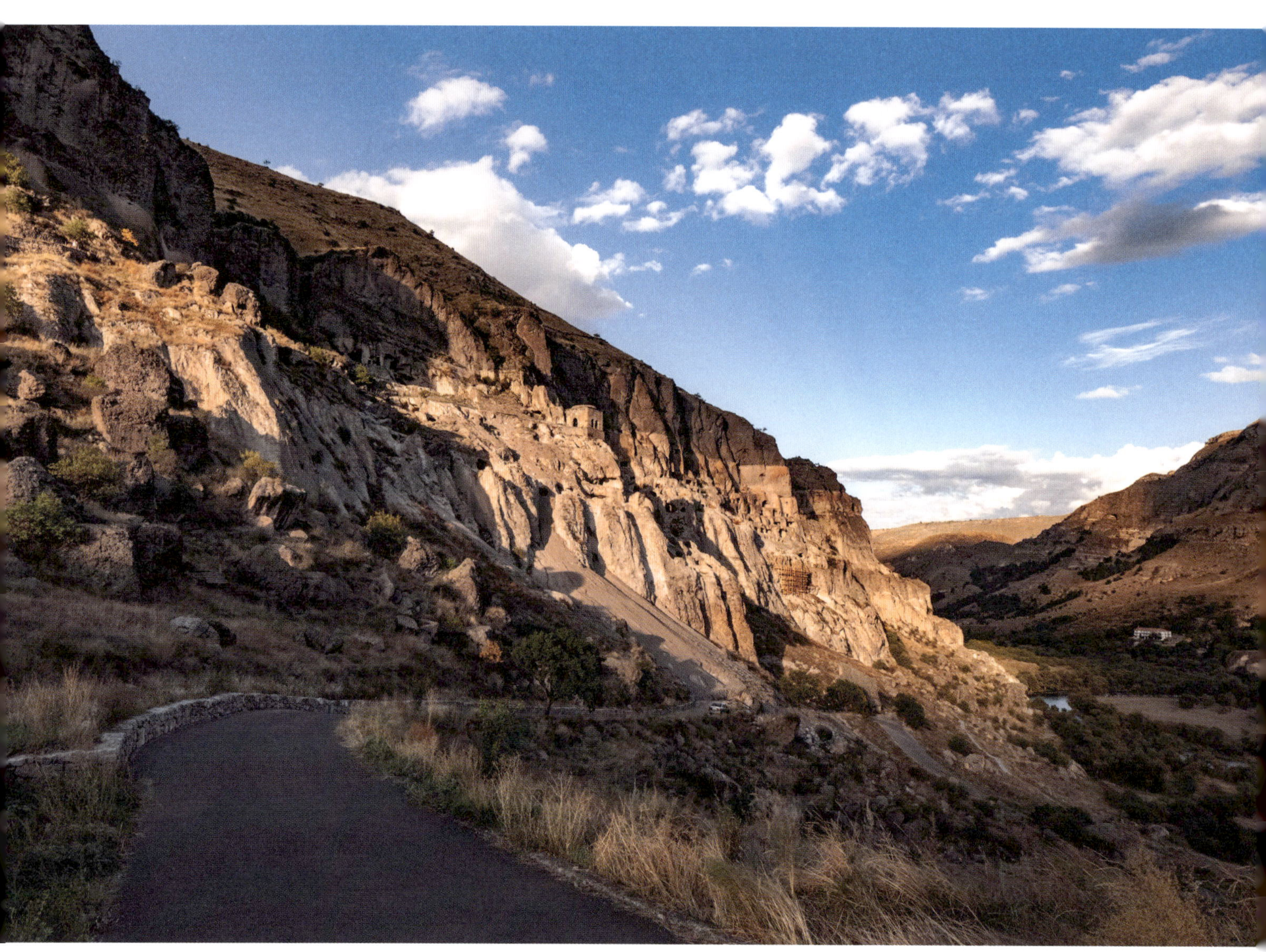

Vardzia, Georgia
41°22'47.8"N 43°16'54.4"E
The Vardzia cave monastery is an extensive
complex carved into the mountainside,
constructed mainly in the course of the
12th century. The drive through the beautiful
valleys is already worth the visit.
// October 2015

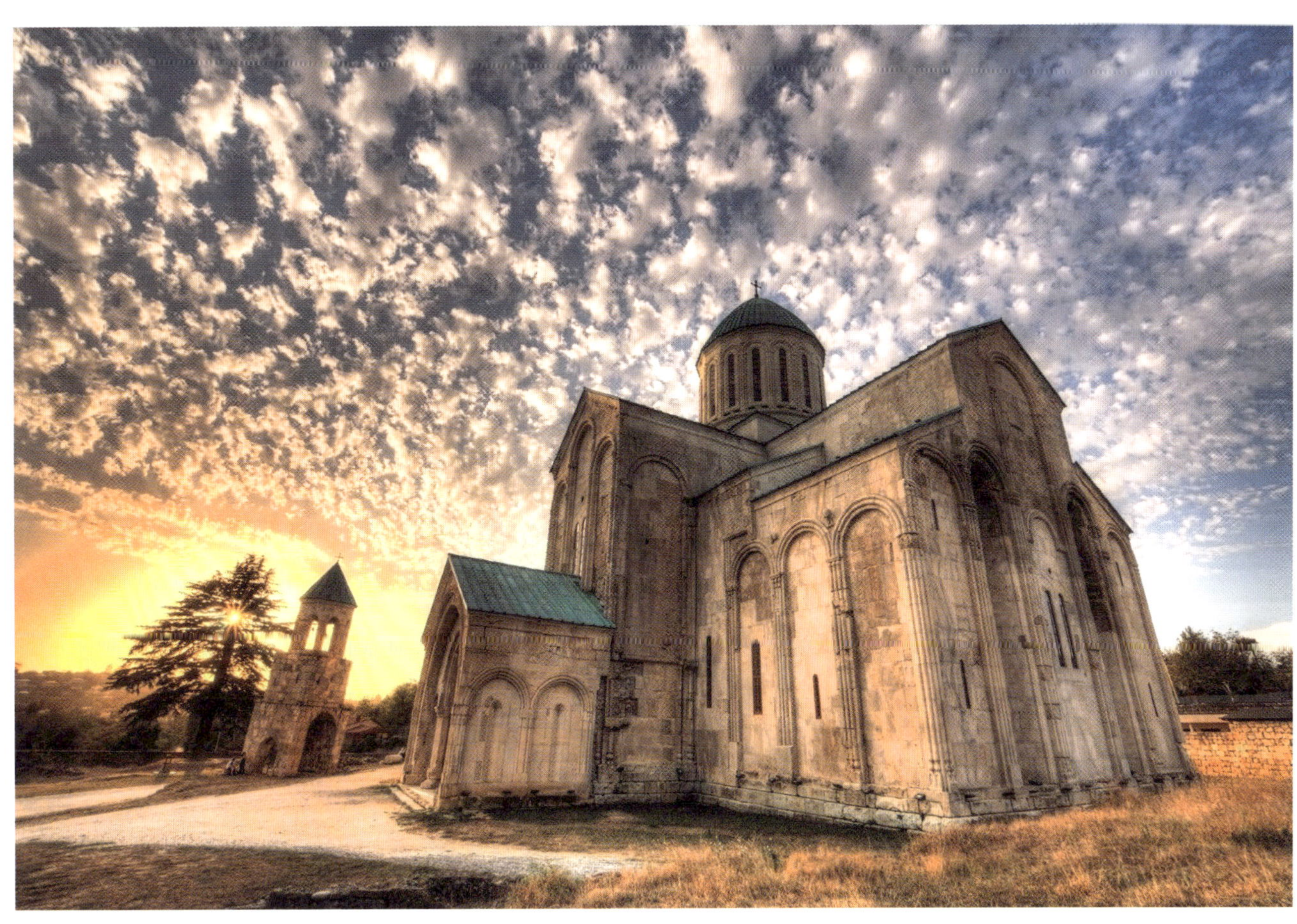

Kutaisi, Georgia
42°16'38.0"N 42°42'15.5"E
While attending a Georgian Orthodox ceremony inside Bagrati Cathedral, the clear sunset sky suddenly turned into a fascinating work of art.
// September 2015

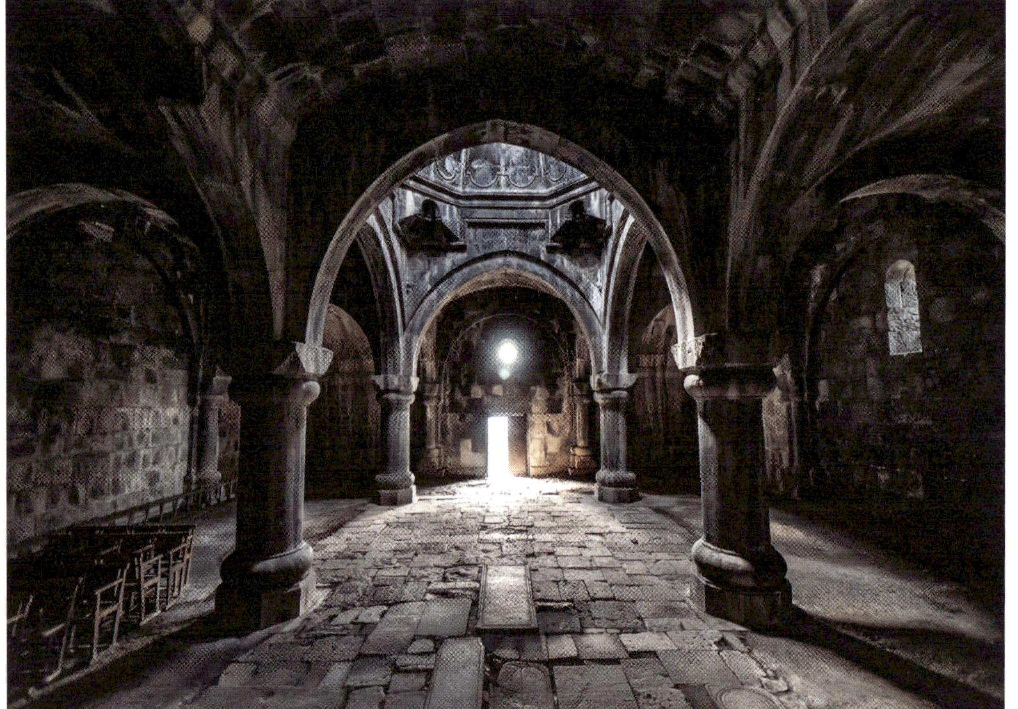

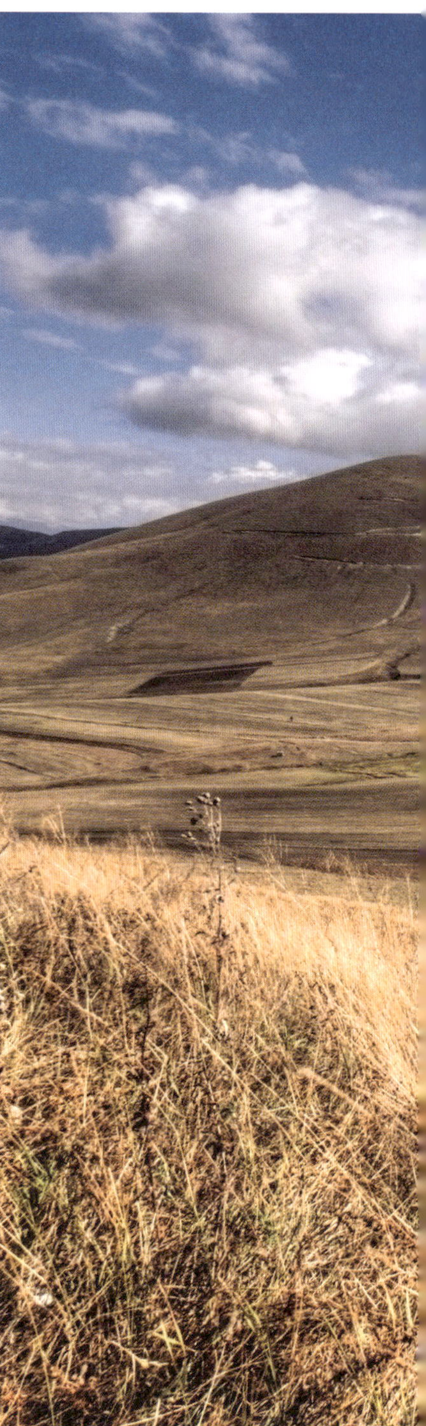

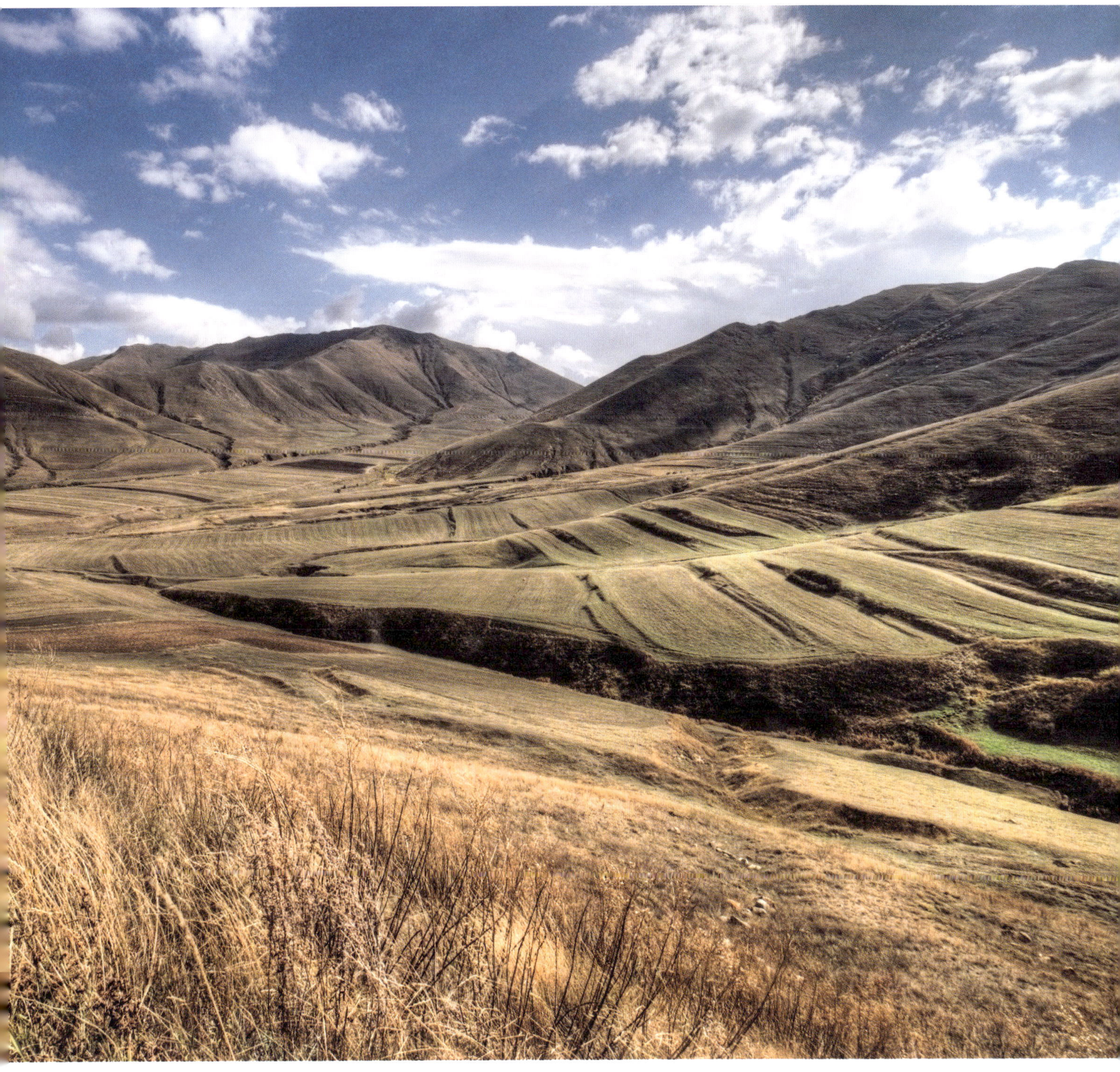

Haghpat, Armenia
41°05'37.4"N 44°42'41.9"E
The dim light and worn floor contribute to the
special ambience inside the Haghpat Monastery.
// October 2015

M3 near Tsilkar, Aragatsotn Province, Armenia
40°44'07.6"N 44°12'06.1"E
Armenia has many wide landscapes such as
this one, enough for plenty of 'wow effects' while
on the road.
// October 2015

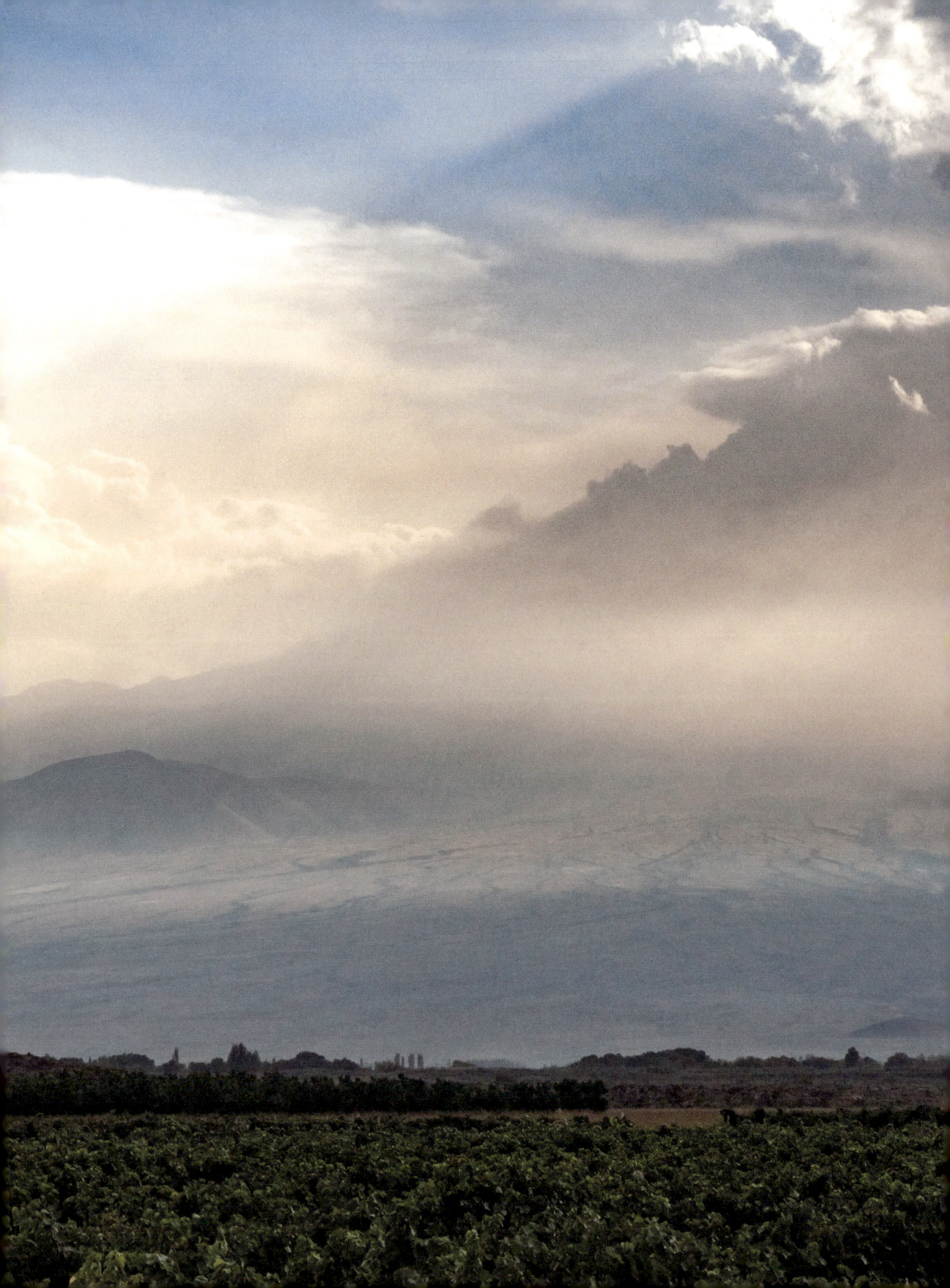

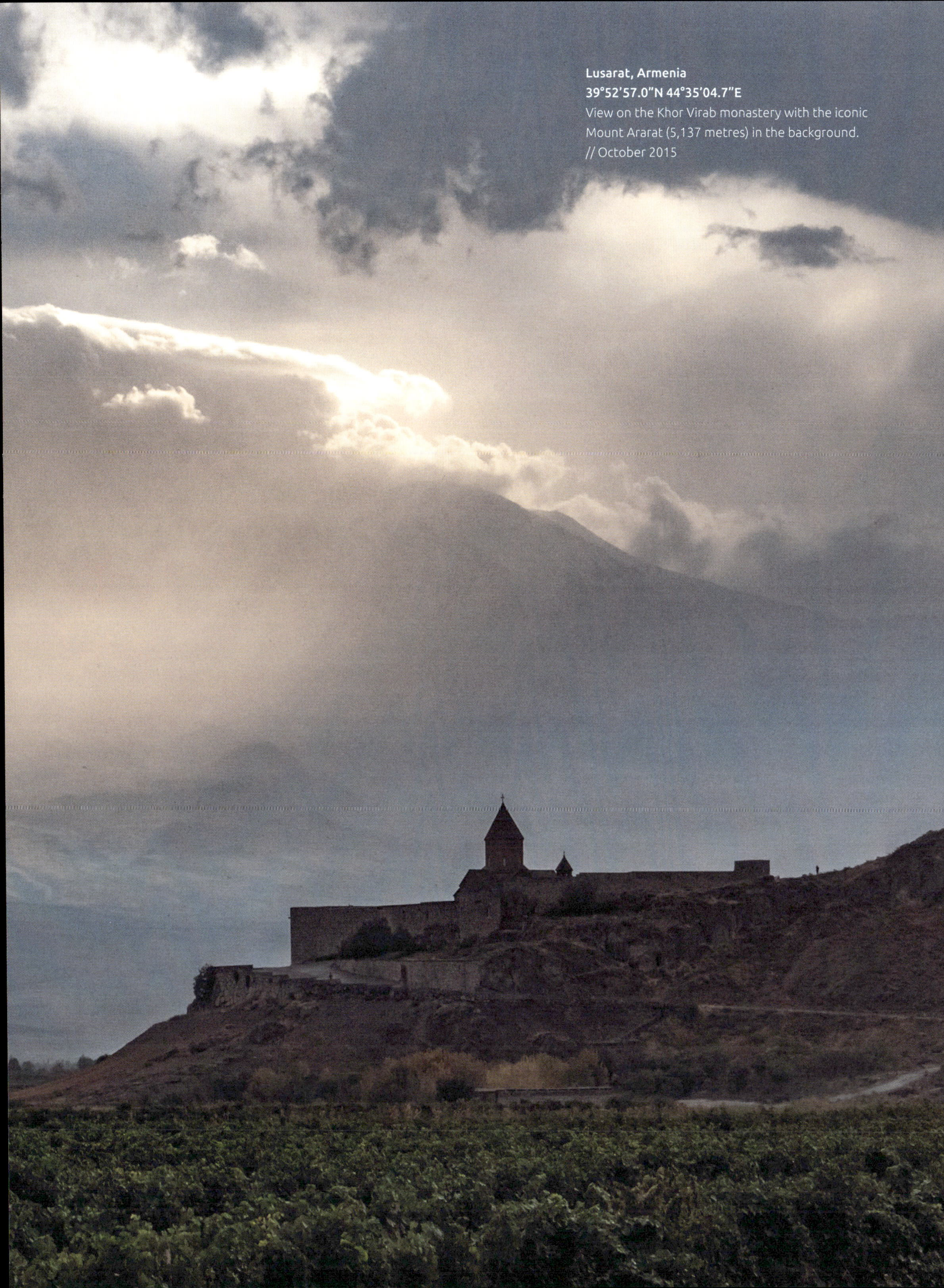

Lusarat, Armenia
39°52'57.0"N 44°35'04.7"E
View on the Khor Virab monastery with the iconic
Mount Ararat (5,137 metres) in the background.
// October 2015

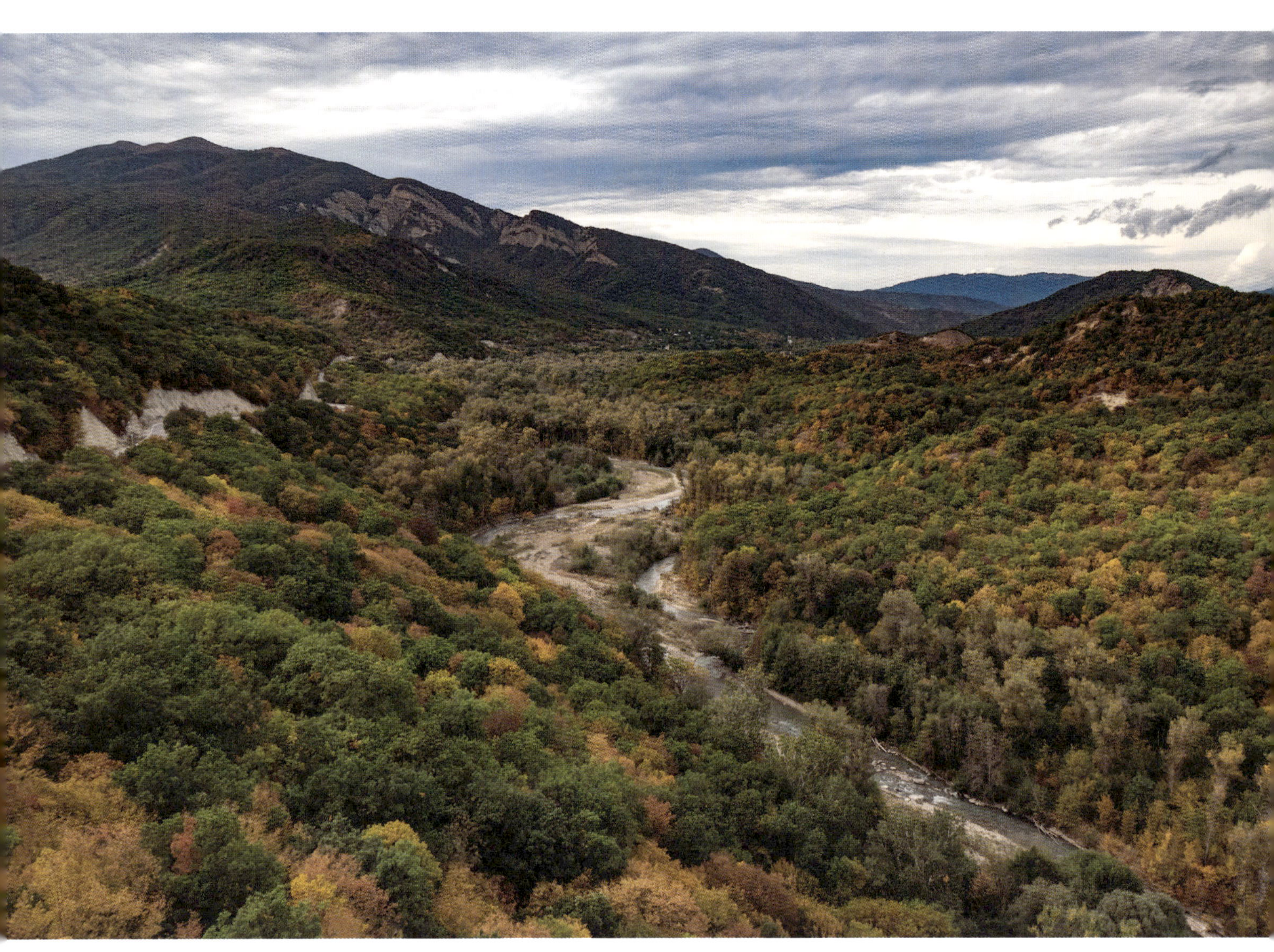

Ujarma, Georgia
41°48'41.0"N 45°09'13.6"E
Autumn is arriving in the lush valleys near Tbilisi.
// October 2015

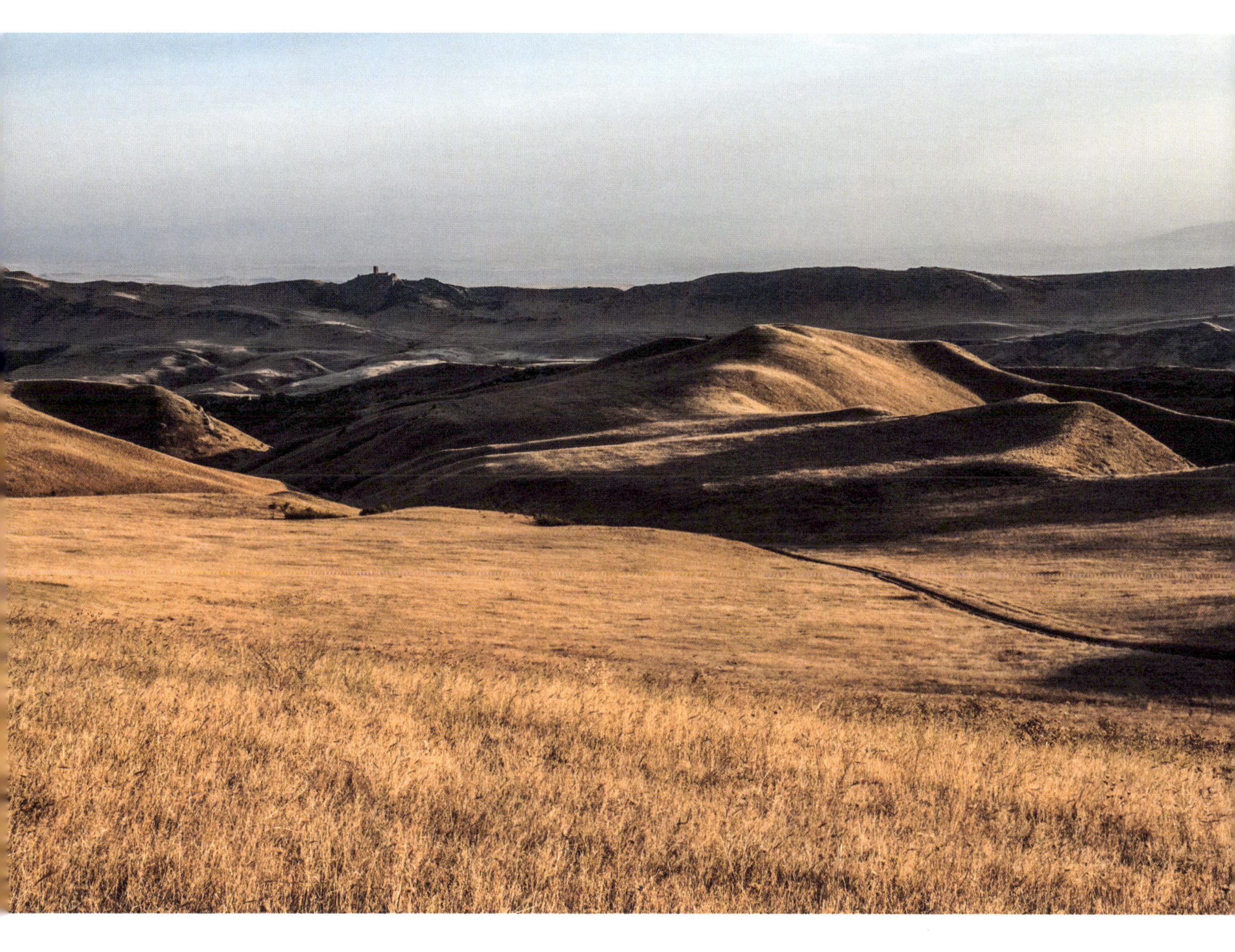

David Gareja, Georgia
41°29'12.3"N 45°21'19.0"E
Of all the kilometres I have driven through Europe
over the years, this journey has been the most
rewarding. The remote and adventurous
atmosphere together with the stunning views
of the golden landscape around David Gareja are
simply unforgettable.
// September 2015

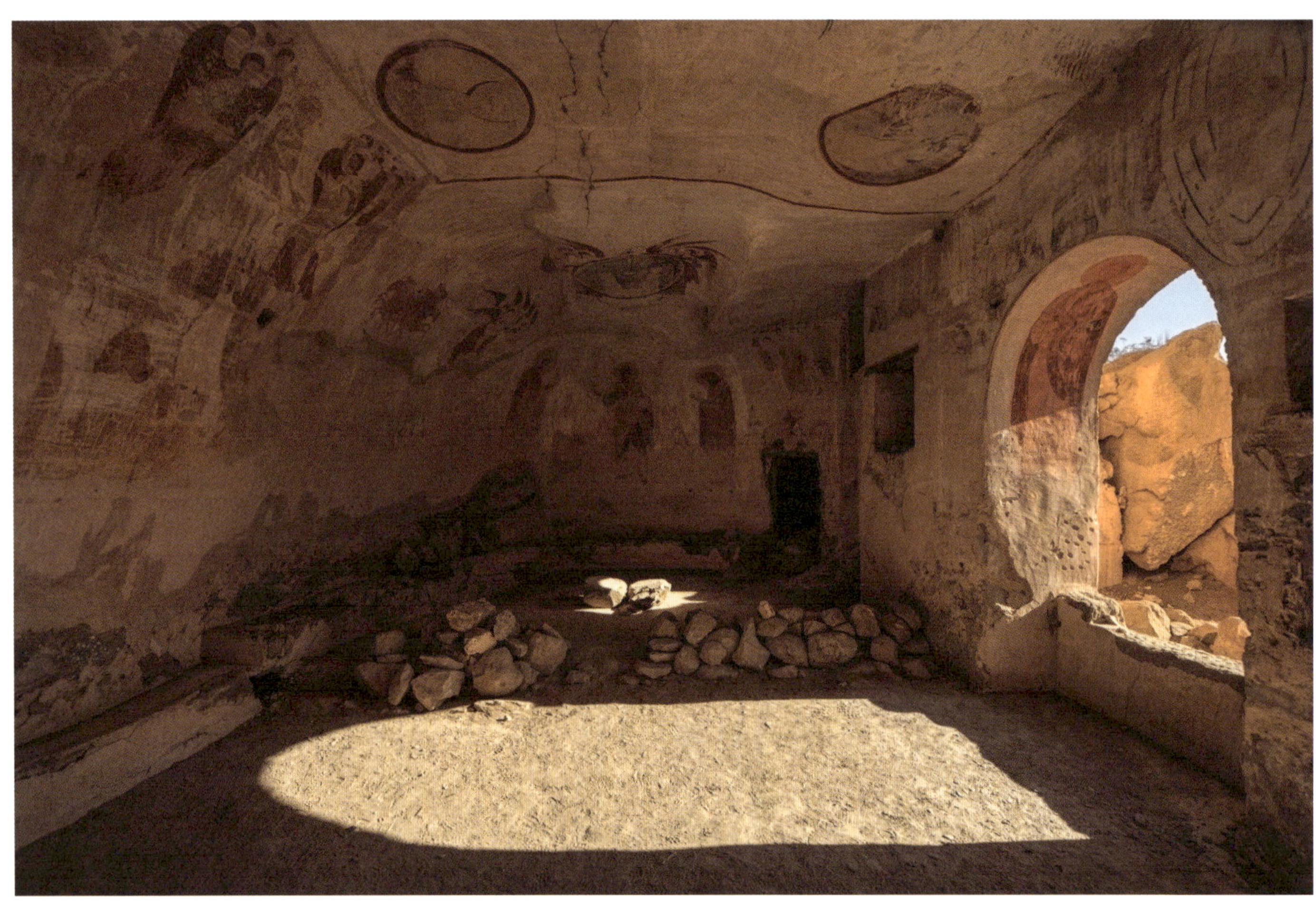

David Gareja, Georgia
41°26'36.3"N 45°22'29.4"E
Ancient frescoes decorate the cave walls of David Gareja. The remote location of this monastery complex with its ridge overlooking both Georgia and Azerbaijan make this one of the most impressive cultural monuments in Europe.
// September 2015

David Gareja, Georgia
41°26'50.2"N 45°22'35.1"E
Decorated door inside the David Gareja monastery.
// September 2015

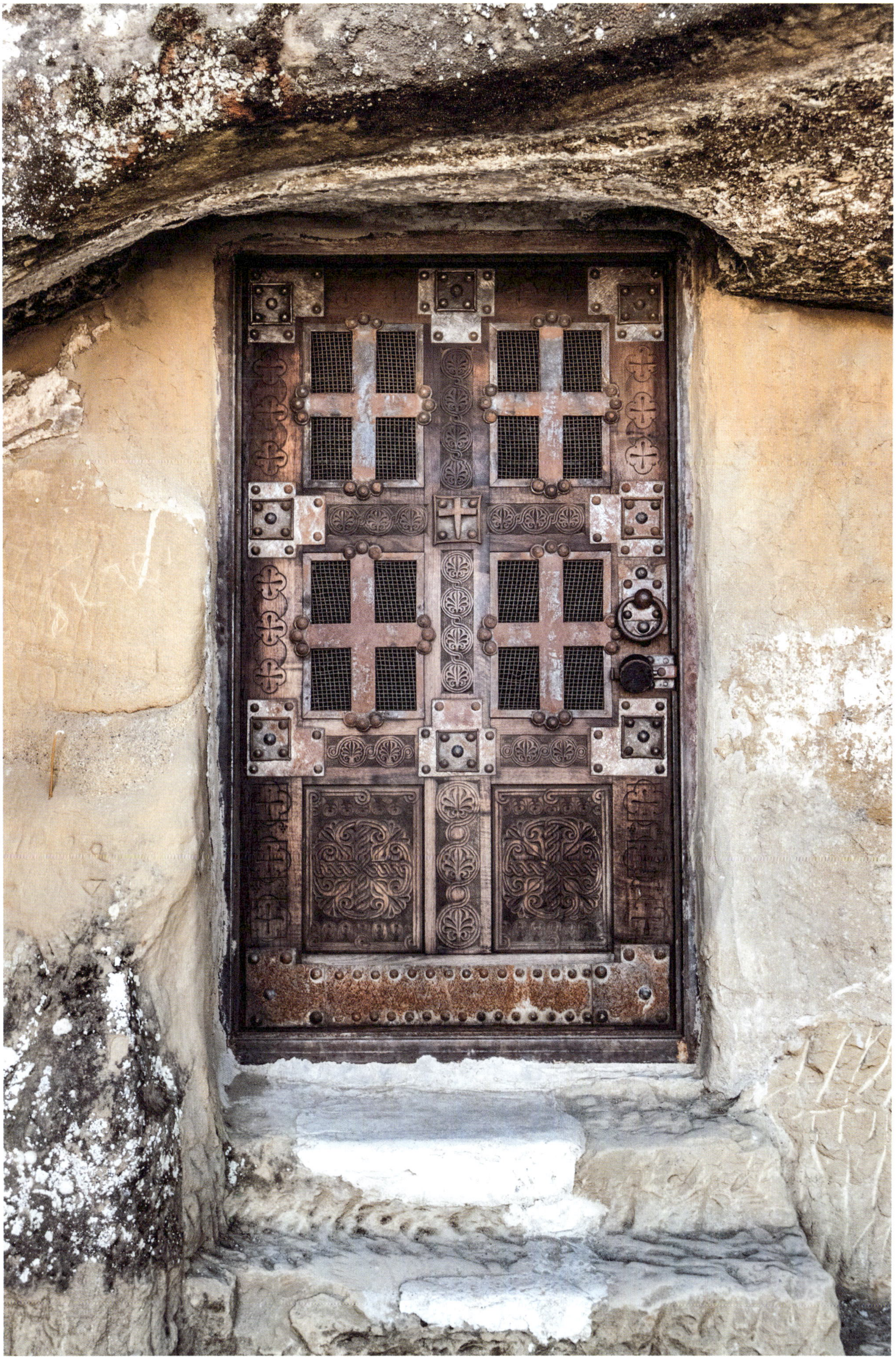

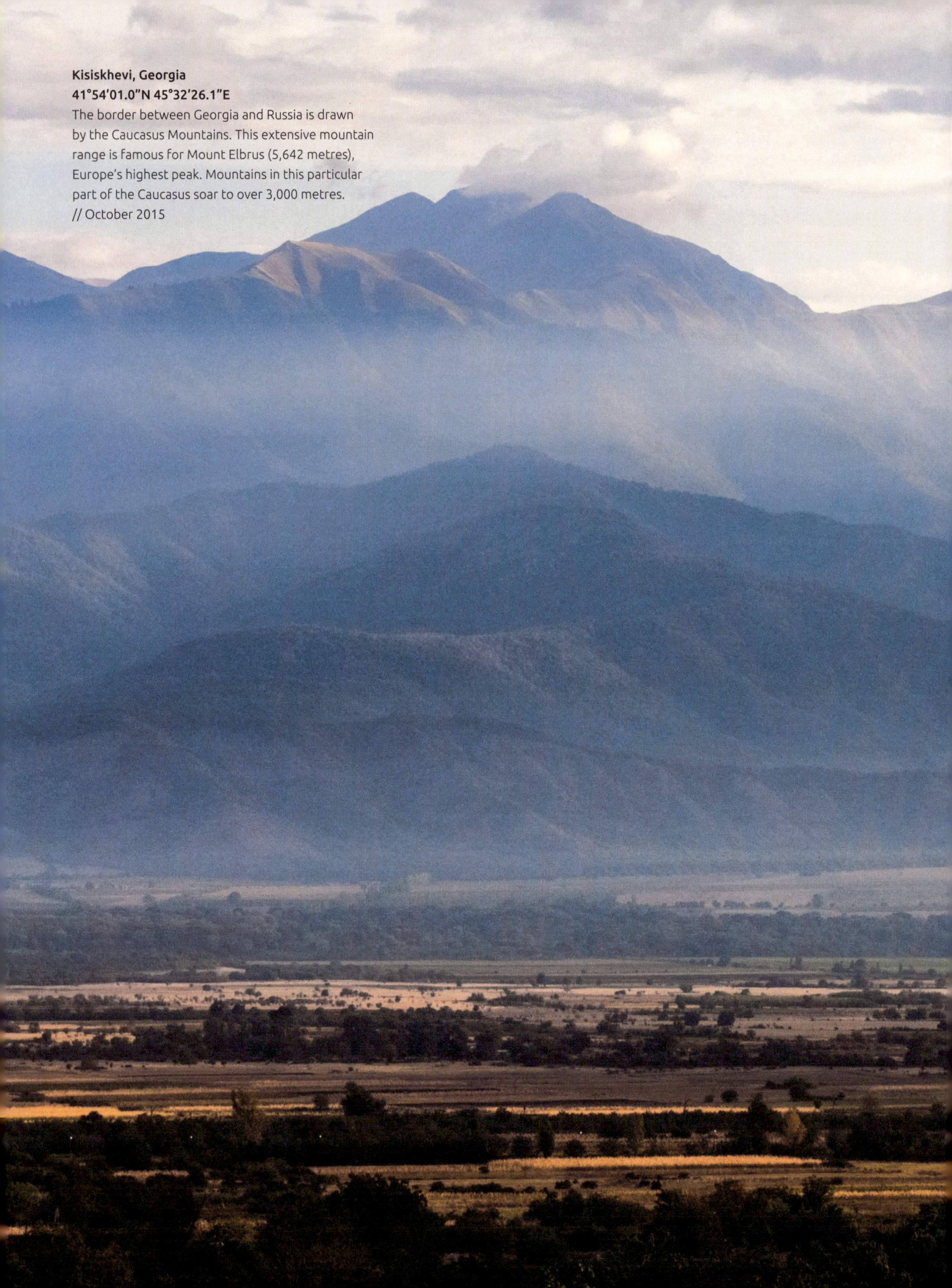

Kisiskhevi, Georgia
41°54'01.0"N 45°32'26.1"E
The border between Georgia and Russia is drawn
by the Caucasus Mountains. This extensive mountain
range is famous for Mount Elbrus (5,642 metres),
Europe's highest peak. Mountains in this particular
part of the Caucasus soar to over 3,000 metres.
// October 2015

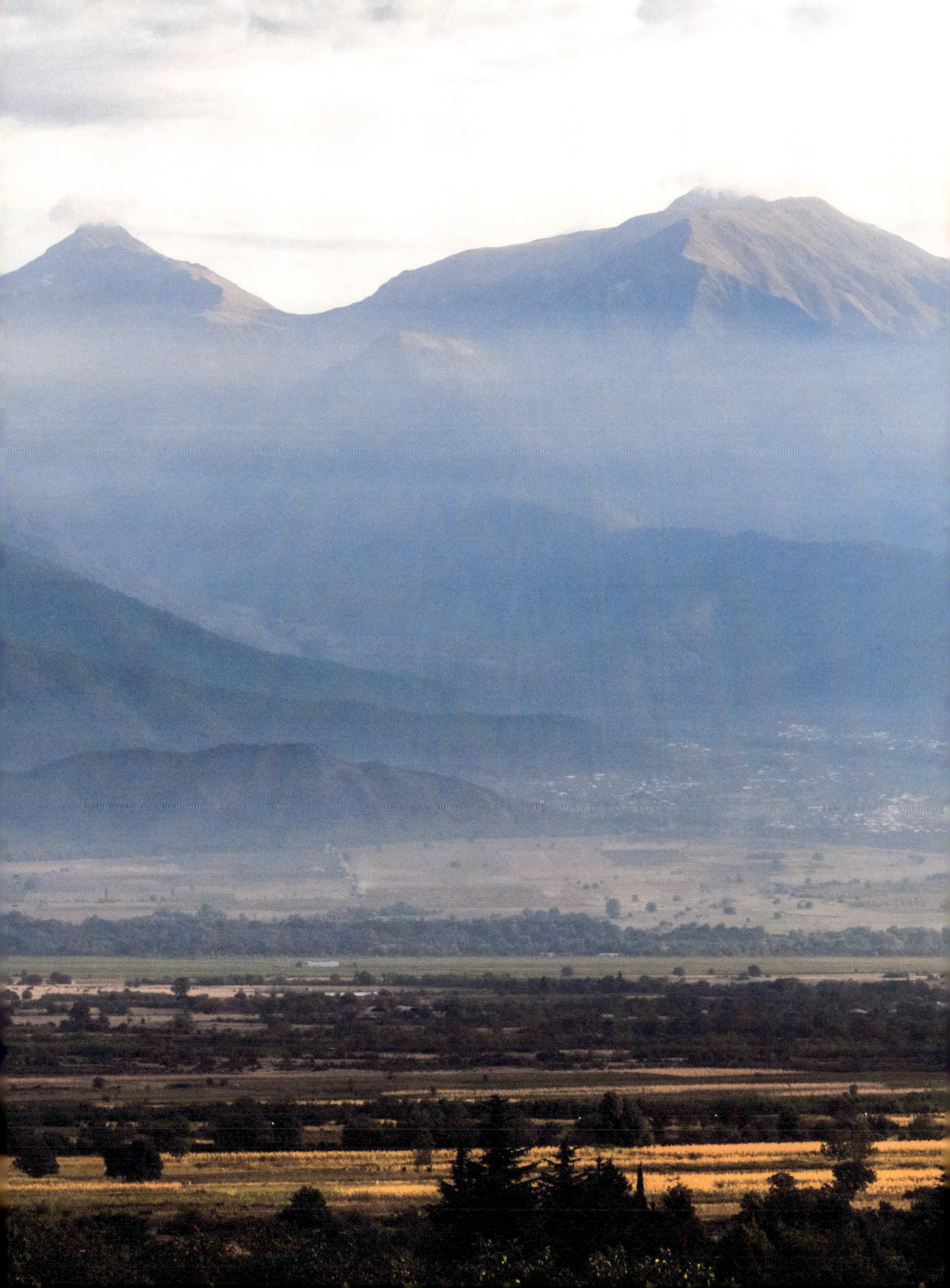

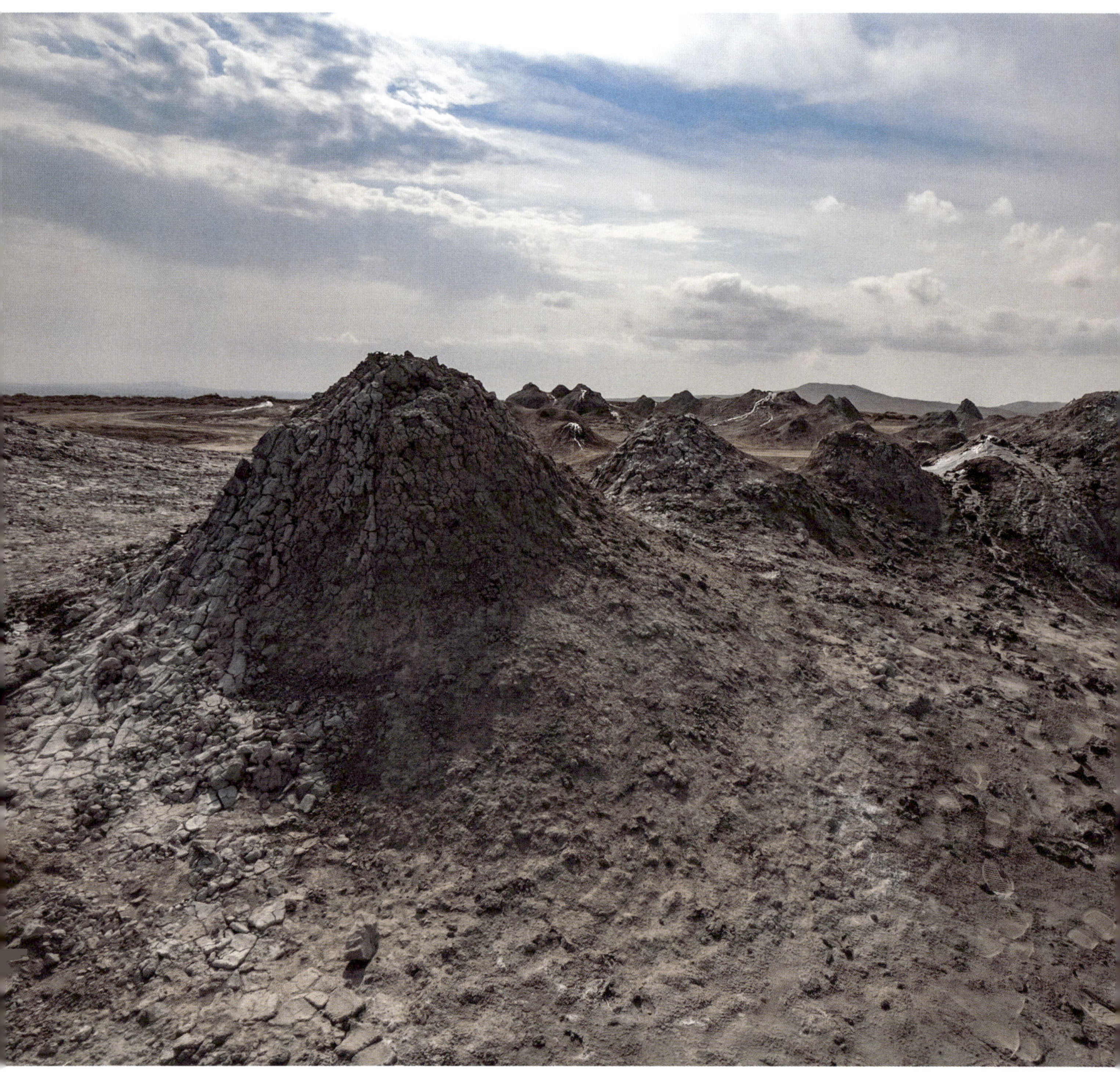

Qobustan, Azerbaijan
39°59'46.8"N 49°24'09.7"E
Mud volcanoes are bubbling constantly in
this strange landscape. Many of the world's mud
volcanoes are found in Azerbaijan, so when you
are here this is not to be missed. Best to be
combined with a visit to the nearby Qobustan
National Park with ancient petroglyphs.
// September 2015

Yanar Dag, Absheron Peninsula, Azerbaijan
40°30'06.7"N 49°53'28.5"E
This permanent fireplace close to the Caspian Sea
is the result of natural gas escaping from porous
sandstone. A worthy natural monument for
a country that itself is known as 'The Land of Fire'.
// September 2015

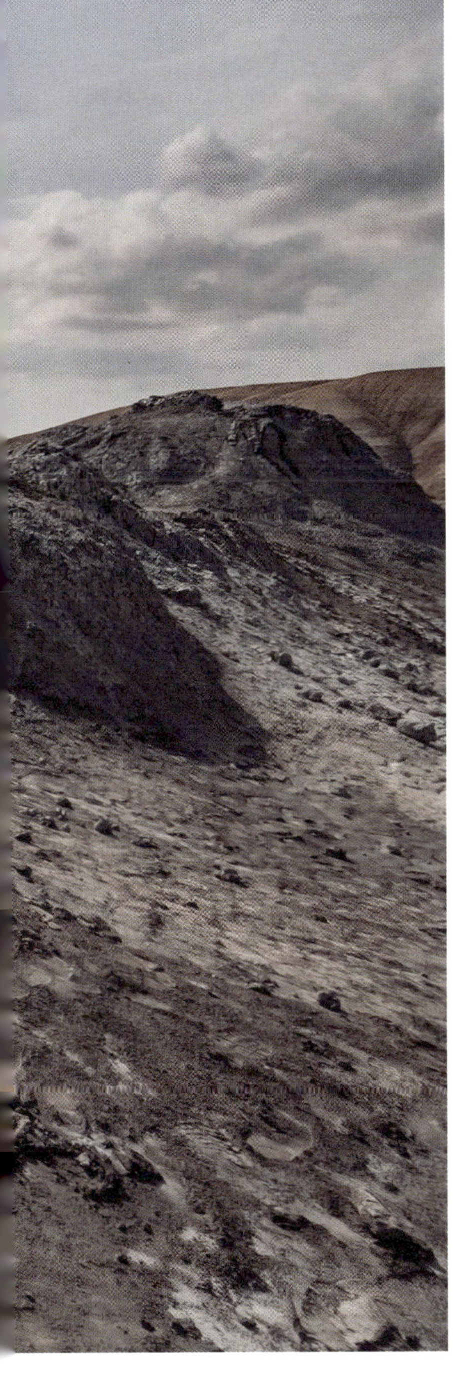

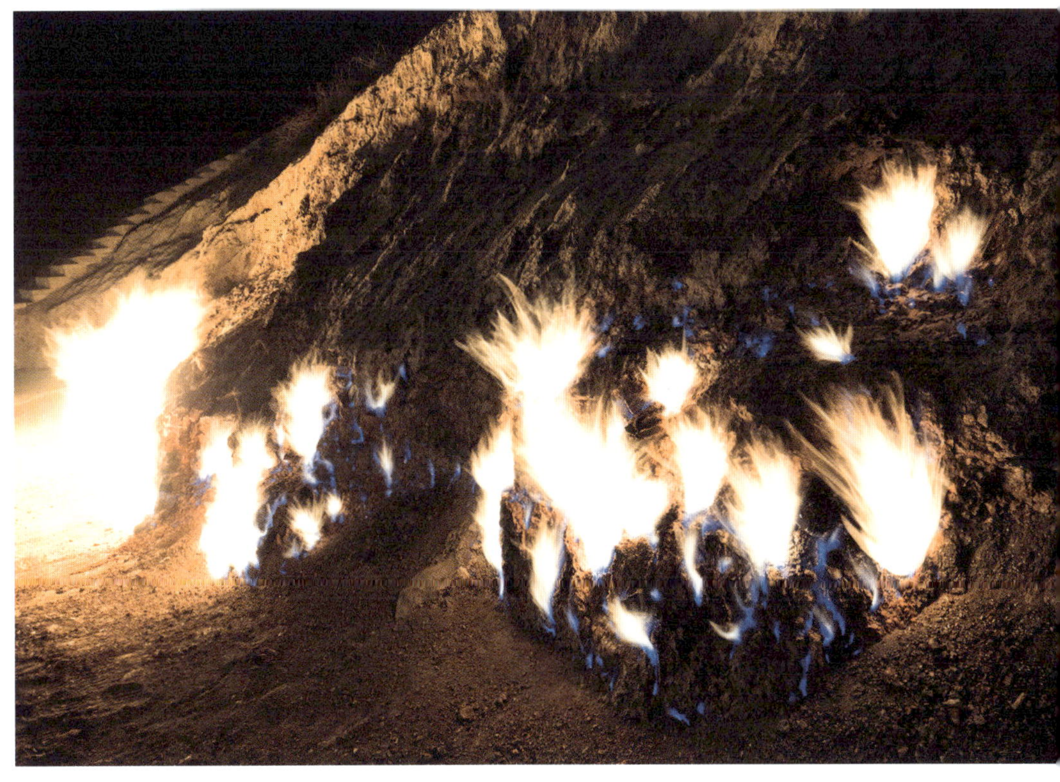

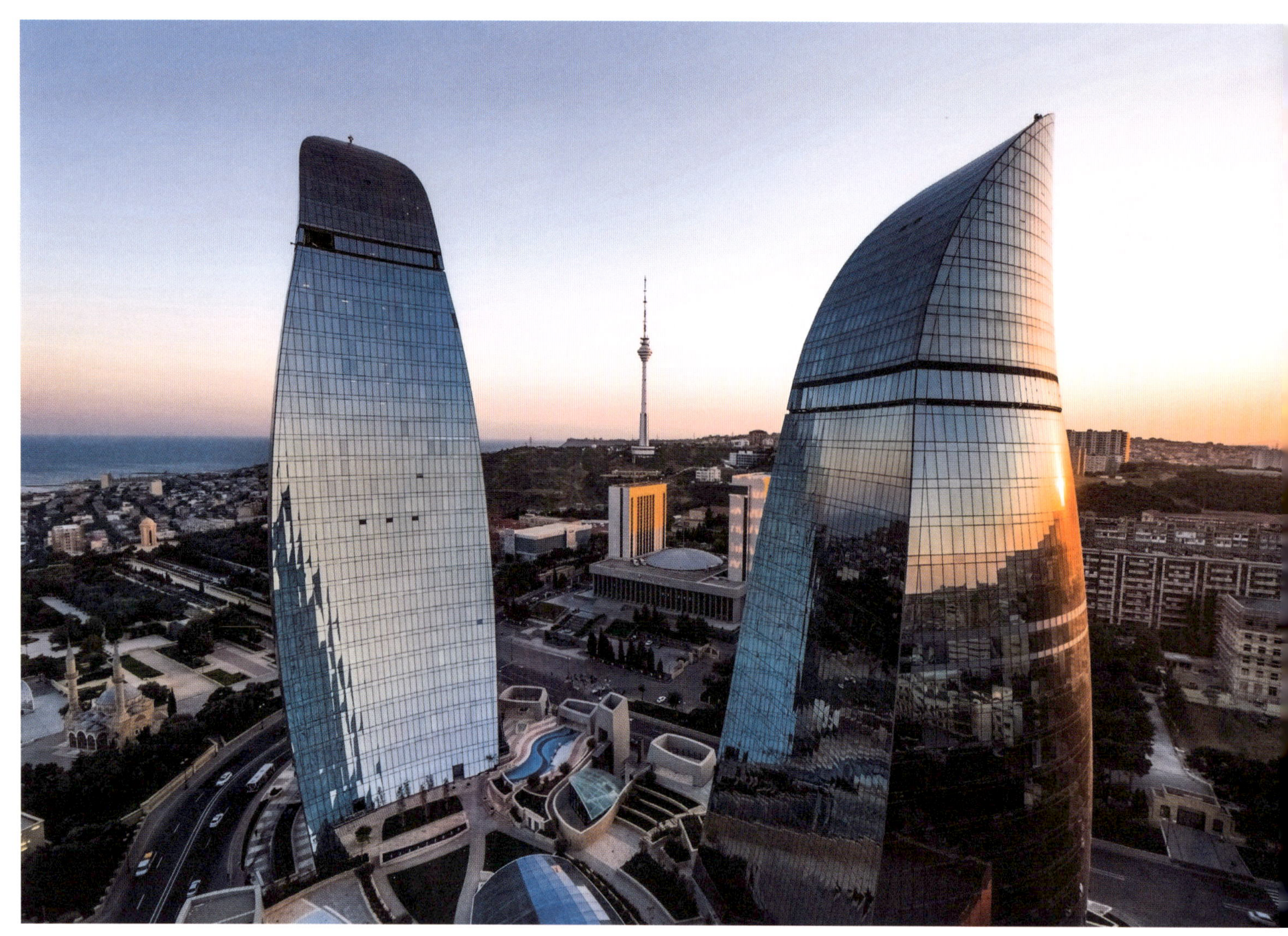

Baku, Azerbaijan
40°21'35.5"N 49°49'35.9"E
On arrival in Baku after a long day of driving and
border crossing hassles, my husband and I treated
ourselves to a stay in one of the buildings of the
famous Baku Flame Towers. Probably the most
futuristic place I have ever spent the night.
// September 2015

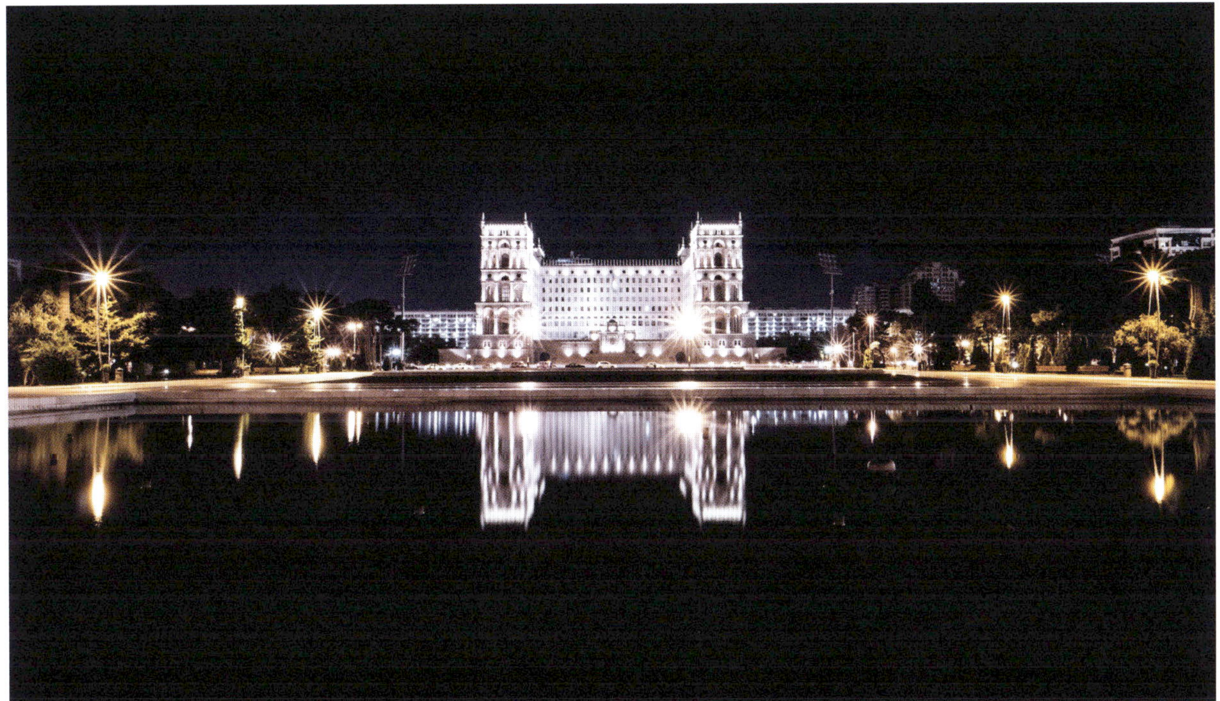

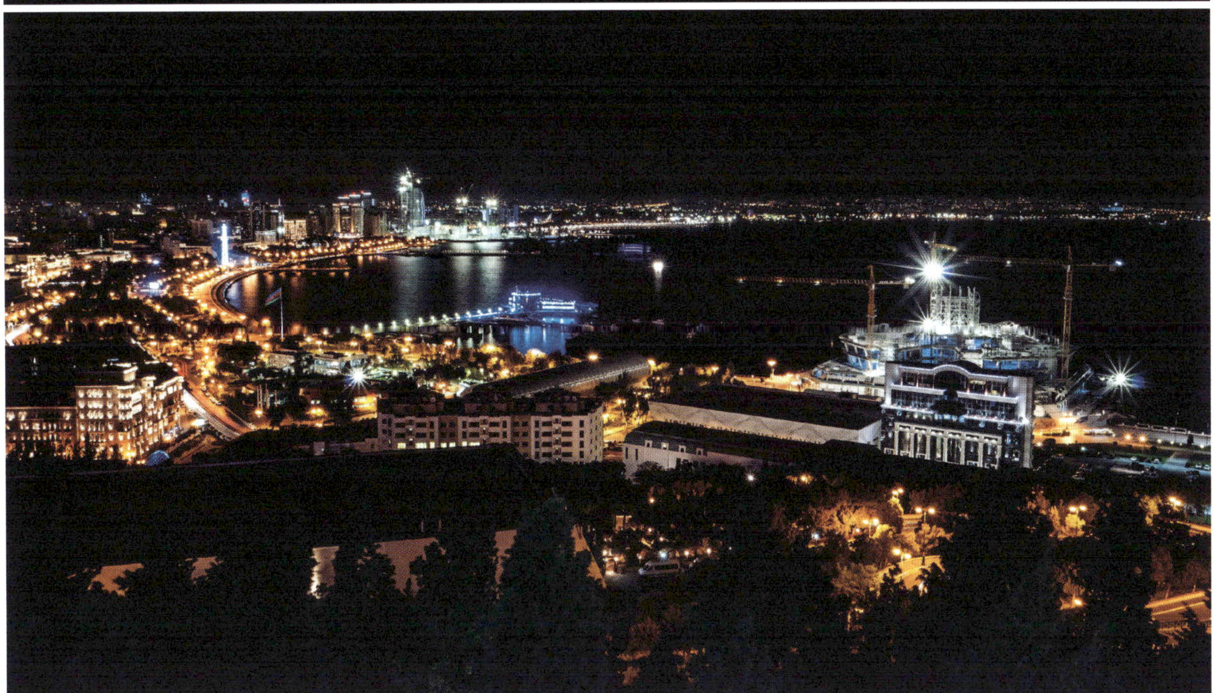

Baku, Azerbaijan
40°22'17.0"N 49°51'14.5"E
A perfect reflection of the Government House
in Baku.
// September 2015

Baku, Azerbaijan
40°21'35.5"N 49°49'35.9"E
Baku by night, as seen from one of
the Flame Towers.
// September 2015

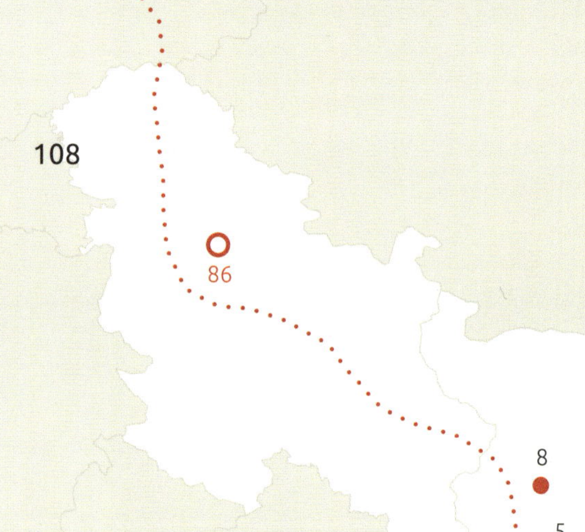

To the Far East
Route and travel suggestions

Scenic regions and nature reserves

1   David Gareja // **Georgia & Azerbaijan**
2   Eastern Anatolia // **Turkey**
3   Greater Caucasus // **Georgia & Russia**
4   Qobustan mud volcanoes // **Azerbaijan**
5   Rila & Pirin // **Bulgaria**

Cities and towns

6   Baku // **Azerbaijan**
7   Safranbolu // **Turkey**
8   Sofia // **Bulgaria**
9   Tbilisi // **Georgia**
10 Plovdiv // **Bulgaria**

Cultural experiences

11 Ani // **Turkey**
12 Bagrati Cathedral // **Kutaisi, Georgia**
13 Haghpat Monastery // **Armenia**
14 Ishak Pasha Palace // **Doğubayazıt, Turkey**
15 Qobustan State Reserve // **Azerbaijan**
16 Tsitsernakaberd, Yerevan // **Armenia**
17 Vardzia // **Georgia**

Spectacular roads and scenic routes

18 E99 between Iğdır and Doğubayazıt // **Turkey**
19 Ilgar Dağı Pass (E691) between Türkgözü
    and Damal // **Turkey**
20 Khertvisi-Vardzia-Mirashkhani // **Georgia**
21 M3 between Spitak and Ohanavan // **Armenia**
22 Ə172, Kakheti Province // **Georgia**
23 Shipka Pass (E85) between Kazanlak
    and Gabrovo // **Bulgaria**

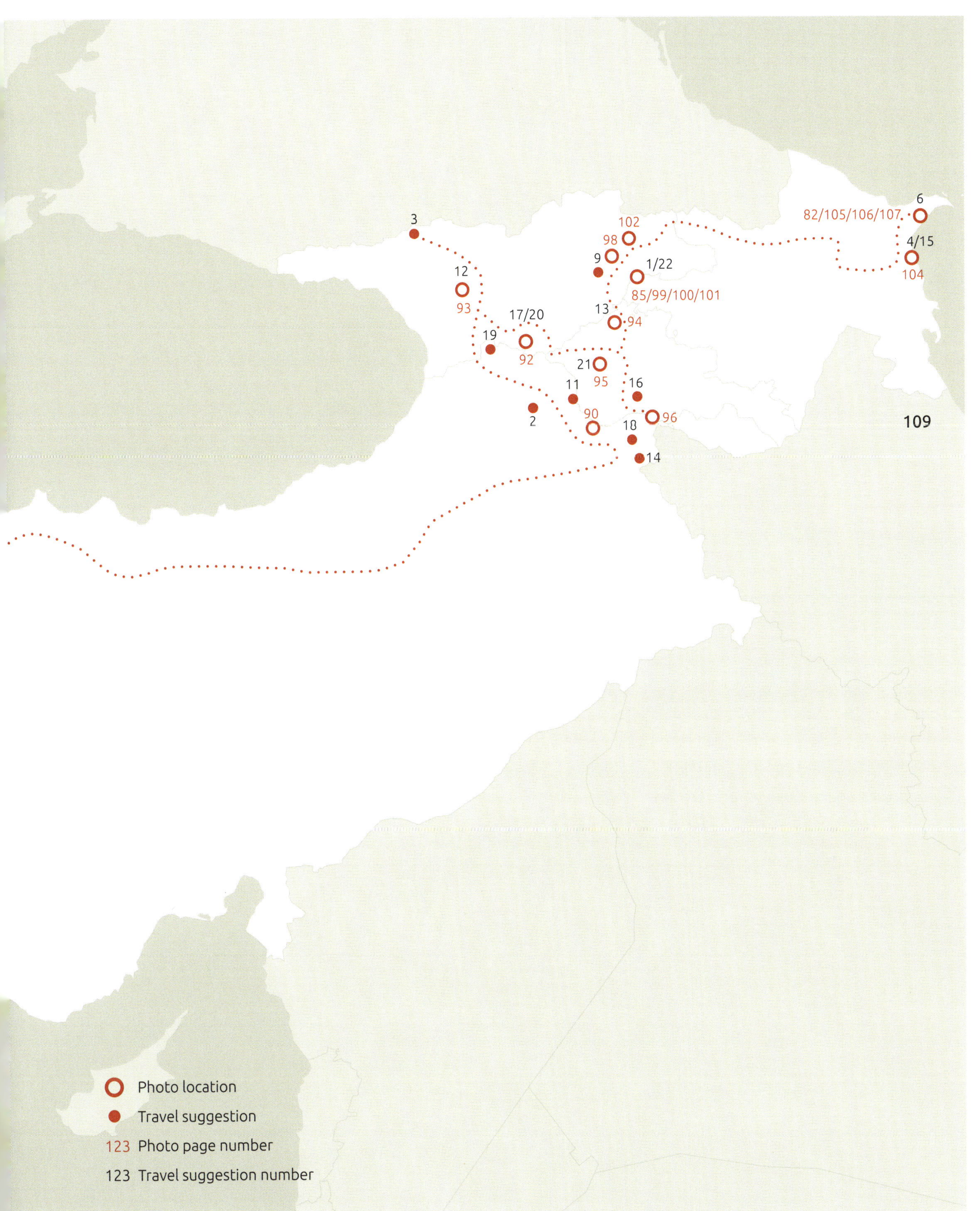

3
12
93
17/20
19
92
9
98
102
1/22
85/99/100/101
13
94
21
95
11
16
2
90
18
96
14
82/105/106/107
6
4/15
104
109
Photo location
Travel suggestion
123 Photo page number
123 Travel suggestion number

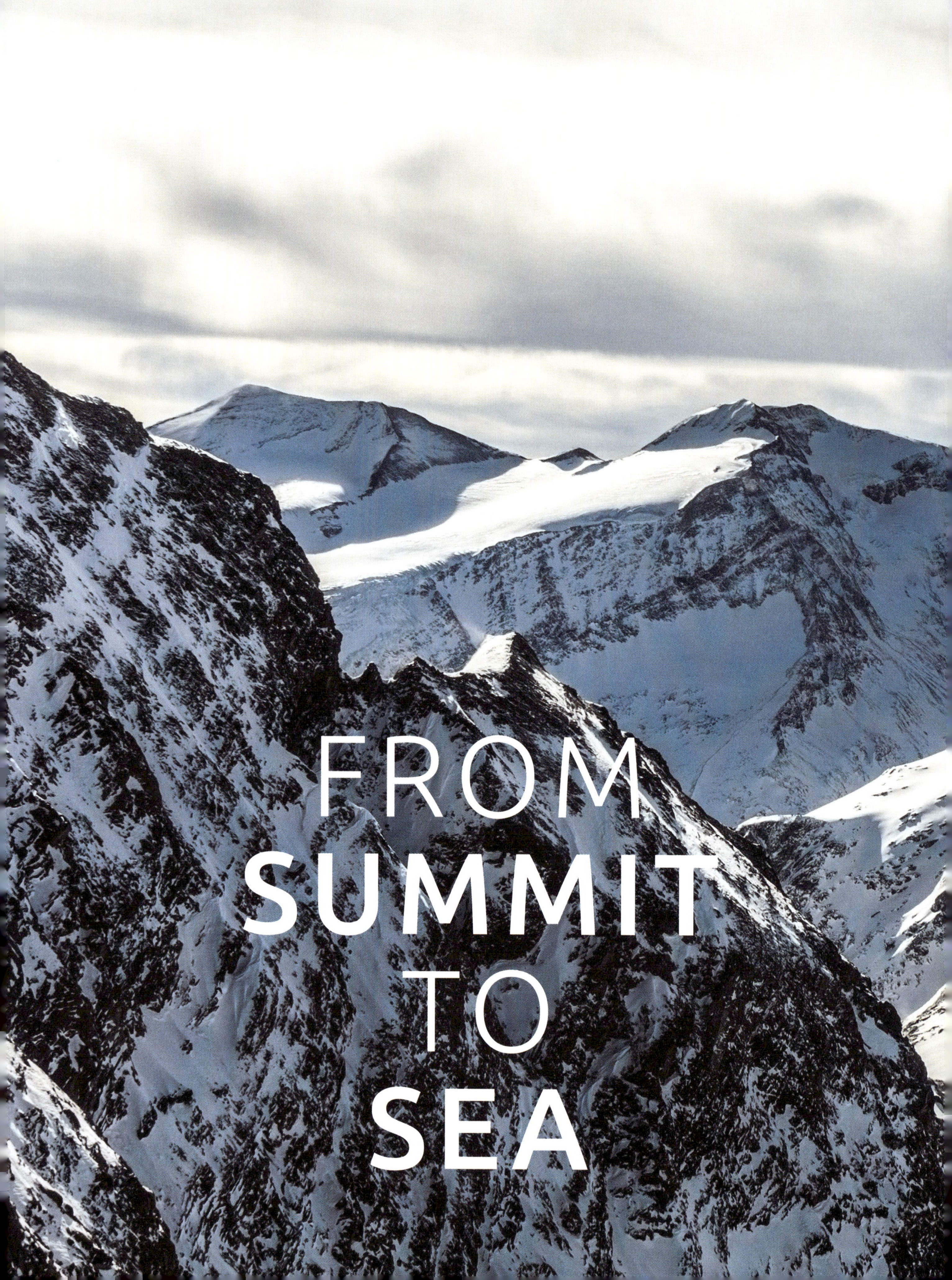

FROM
SUMMIT
TO
SEA

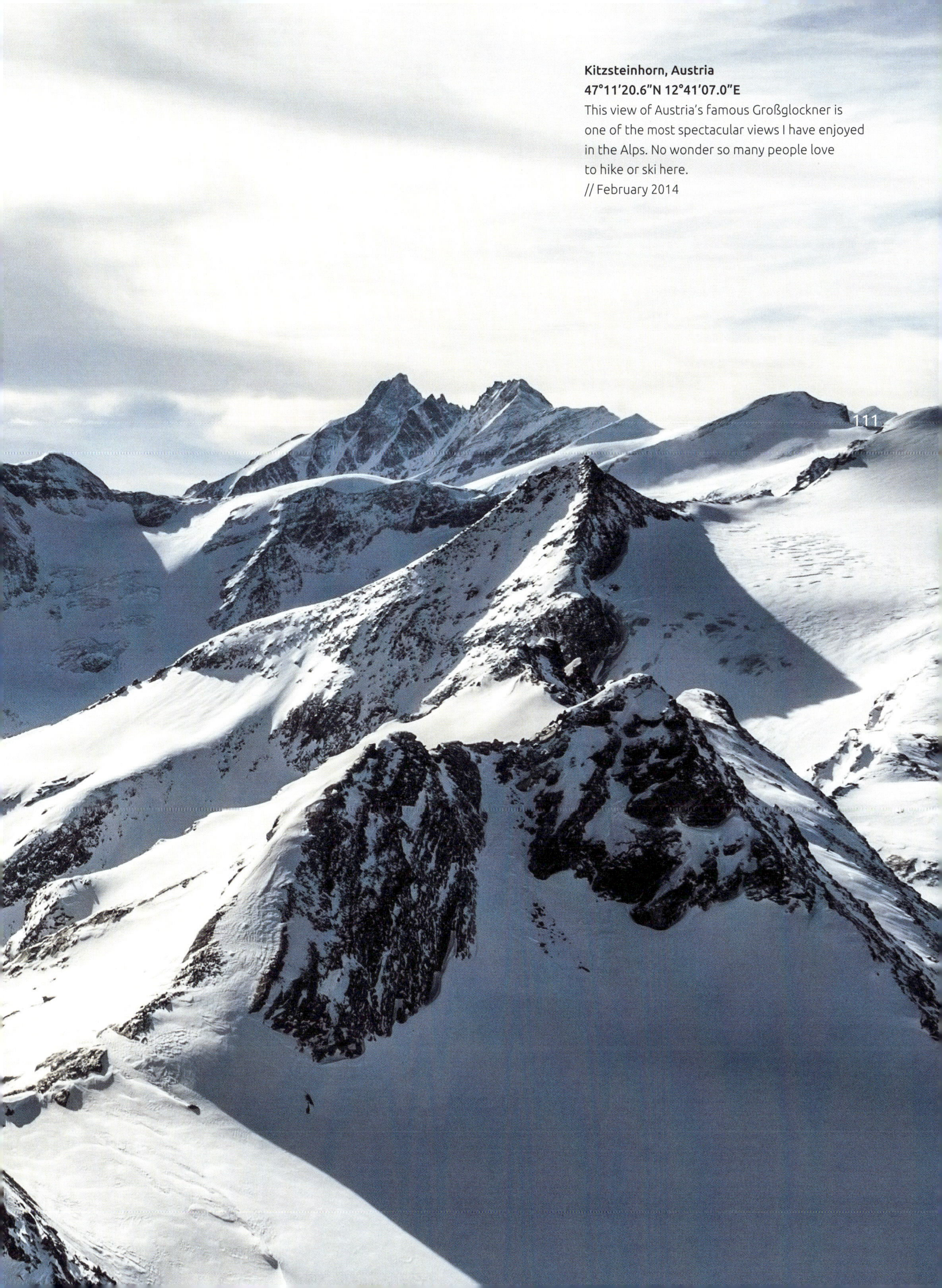

Kitzsteinhorn, Austria
47°11'20.6"N 12°41'07.0"E
This view of Austria's famous Großglockner is
one of the most spectacular views I have enjoyed
in the Alps. No wonder so many people love
to hike or ski here.
// February 2014

111

TRAVELLING from the Netherlands to the southeast, the Alps mark the start of a long curve of connected mountain ranges extending all the way to the end of the Peloponnese in Greece. Thousands of peaks dominate the landscape and separate medieval Ottoman villages from bustling ports, and green Alpine meadows from remote wildlife reserves.

Some mountain ranges are popular tourist destinations, others are yet to be discovered. Whether you prefer hiking, rock climbing, skiing, or any other outdoor mountain activity, the peaks and slopes of the Alps and Balkans offer more challenges than you will ever be able to face.

The Alps are in a class of their own. With over 500 peaks that exceed 3,000 metres and over 14 million inhabitants, the Alps show striking contrasts between rough Alpine environments and cosy villages full of life. Located at the heart of Europe with a strongly-developed tourism industry, it is no wonder so many people visit the Alps year after year. In my opinion, it is both the strength and the weakness of the Alps. Nevertheless, the landscapes are fantastic and worth returning to time after time to explore new peaks and valleys.

What I love about the Balkans in particular is the diversity in landscape and culture all within one or two days of driving. Mediterranean seaside towns, authentic mountain villages and charming capitals make the drive along the Adriatic coastline and the inland mountain ranges a journey full of surprises. Towns and villages I recommend visiting are Berat in Albania, Sarajevo in Bosnia and Herzegovina, and Prizren in Kosovo.

In addition, three scenic routes are at the top of my European list of favourites: the P14 between Pluzine and Žabljak in Montenegro, the SH20 between Lake Skadar and Tamarë in Albania, and the E92 between Koridallos and Kastraki in Greece. These roads offer spectacular views and are a real joy to drive. Together they highlight the surprising beauty of the Balkans.

'The peaks and slopes of the Alps and Balkans offer more challenges than you will ever be able to face.'

Kastraki, Greece
39°42'59.1"N 21°37'26.6"E
A heavy thunderstorm struck the village of Kastraki on a warm and sunny September night. I was determined to capture a few of those thunder bolts on camera from the window of our room. An impressive act of meteorology.
// September 2015

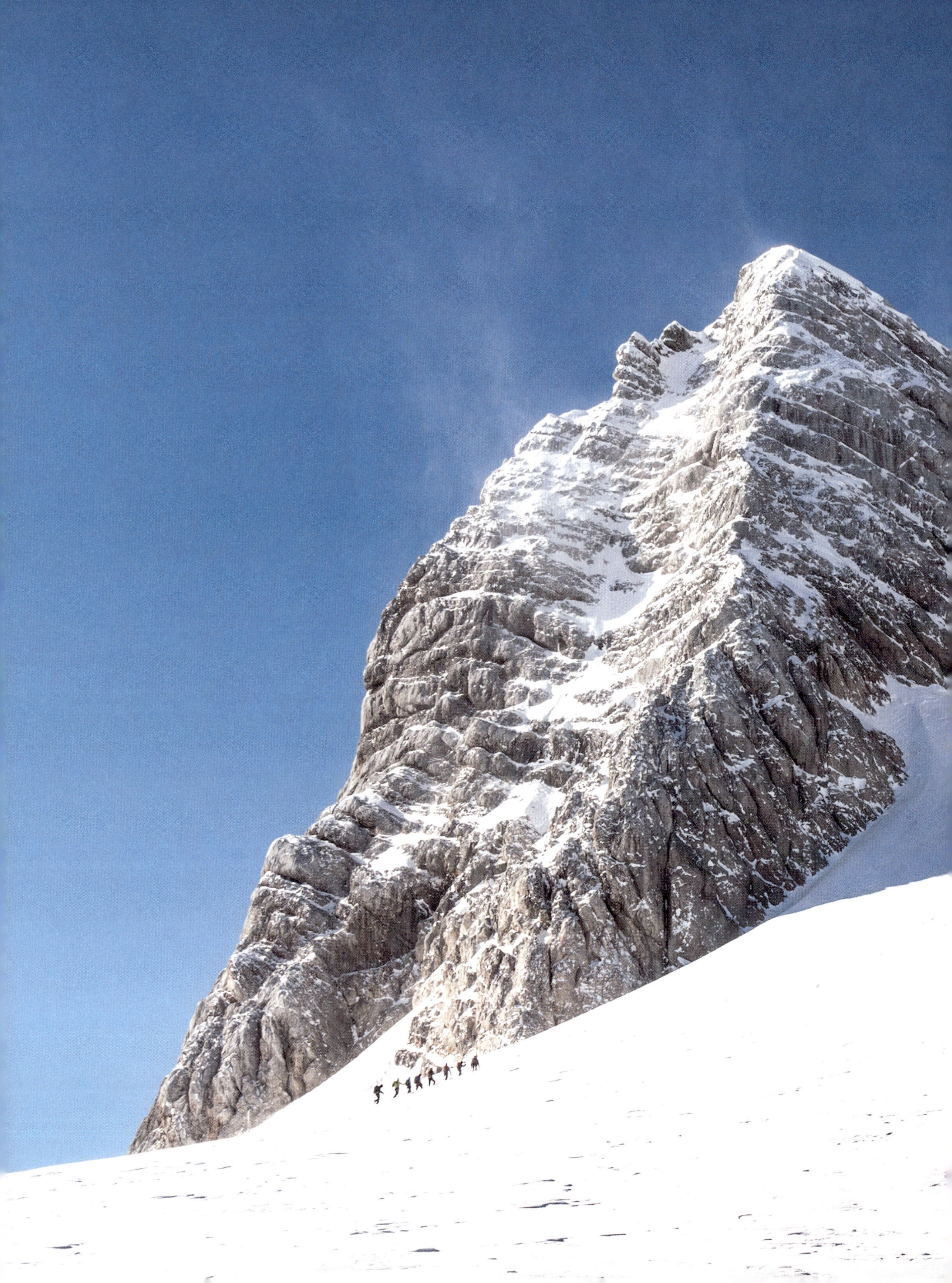

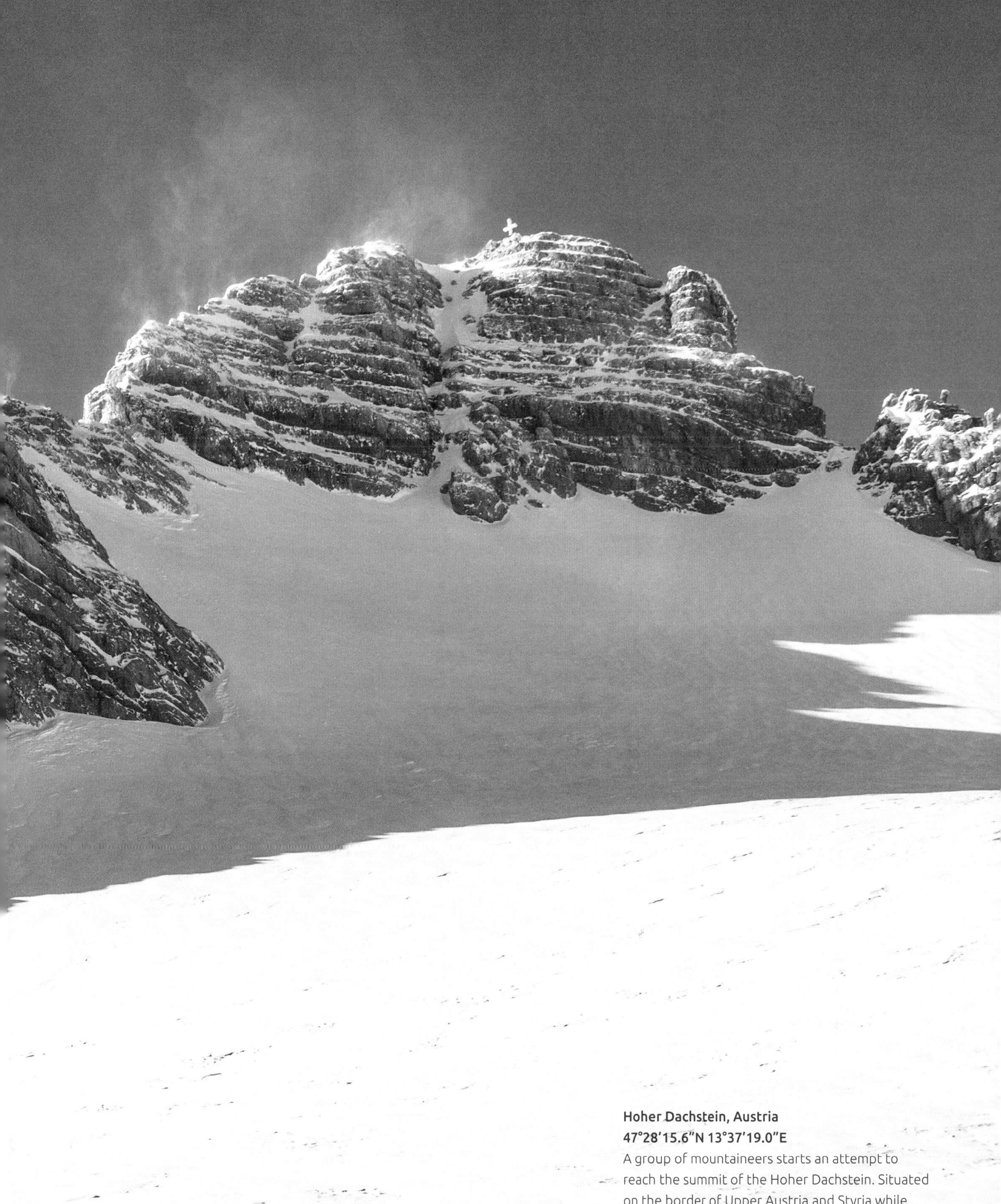

Hoher Dachstein, Austria
47°28'15.6"N 13°37'19.0"E
A group of mountaineers starts an attempt to reach the summit of the Hoher Dachstein. Situated on the border of Upper Austria and Styria while having parts also located in Salzburg, this mountain is known in German as the 'Drei-Länder-Berg'.
// February 2014

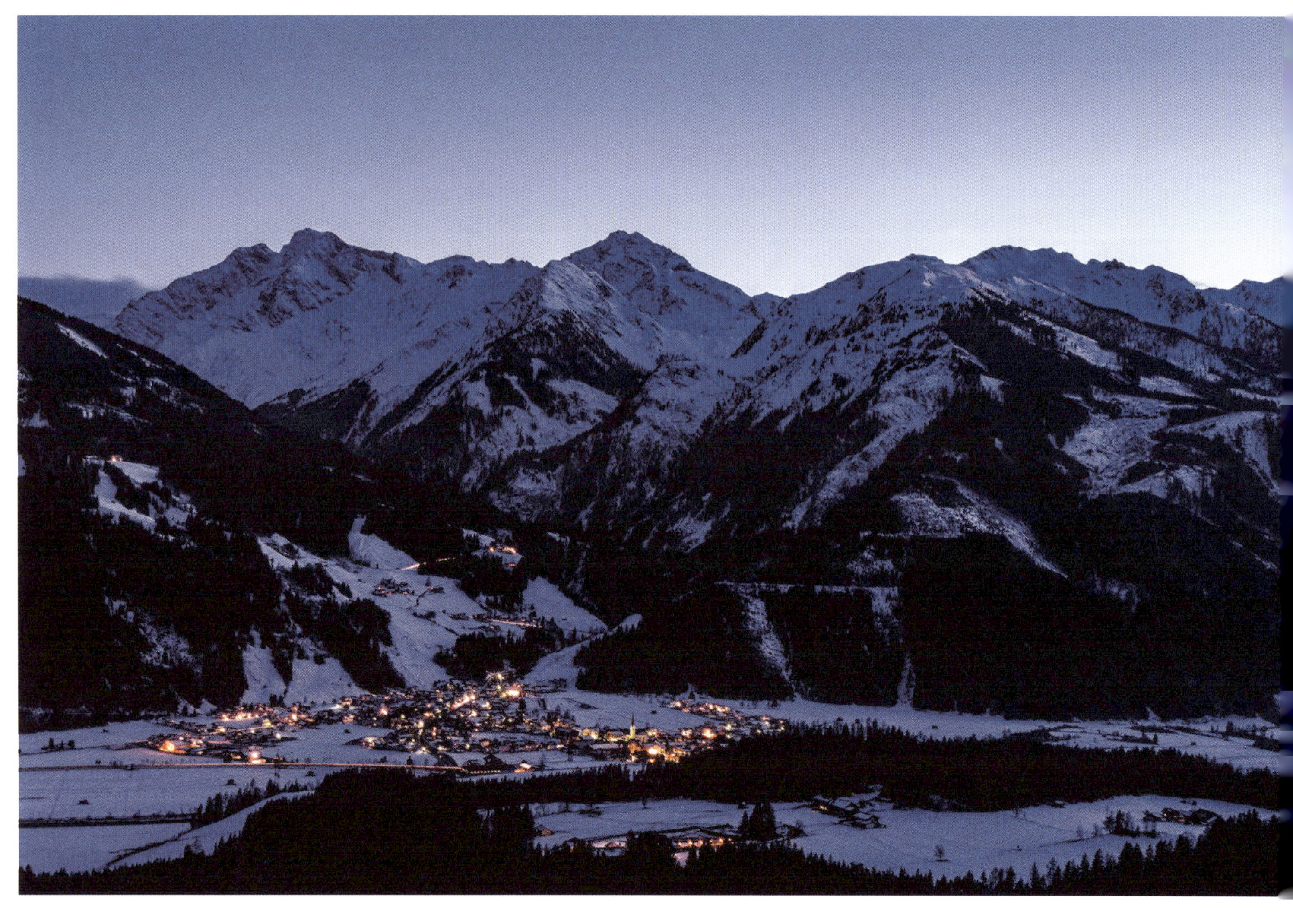

Hollersbach im Pinzgau, Austria
47°17'59.3"N 12°24'39.3"E
As the sun sets behind the Alps, the village lights
transform the harsh winter environment into
a fairytale scene.
// February 2014

Ptuj, Slovenia
46°25'14.2"N 15°52'05.5"E
View across Ptuj on a cold winter morning.
// December 2018

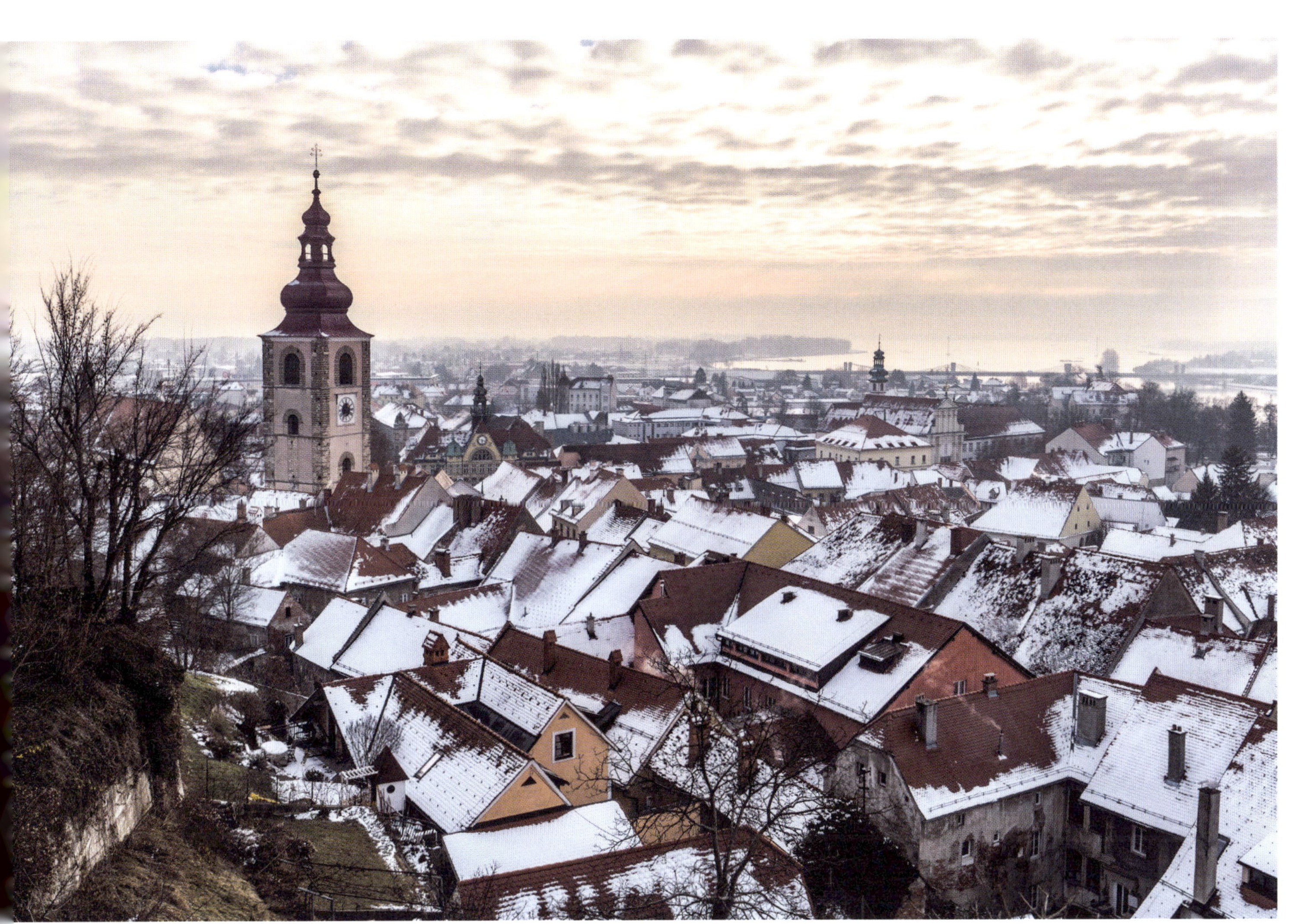

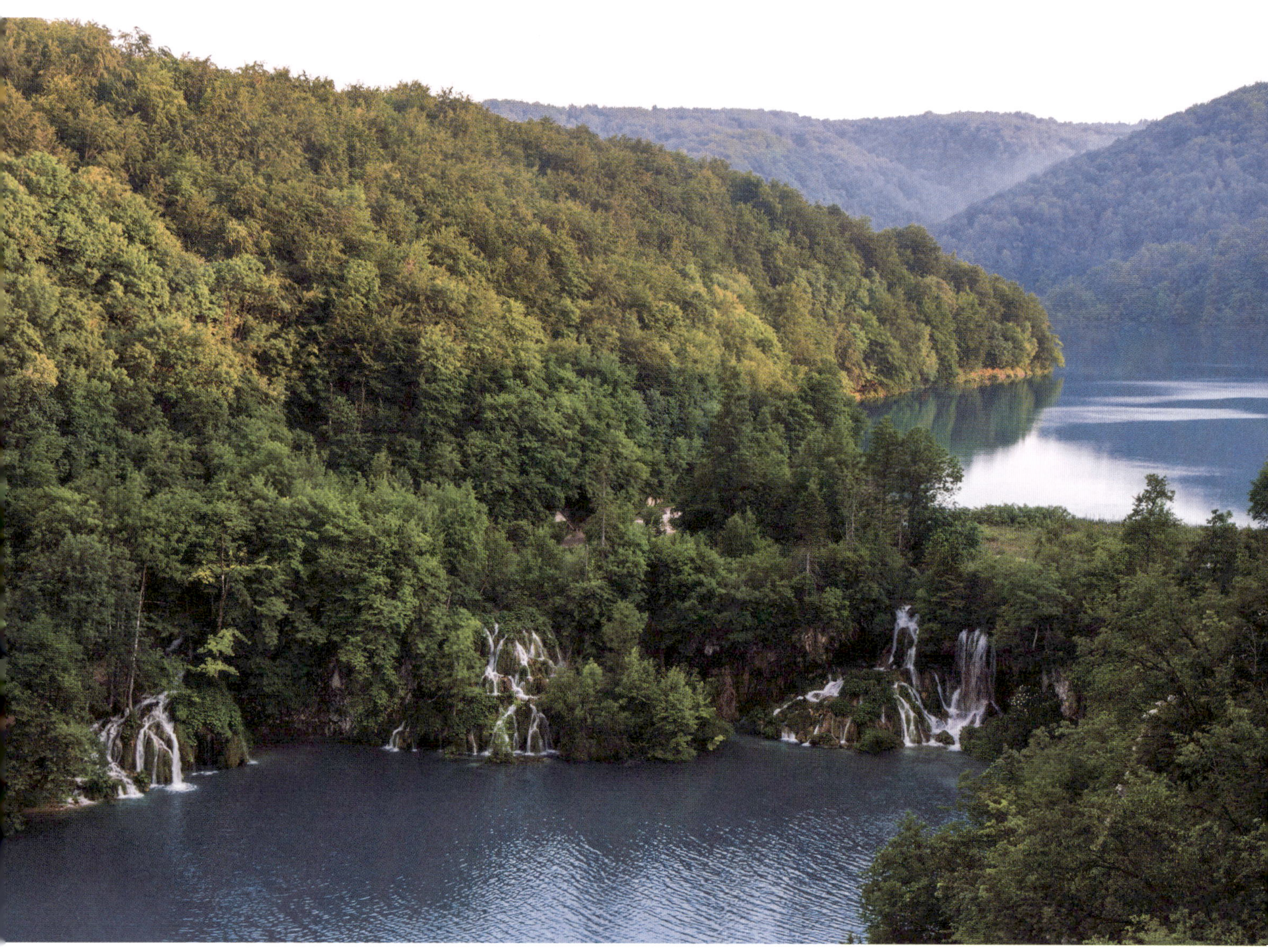

Plitvice Lakes National Park, Croatia
44°52'33.2"N 15°35'55.4"E
The lakes of Plitvice are one of the most beautiful
natural wonders on Earth. Big crowds spoil the
place during the day, but around sunset its magical
atmosphere returns. I will never forget how
thousands of fireflies completed the fairytale
experience at night.
// June 2013

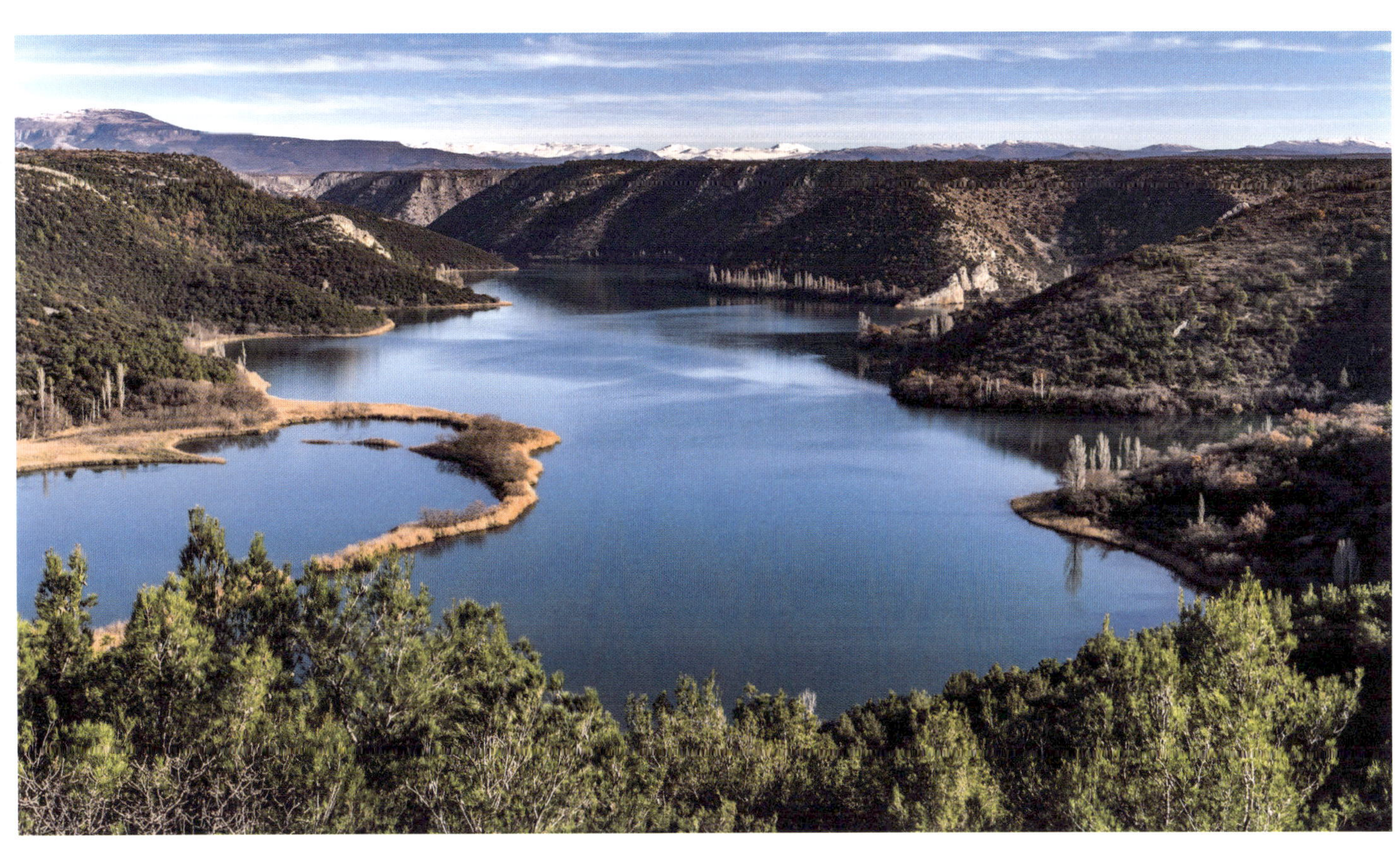

Krka National Park, Croatia
43°48'06.9"N 15°58'20.8"E
A wide view over the Krka river.
// December 2018

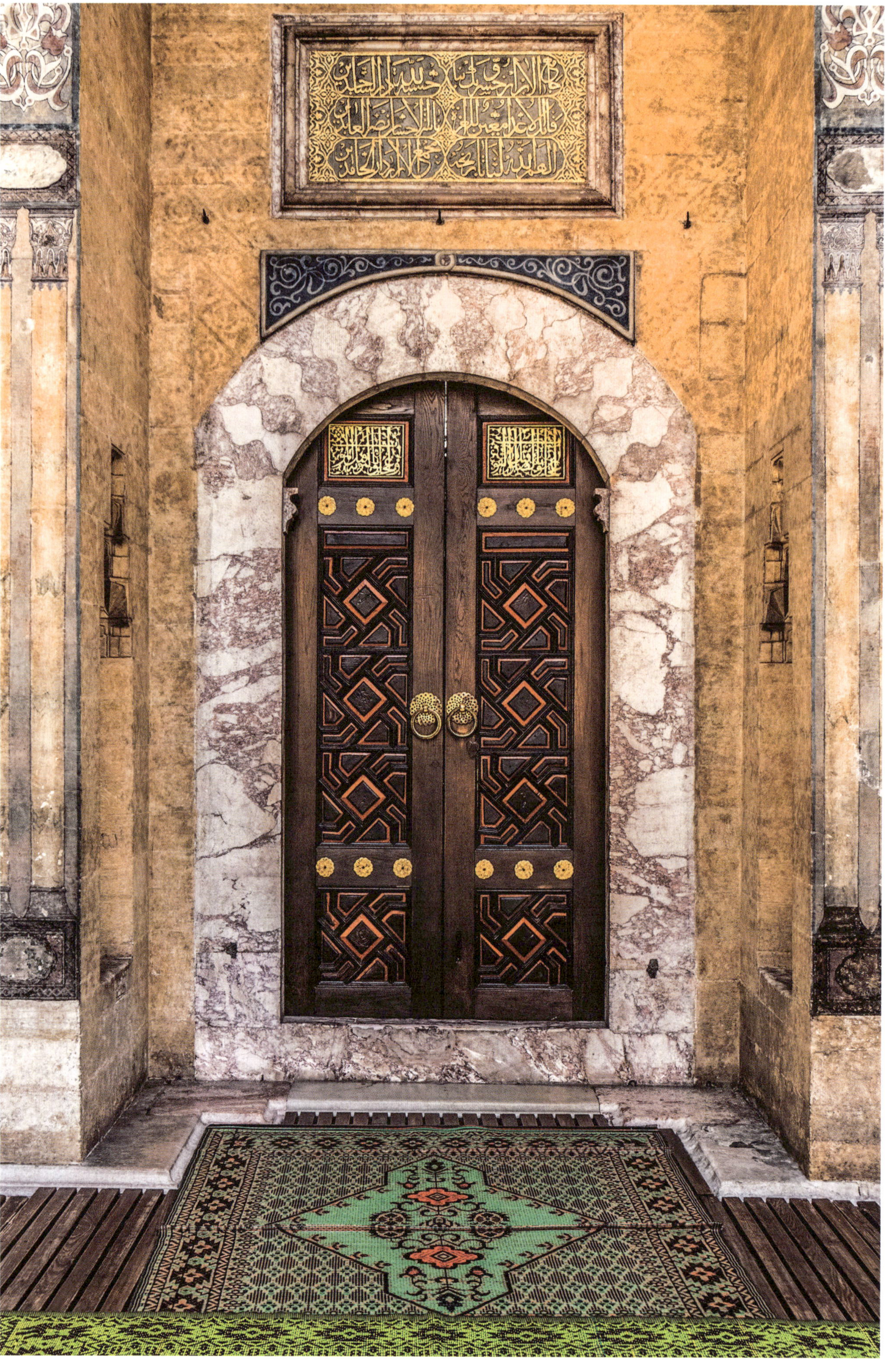

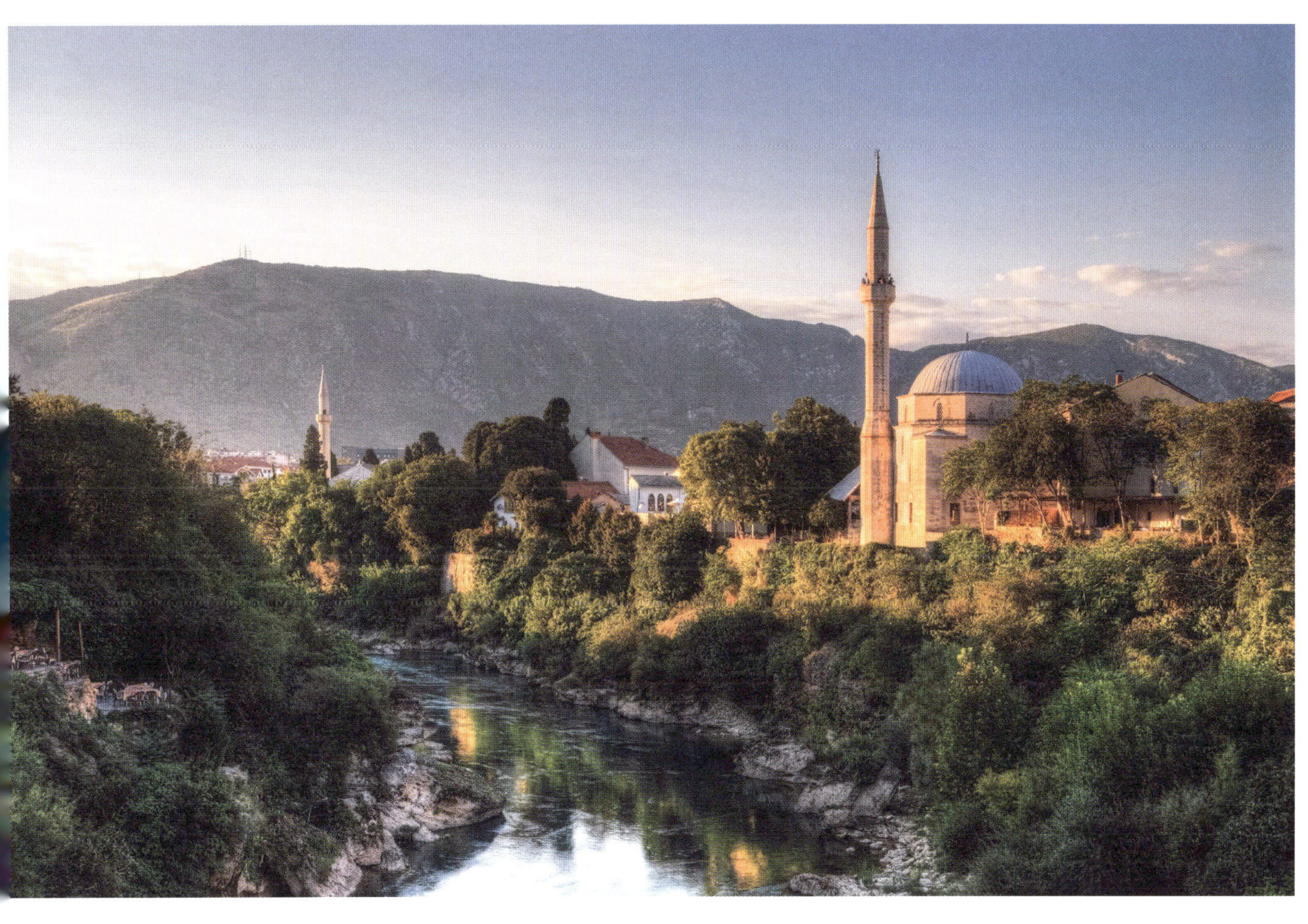

Sarajevo, Bosnia and Herzegovina
43°51′33.3″N 18°25′44.7″E
An entrance to the beautiful Gazi Husrev-beg
Mosque in Sarajevo.
// September 2015

Mostar, Bosnia and Herzegovina
43°20′14.3″N 17°48′54.0″E
The view from the Stari Most ('Old Bridge'),
a famous landmark of Mostar in the south of
Bosnia and Herzegovina. Sadly, the bridge was
destroyed during the Bosnian War in 1993.
It was rebuilt from 2001 to 2004, reconnecting
the two historic parts of Mostar.
// September 2015

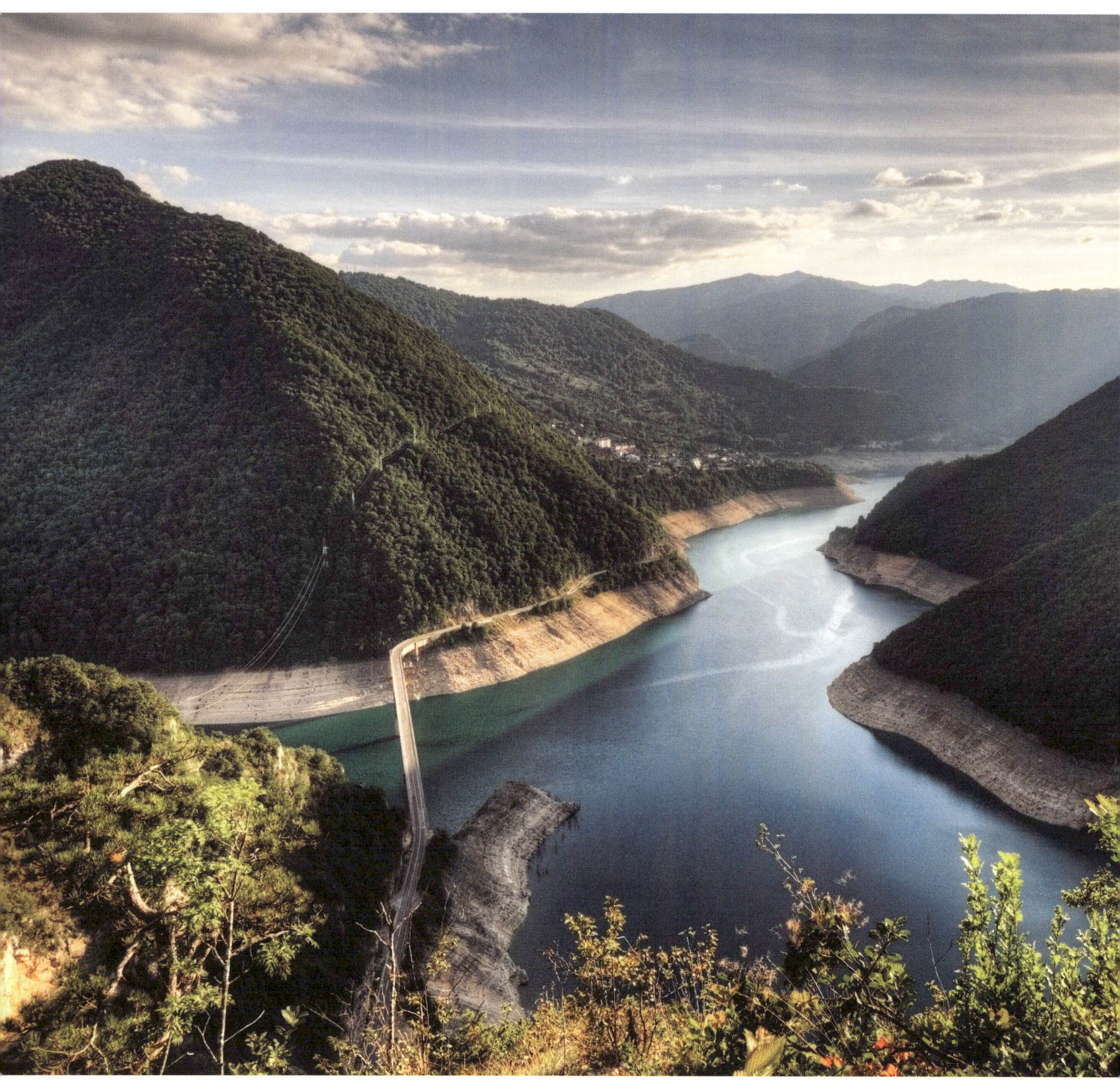

Piva Lake, Montenegro
43°10'26.7"N 18°51'29.6"E
One of the best views I have ever had for dinner,
along the P14 near Piva Lake.
// September 2015

P14 near Piva Lake, Montenegro
43°10'26.0"N 18°51'35.4"E
This small tunnel on the start of road P14 leading
through Durmitor National Park is a typical view
for this region of Montenegro – a gem for both
nature lovers and road trip adventurers.
// September 2015

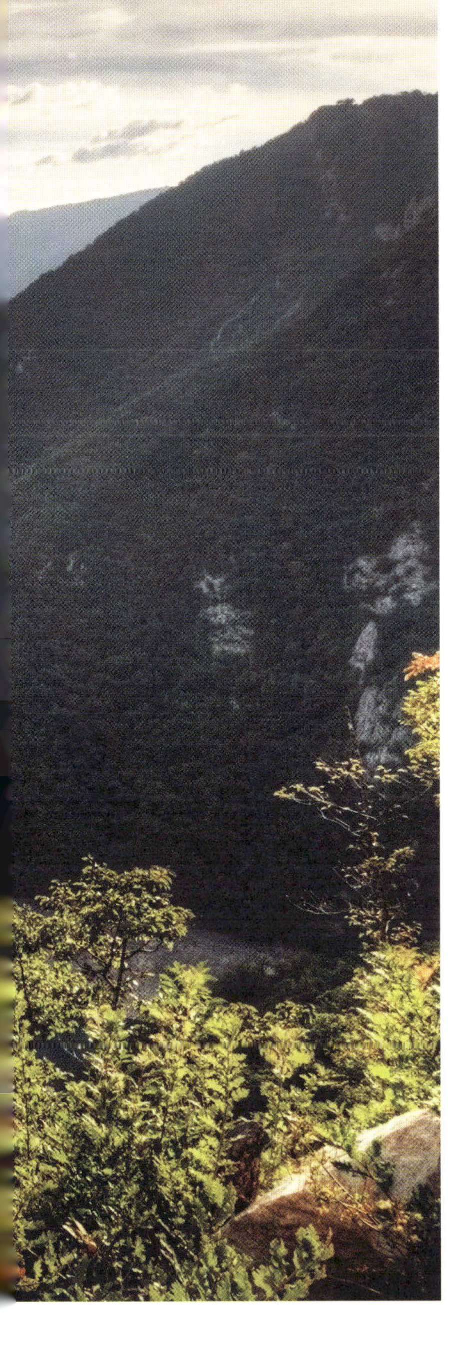

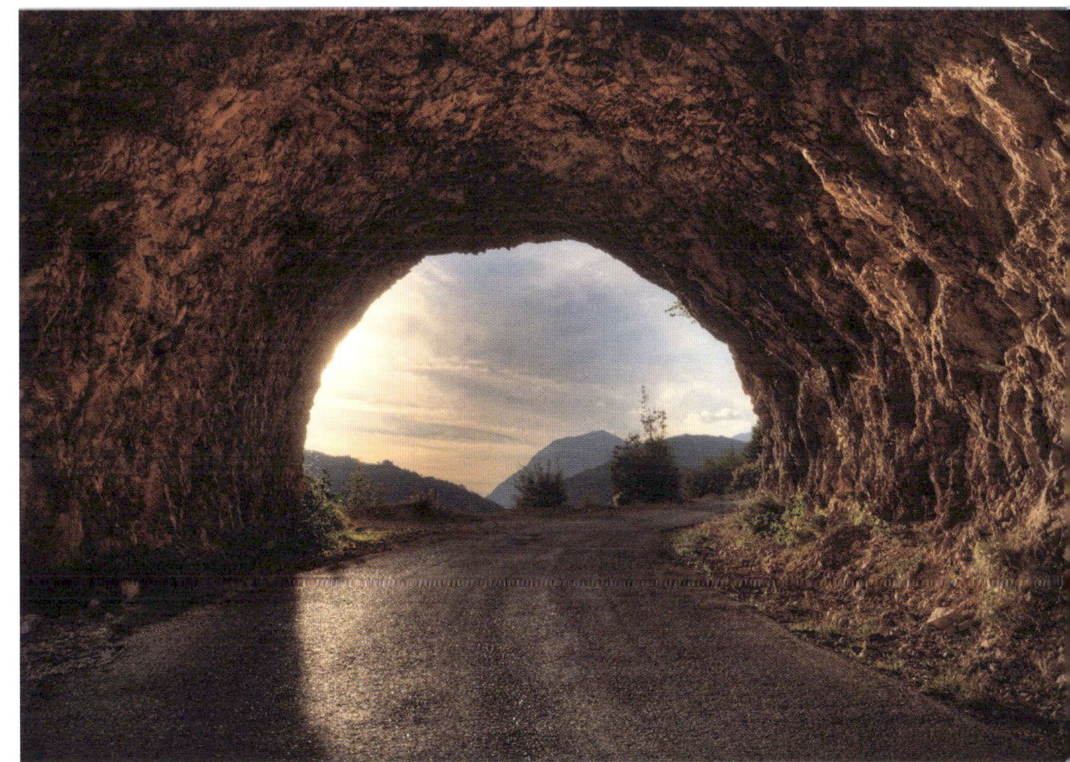

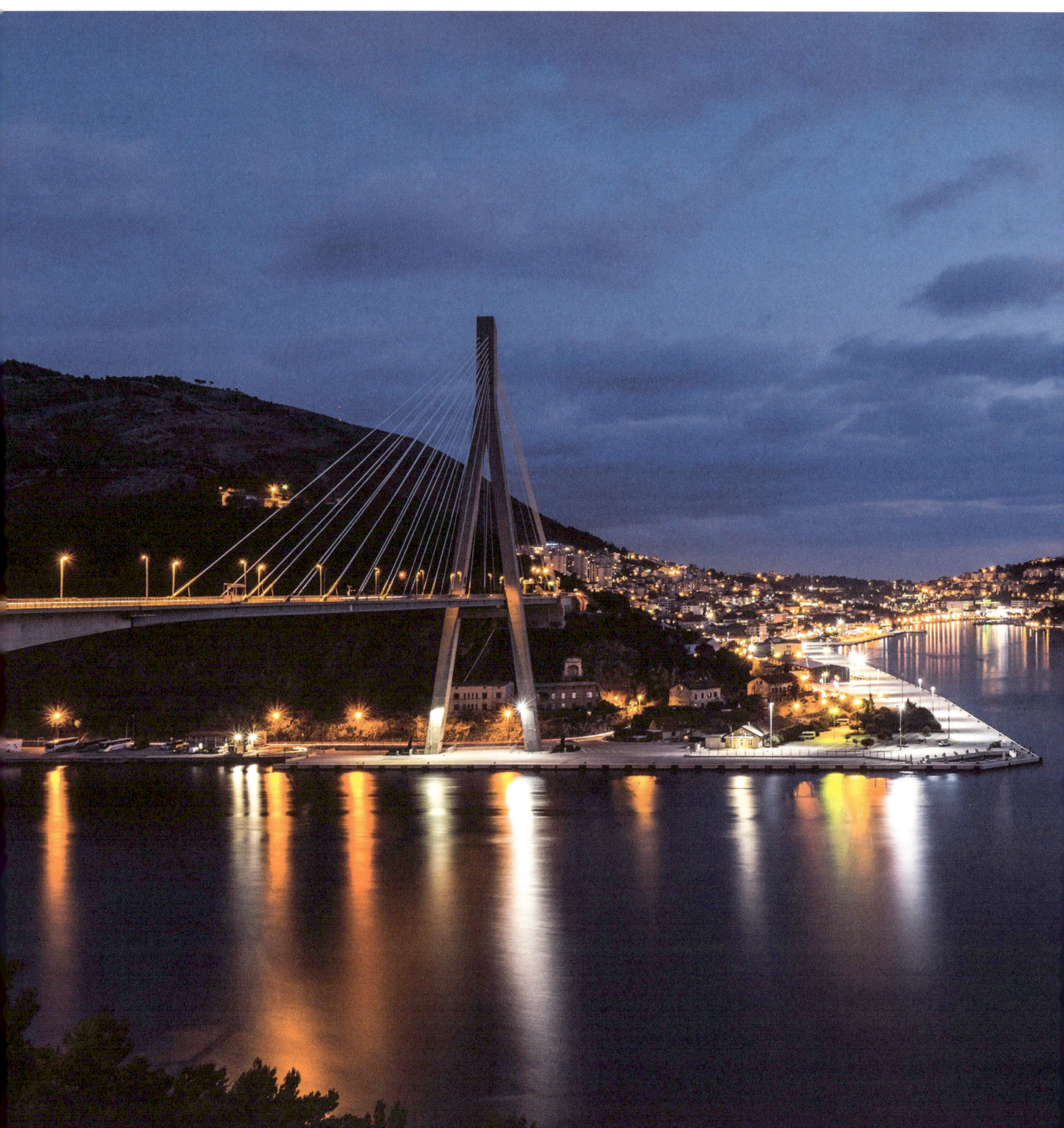

Dubrovnik, Croatia
42°40'11.6"N 18°04'37.5"E
A scenic entree to the city of Dubrovnik.
// December 2018

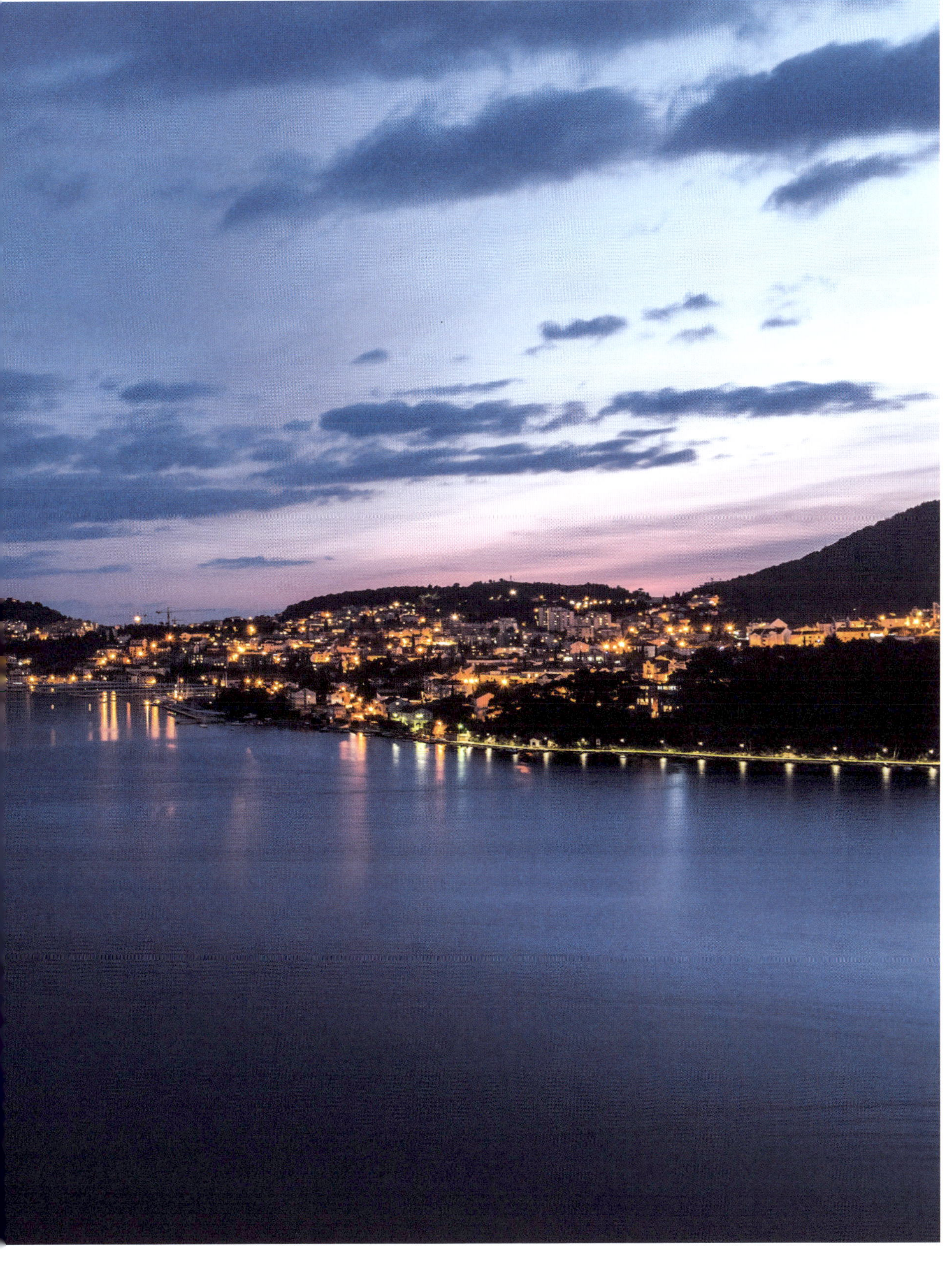

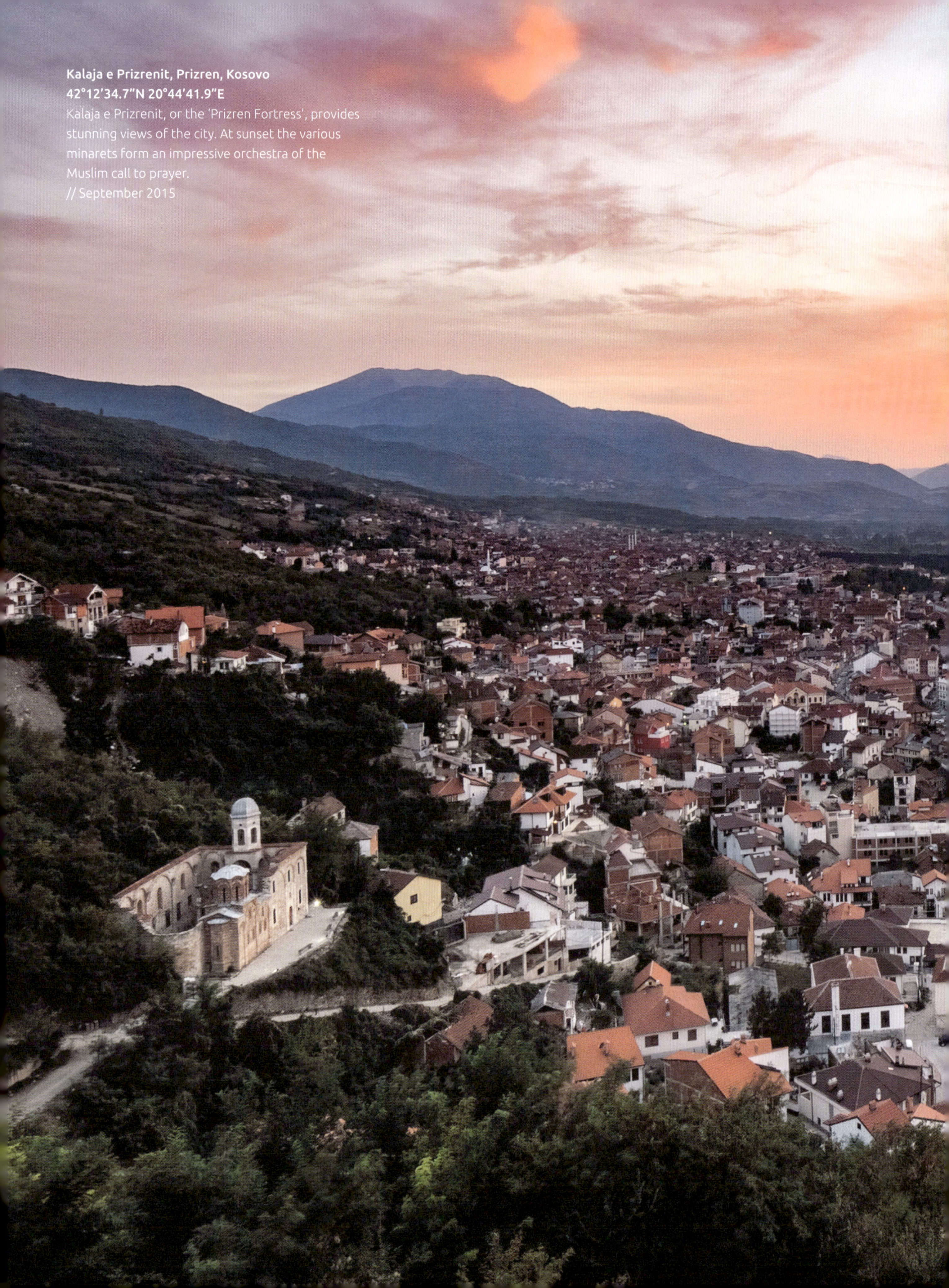

Kalaja e Prizrenit, Prizren, Kosovo
42°12'34.7"N 20°44'41.9"E
Kalaja e Prizrenit, or the 'Prizren Fortress', provides
stunning views of the city. At sunset the various
minarets form an impressive orchestra of the
Muslim call to prayer.
// September 2015

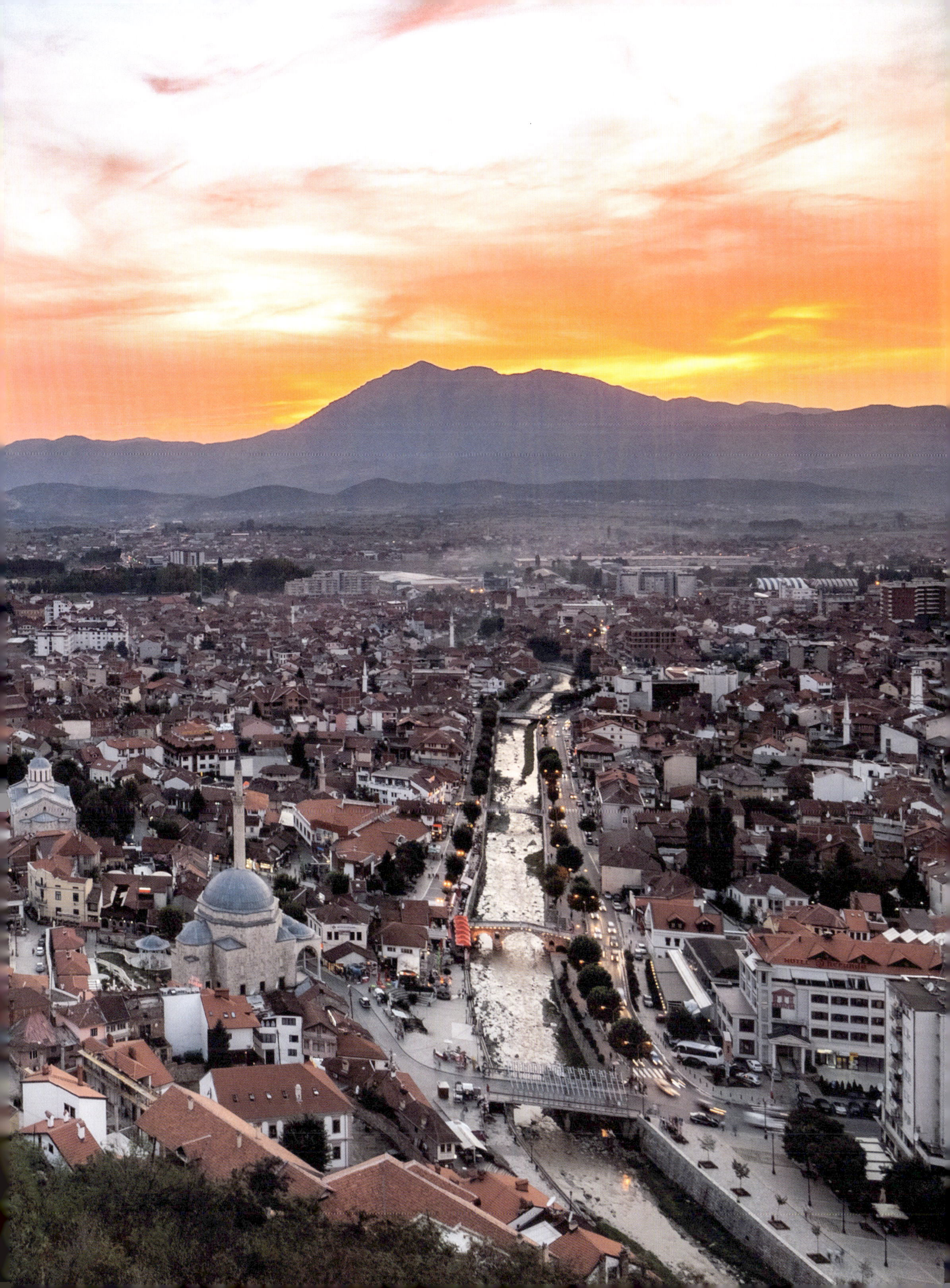

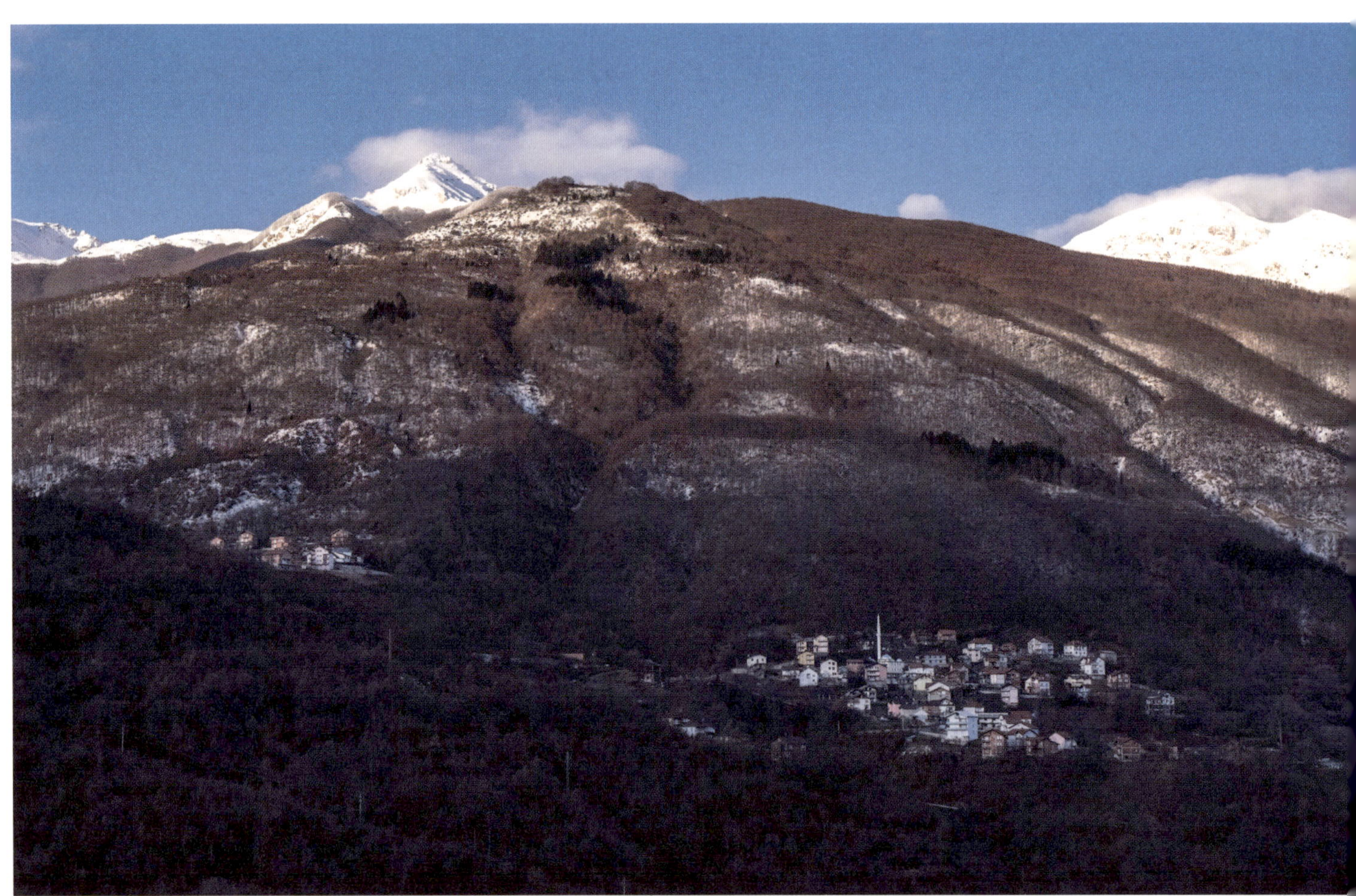

Janche, North Macedonia
41°35'15.2"N 20°37'38.0"E
The beautiful view from a mountain village cottage
in the southeastern part of Mavrovo National Park.
// January 2019

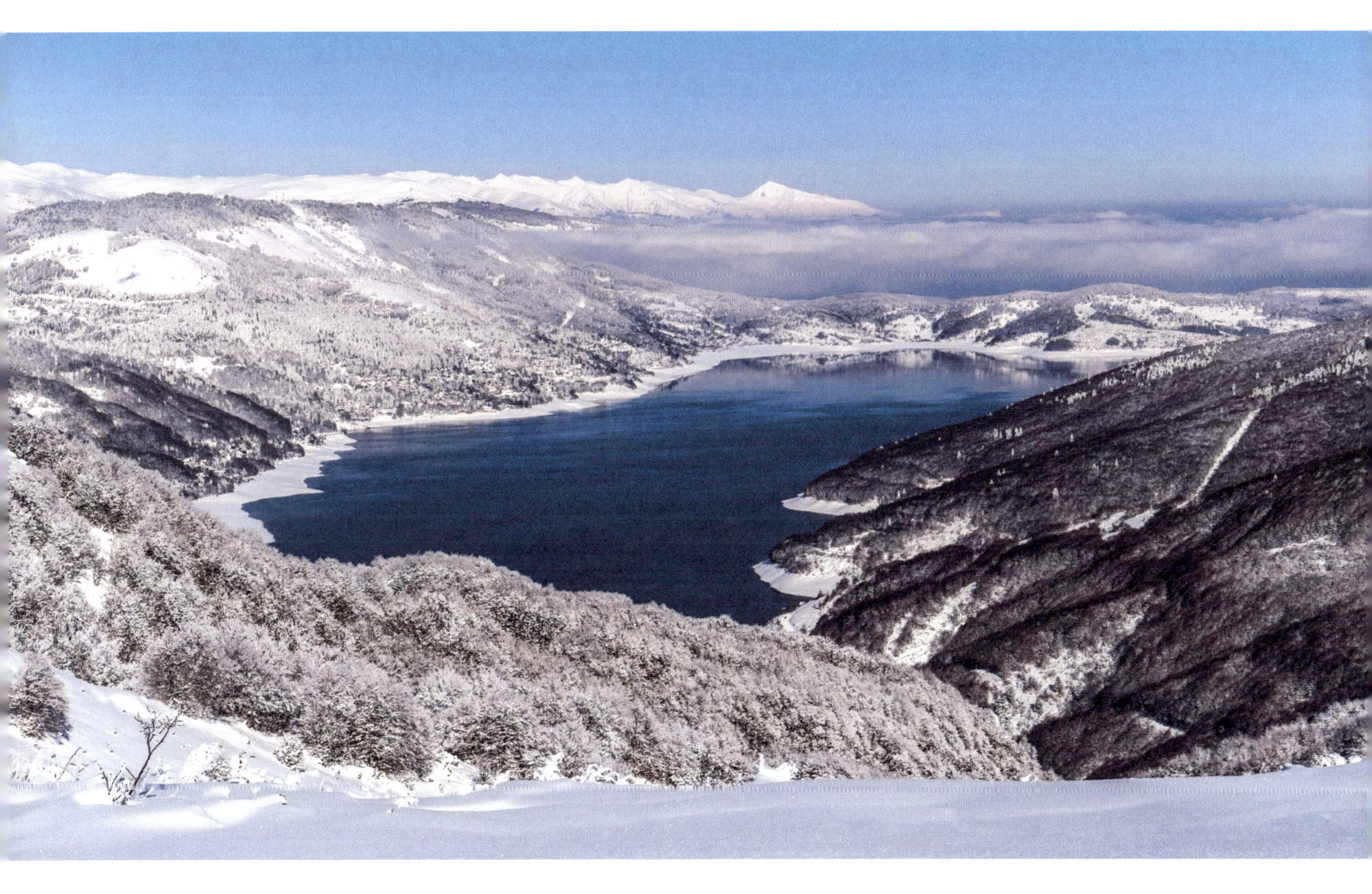

Mavrovo, North Macedonia
41°38'21.7"N 20°43'20.0"E
A frozen world around Mavrovo Lake.
// January 2019

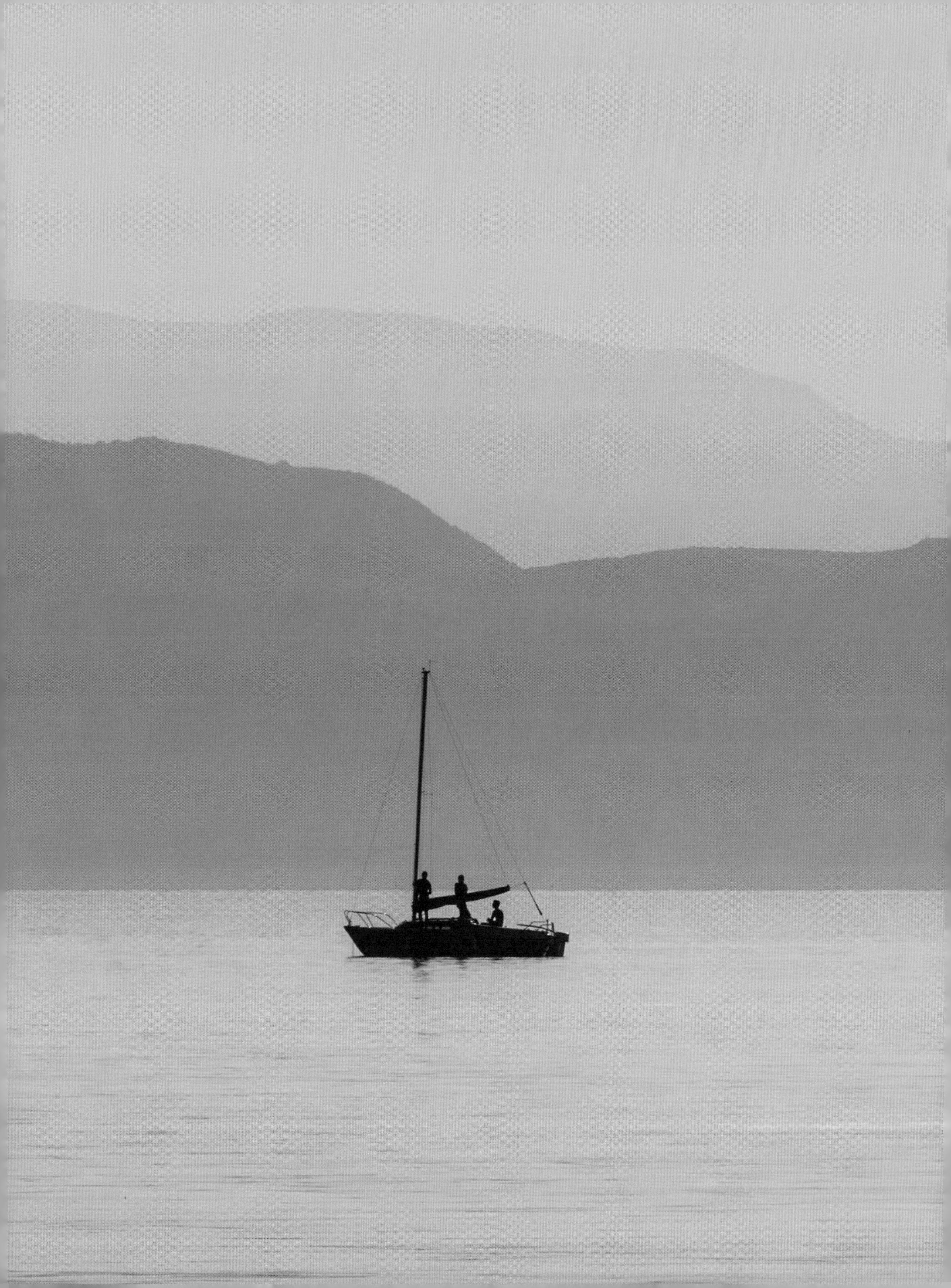

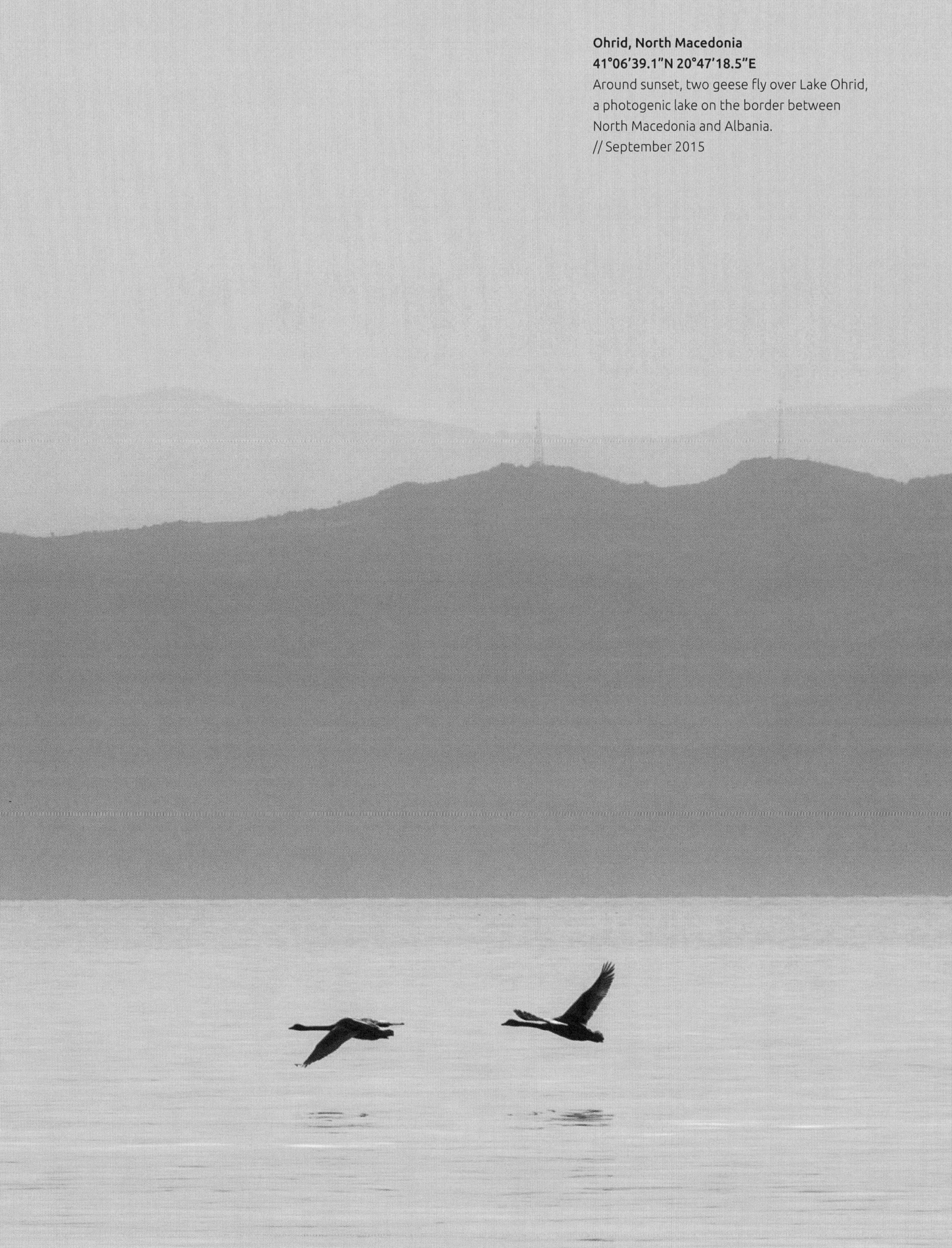

Ohrid, North Macedonia
41°06'39.1"N 20°47'18.5"E
Around sunset, two geese fly over Lake Ohrid,
a photogenic lake on the border between
North Macedonia and Albania.
// September 2015

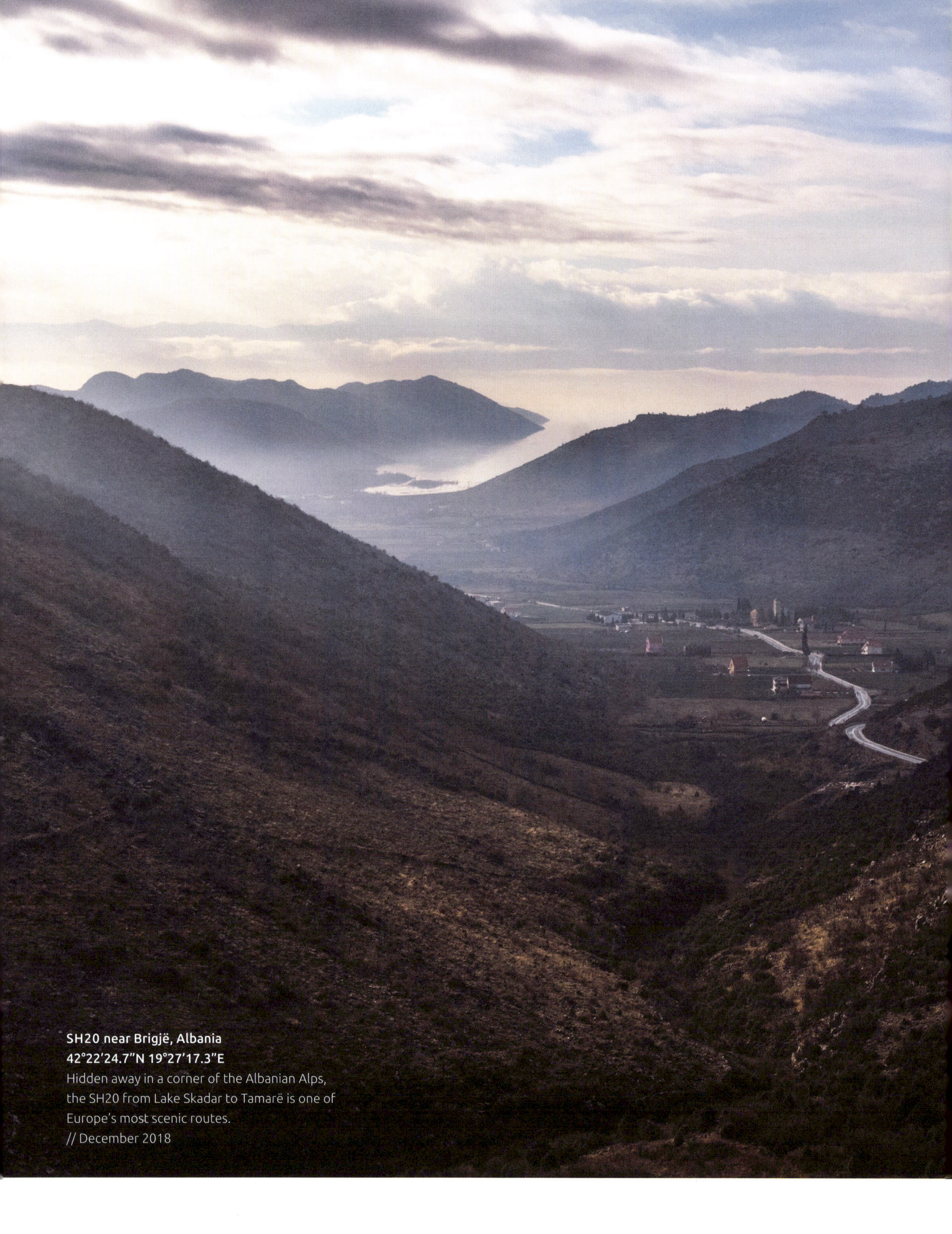

SH20 near Brigjë, Albania
42°22'24.7"N 19°27'17.3"E
Hidden away in a corner of the Albanian Alps,
the SH20 from Lake Skadar to Tamarë is one of
Europe's most scenic routes.
// December 2018

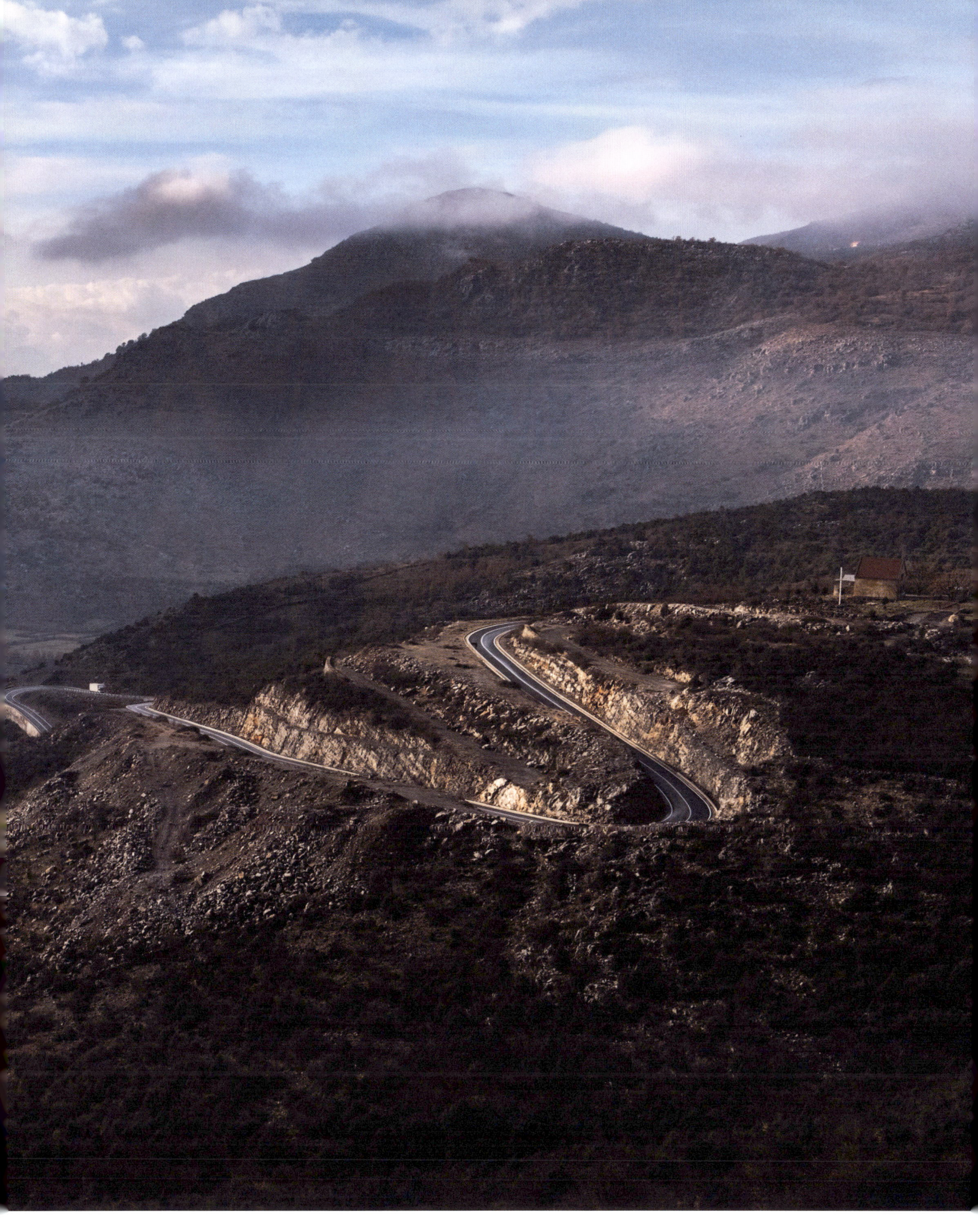

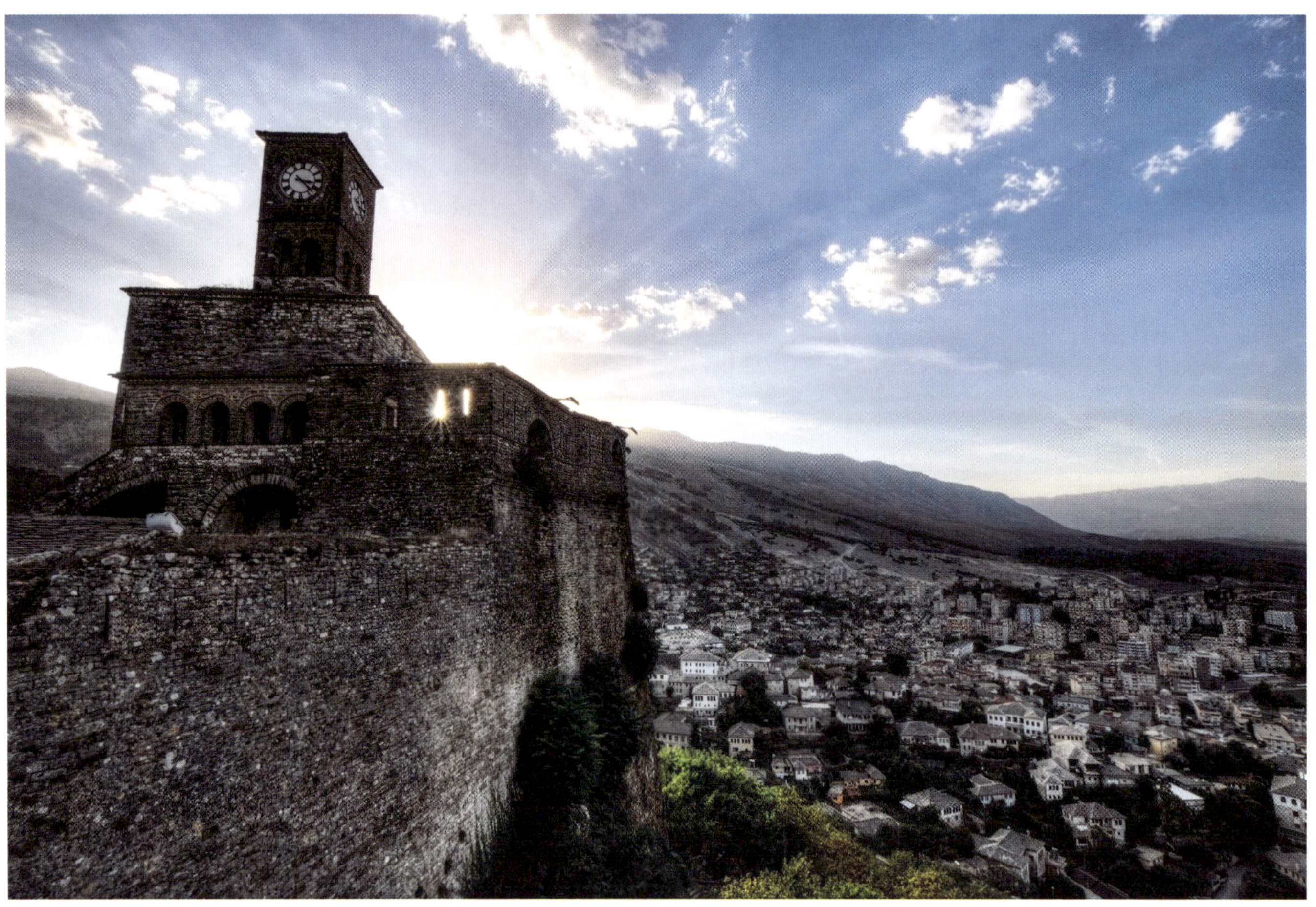

Gjirokastër, Albania
40°04'27.1"N 20°08'27.1"E
The Gjirokastër Castle offers an excellent
viewpoint to overlook the numerous Ottoman
houses that make this city unique.
// September 2015

Berat, Albania
40°42'08.1"N 19°56'54.2"E
Albania is home to some of the best-preserved
Ottoman towns, such as Gjirokastër in the South
of Albania and Berat along the river Osum.
// September 2015

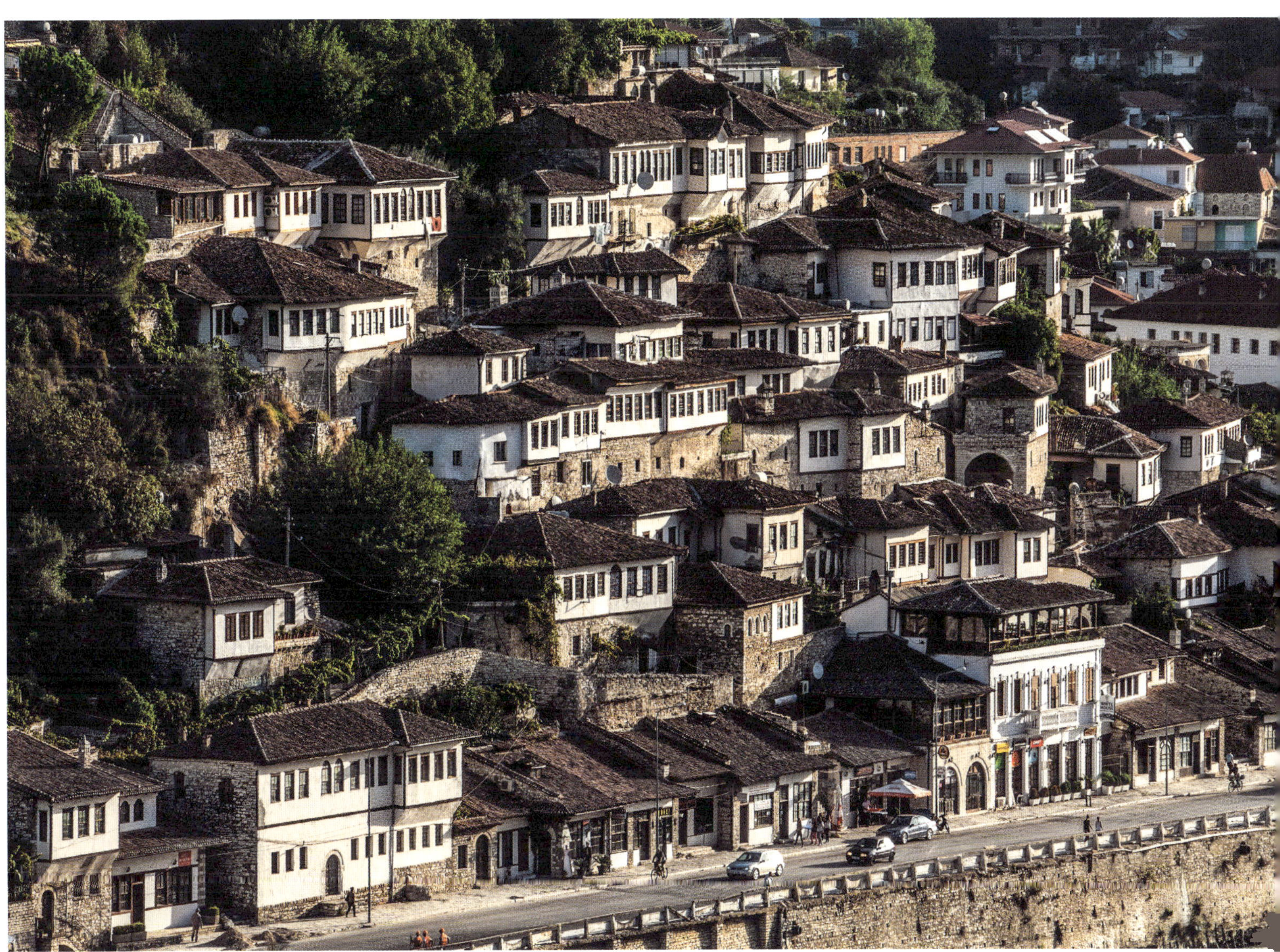

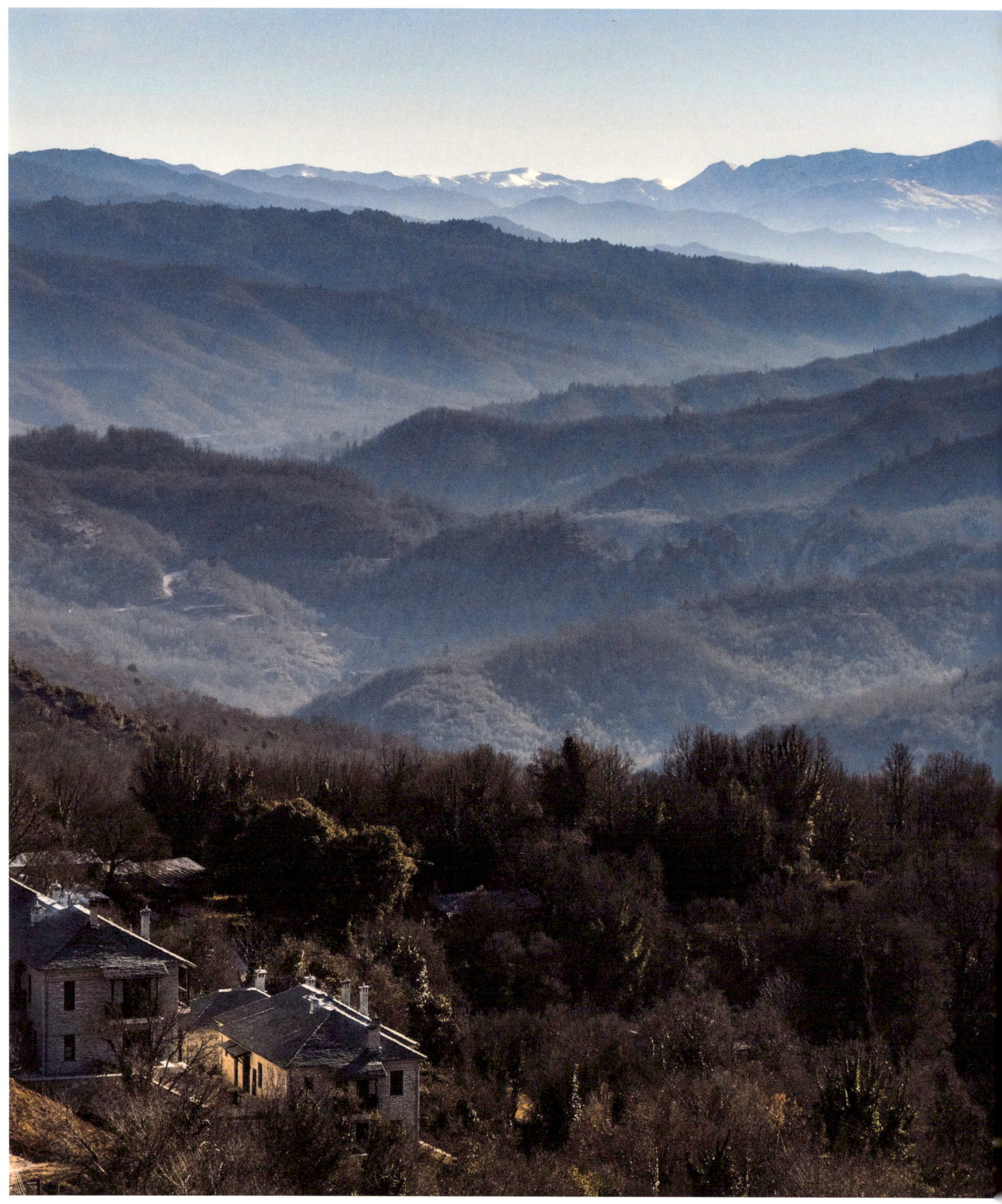

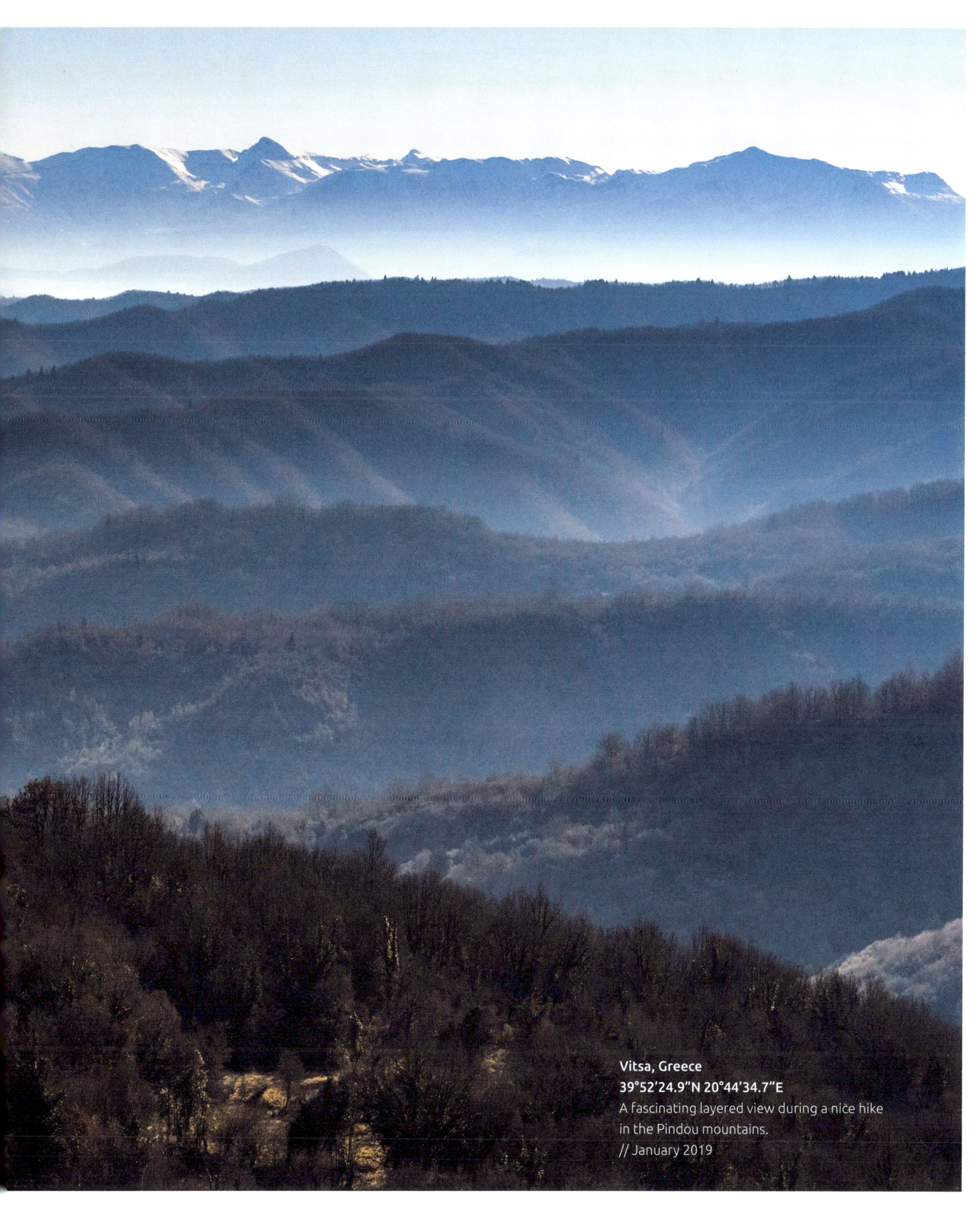

Vitsa, Greece
39°52'24.9"N 20°44'34.7"E
A fascinating layered view during a nice hike
in the Pindou mountains.
// January 2019

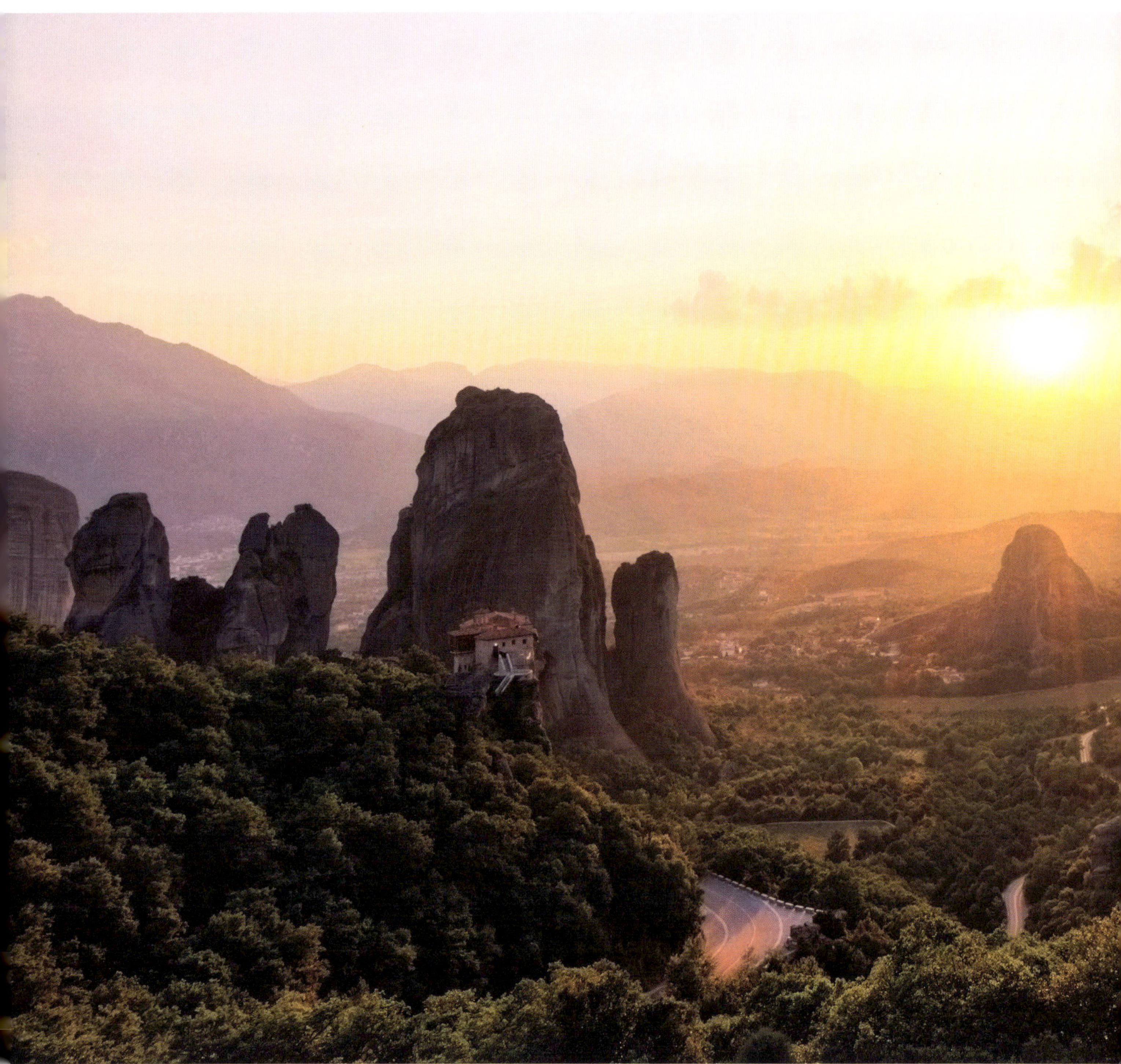

Meteora, Greece
39°43'15.7"N 21°38'01.4"E
This is one of the most beautiful places I have
ever visited. Once the crowds have left Meteora
at sunset, it is truly magical.
// September 2015

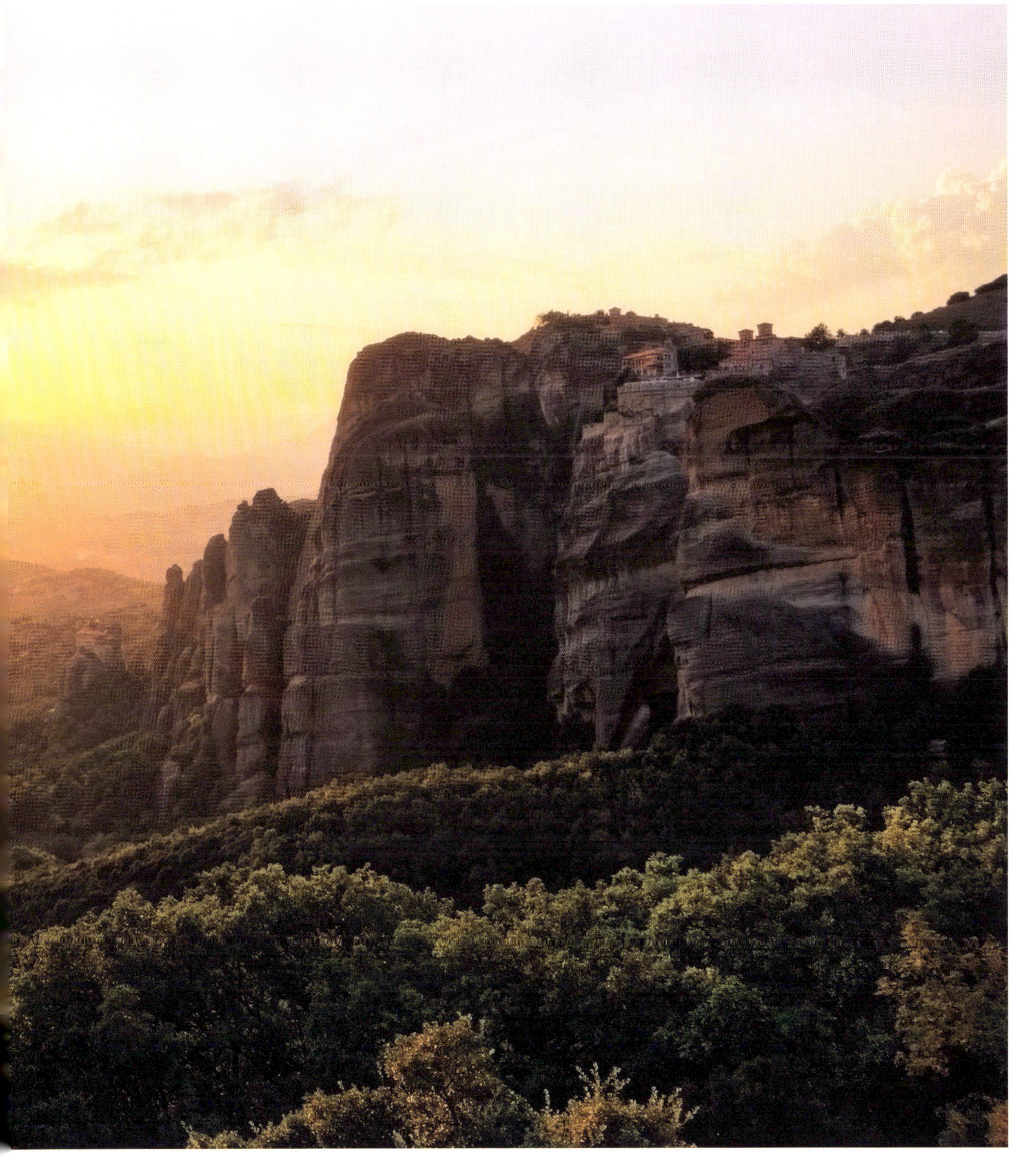

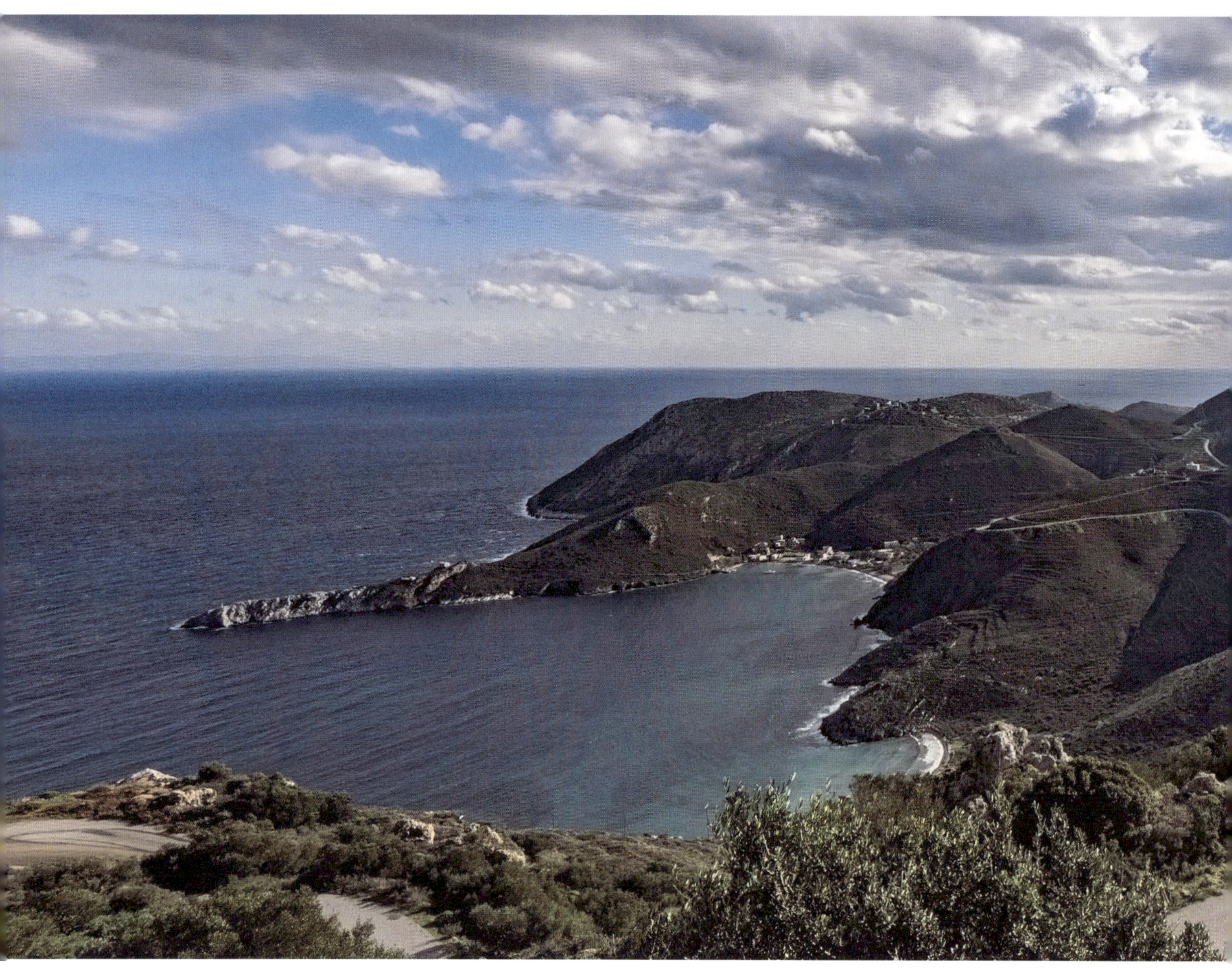

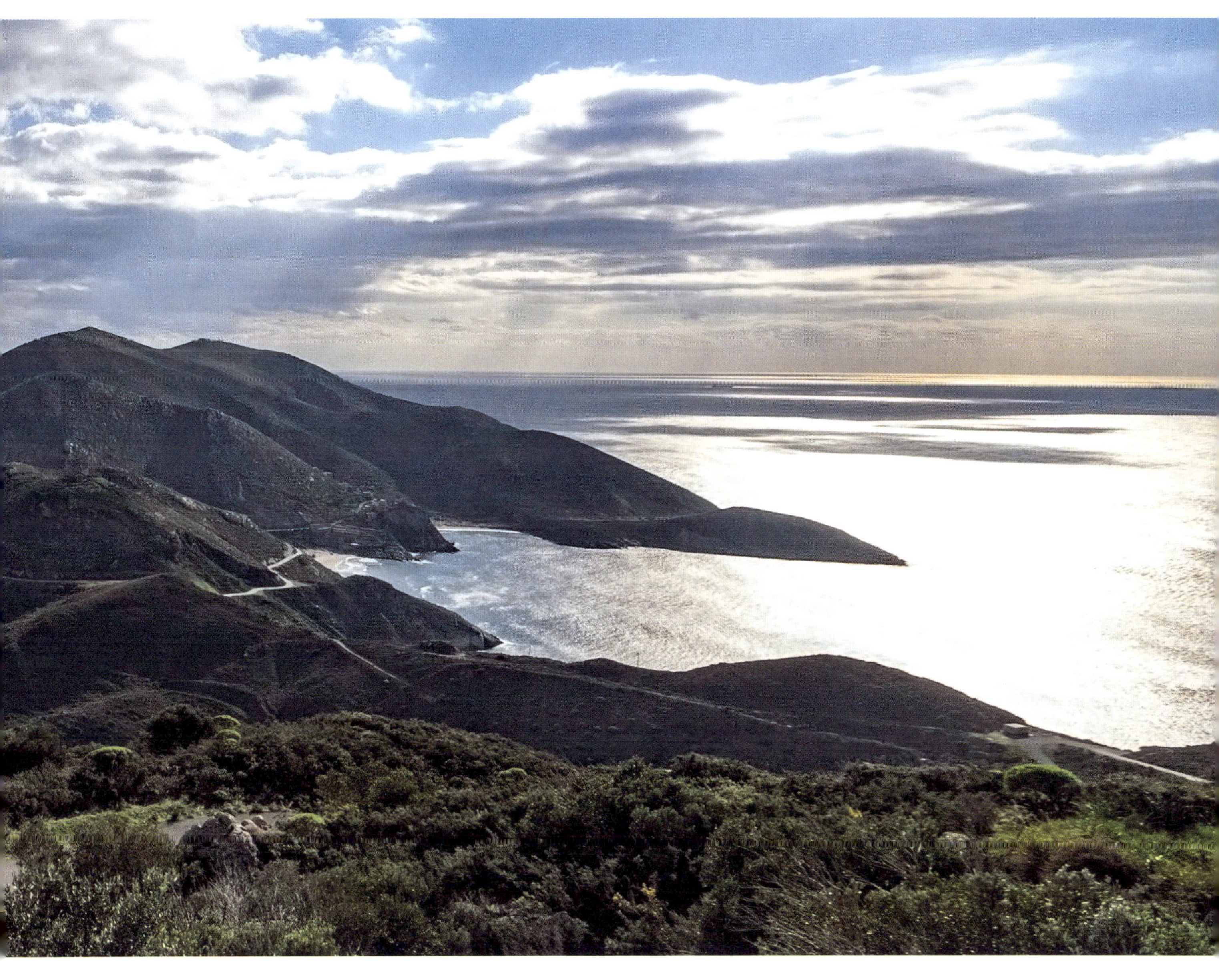

Mani Peninsula, Peloponnese, Greece
36°26′13.7″N 22°28′39.3″E
A panoramic view of Mani Peninsula,
the southernmost tip of mainland Greece.
// December 2018

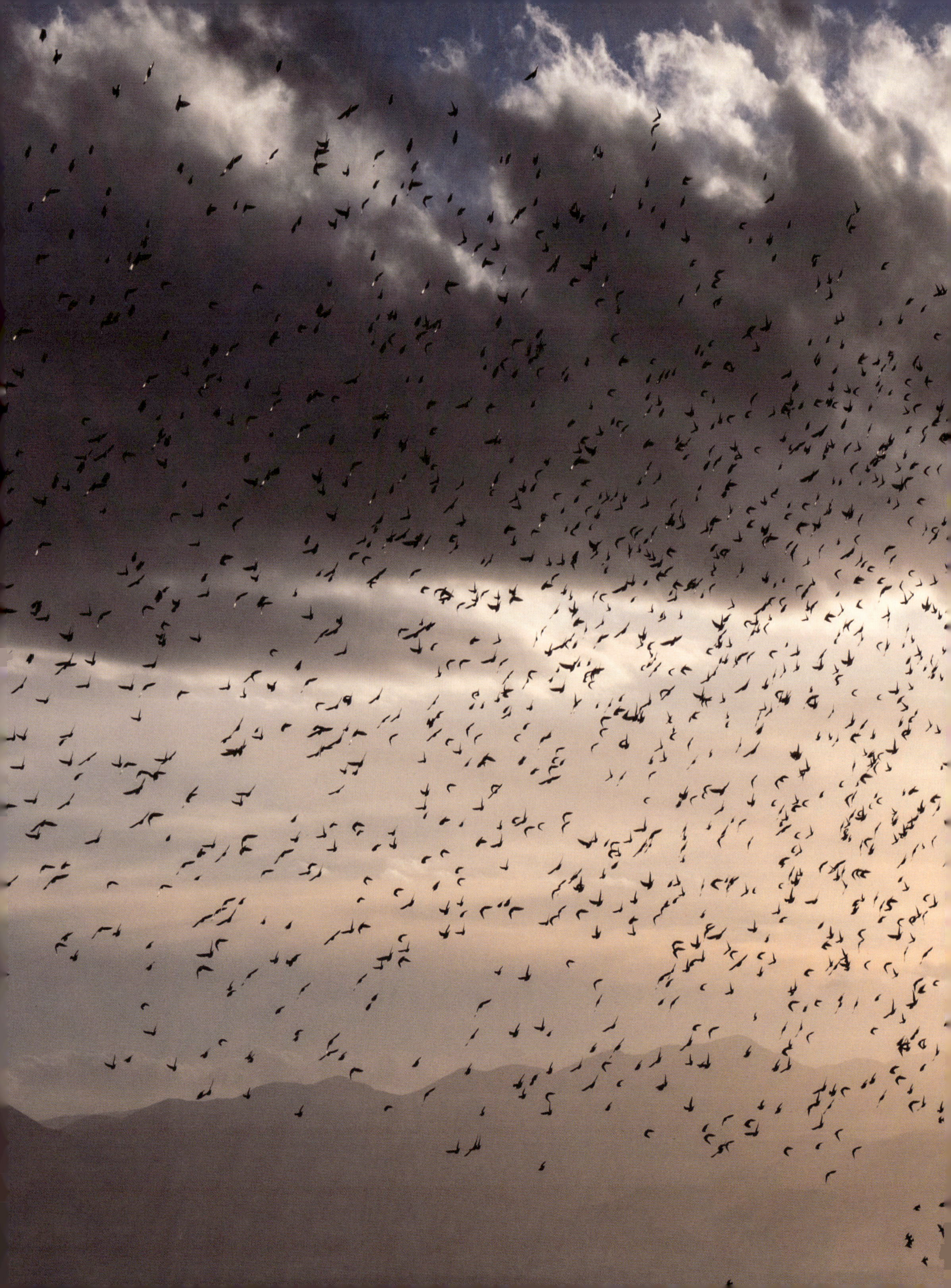

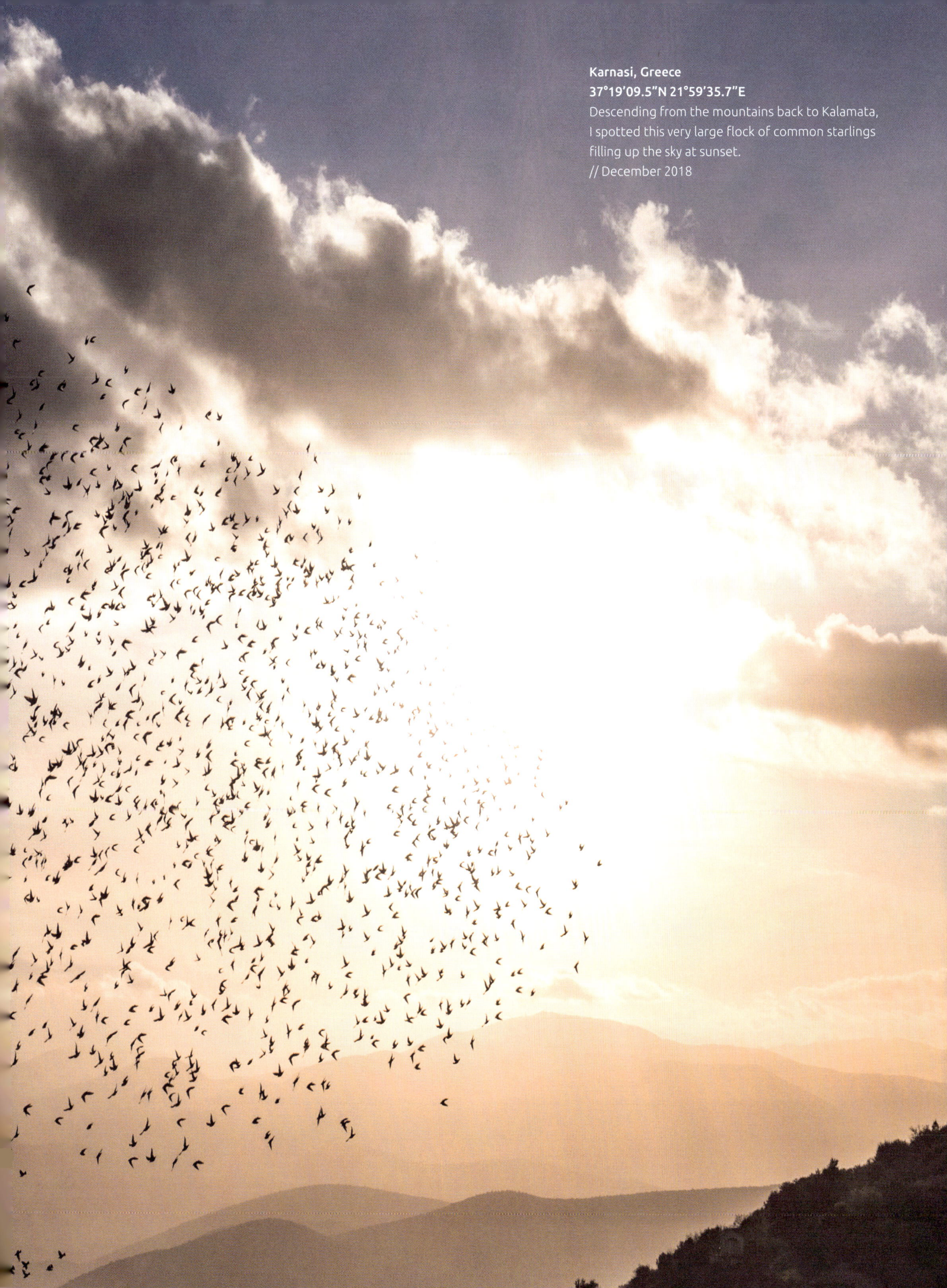

Karnasi, Greece
37°19'09.5"N 21°59'35.7"E
Descending from the mountains back to Kalamata,
I spotted this very large flock of common starlings
filling up the sky at sunset.
// December 2018

From Summit to Sea
Route and travel suggestions

Scenic regions and nature reserves
1 Dachstein // **Austria**
2 Durmitor & Tara Canyon // **Montenegro**
3 Krka // **Croatia**
4 Pindos // **Greece**
5 Šar Mountains // **Kosovo & North Macedonia**

Cities and towns
6 Berat // **Albania**
7 Monemvasia // **Greece**
8 Mostar // **Bosnia and Herzegovina**
9 Ohrid // **North Macedonia**
10 Prizren // **Kosovo**
11 Salzburg // **Austria**
12 Sarajevo // **Bosnia and Herzegovina**

Cultural experiences
13 Gazi Husrev-beg Mosque, Sarajevo // **Bosnia and Herzegovina**
14 Meteora // **Greece**
15 Schönbrunn Palace, Vienna // **Austria**
16 Tunel Spasa, Sarajevo // **Bosnia and Herzegovina**
17 Visoki Dečani, Deçan/Dečani // **Kosovo**

Spectacular roads and scenic routes
18 E92 between Koridallos and Megali Kerasia // **Greece**
19 M20 & M18 between Čemerno and Vučevo // **Bosnia and Herzegovina**
20 P14 between Pluzine and Žabljak // **Montenegro**
21 R115 between Prizren and Brod // **Kosovo**
22 SH20 between Lake Skadar and Tamarë // **Albania**
23 The Magistral (E65) between Senj and Starigrad // **Croatia**

○ Photo location
● Travel suggestion
123 Photo page number
123 Travel suggestion number

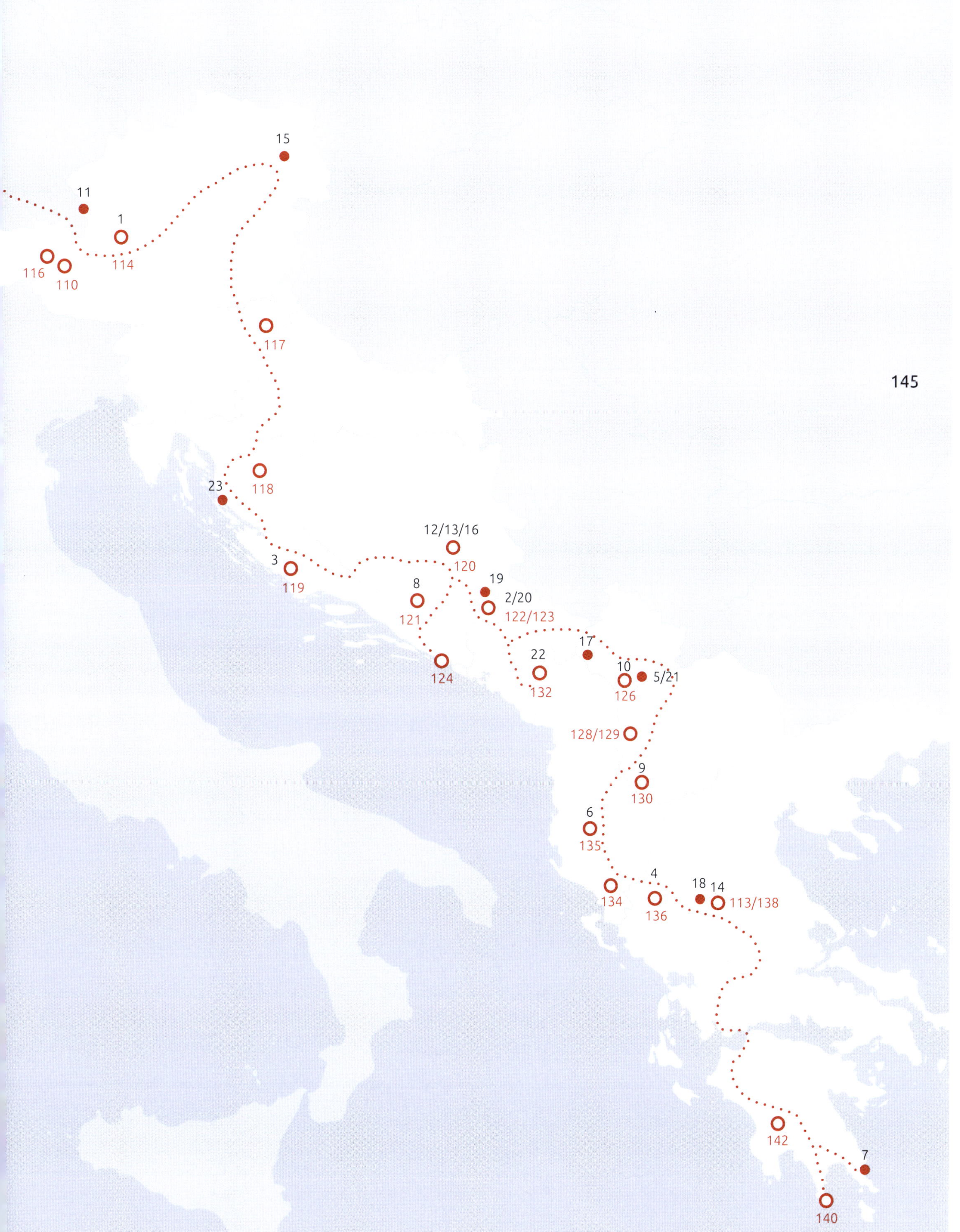

15
11
1
116
110
114
117
118
23
12/13/16
120
3
119
8
121
19
2/20
122/123
124
22
132
17
10
5/21
126
128/129
9
130
6
135
4
18
14
134
136
113/138
142
7
140

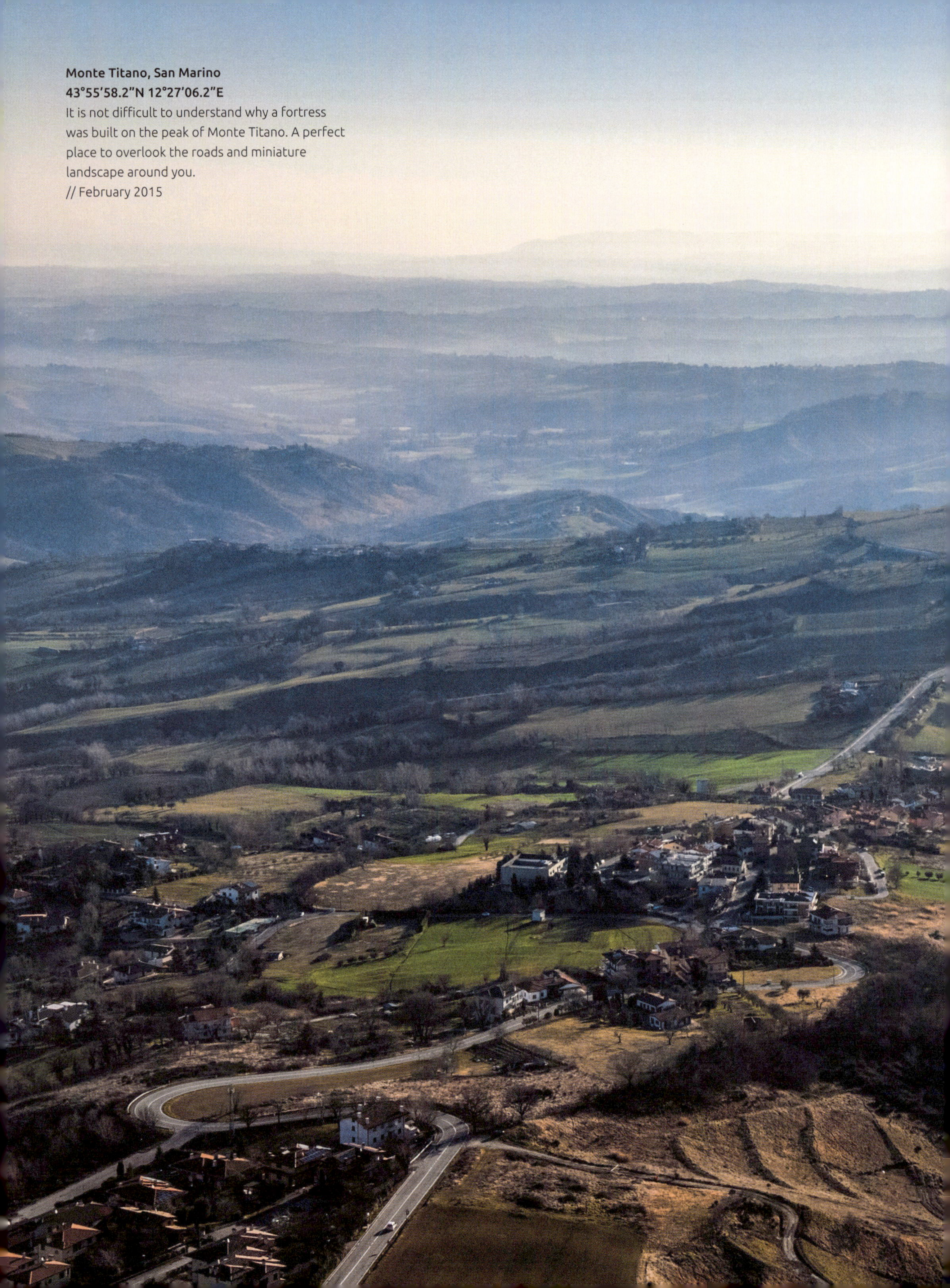

Monte Titano, San Marino
43°55'58.2"N 12°27'06.2"E
It is not difficult to understand why a fortress
was built on the peak of Monte Titano. A perfect
place to overlook the roads and miniature
landscape around you.
// February 2015

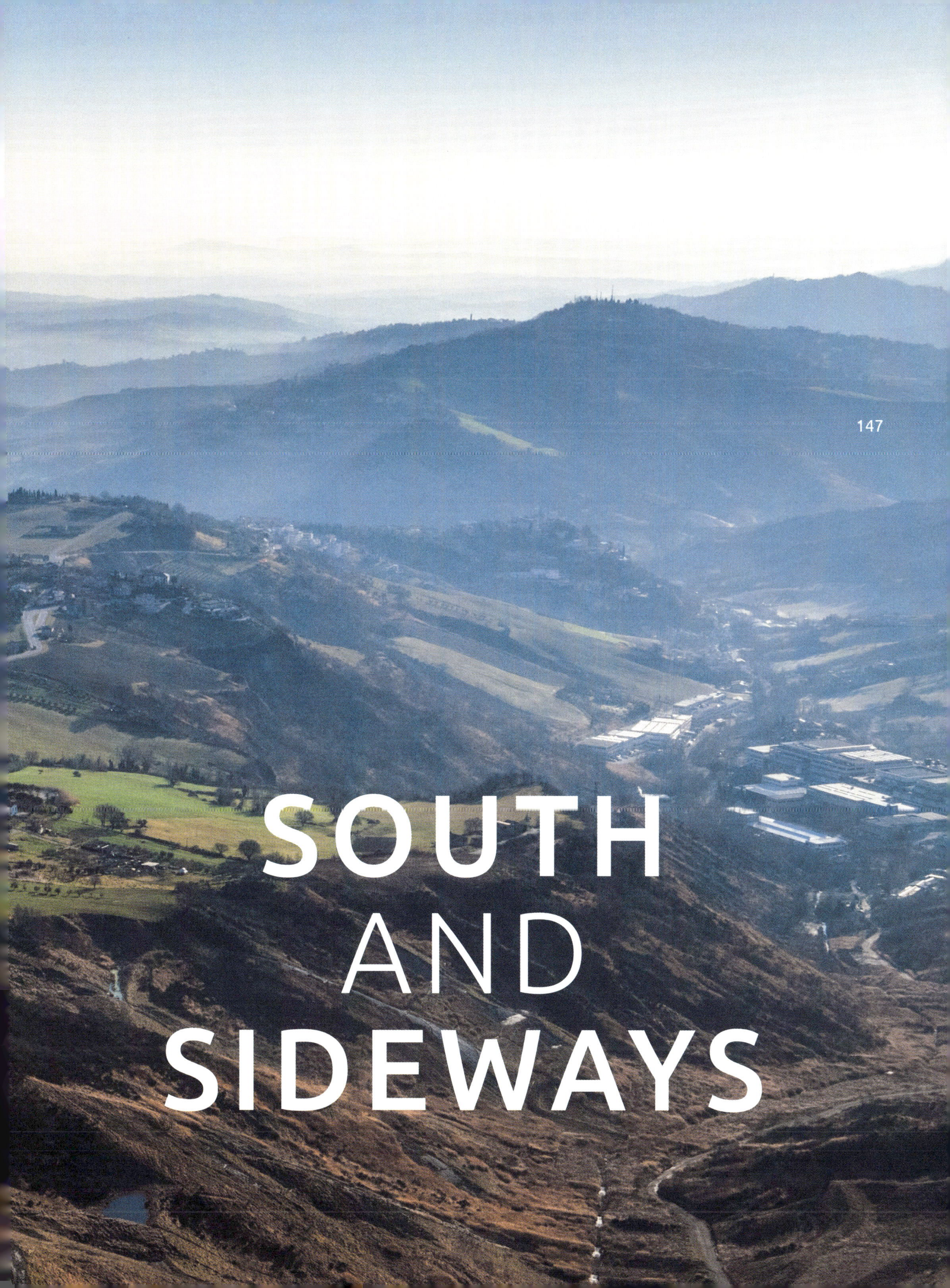

SOUTH AND SIDEWAYS

'Moving south through Italy shows how nature and culture have shaped the country over the past thousands of years.'

A LONG SCENIC ROUTE leads all the way to Sicily in Italy. As a first stop along the way, a surprisingly beautiful destination is the rocky forest in the east of Luxembourg. The rock formations around the Mullerthal Trail and climbing paradise Berdorf are one of the most wonderful nature scenes to be found within a four-hour drive of Rotterdam.

Next on this trip are the wide mountain panoramas of Switzerland and the rough peaks in the north of Italy, such as those in the Aosta valley and the Dolomites more to the east. Moving further south through Italy, one passes picturesque regions like Cinque Terre and Crete Senesi (in Tuscany), impressive volcanoes, numerous wine regions and many historic sites showing how nature and culture have shaped the country over the past thousands of years.

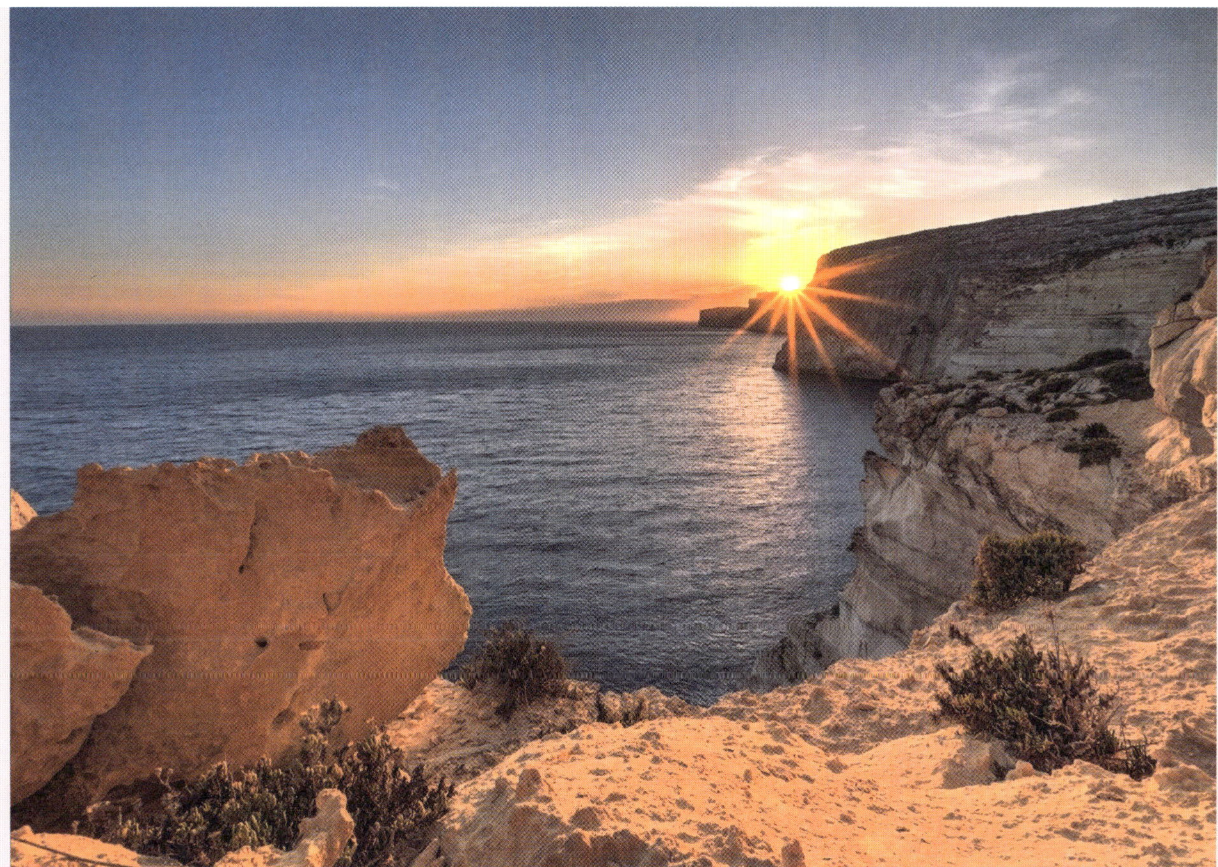

Taking the ferry to Malta brings us to an entirely different world. An island full of cacti, with street scenes and architecture clearly influenced by prehistoric, British and Arabic cultures, Malta is more than an intriguing destination. Although only a small archipelago consisting of the islands of Malta, Gozo and Comino, there are plenty of natural and cultural monuments to justify a longer stay here.

We fly 'sideways' from Malta to Cyprus to explore this island in the eastern corner of the Mediterranean. The south has a Greek atmosphere, the north shows the clear influence of Turkish culture, thus dividing the island in two regions. It is a culture-rich destination with so many ancient Greek ruins on the island.

In the far northeast lies my favourite destination on the island. Travelling to the tip of the Peninsula of Karpasia offers some of the best scenes to be found in Cyprus. Beware that cars are guests; donkeys actually rule the roads here.

Ta'Cenc Cliffs, Gozo, Malta
36°01'02.3"N 14°15'14.1"E
The steep, erosive cliffs of Ta'Cenc form part of the impressive southern coastline of Gozo. It is home to a large number of birds, such as the threatened yelkouan shearwater.
// May 2016

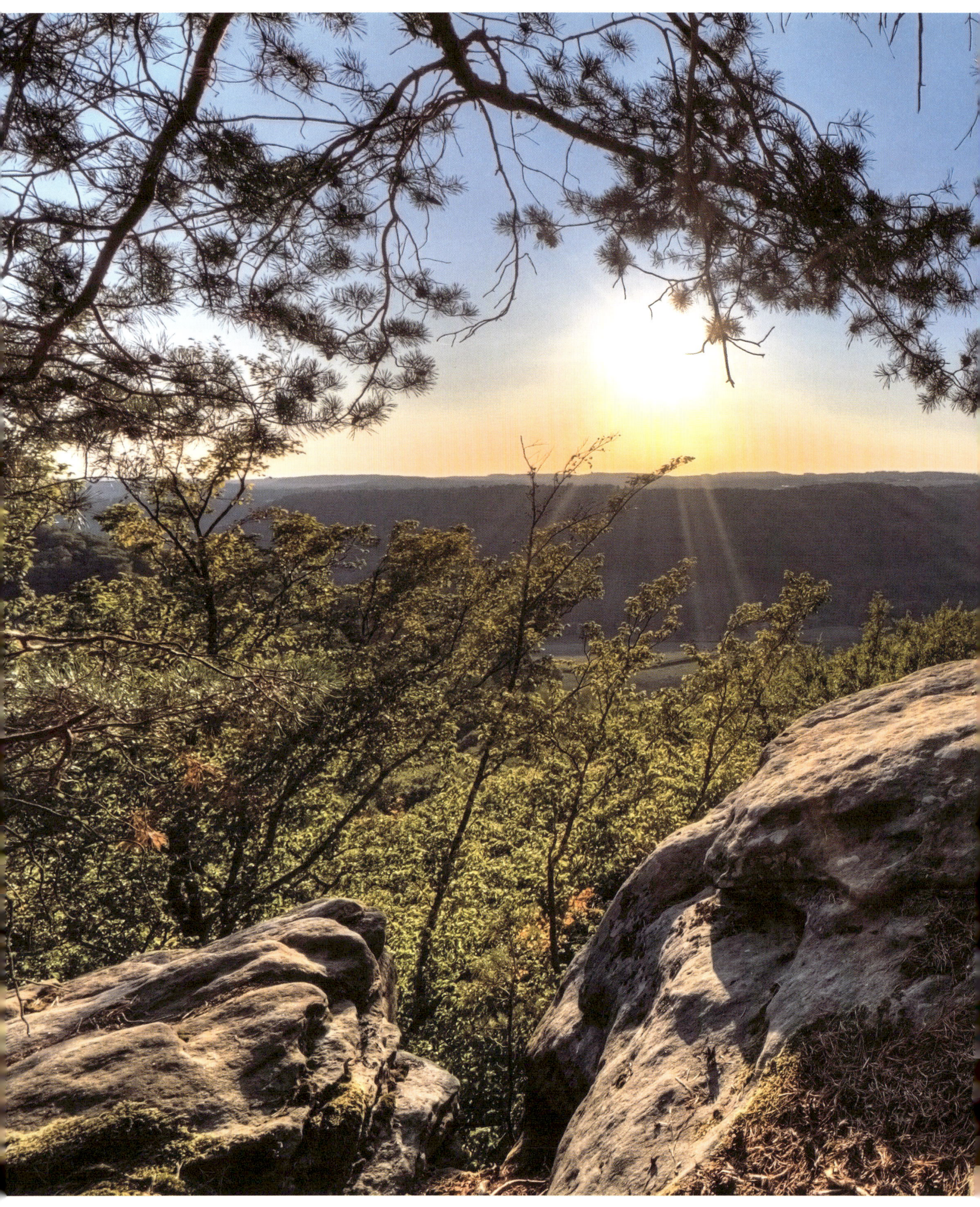

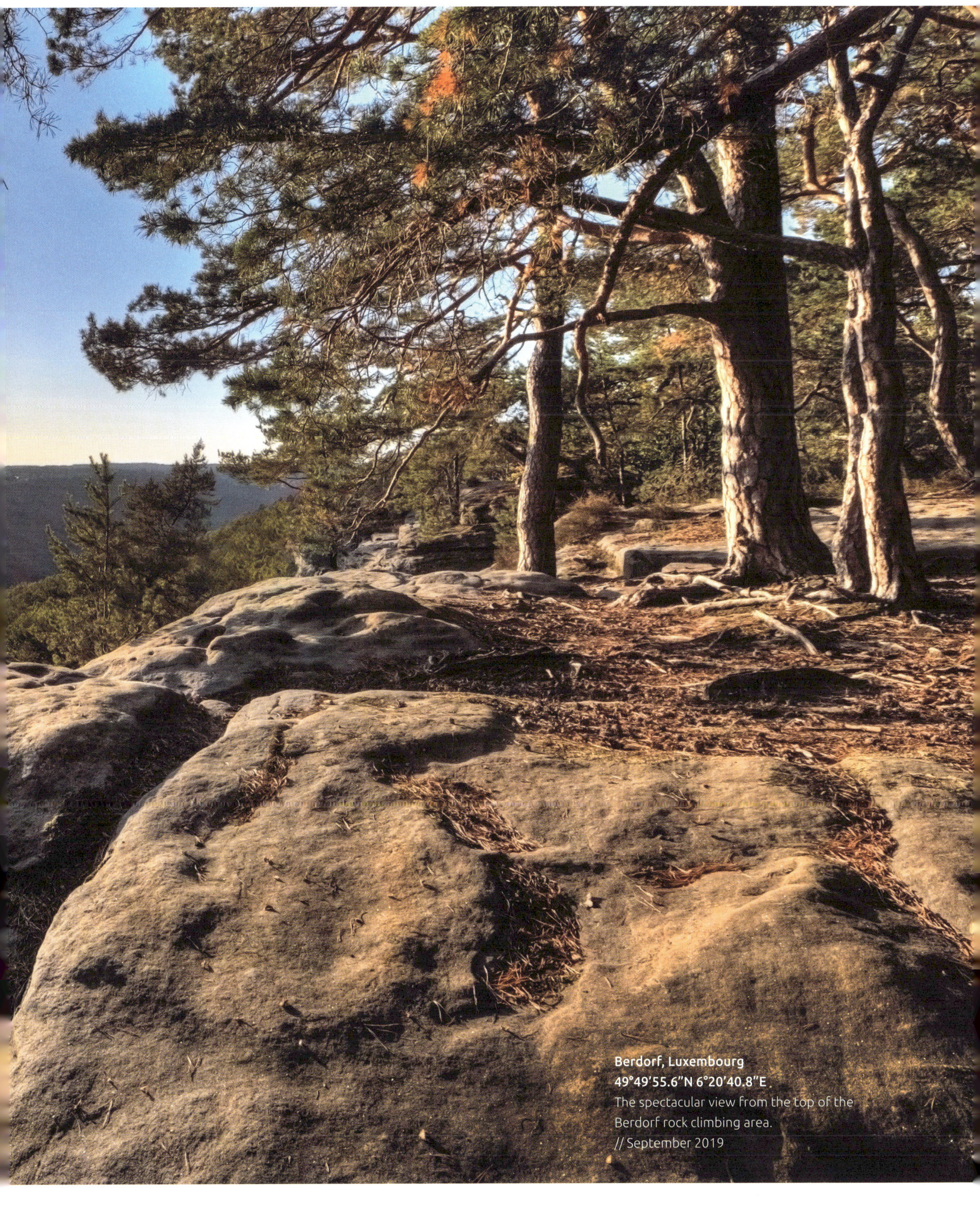

Berdorf, Luxembourg
49°49'55.6"N 6°20'40.8"E
The spectacular view from the top of the
Berdorf rock climbing area.
// September 2019

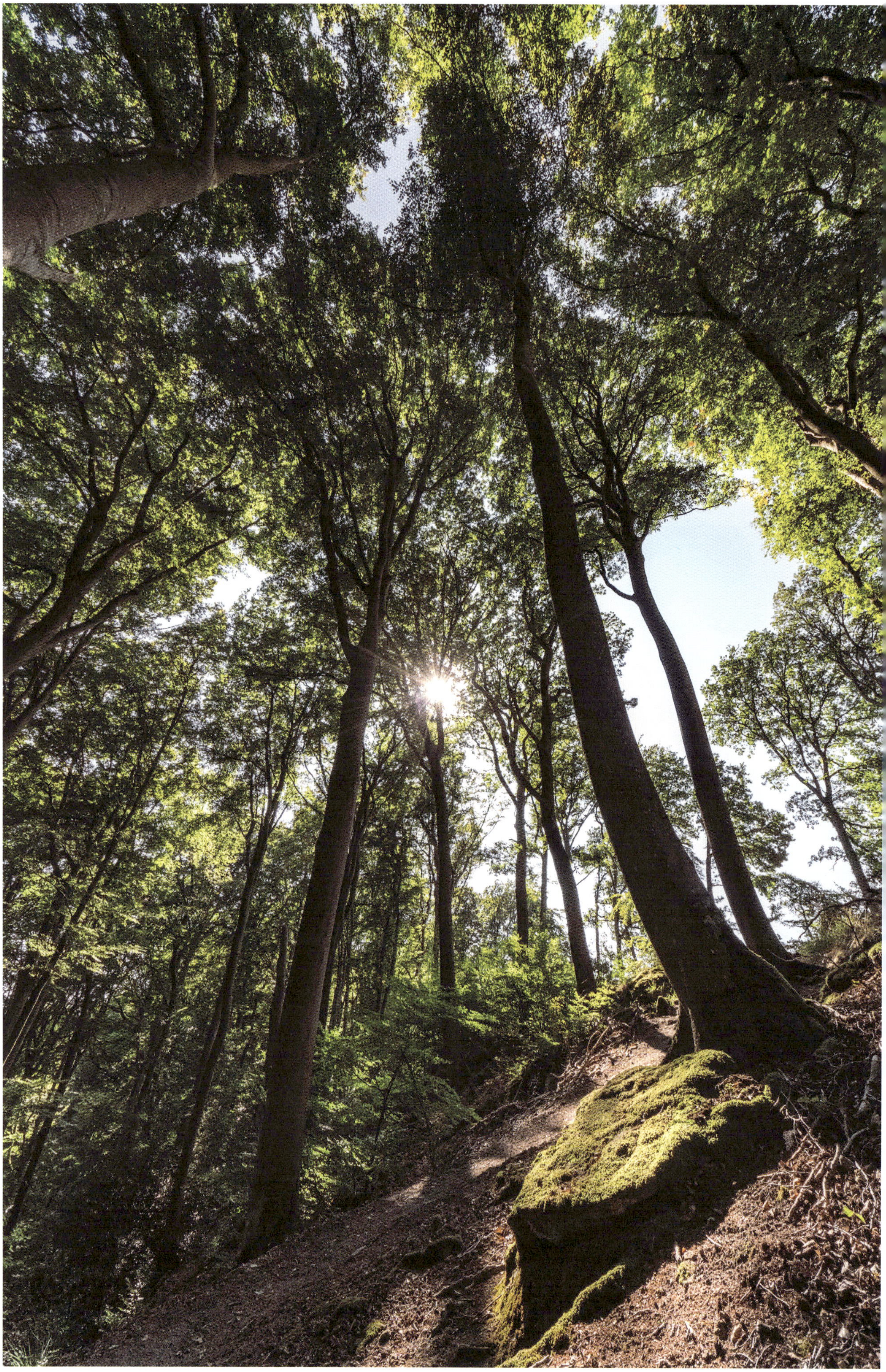

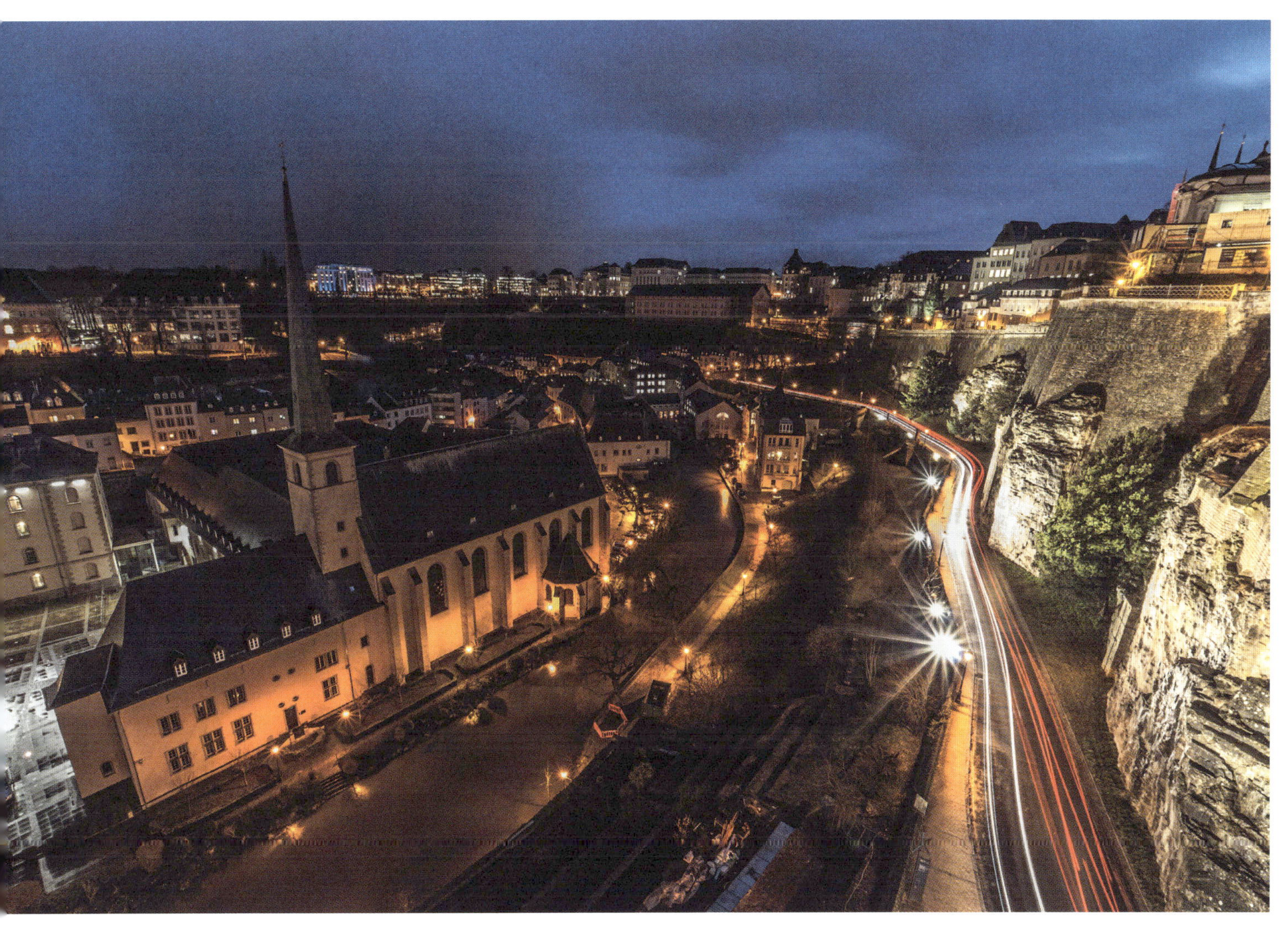

Beaufort, Luxembourg
49°49'37.8"N 6°19'22.9"E

The magical forest around Beaufort features large
boulders, long steps and a surprising variation
in altitude for this part of Europe.
// September 2019

Luxembourg City, Luxembourg
49°36'42.5"N 6°08'14.1"E

Long spells of rain disturbed this winter evening
in Luxembourg City. Only for a few minutes
the weather improved, but that was sufficient
for this shot.
// February 2015

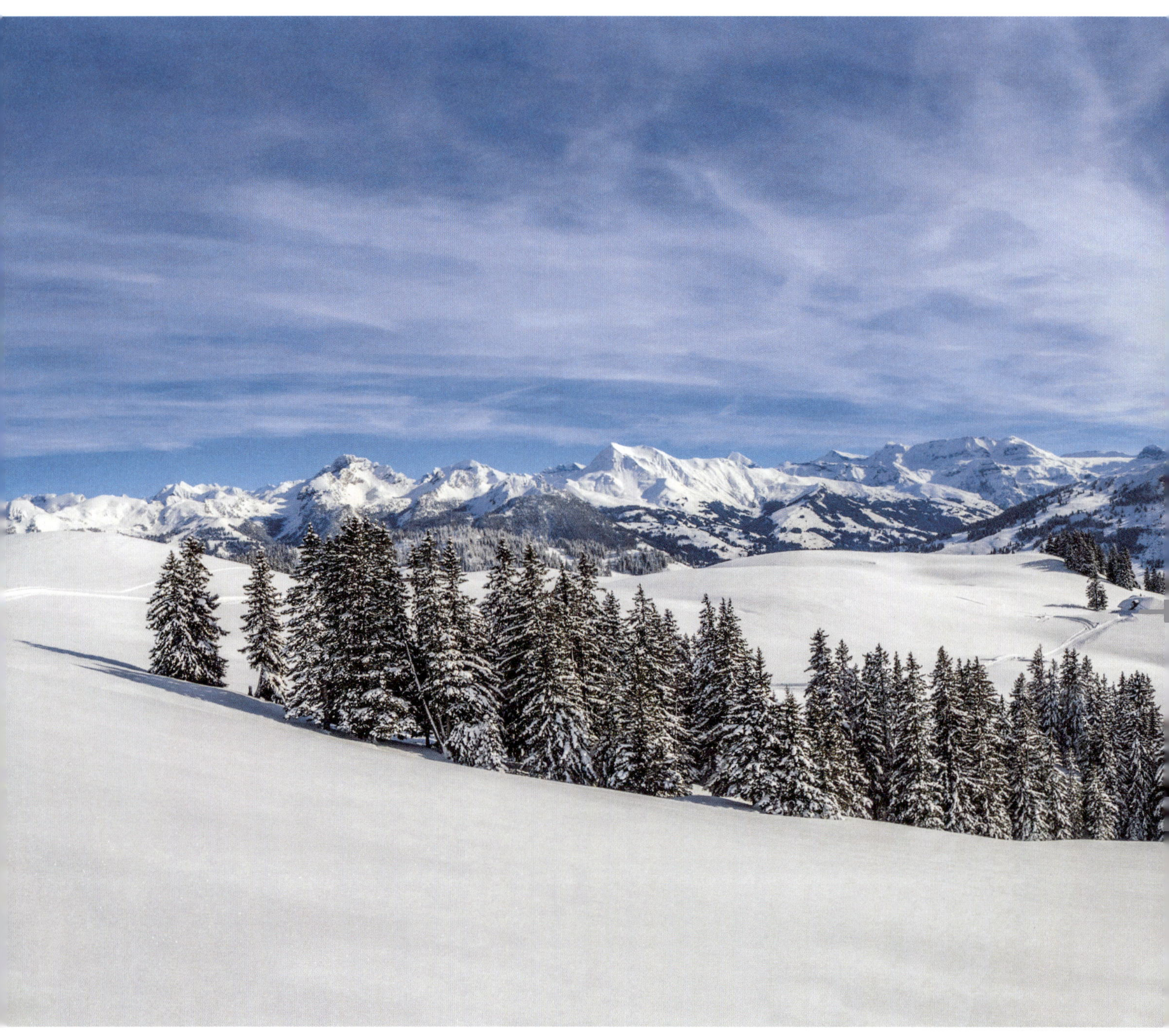

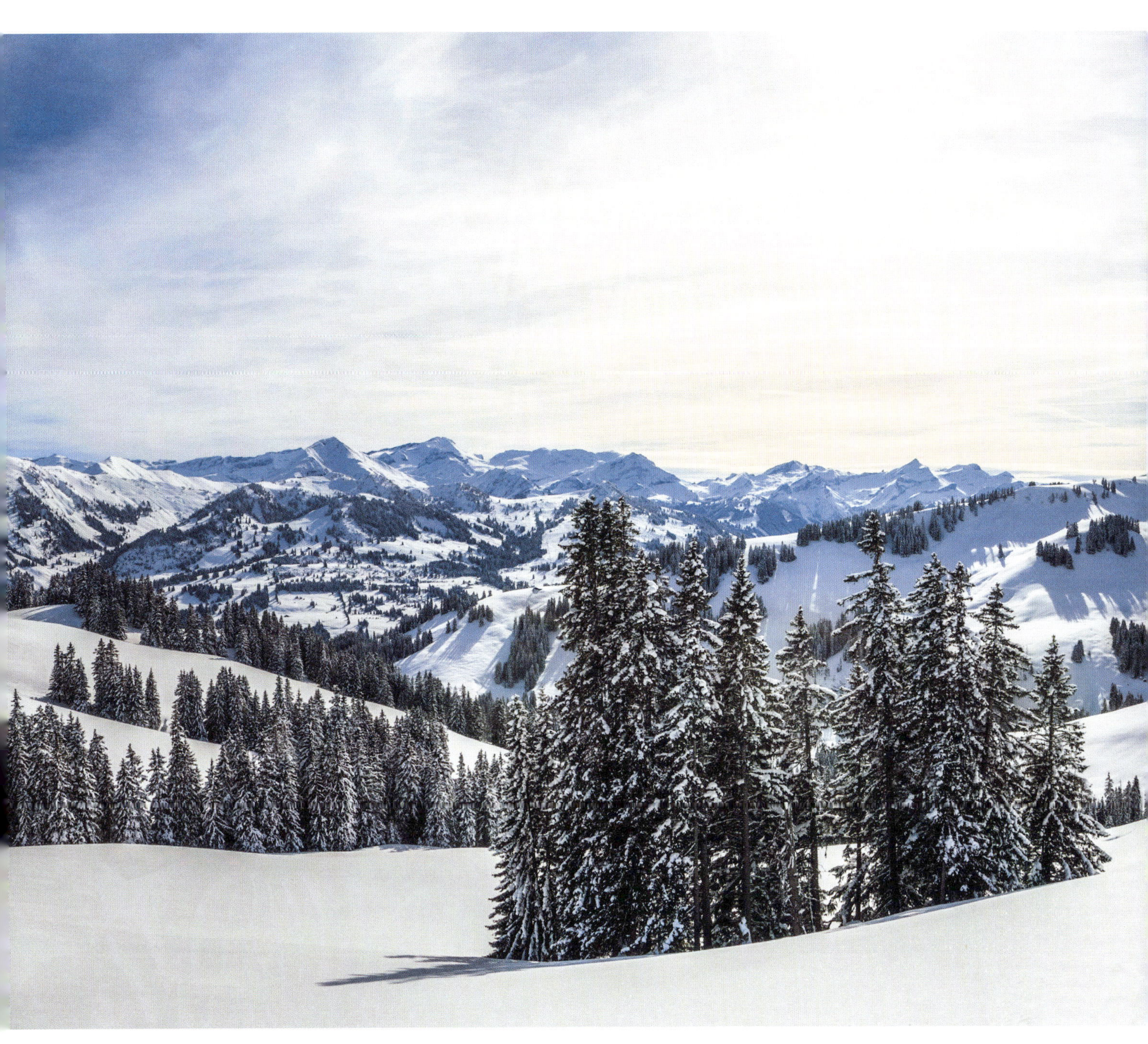

Sparenmoos, Zweisimmen, Switzerland
46°33'17.3"N 7°20'19.5"E
Sparenmoos is a beautiful region to enjoy a winter
wonderland scene without the hectics of ski
resorts. You can hike, cross-country ski or enjoy
other winter activities in peace on this charming
mountain plateau at 1,640 metres.
// February 2013

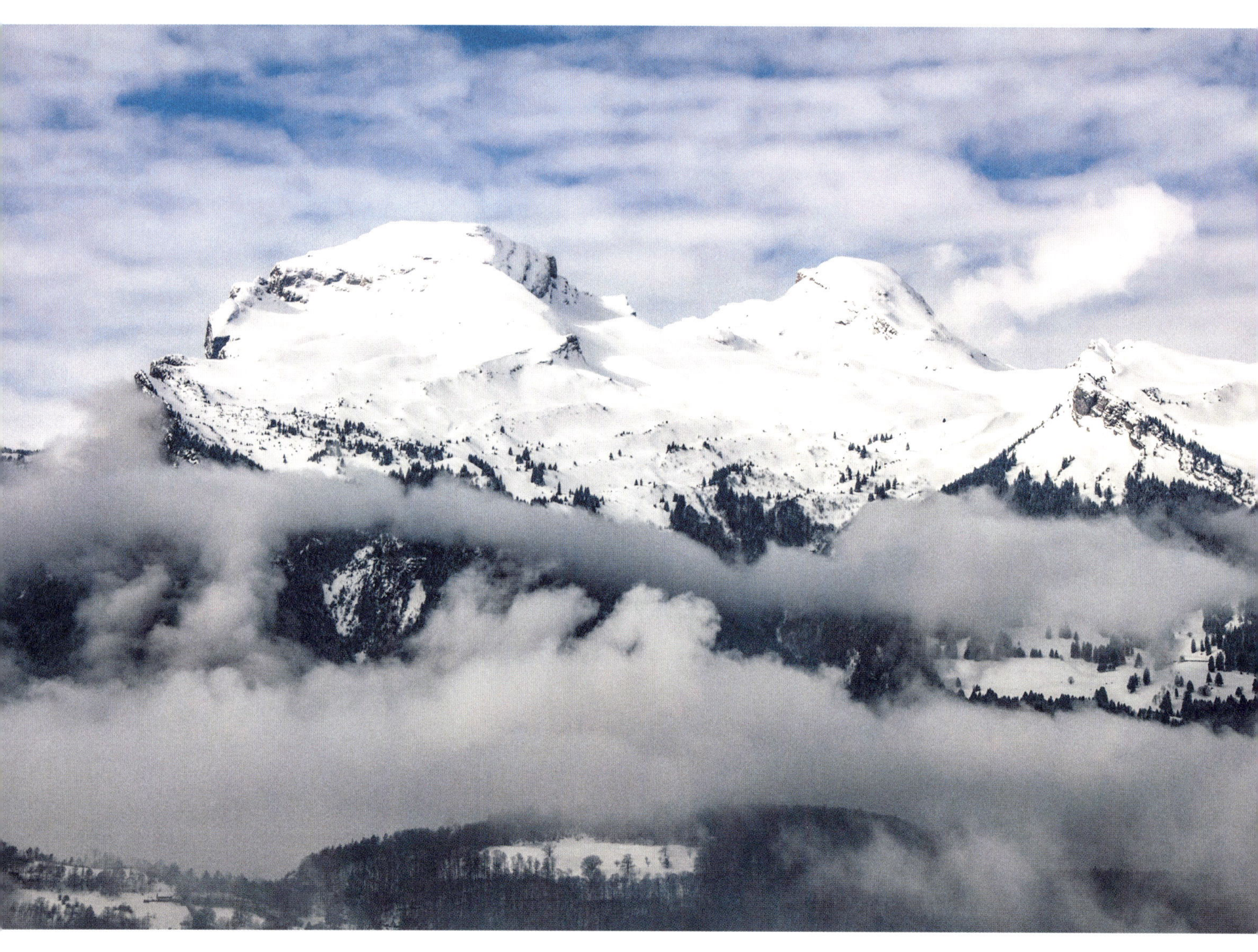

Vaduz, Liechtenstein
47°08'20.8"N 9°31'32.8"E
Liechtenstein is one of the seven Alpine countries,
landlocked between its two big neighbours
Switzerland and Austria. This microstate may be
tiny in size, but its mountains are not small at all.
// February 2013

Corippo, Switzerland
46°14'05.2"N 8°50'46.1"E
A mountain village in the Swiss Alps, close to
the Italian border.
// May 2016

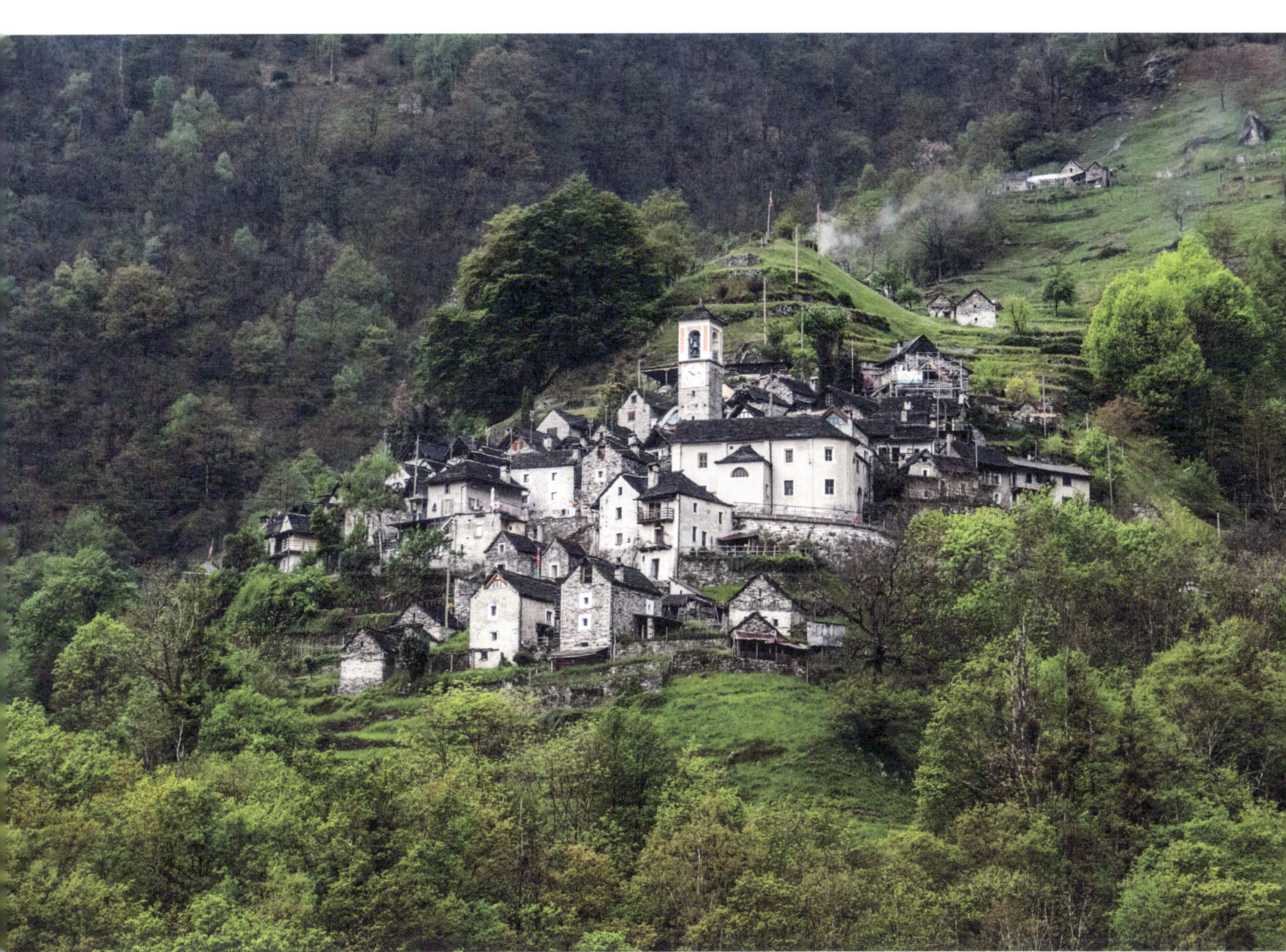

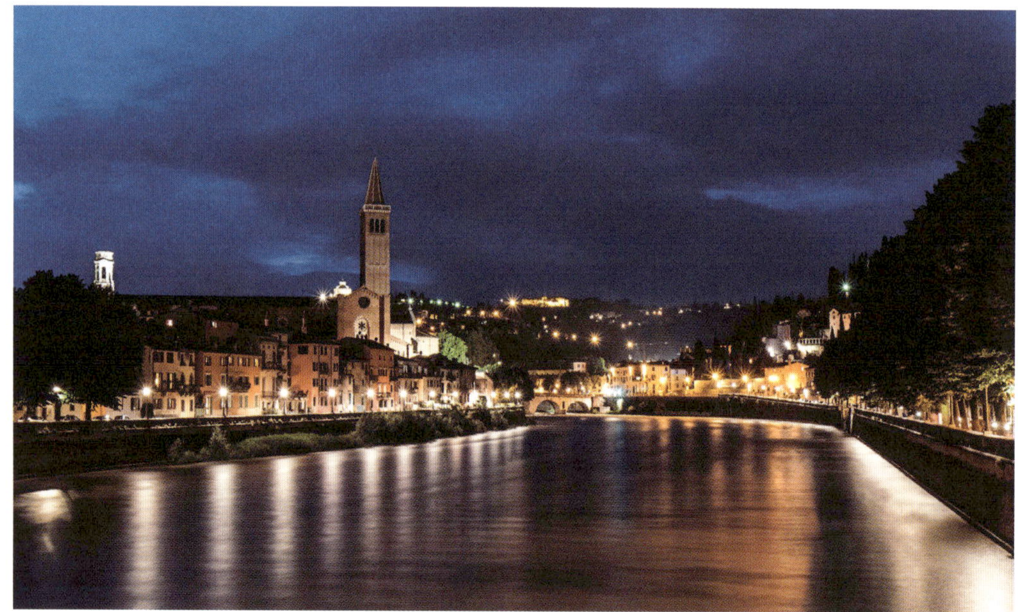

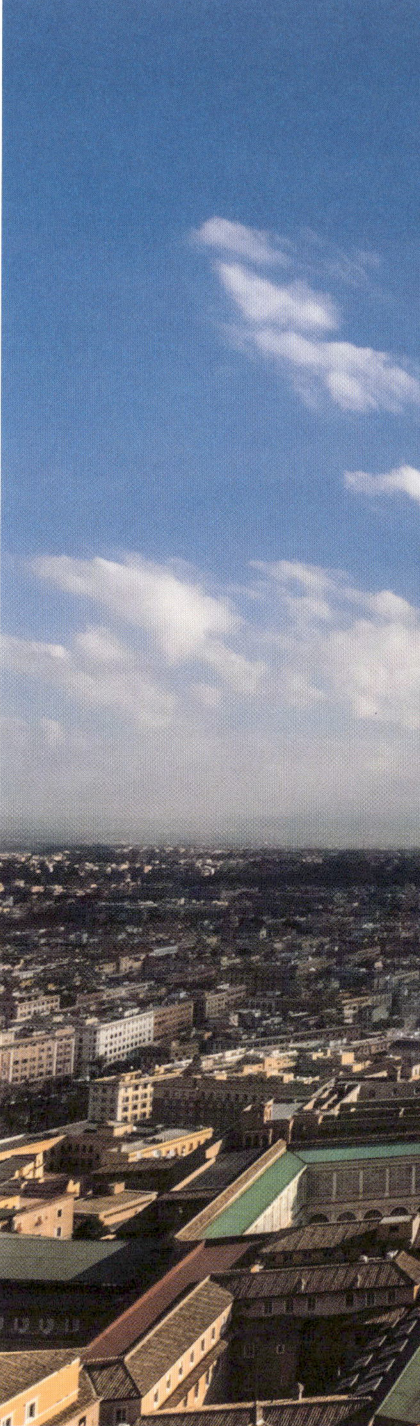

Verona, Italy
45°26'41.3"N 11°00'07.7"E
The 'blue hour' turned Verona into a colourful
light show on this rainy spring evening.
// May 2016

Vatican City
41°54'07.5"N 12°27'12.3"E
The crowds have left Piazza San Pietro after
the speech of Pope Francis earlier that day.
I did not plan to be here at the time of such
a ceremonial event, so it was one of my lucky
moments of being at the right place at the
right time.
// February 2015

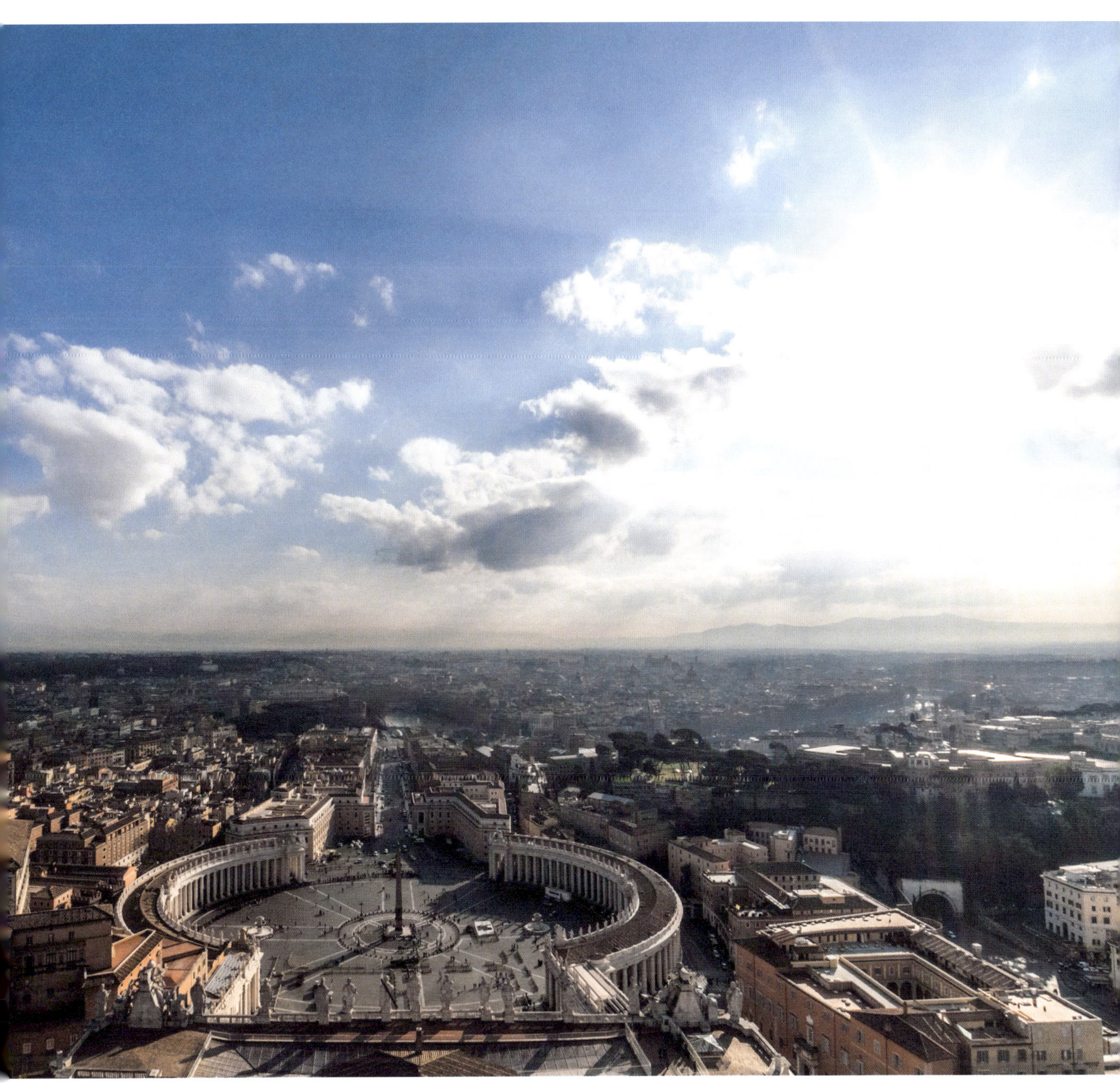

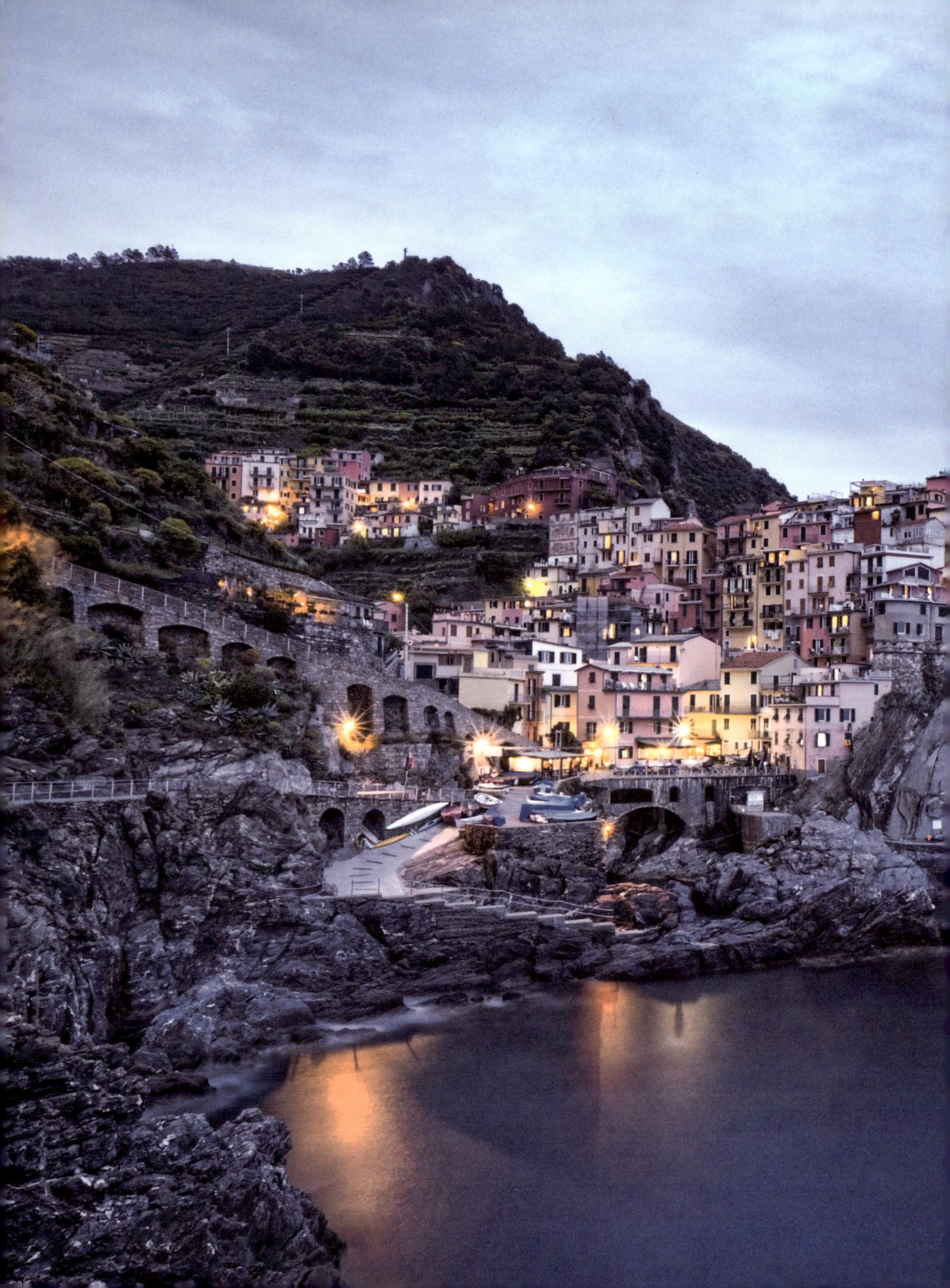

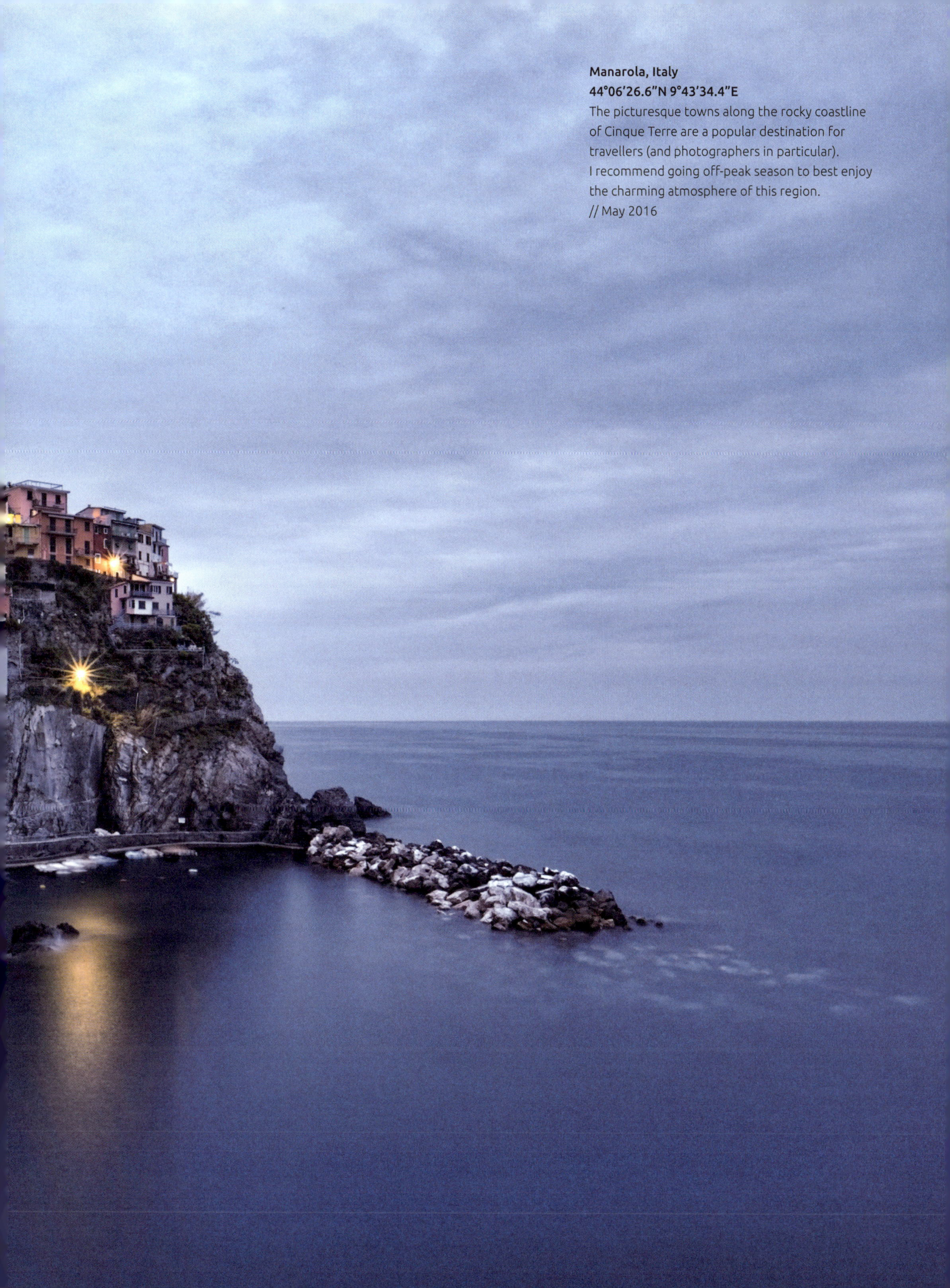

Manarola, Italy
44°06'26.6"N 9°43'34.4"E
The picturesque towns along the rocky coastline
of Cinque Terre are a popular destination for
travellers (and photographers in particular).
I recommend going off-peak season to best enjoy
the charming atmosphere of this region.
// May 2016

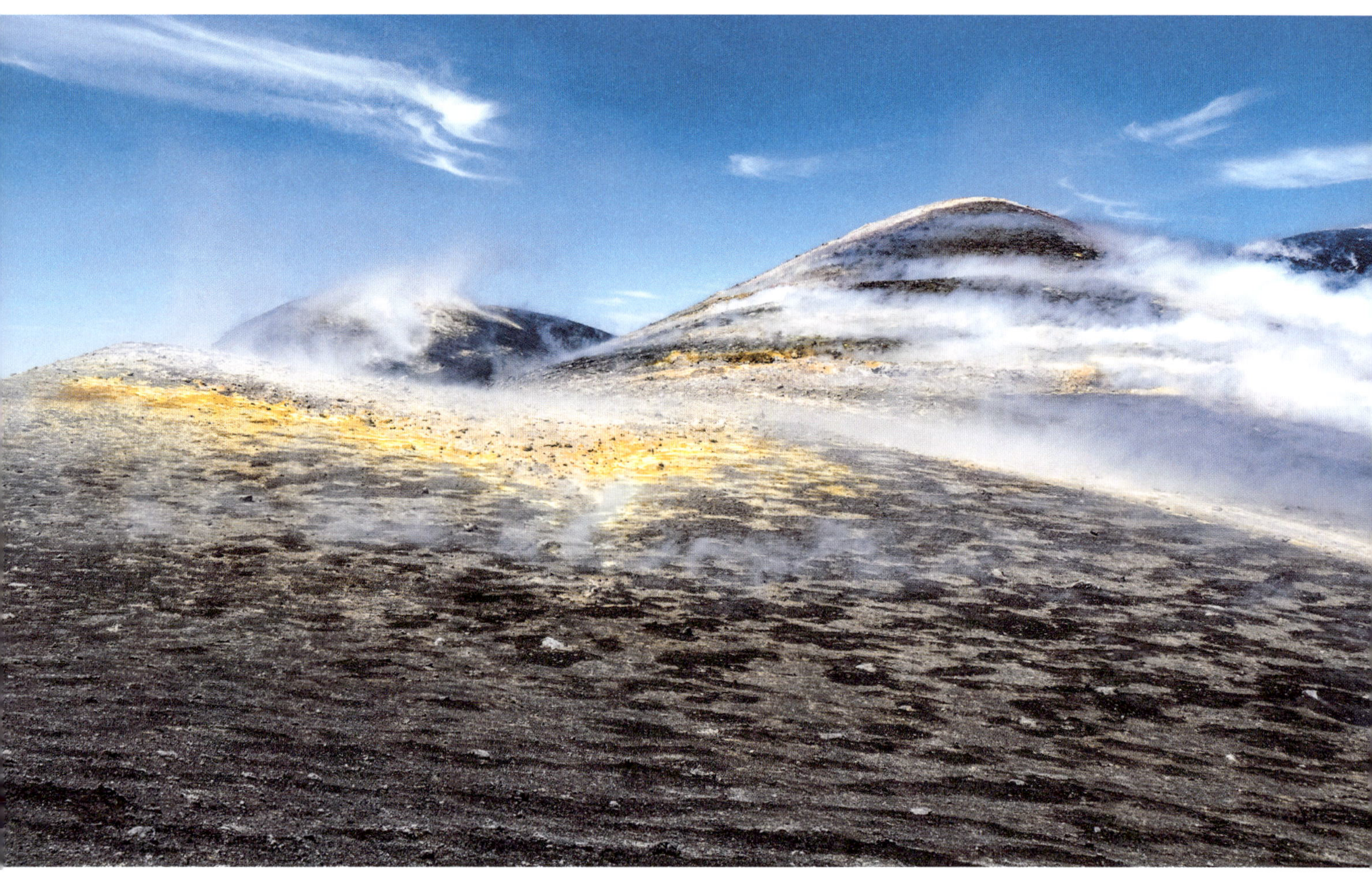

Mount Etna, Sicily, Italy
37°44'55.2"N 14°59'51.7"E
Toxic fumes escape from the sulphur-covered
landscape around the summit of Mount Etna, while
I closely follow the trail of my volcanologist guide
on this adventurous hike.
// May 2016

Poggioreale, Sicily, Italy
37°47'26.7"N 13°01'28.1"E
The old town of Poggioreale was destroyed by
an earthquake in 1968. Although it has been rebuilt
at a new location a couple of kilometres away,
the deserted town was never demolished. An ideal
photographic location for urban explorers.
// May 2016

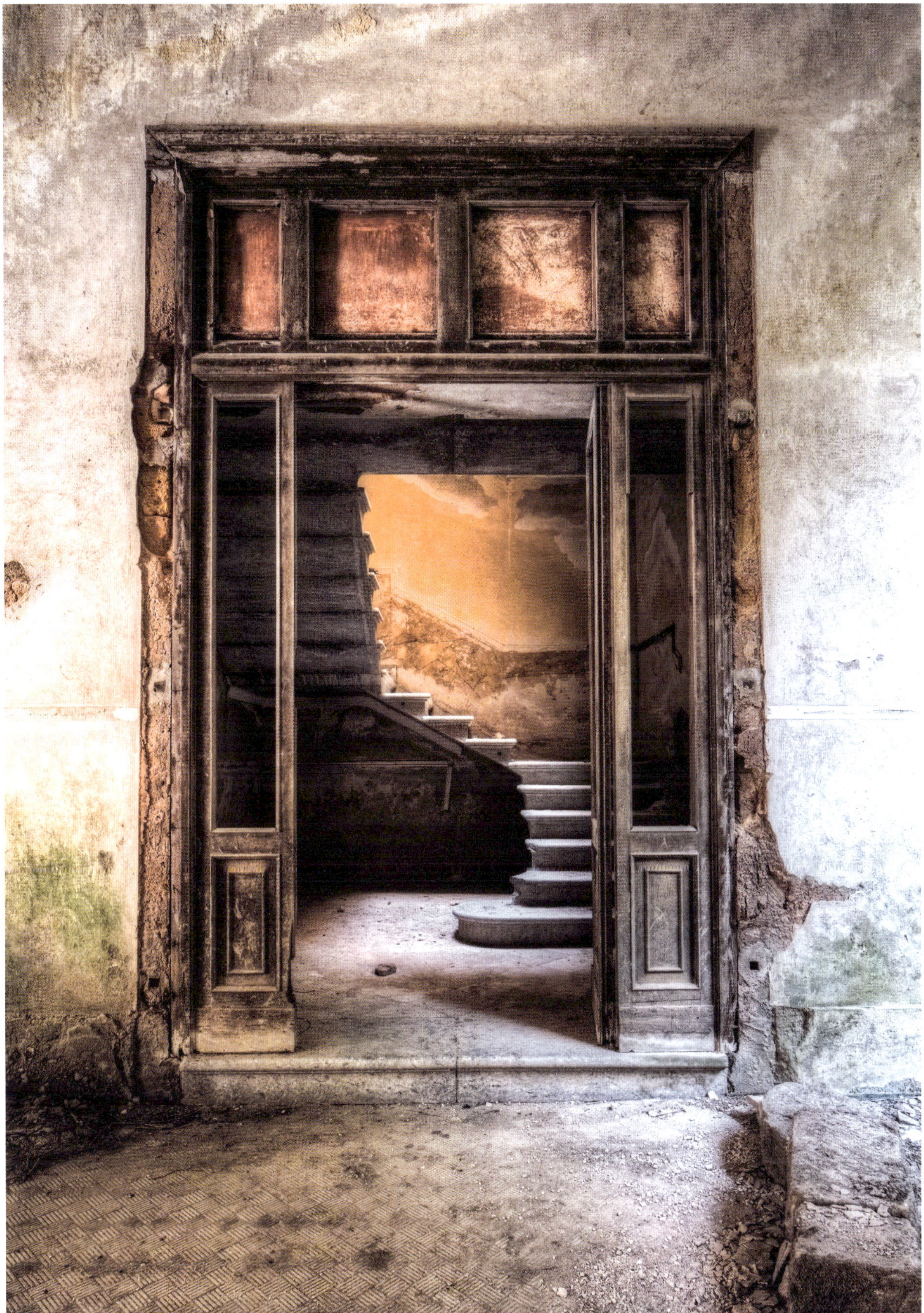

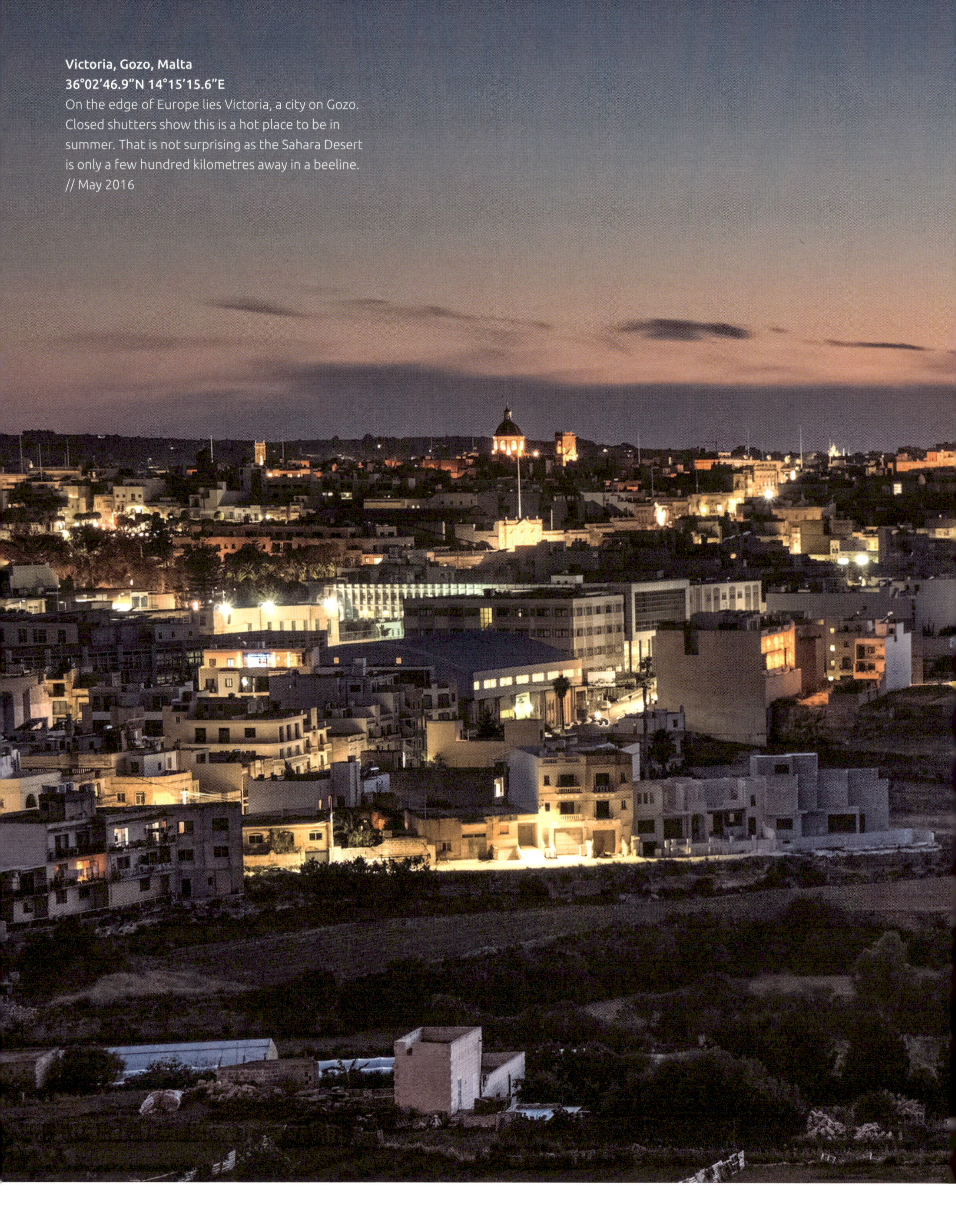

Victoria, Gozo, Malta
36°02'46.9"N 14°15'15.6"E
On the edge of Europe lies Victoria, a city on Gozo.
Closed shutters show this is a hot place to be in
summer. That is not surprising as the Sahara Desert
is only a few hundred kilometres away in a beeline.
// May 2016

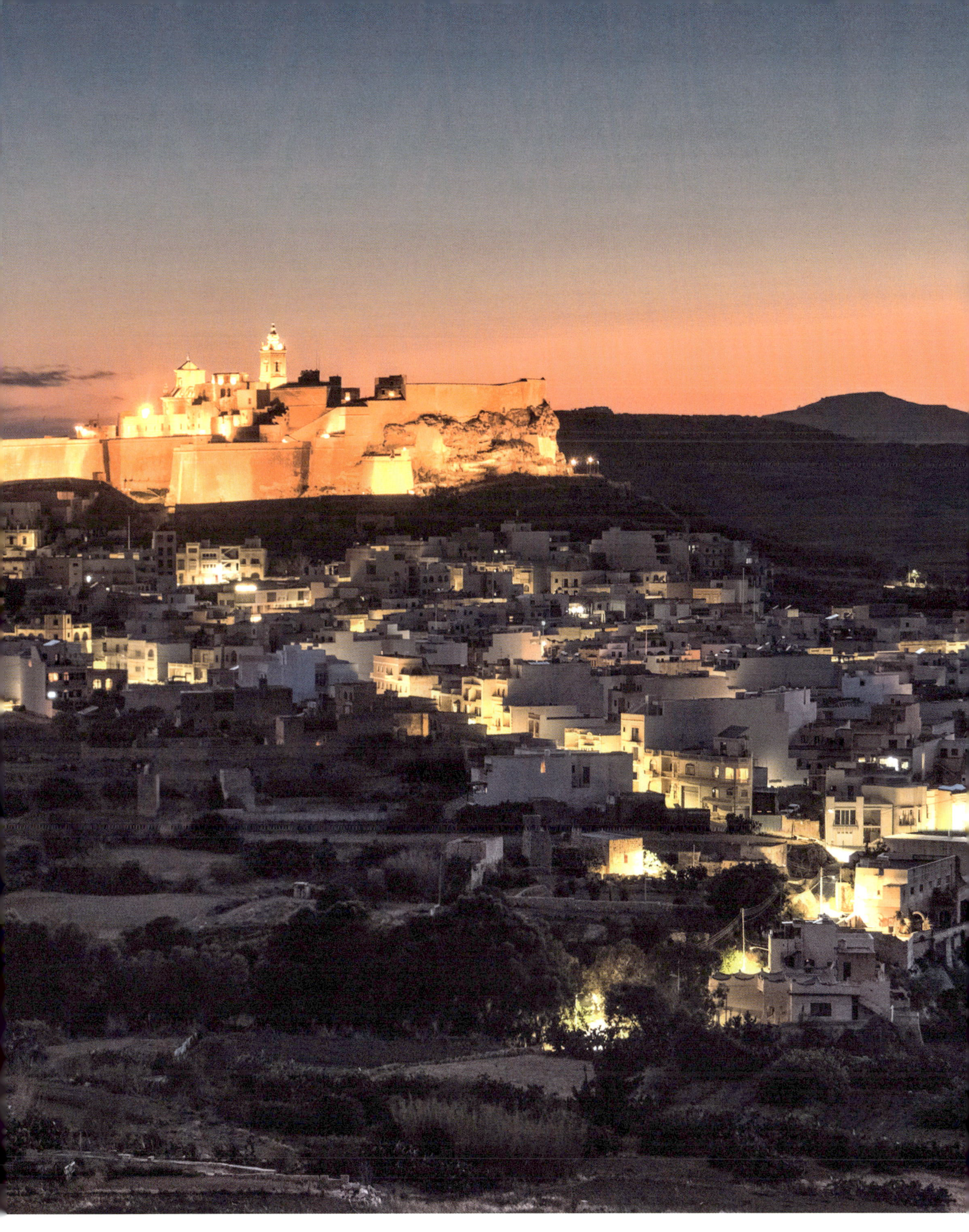

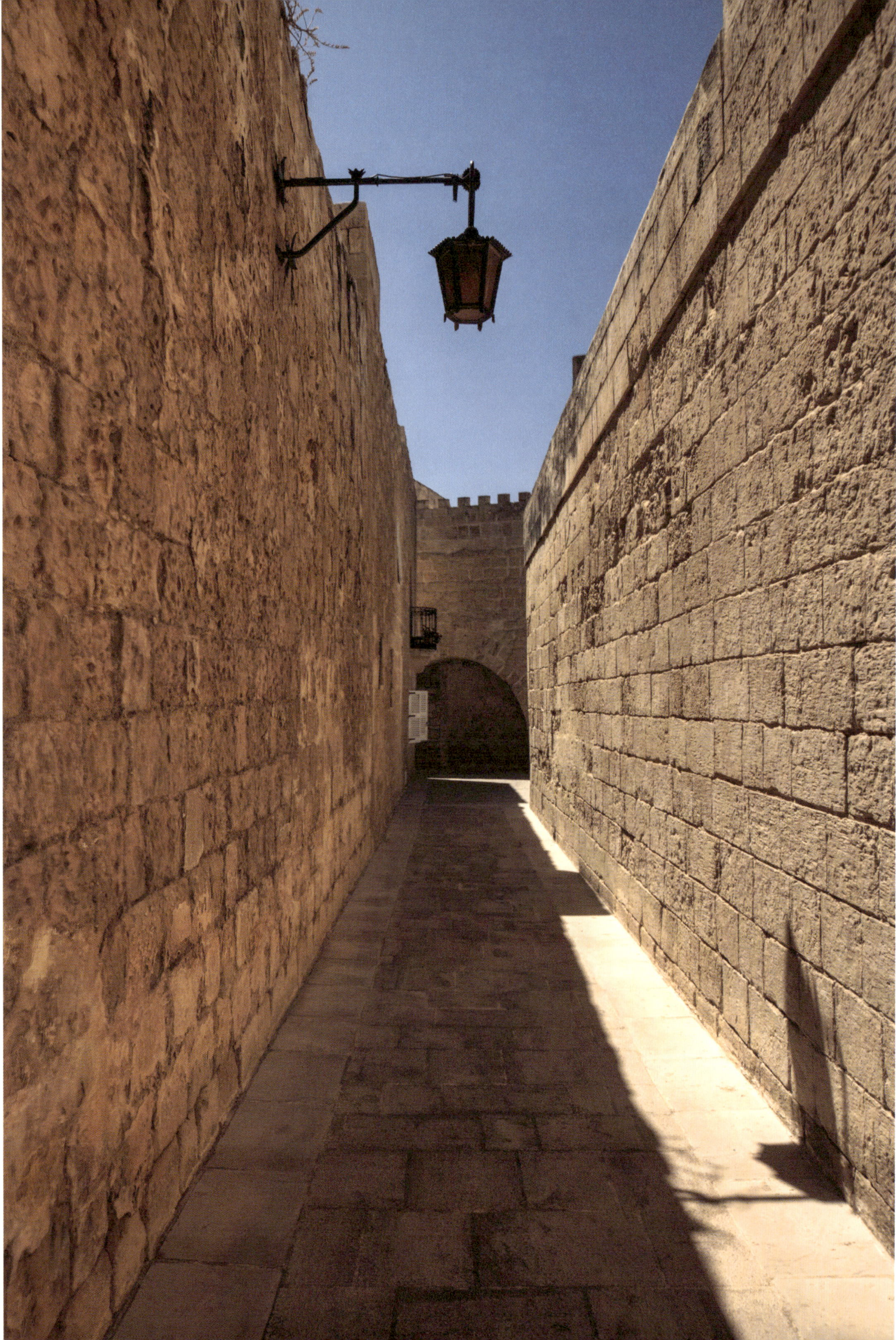

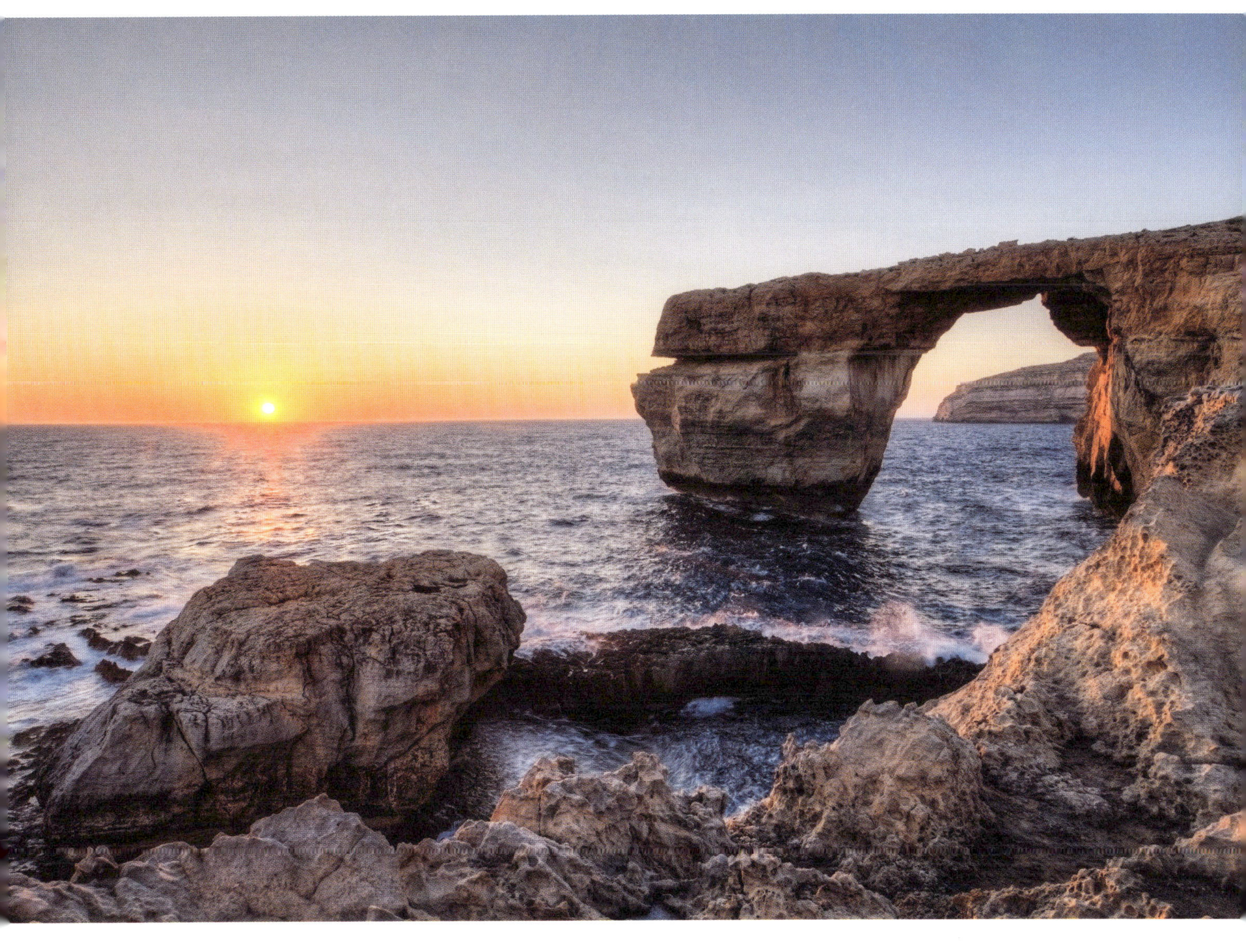

Mdina, Malta
35°53'09.0"N 14°24'08.3"E
Even after many centuries, the fortified city
of Mdina – the former capital of Malta – is still
confined to its old city walls.
// May 2016

Azure Window, Gozo, Malta
36°03'10.0"N 14°11'19.3"E
I visited the famous Azure Window on Gozo in its
last year of existence – this beautiful rock arch
sadly collapsed after a heavy storm in March 2017.
// May 2016

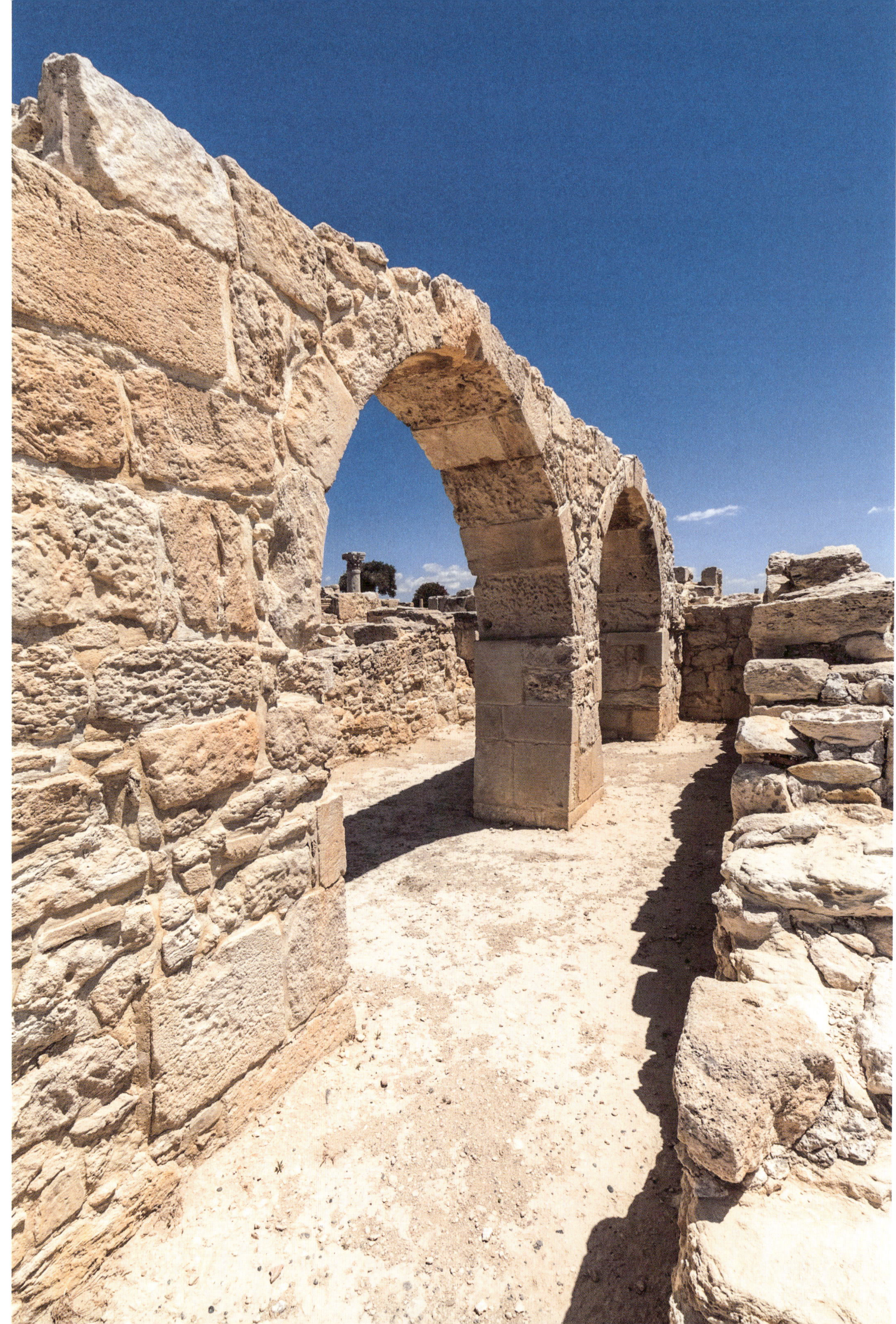

Kourion, Cyprus
34°39'58.0"N 32°53'01.8"E
Kourion, an ancient city on the southwest coast
of Cyprus.
// May 2016

Famagusta, Cyprus
35°07'30.0"N 33°56'33.4"E
The Lala Mustafa Pasha Mosque in Famagusta
shows an interesting mixture of cultures. It was
once a cathedral, but the Ottomans converted it
into a mosque after they captured the city in 1571.
// May 2016

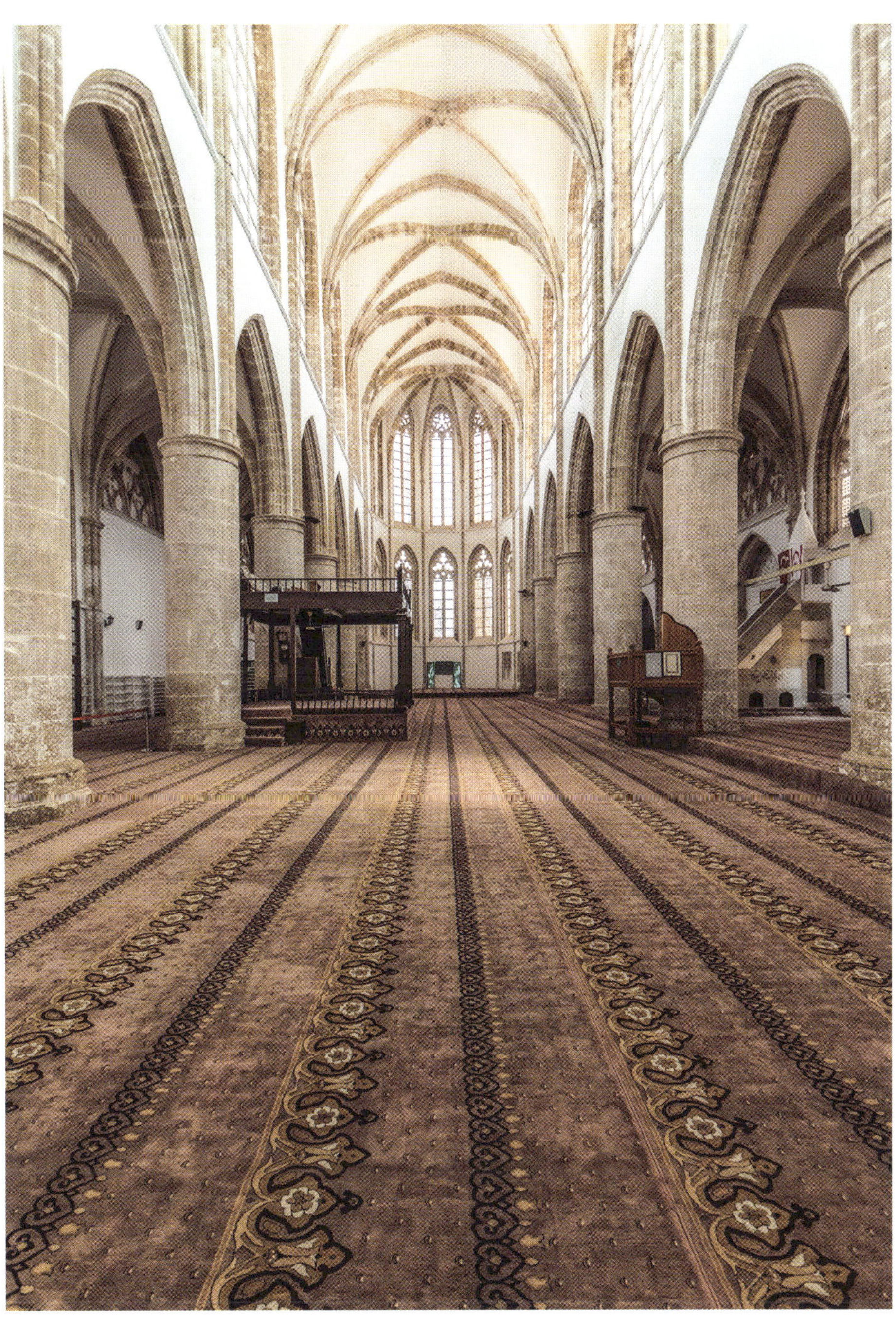

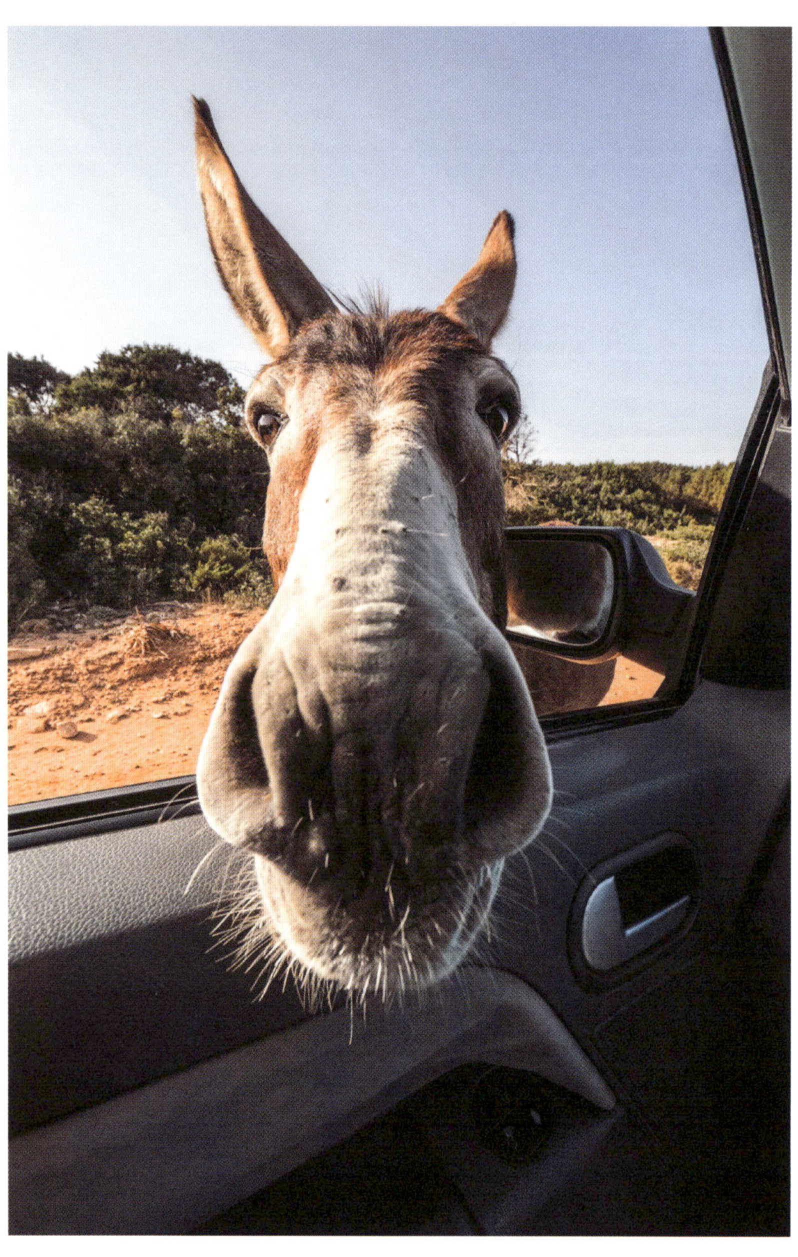

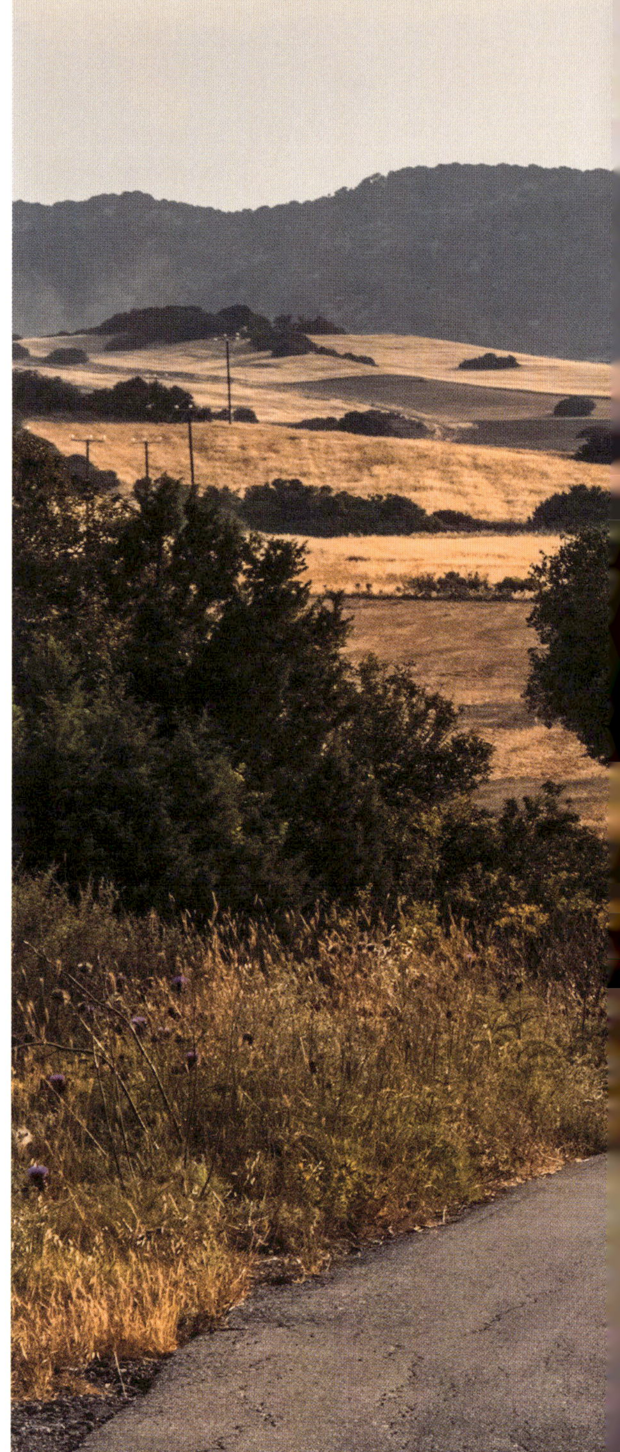

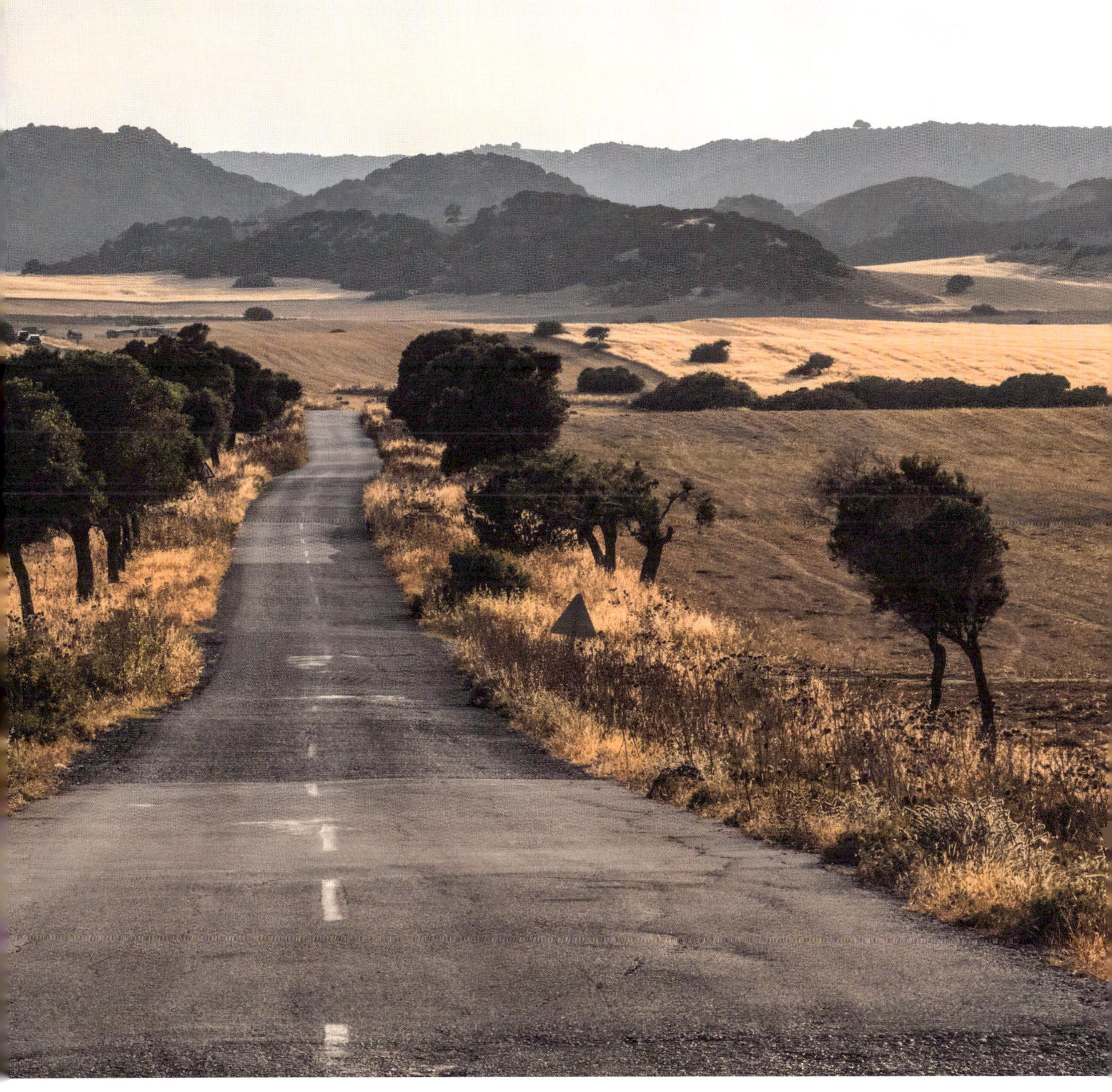

Peninsula of Karpasia, Cyprus
35°39'50.3"N 34°34'19.5"E
Somewhere on a remote gravel road on the
Peninsula of Karpasia, a curious donkey stops
the car. He walks over to say hello – probably
in the hope of getting a tasty snack.
// May 2016

Peninsula of Karpasia, Cyprus
35°37'05.7"N 34°27'33.5"E
At the end of a sunny day, this scenic road through
the Peninsula of Karpasia is a real pleasure to drive
and photograph.
// May 2016

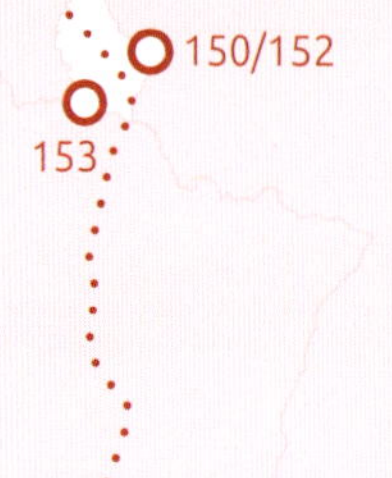

South and Sideways
Route and travel suggestions
172
150/152
153
156
8
154
21
22
1/19
157
3
12
158
14
160
146
17
2
11
159
15
7
4
18
163
162
5
149/164/167
9/13
166
Photo location
Travel suggestion
123 Photo page number
123 Travel suggestion number

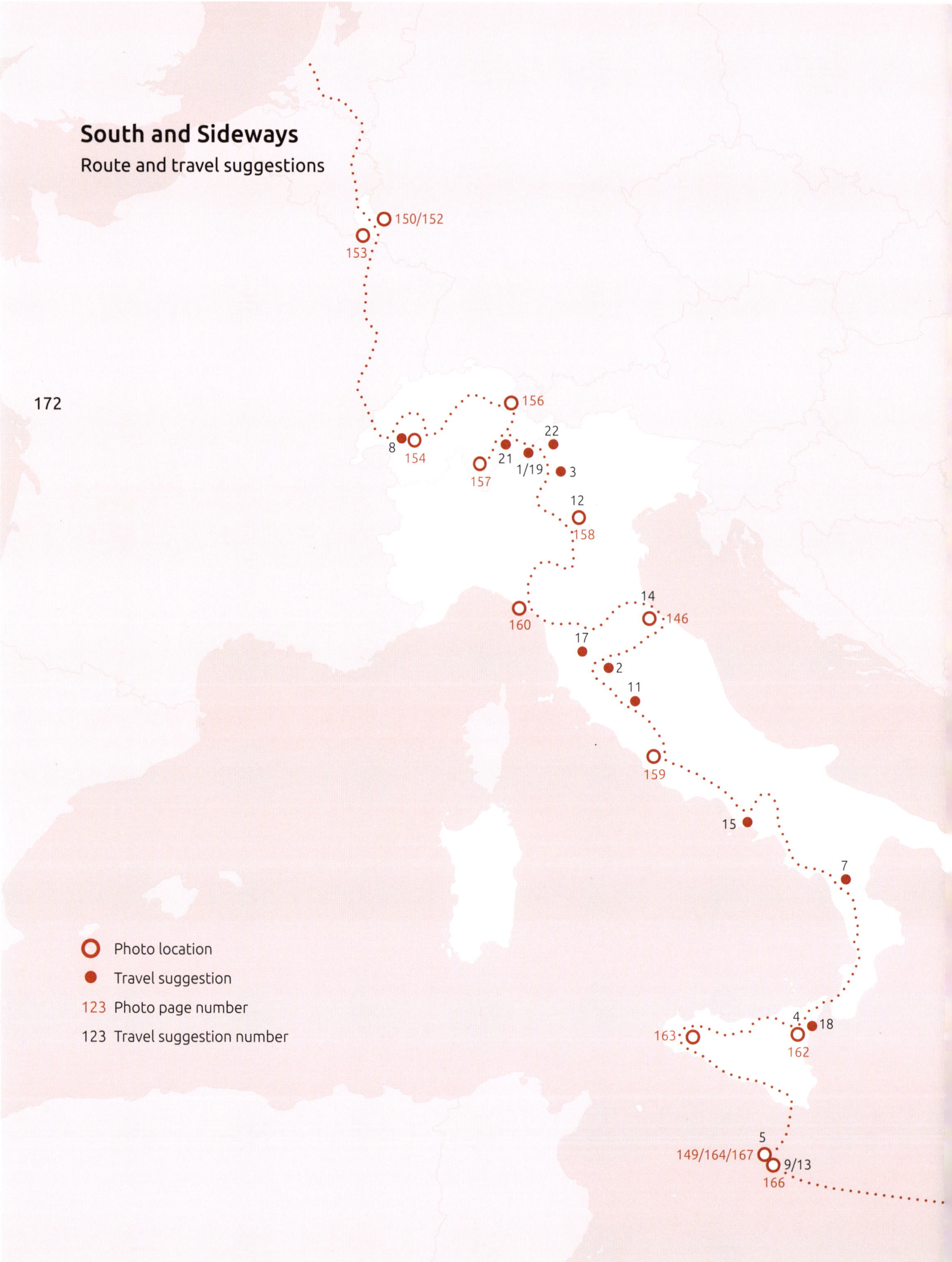

Scenic regions and nature reserves

1 Bernina // **Switzerland & Italy**
2 Crete Senesi // **Italy**
3 Dolomiti di Brenta // **Italy**
4 Etna, Sicily // **Italy**
5 Gozo // **Malta**
6 Peninsula of Karpasia // **Cyprus**
7 Pollino // **Italy**

Cities and towns

8 Gruyères // **Switzerland**
9 Mdina // **Malta**
10 Nicosia // **Cyprus**
11 Orvieto // **Italy**
12 Verona // **Italy**

Cultural experiences

13 Mnajdra, Qrendi // **Malta**
14 Monte Titano // **San Marino**
15 Napoli Sotterranea, Naples // **Italy**
16 Salamis // **Cyprus**
17 San Gimignano, Tuscany // **Italy**
18 Taormina Ancient Theatre, Sicily // **Italy**

Spectacular roads and scenic routes

19 Bernina Pass // **Switzerland**
20 Karpaz Anayolu // **Cyprus**
21 Splügen Pass // **Switzerland & Italy**
22 Stelvio Pass // **Switzerland & Italy**

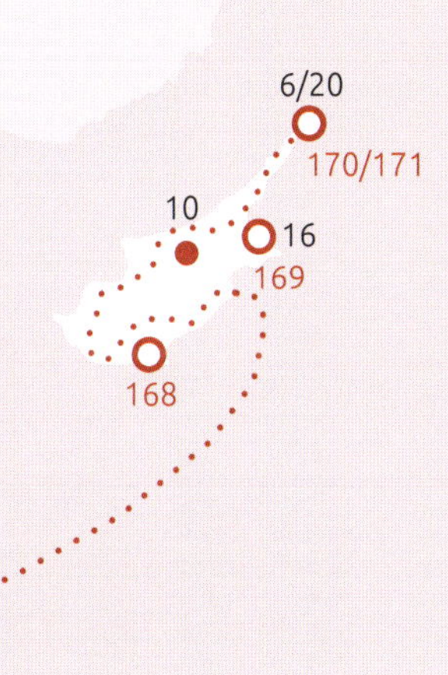

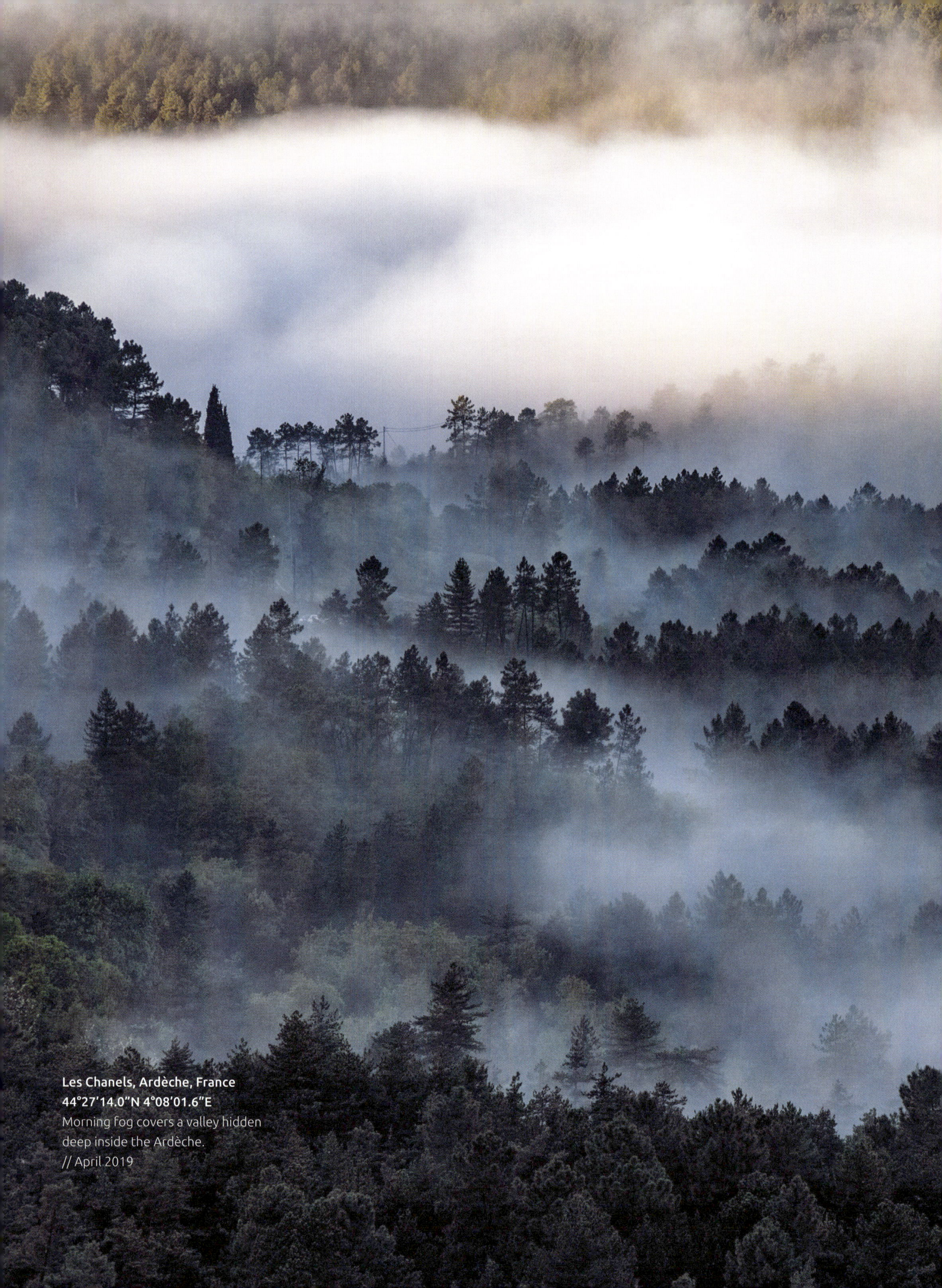

Les Chanels, Ardèche, France
44°27'14.0"N 4°08'01.6"E
Morning fog covers a valley hidden
deep inside the Ardèche.
// April 2019

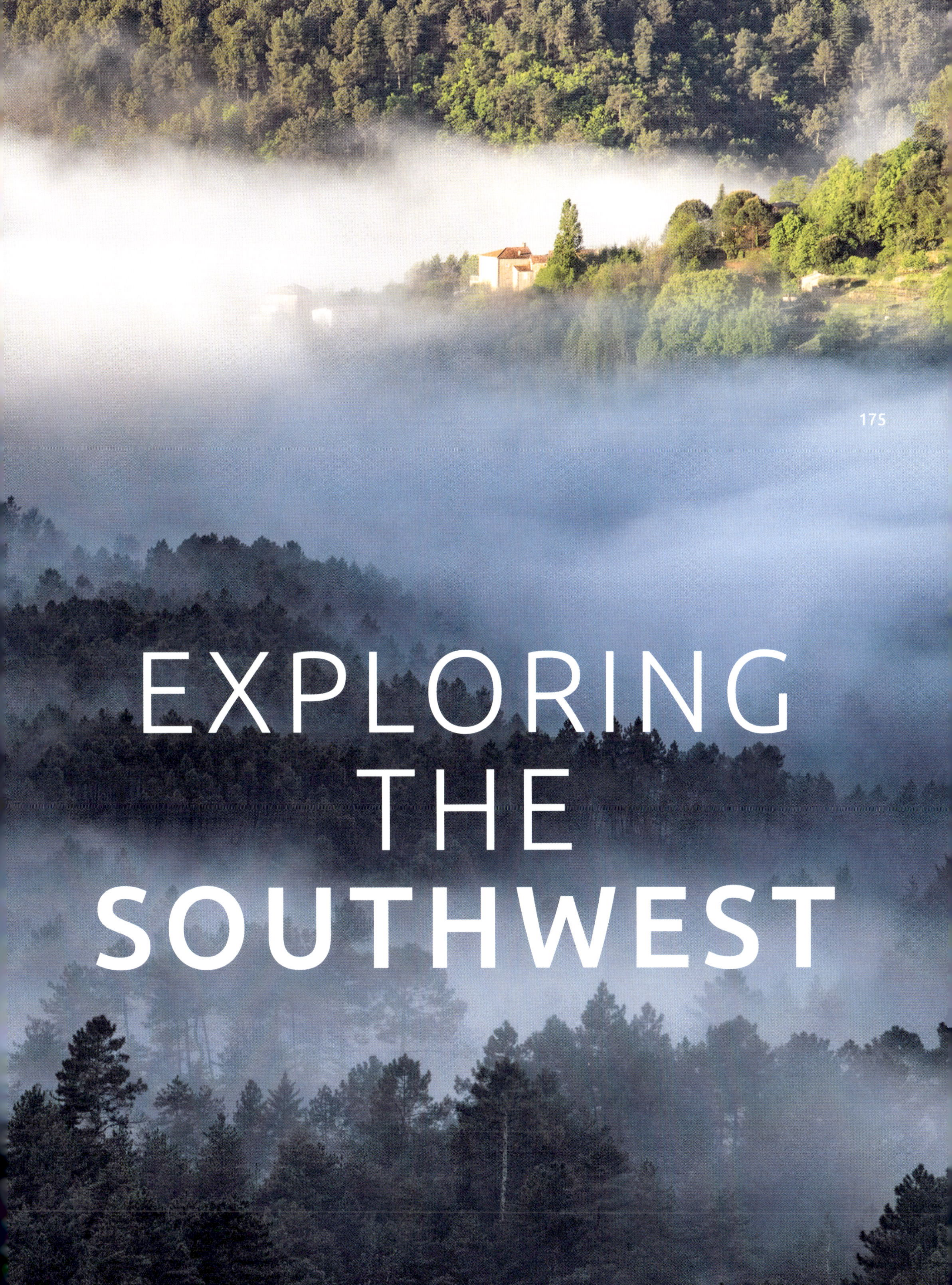

EXPLORING THE SOUTHWEST

'Those who have only visited Spain's Mediterranean coastline have seen just a fraction of what the Iberian Peninsula has to offer.'

TRAVELLING SOUTHWEST

through Belgium we can take a break in one of the picturesque cities of Flanders, the Dutch-speaking northern and western part of the country. Or explore the great outdoors in the Ardennes, where you can engage in challenging activities such as rock climbing, canyoning or mountain biking.

Driving further south soon brings us to France. More than 50 nature reserves are dotted across the country, with varied landscapes and regions rich in wildlife. The west of France has a distinct Atlantic character and climate; while stone pines populate the mild Mediterranean southeast. The Alsace region in the northeast is an interesting blend of French and German cultures with vineyards and half-timbered buildings colouring the landscape, while the Monts du Cantal in the Auvergne form a photogenic mountainous landscape made up of volcanic remnants.

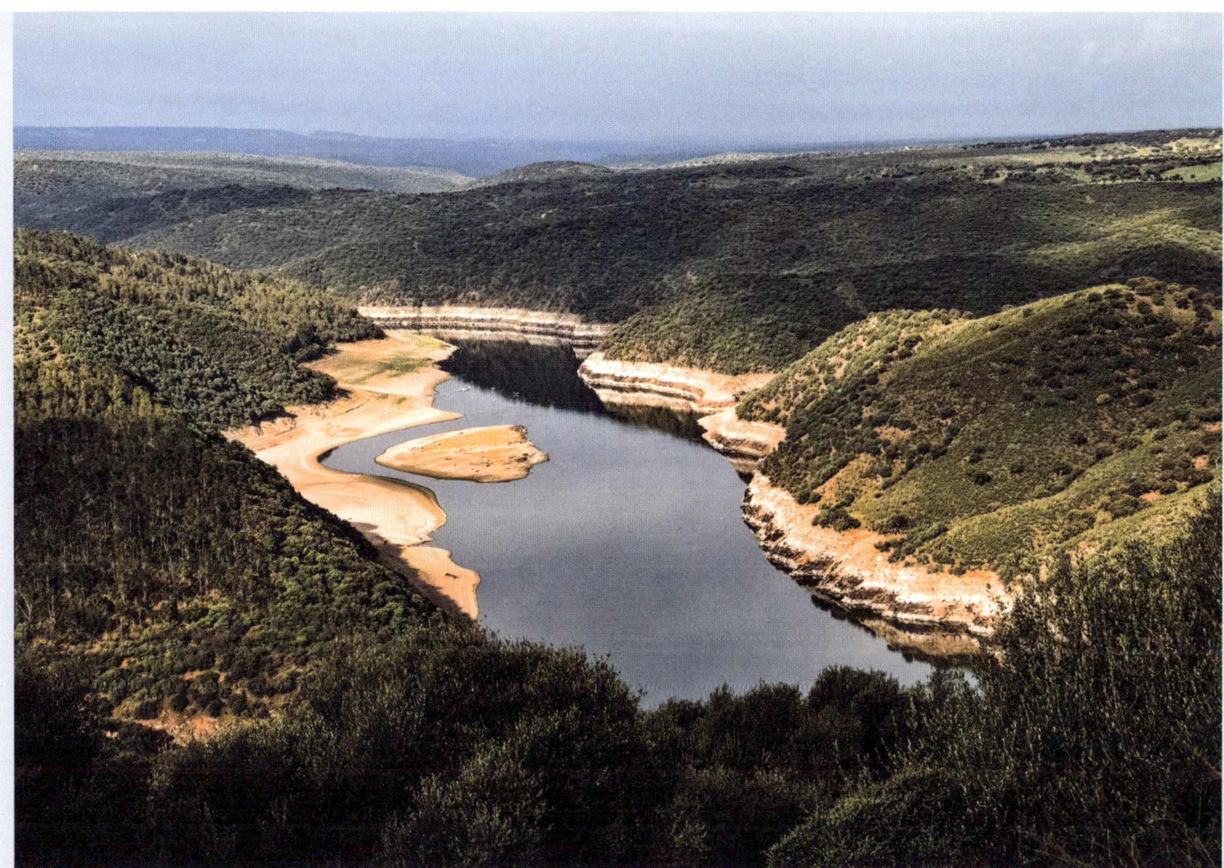

The borders with Switzerland and Italy are home to some of the Alps' most impressive and well-known mountains, whereas the Pyrenees in the south are characterised by lofty waterfalls and isolated valleys and cirques. France has landscapes for everyone to explore.

Those who have only visited Spain's Mediterranean coastline have seen just a fraction of what the Iberian Peninsula has to offer. The real surprises are found far away from the coast, such as Monfragüe in Extremadura with its vultures and cork oaks, La Rioja with its scenic slopes and sun-drenched vineyards, and the Sierra Nevada with rare flora and fauna on the slopes of 3000ers like Mulhacén and Alcazaba.

The Portuguese region of Alentejo is also one of many faces. Landscapes full of olive trees or rice fields. The many deserted beaches of sand and rock range from quiet inlets to rough surfing spots with breath-taking waves.

A road trip through France and the Iberian Peninsula (including their microstates) is one of natural, cultural and culinary surprises, provided you look further than just the pristine beaches and reputed ski resorts.

Monfragüe, Extremadura, Spain
39°49'41.6"N 6°03'07.7"W
Hidden deep inside Spain lies Monfragüe, a landscape shaped by the river Tajo in the Extremadura region. The region is home to many birds, including the impressive black vulture.
// May 2012

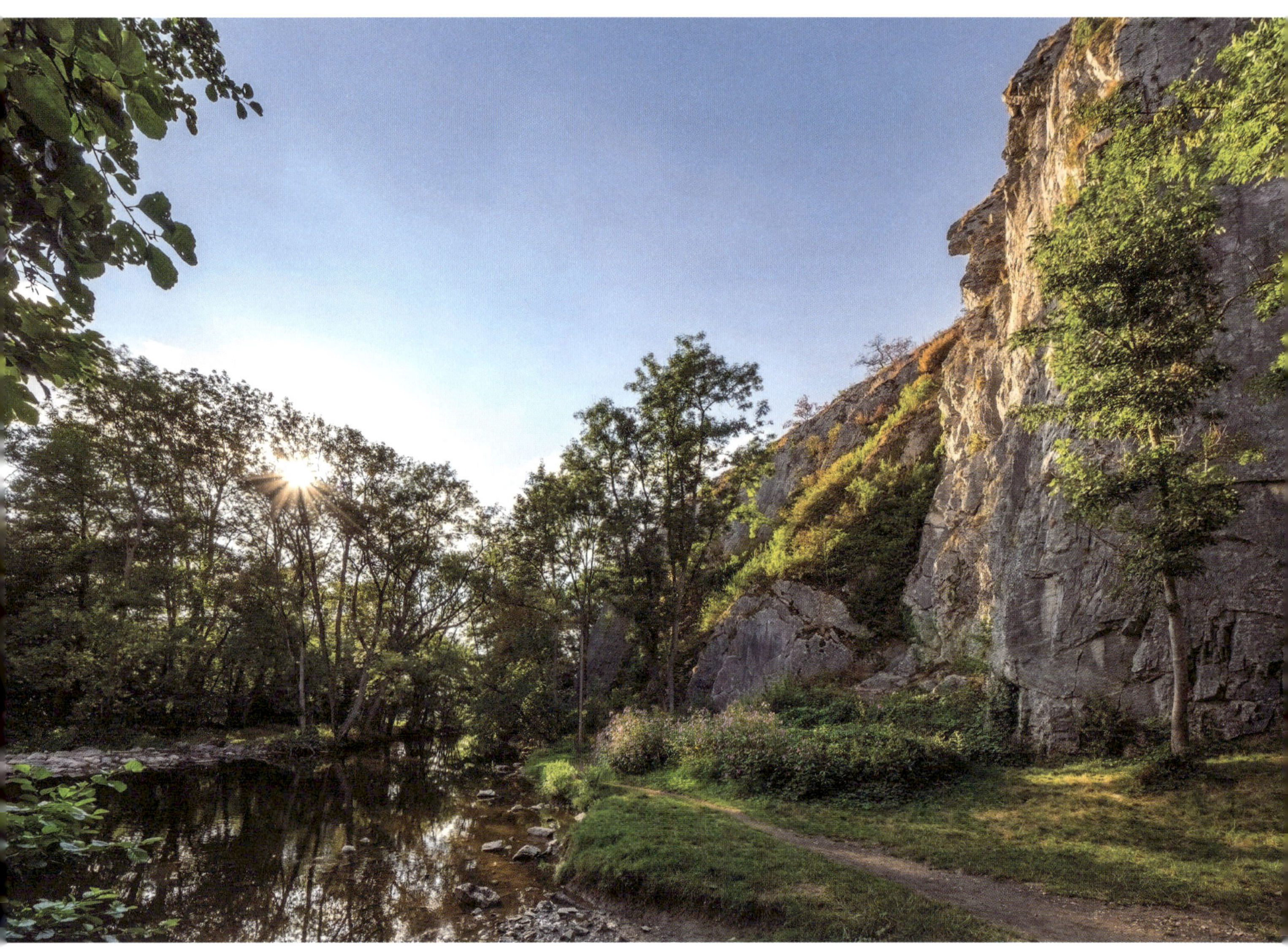

Hotton, Belgium
50°15′58.5″N 5°27′30.0″E
Rock climbing has taken me to beautiful sites
that I would probably not have visited otherwise.
This photogenic climbing area in the heart of
Wallonia is a great place for those who like
to challenge gravity.
// August 2018

Leuven, Belgium
50°53′06.5″N 4°41′55.8″E
Soft winter light emphasises the texture and
patterns of the bricks in this quiet street
in the heart of Leuven.
// January 2016

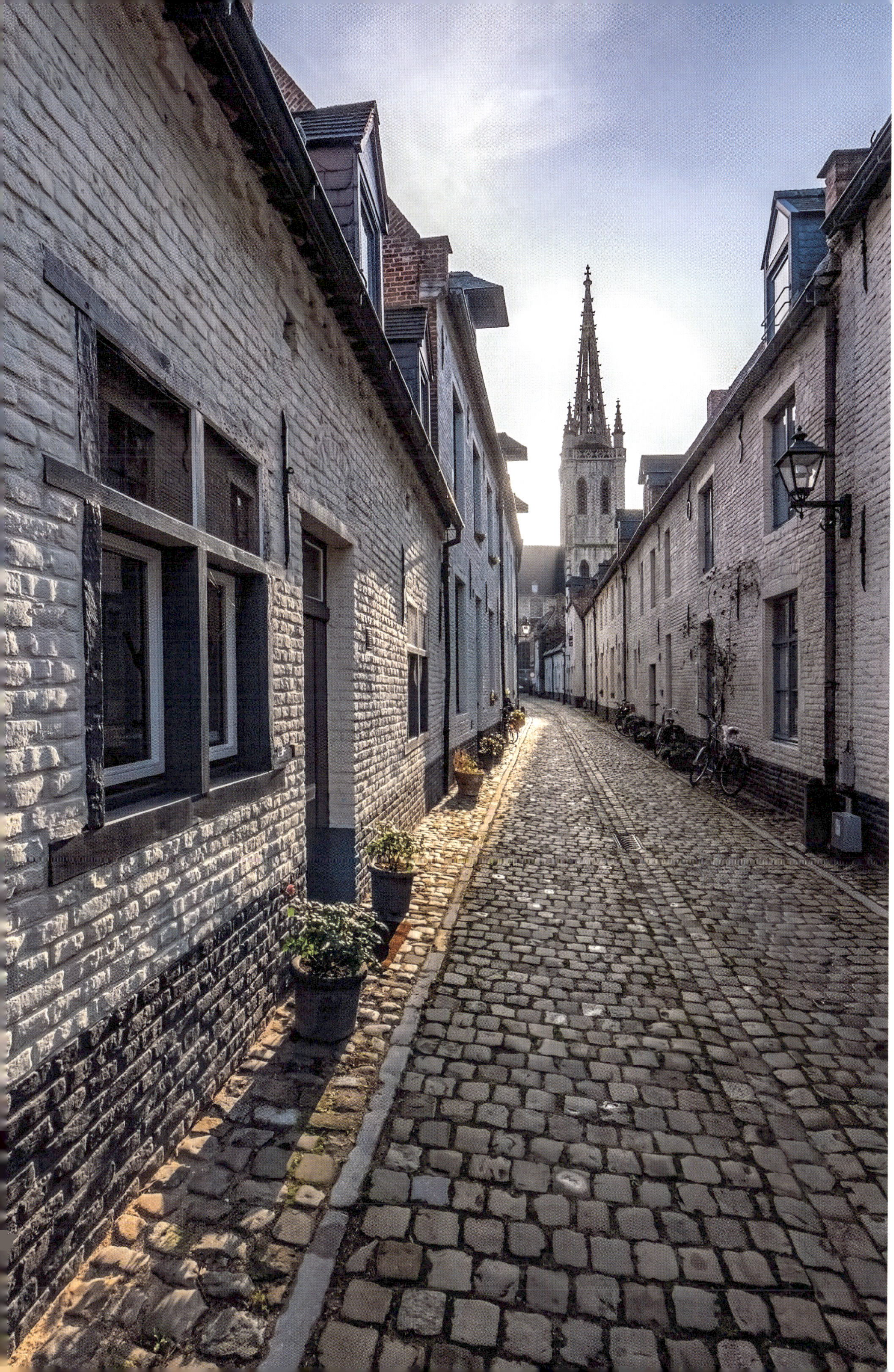

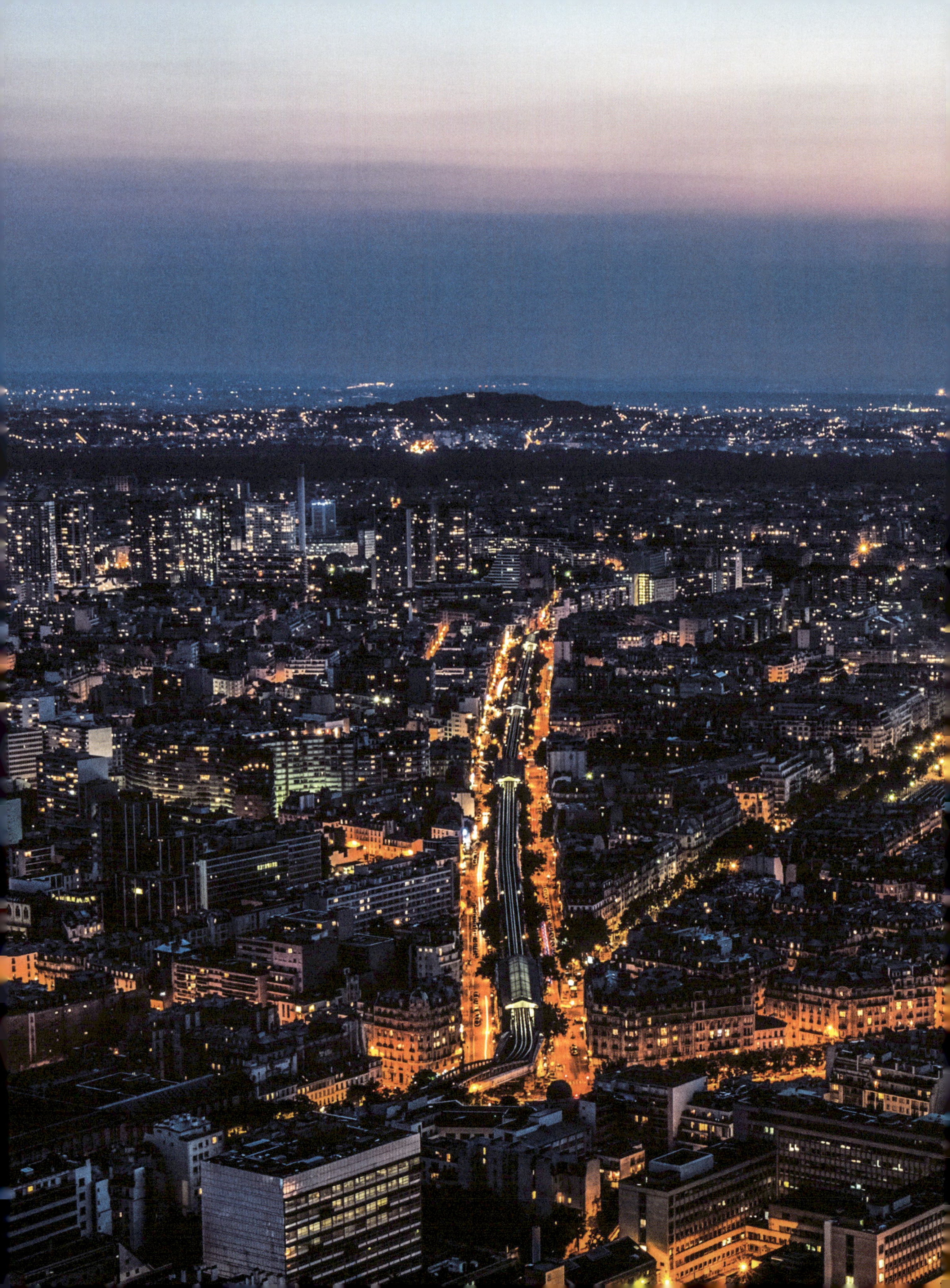

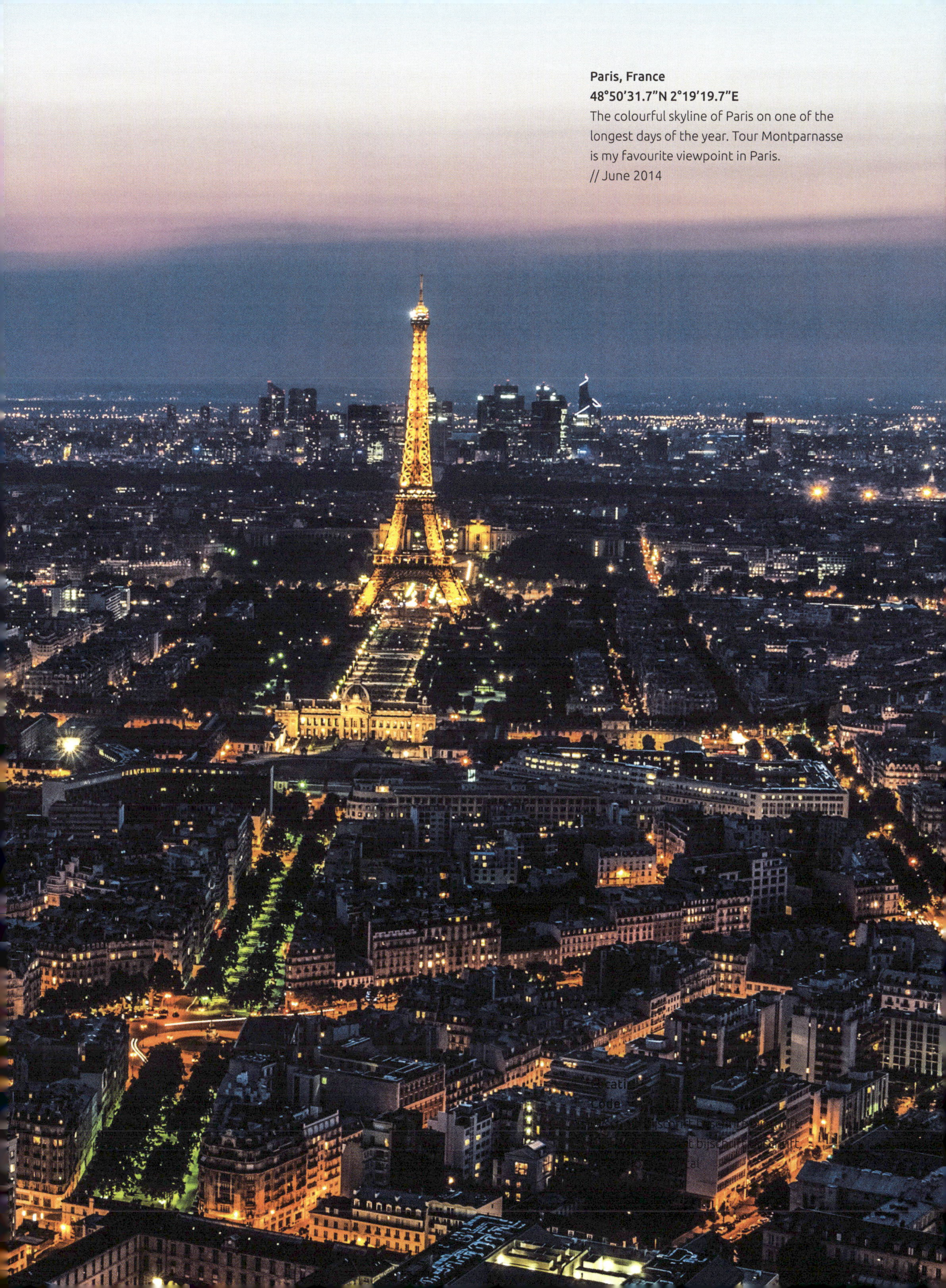

Paris, France
48°50'31.7"N 2°19'19.7"E
The colourful skyline of Paris on one of the
longest days of the year. Tour Montparnasse
is my favourite viewpoint in Paris.
// June 2014

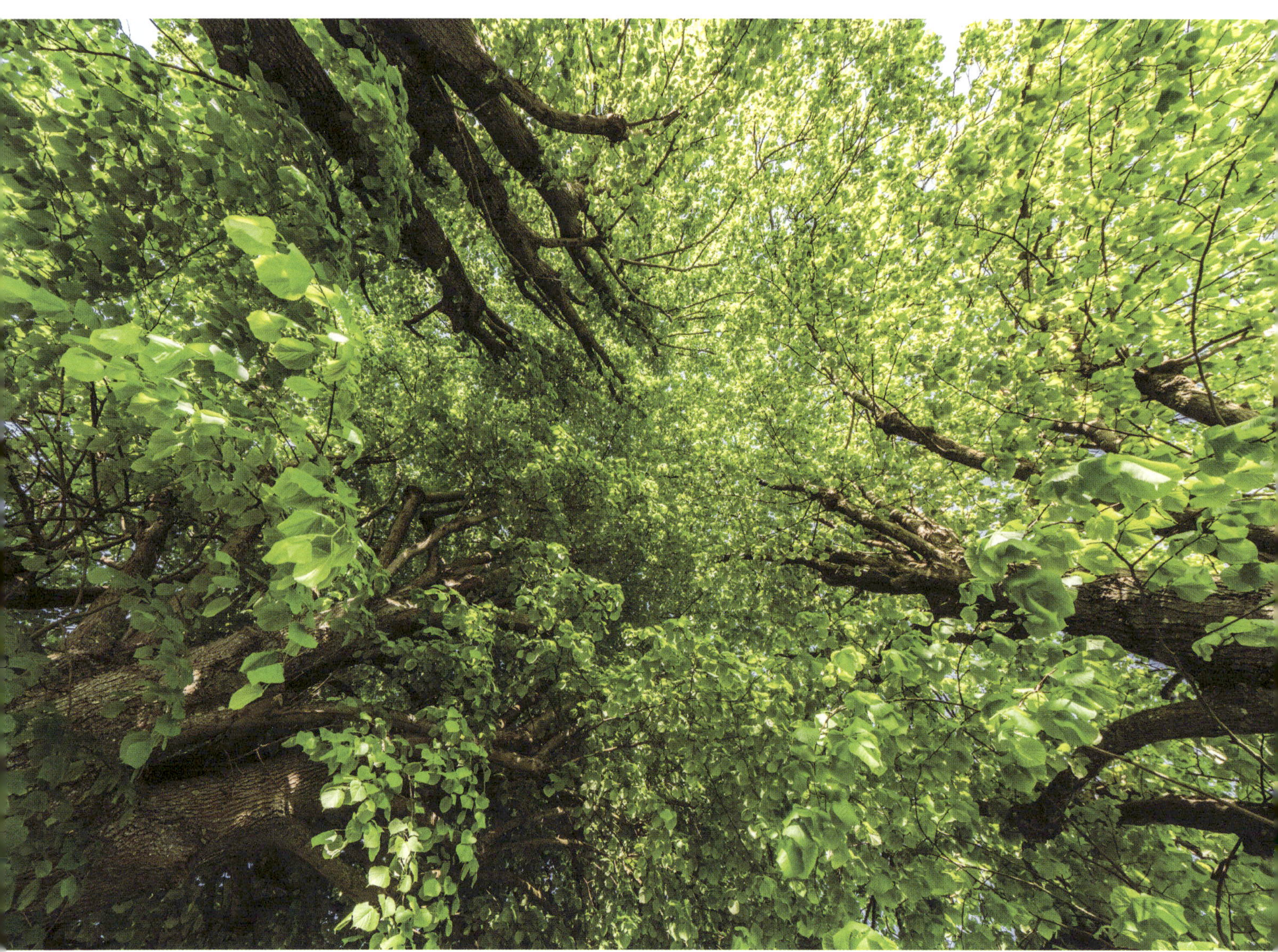

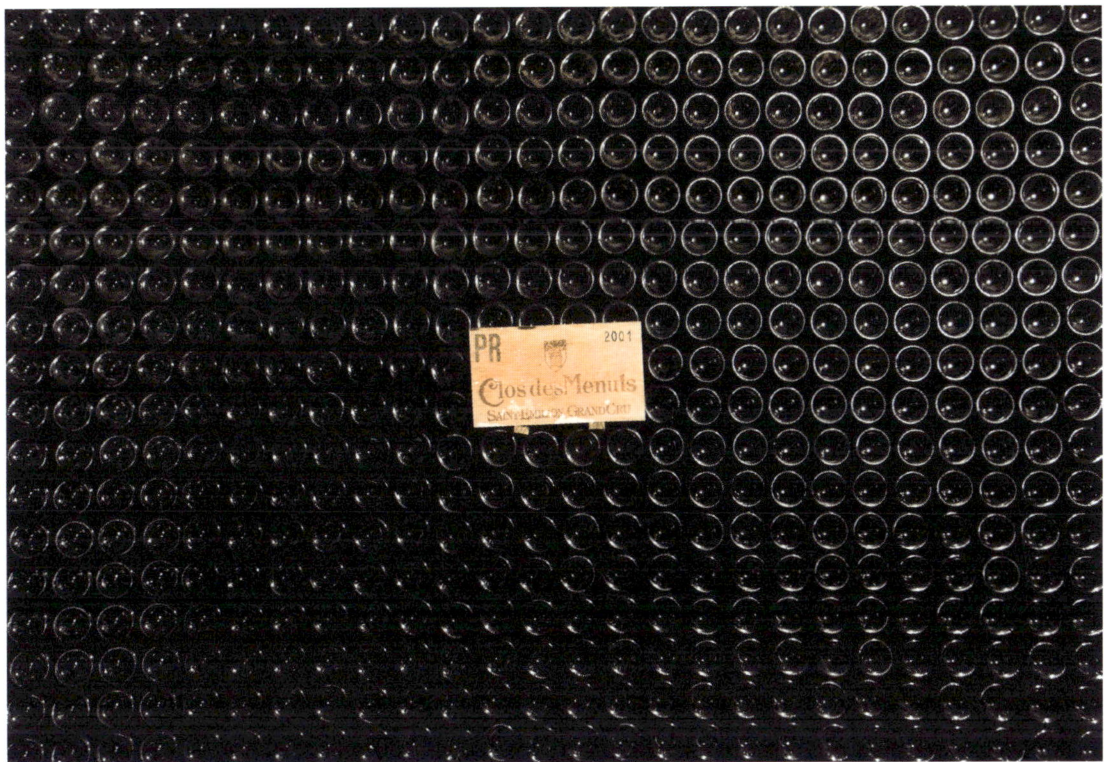

Féricy, France
48°27'34.9"N 2°48'29.7"E
The canopy of a group of three linden trees meets
high above me. There are no other trees around,
so you can see this triangle of trees already from
far away.
// April 2018

Saint-Émilion, France
44°53'41.1"N 0°09'17.8"W
Hundreds of wine bottles are stacked in a wine
cellar in Saint-Émilion, an important wine region
which history goes all the way back to the Roman
era. Wine is still the main attraction here, with
grapes even growing as weed between the setts.
// April 2012

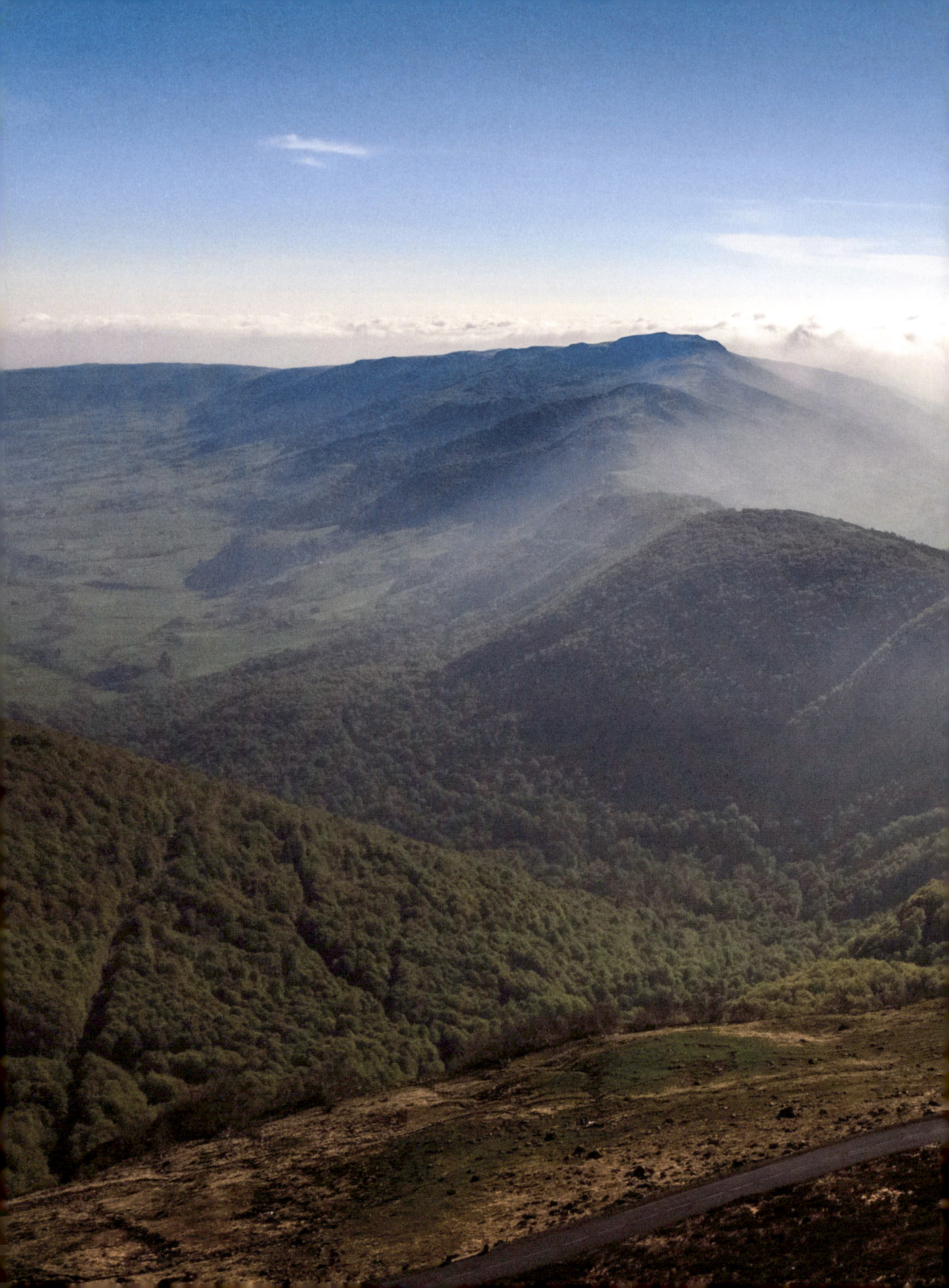

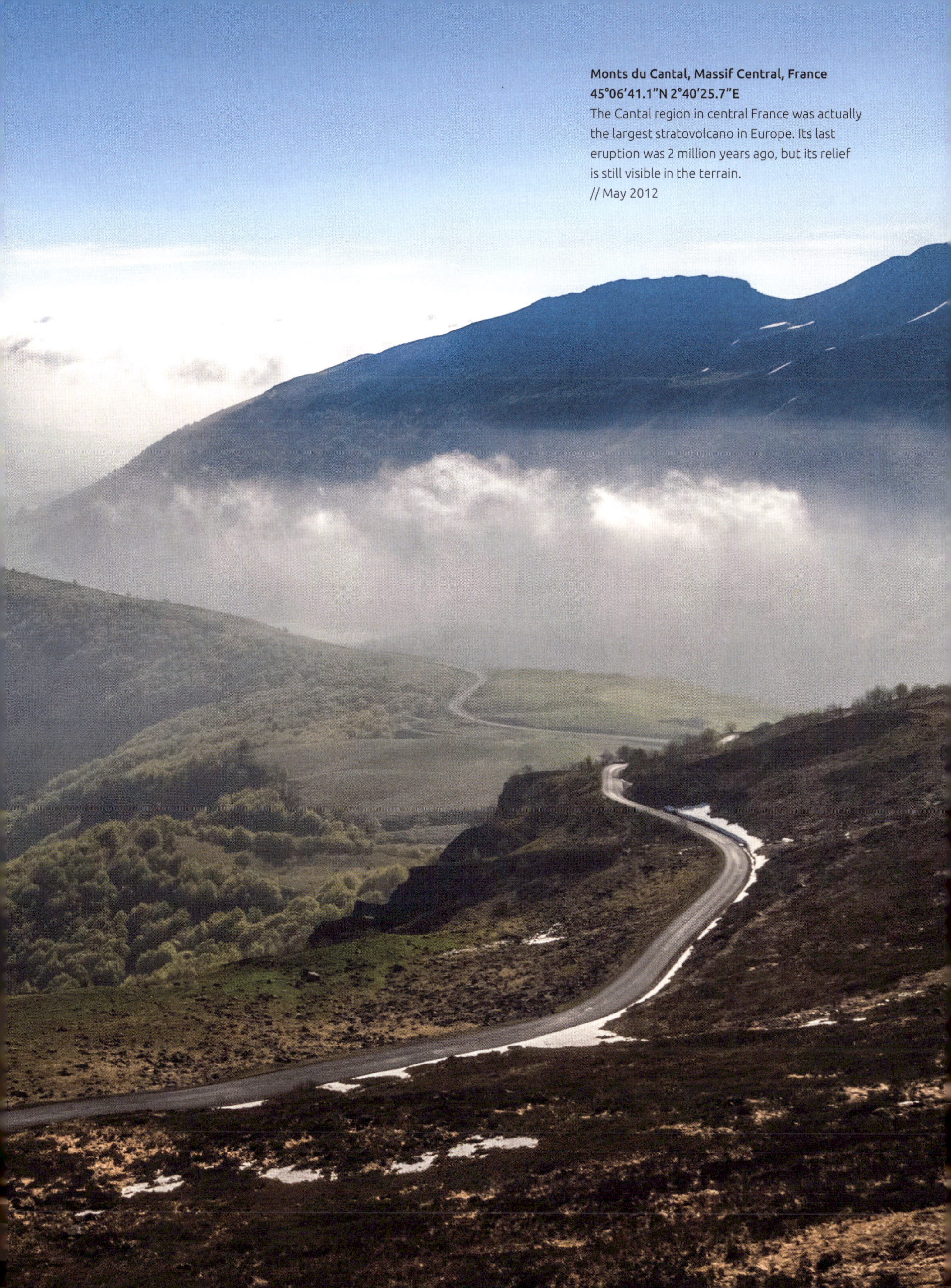

Monts du Cantal, Massif Central, France
45°06'41.1"N 2°40'25.7"E
The Cantal region in central France was actually
the largest stratovolcano in Europe. Its last
eruption was 2 million years ago, but its relief
is still visible in the terrain.
// May 2012

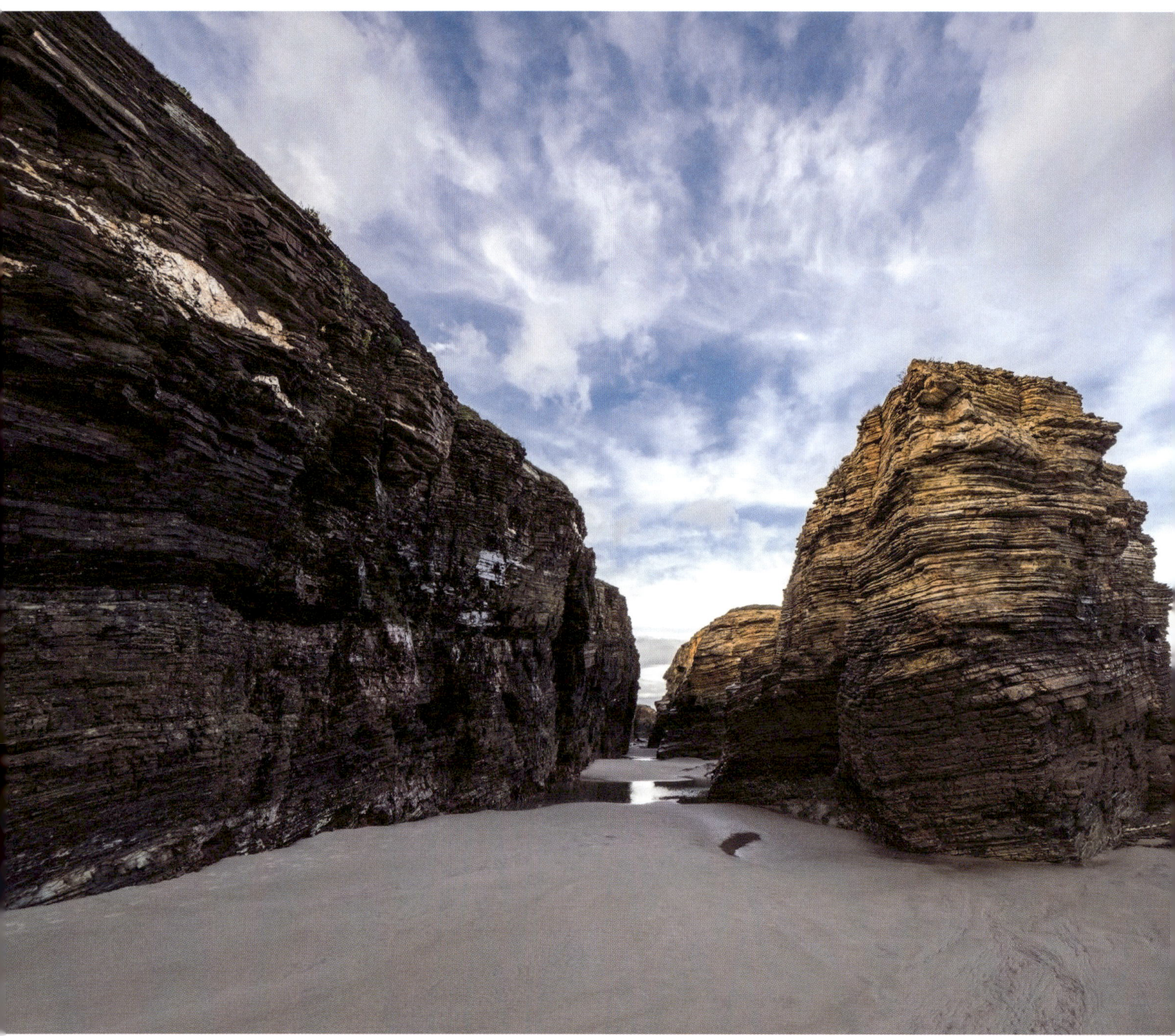

Praia de Augas Santas, Spain
43°33'14.6"N 7°09'26.5"W
Beautiful rock formations can be found in various
places in Europe, but in particular on Praia de
Augas Santas (also known as Cathedral Beach)
along the spectacular shoreline of Galicia.
// January 2018

Dune du Pilat, Arcachon, France
44°35'30.1"N 1°12'36.4"W
You may think this is the Sahara, but located in
France is the tallest sand dune in Europe. Dune
du Pilat measures roughly 500 by 2,700 metres
and has an altitude of around 110 metres.
Best visited early in the morning, before the
crowds arrive.
// May 2012

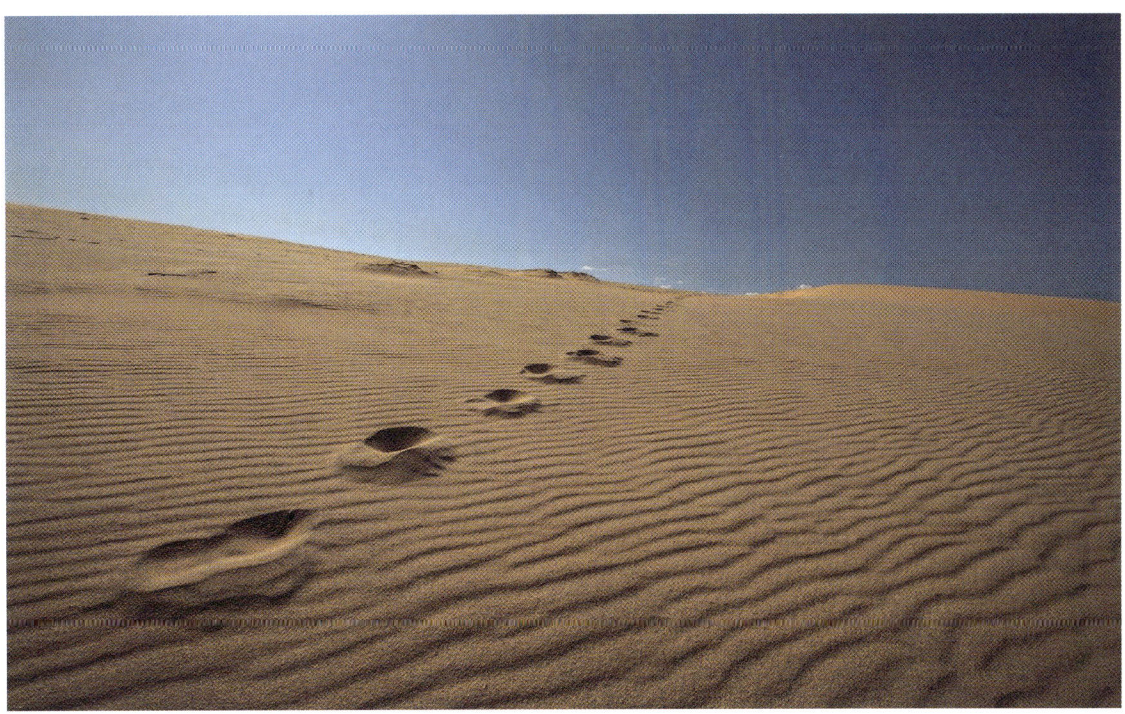

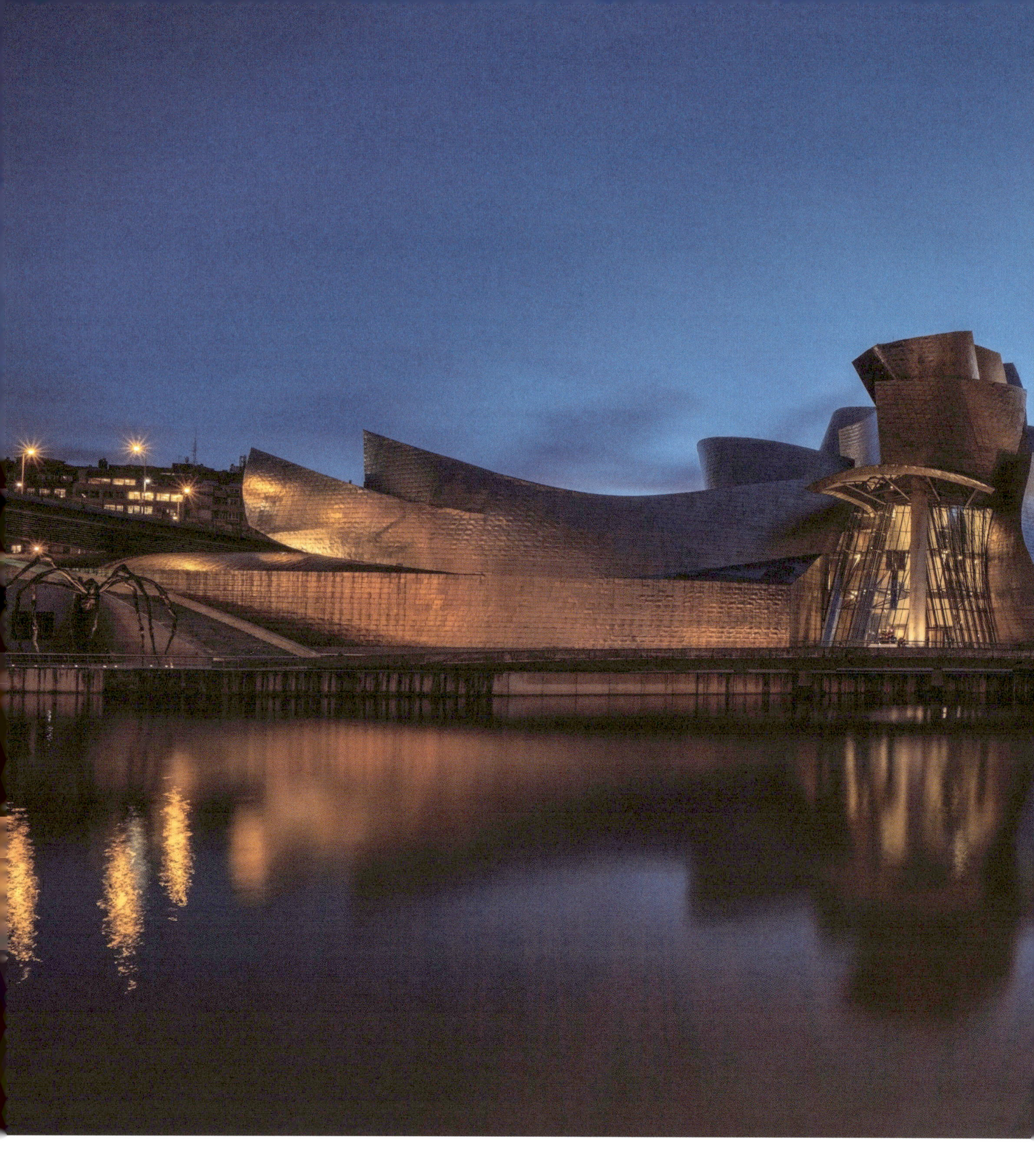

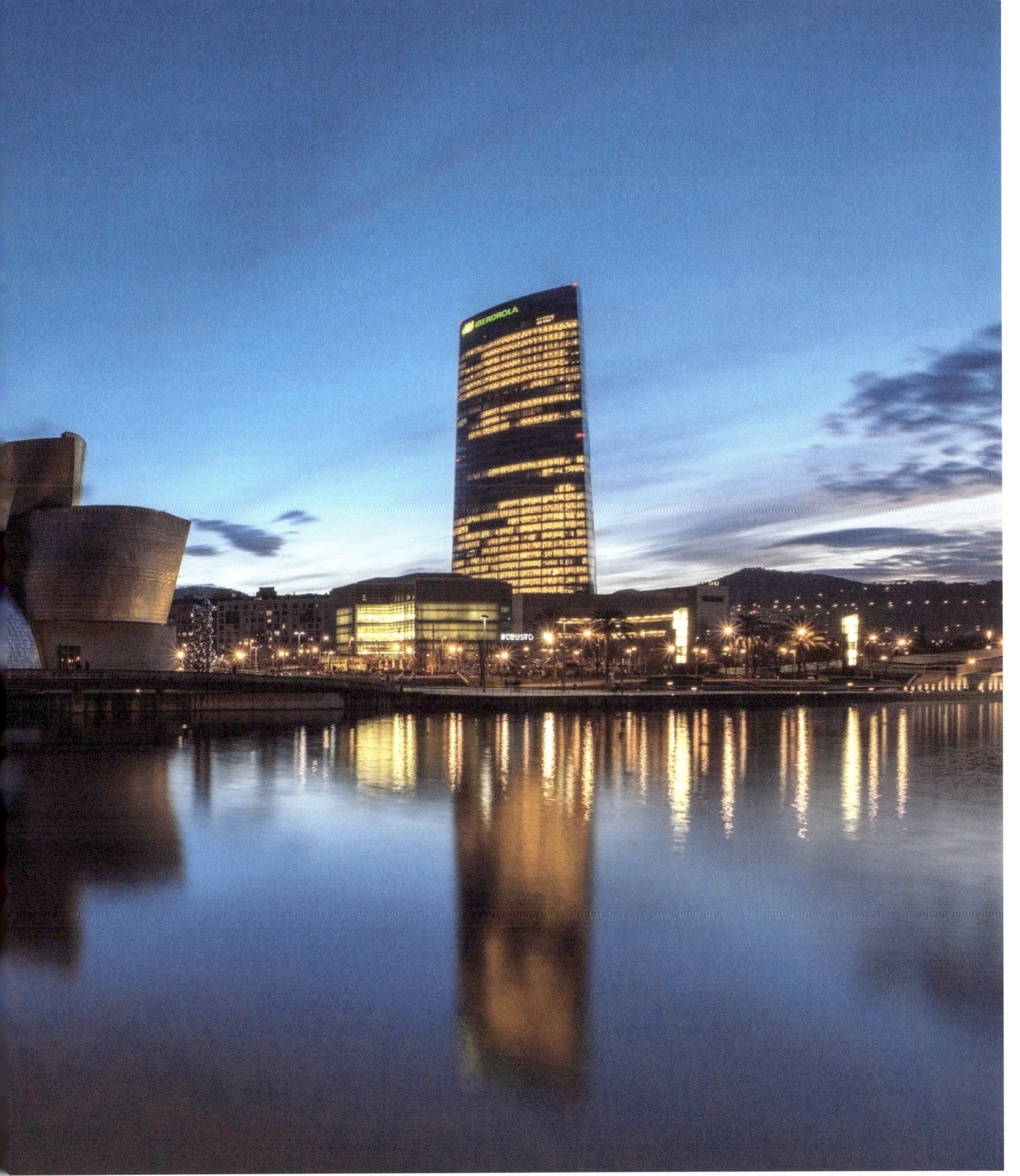

Bilbao, Spain
43°16'12.0"N 2°56'01.4"W
The unusual flowing shapes of Bilbao's
Guggenheim Museum give this modern city
in Basque Country a futuristic look and feel.
// January 2018

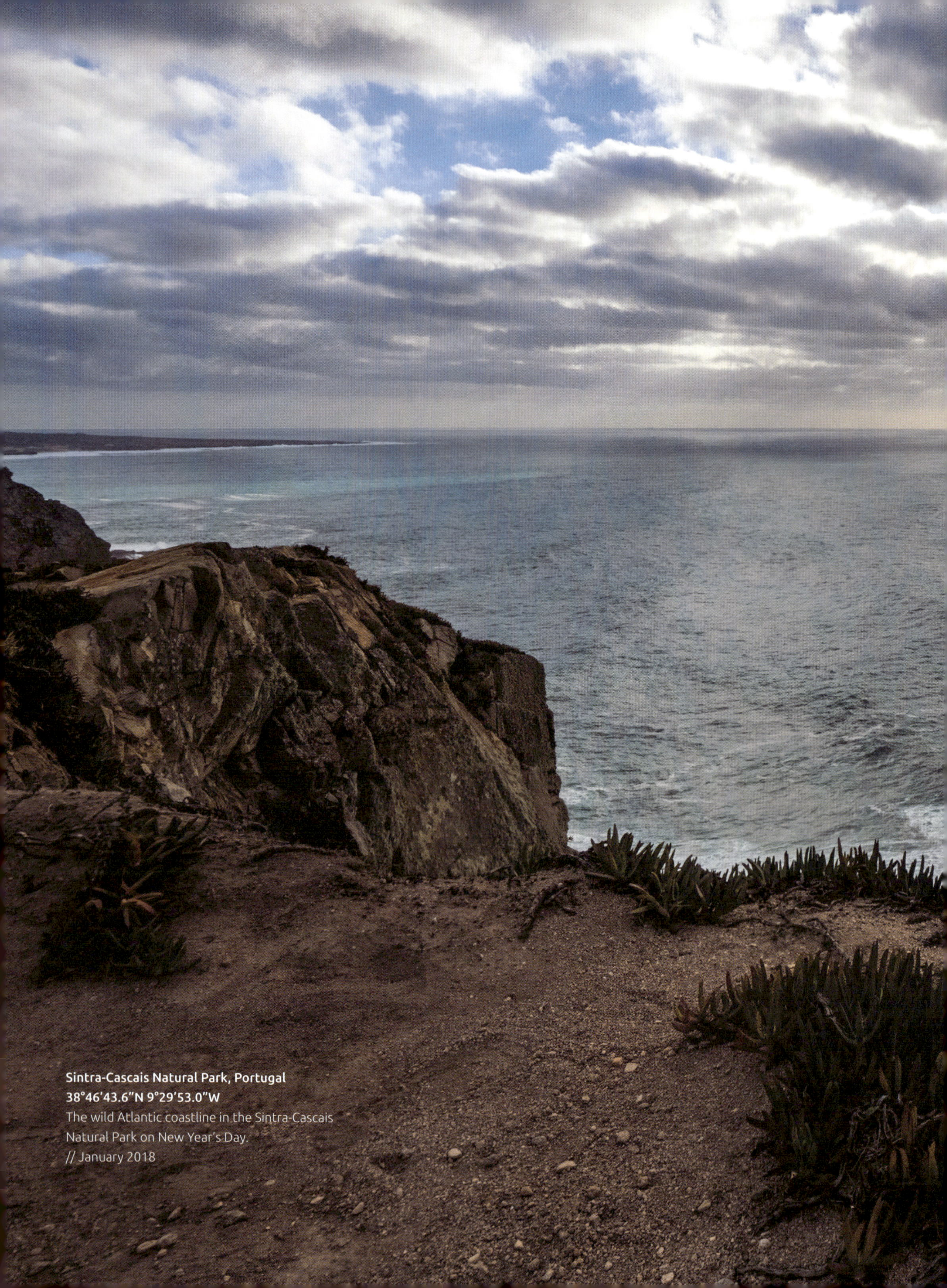

Sintra-Cascais Natural Park, Portugal
38°46'43.6"N 9°29'53.0"W
The wild Atlantic coastline in the Sintra-Cascais
Natural Park on New Year's Day.
// January 2018

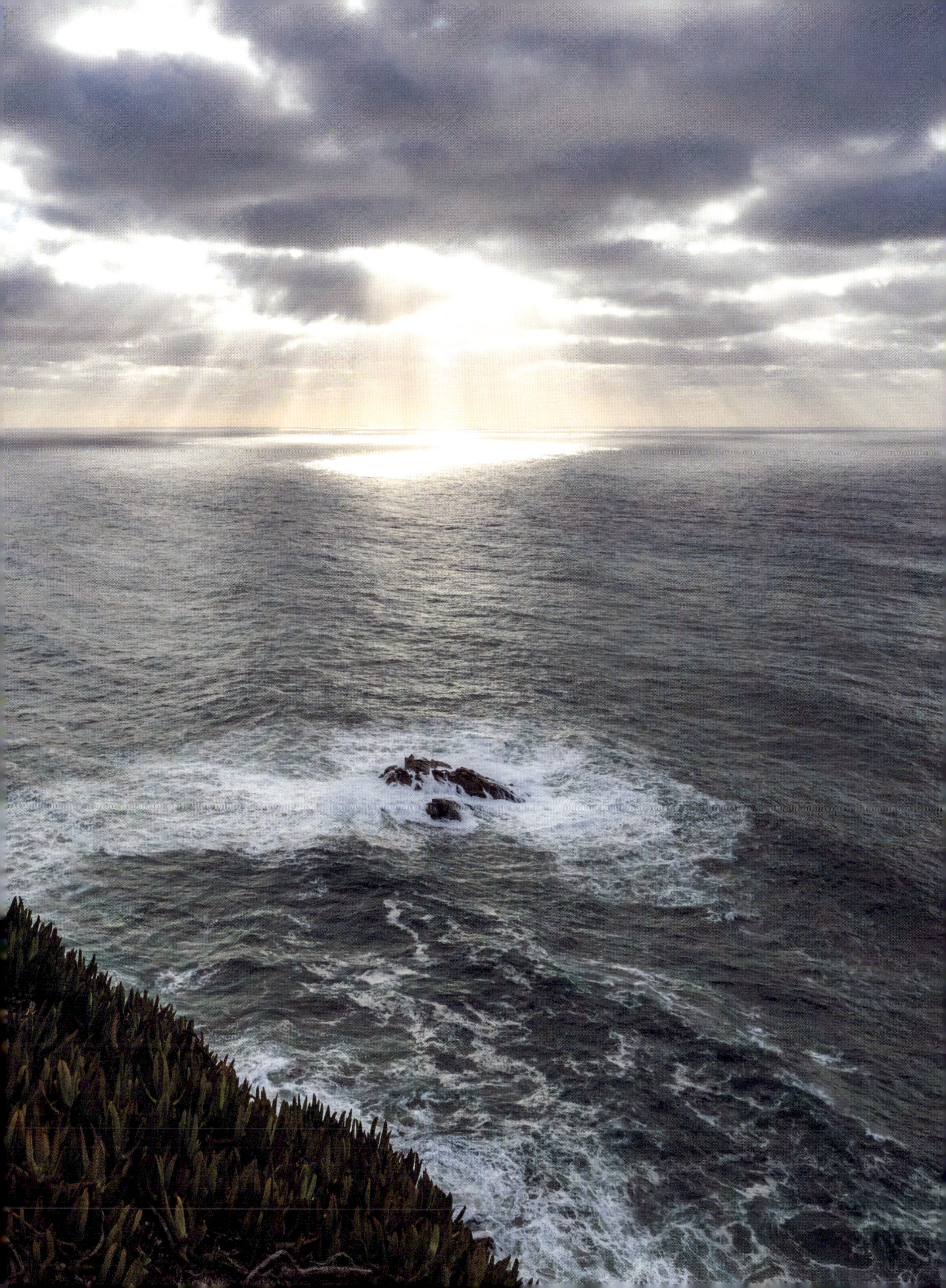

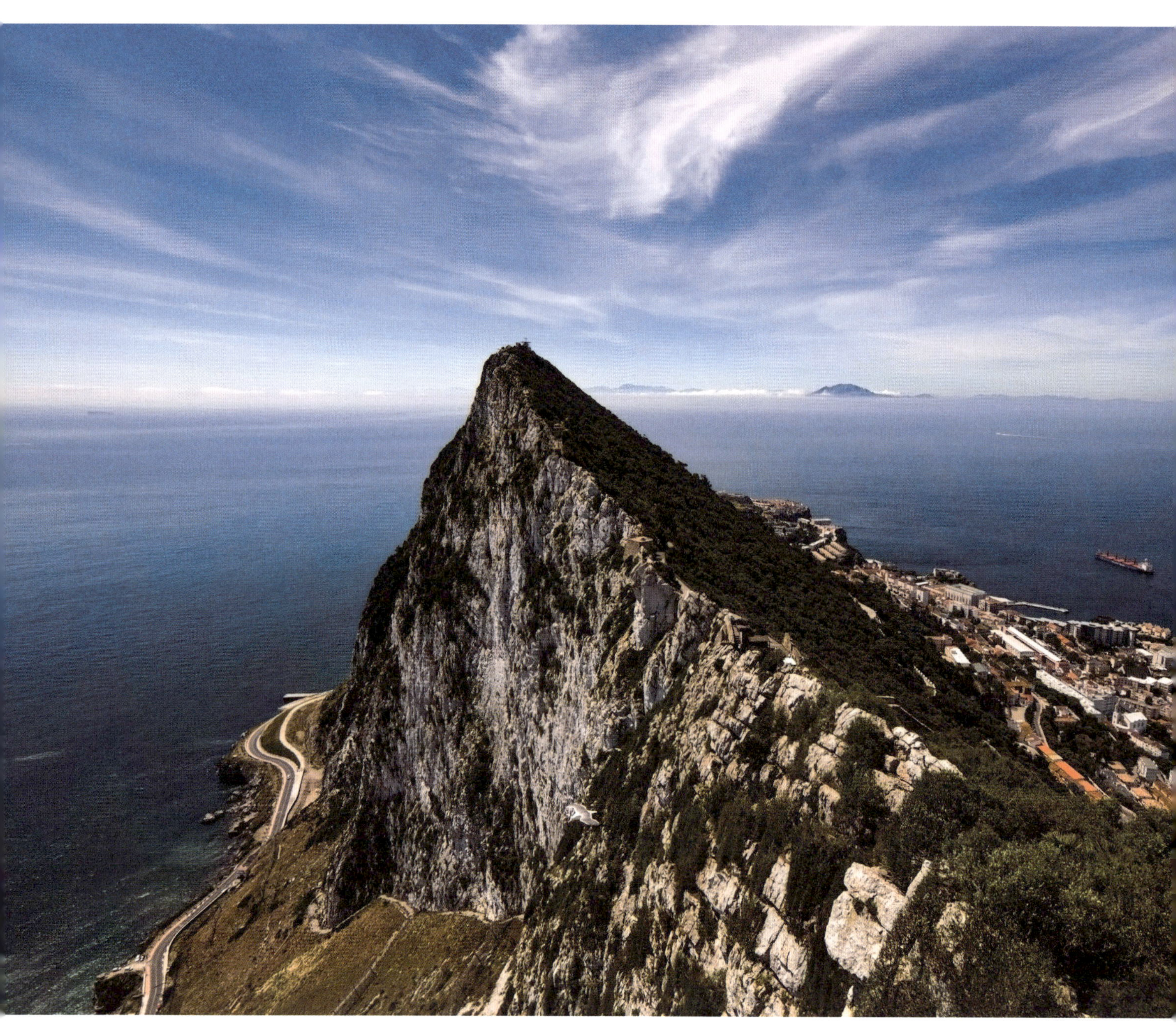

Gibraltar
36°07'55.2"N 5°20'44.5"W
The Rock of Gibraltar is a weird mixture of
Mediterranean climate and British culture.
Touristic but definitely intriguing.
// May 2012

Ardales, Spain
36°52'42.3"N 4°50'51.9"W
Ardales is a small town near Málaga in the
picturesque region of Andalusia. It is an ideal place
to stay for visiting the Caminito del Rey walkway.
// December 2017

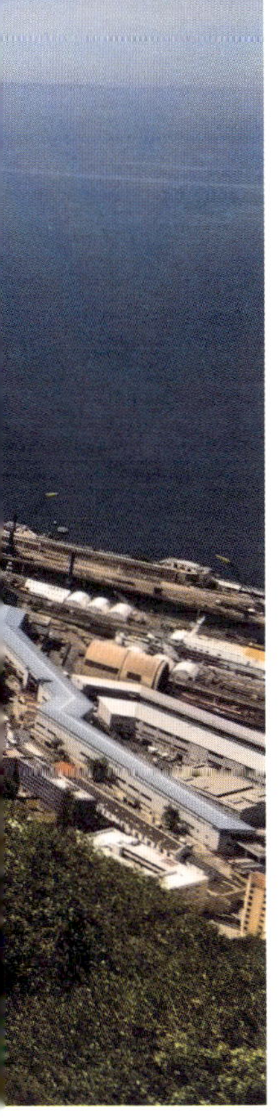

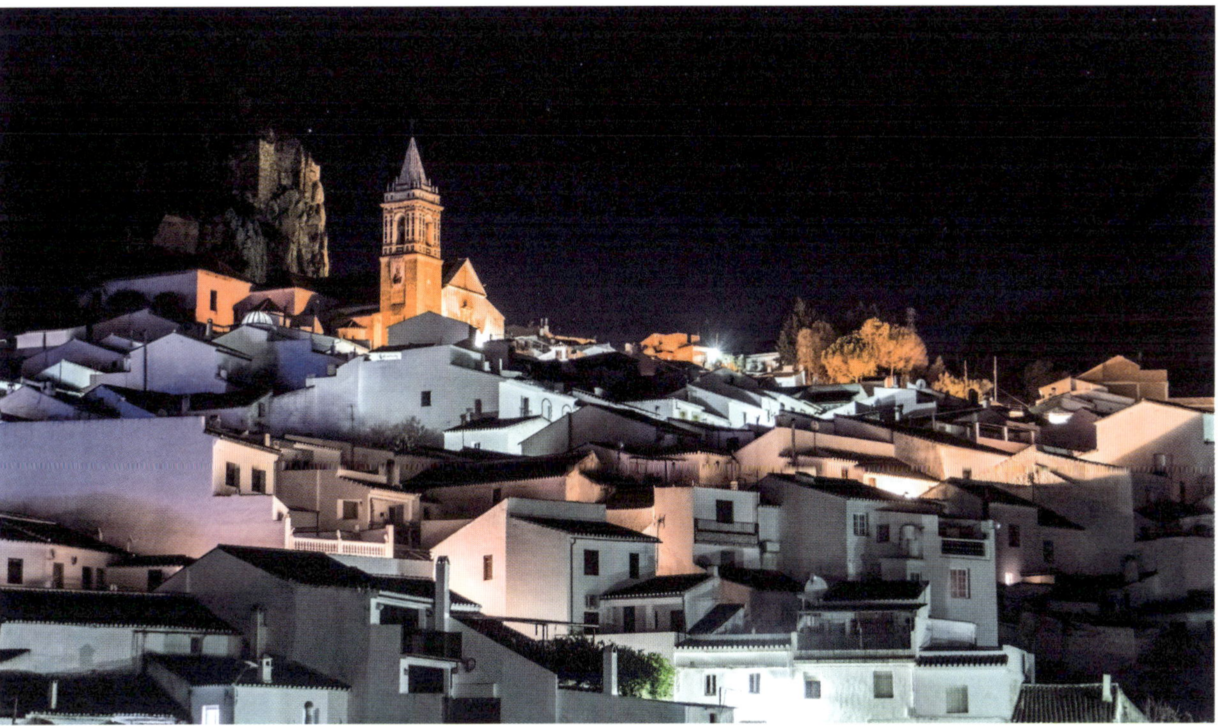

194

Ardales, Spain
36°54′58.4″N 4°46′25.2″W
These peaks form an impressive decor along
El Caminito del Rey, a famous hiking path through
the El Chorro gorge in Andalusia.
// December 2017

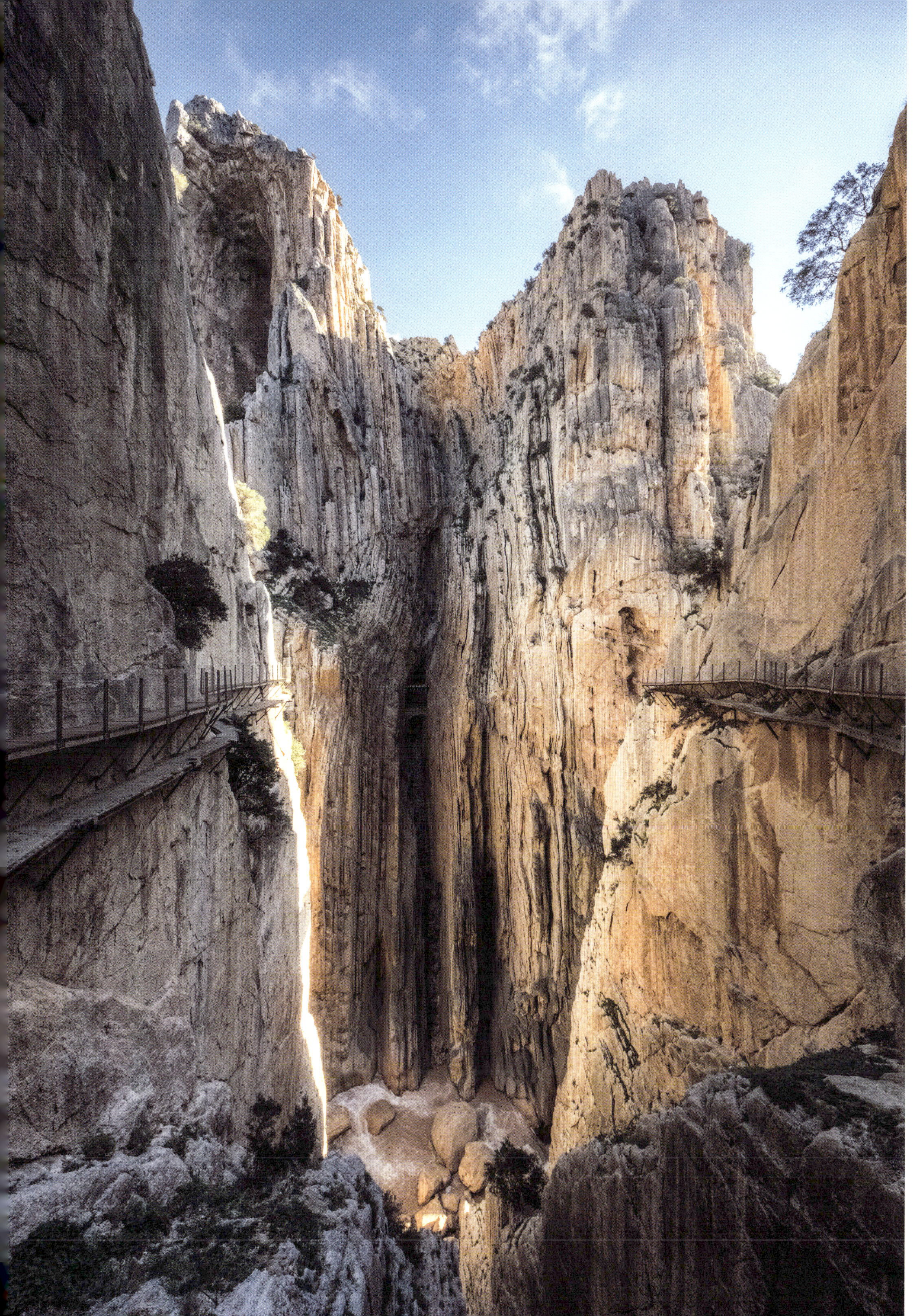

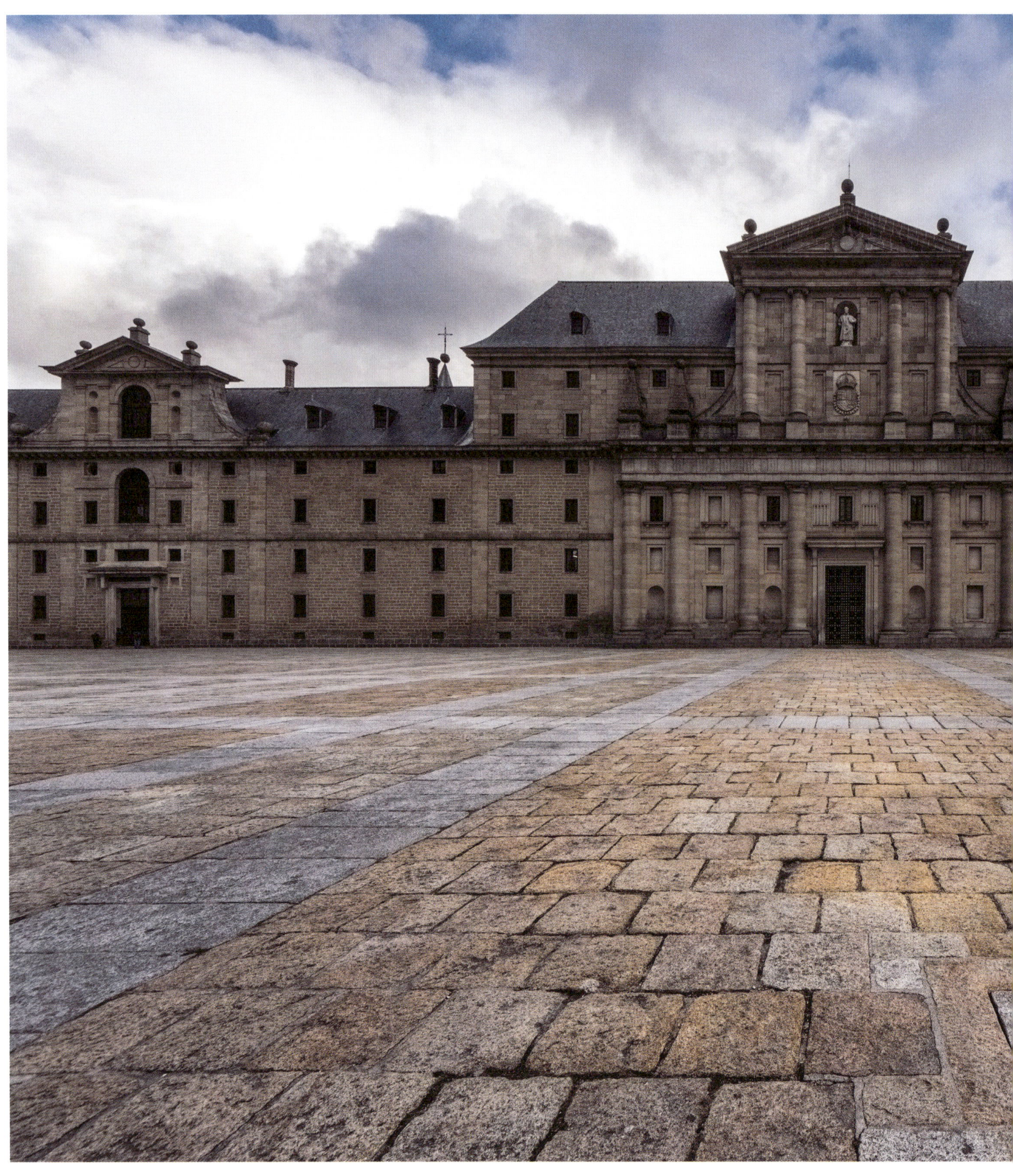

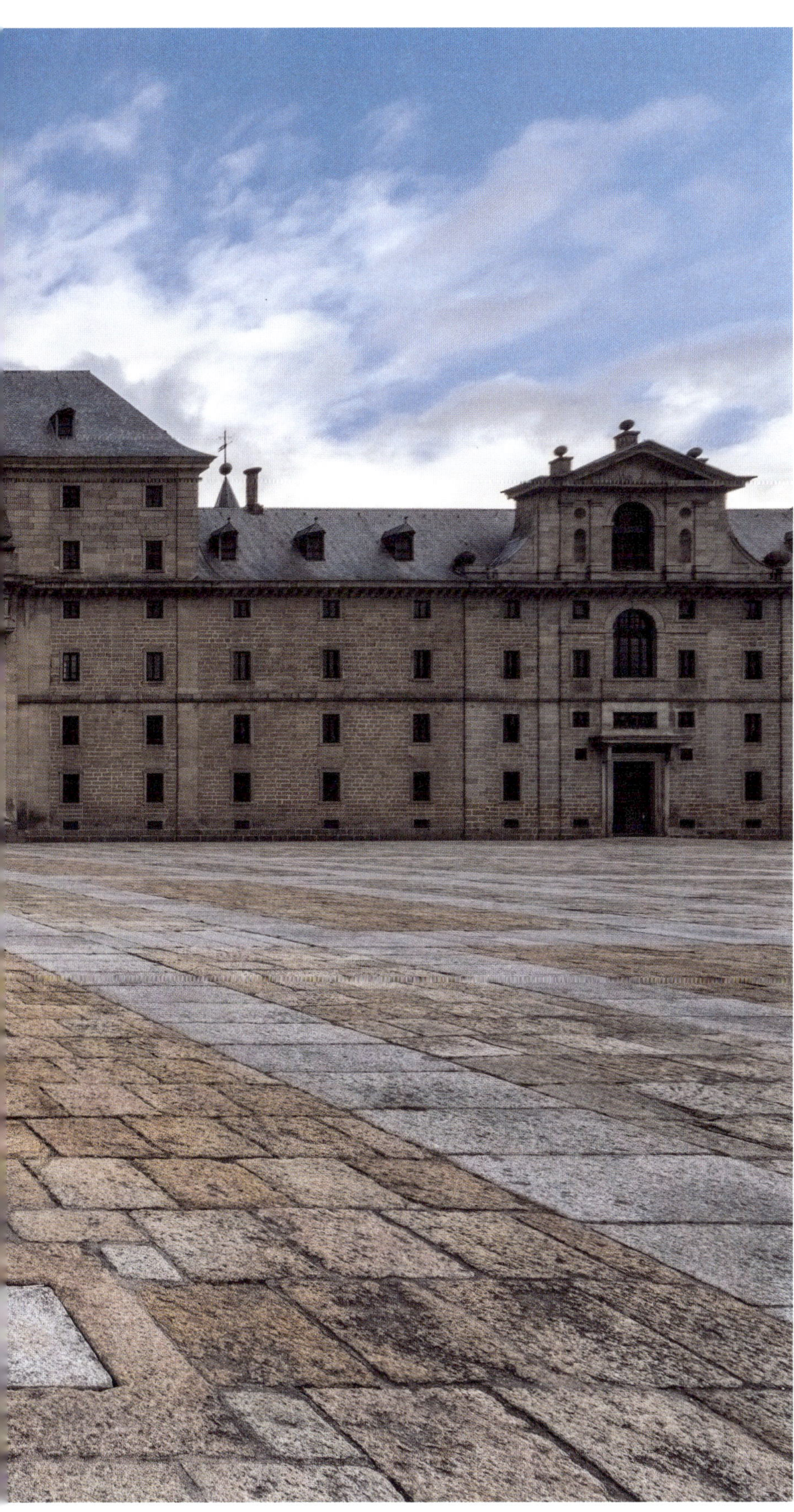

San Lorenzo de El Escorial, Spain
40°35'21.6"N 4°08'58.2"W
The Royal Site of San Lorenzo de El Escorial is
a large, historic residence of the King of Spain.
The building is very impressive. Although it is
a popular destination for visitors to Madrid, it was
deserted when I visited it on a December weekday.
// December 2017

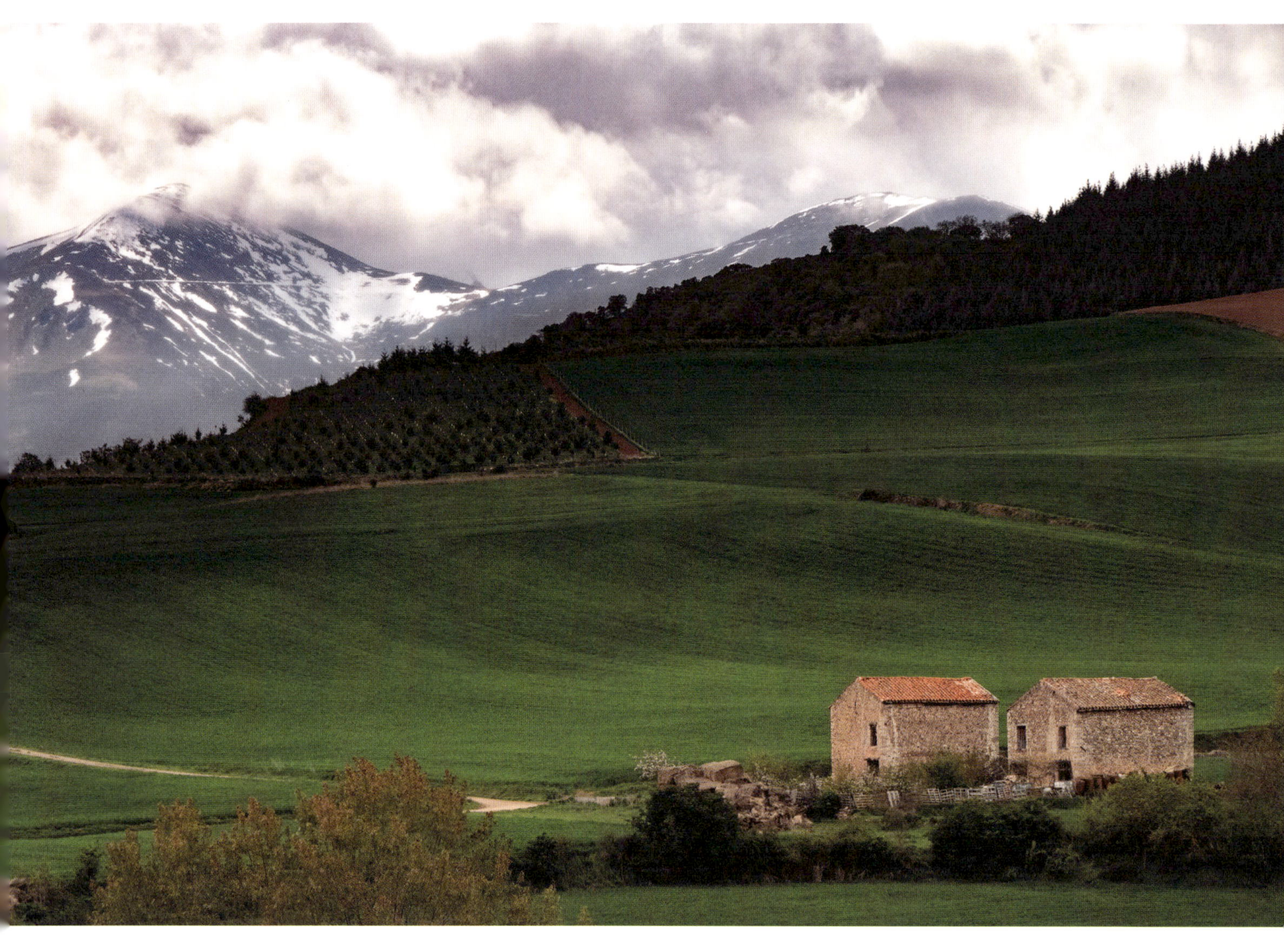

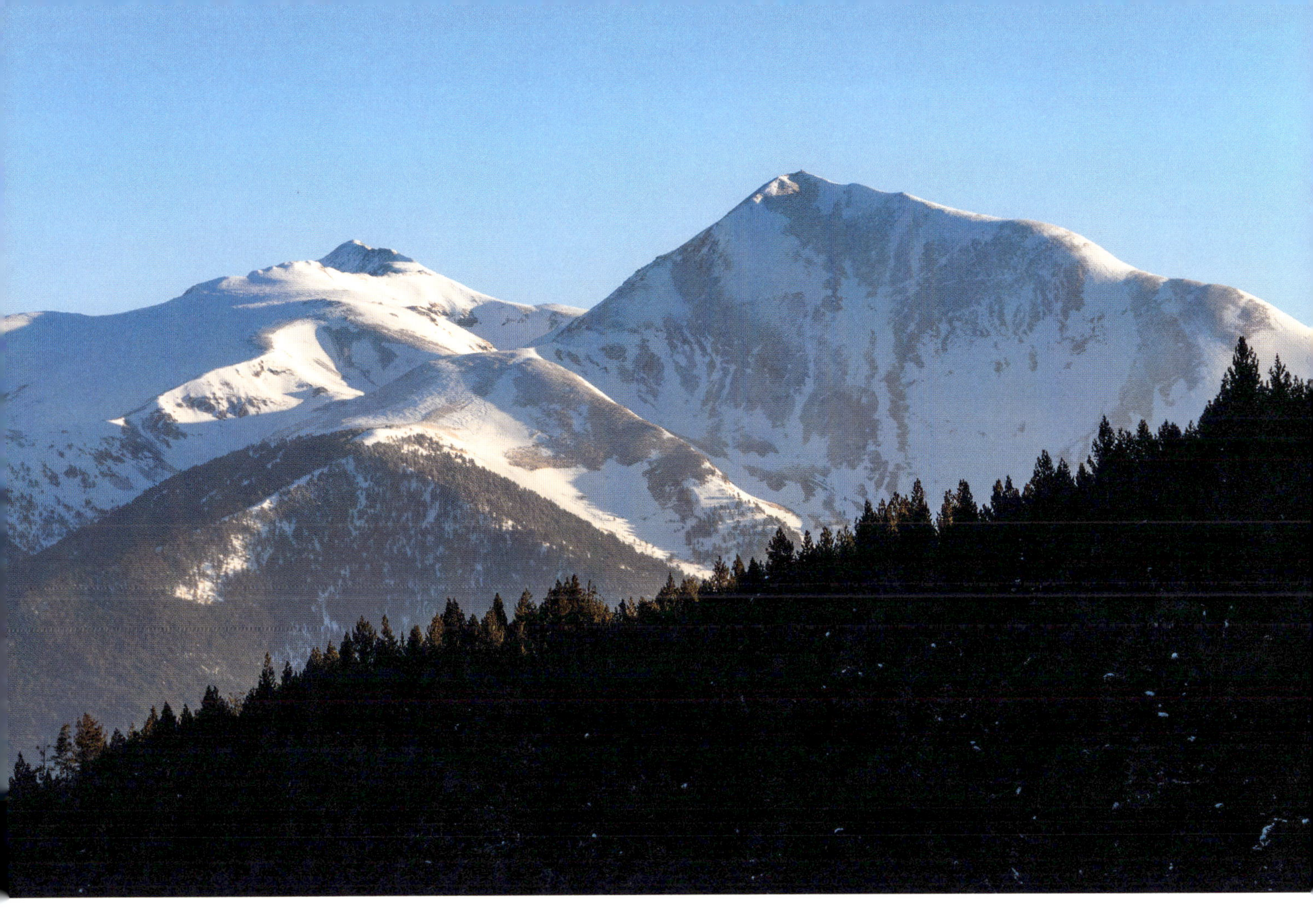

Berceo, Spain
42°20′36.4″N 2°50′55.5″W
La Rioja is famous for its wines, but it also offers many scenic views and, surprisingly, even a ski resort.
// May 2012

Grandvalira, Andorra
42°31′40.4″N 1°40′13.0″E
The majestic peaks of the Grandvalira.
// February 2015

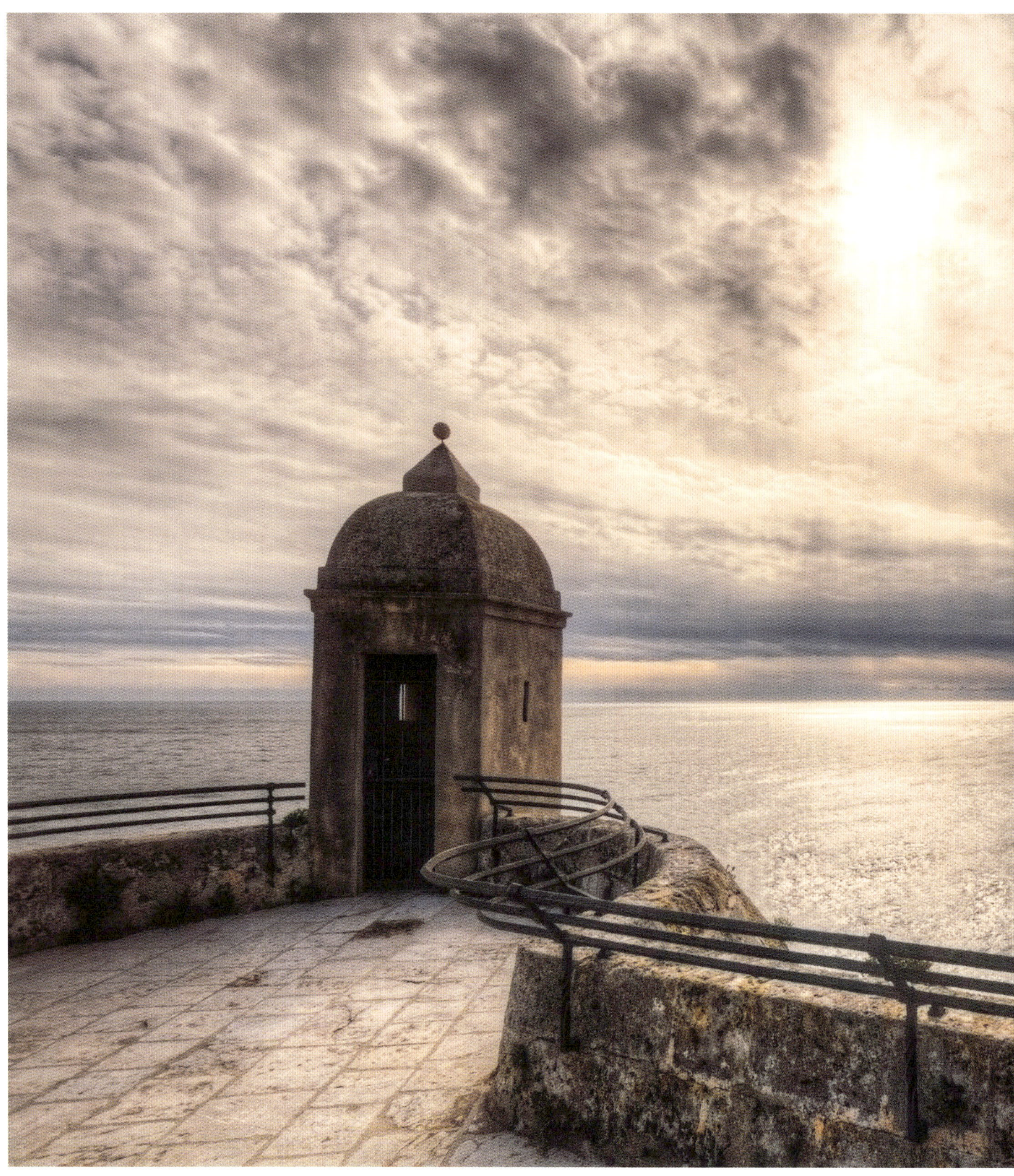

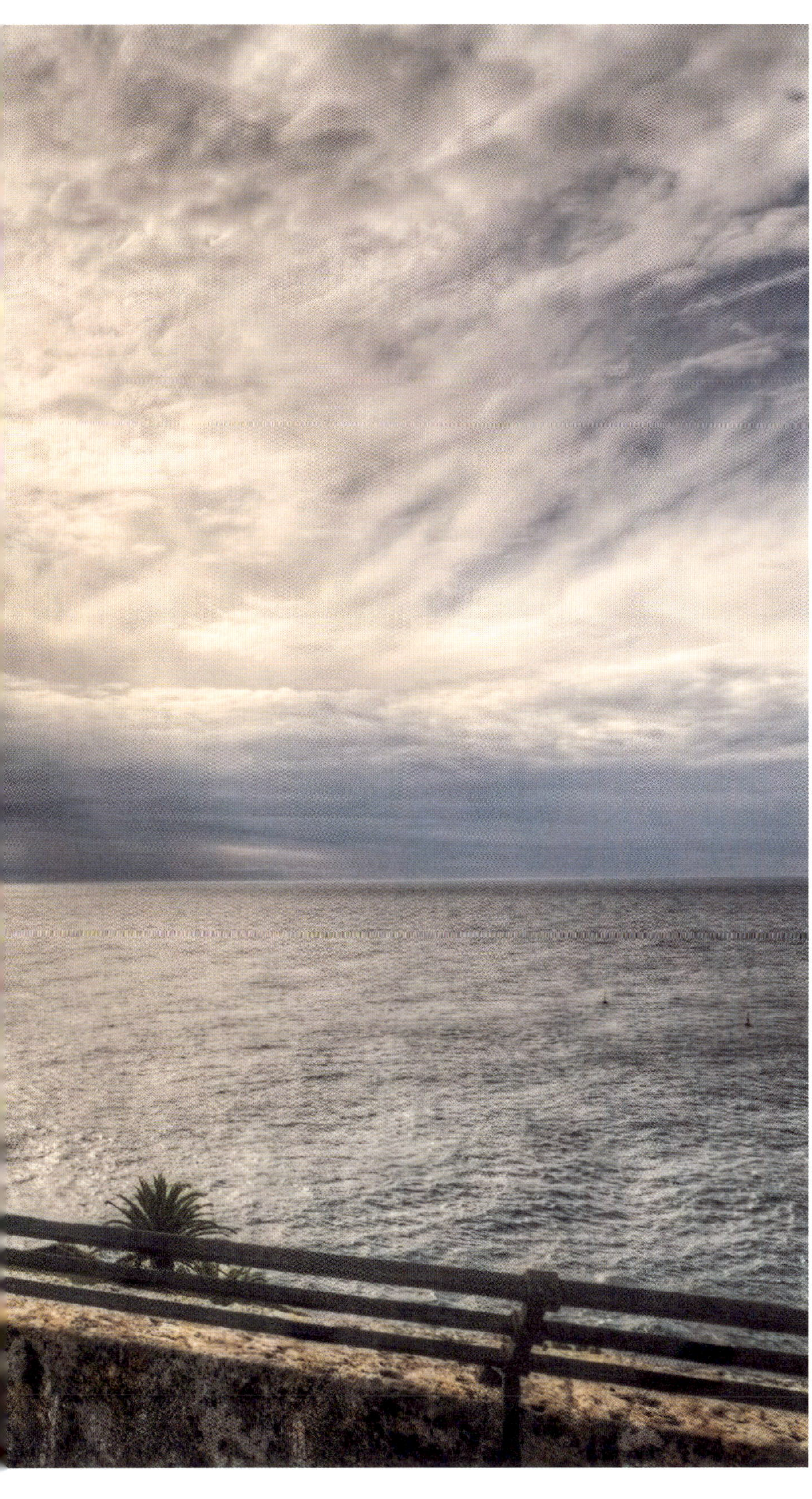

Monaco
43°43′52.6″N 7°25′34.8″E
An almost surreal blanket of clouds fills
the winter sky in Monaco.
// February 2015

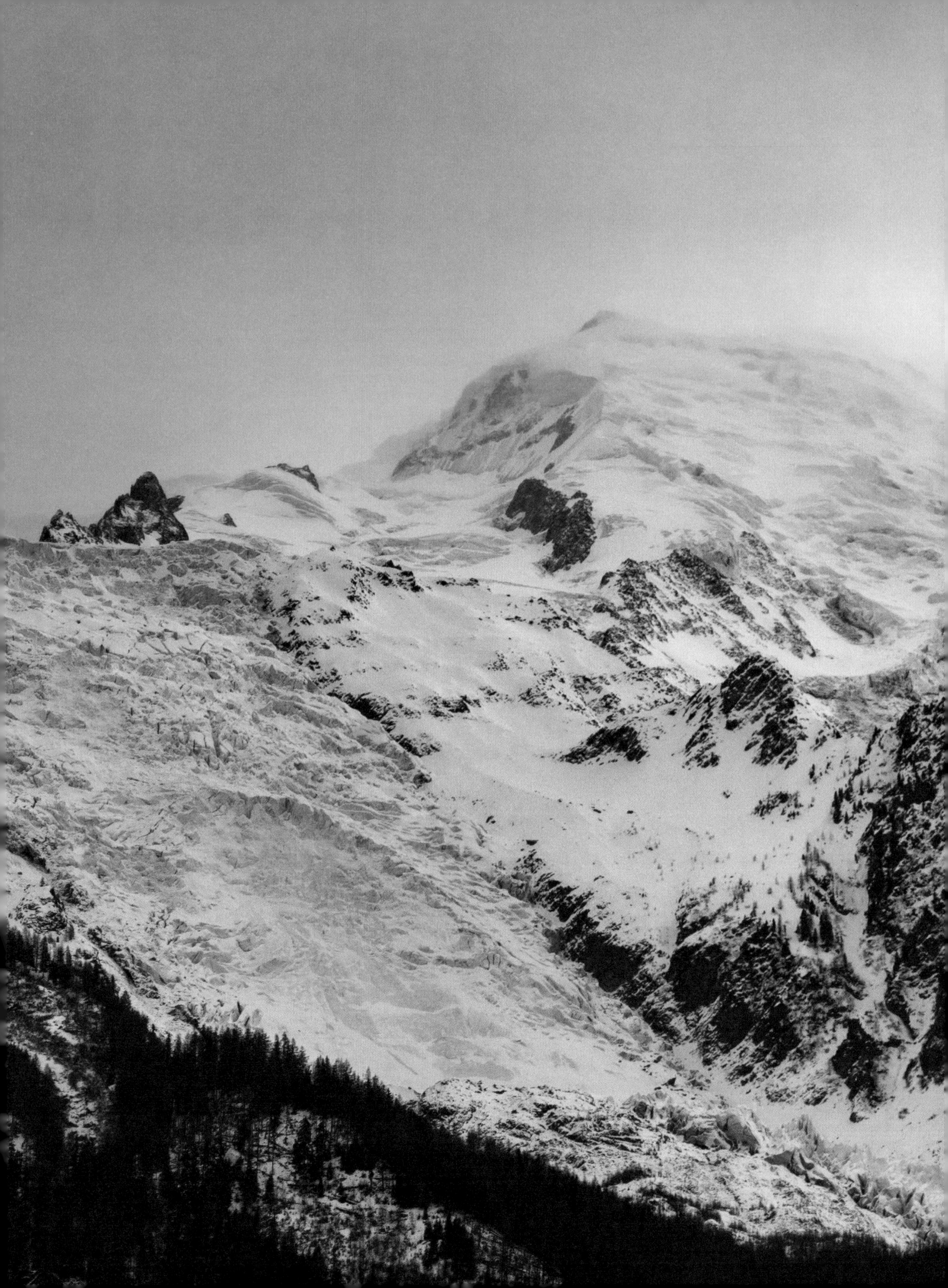

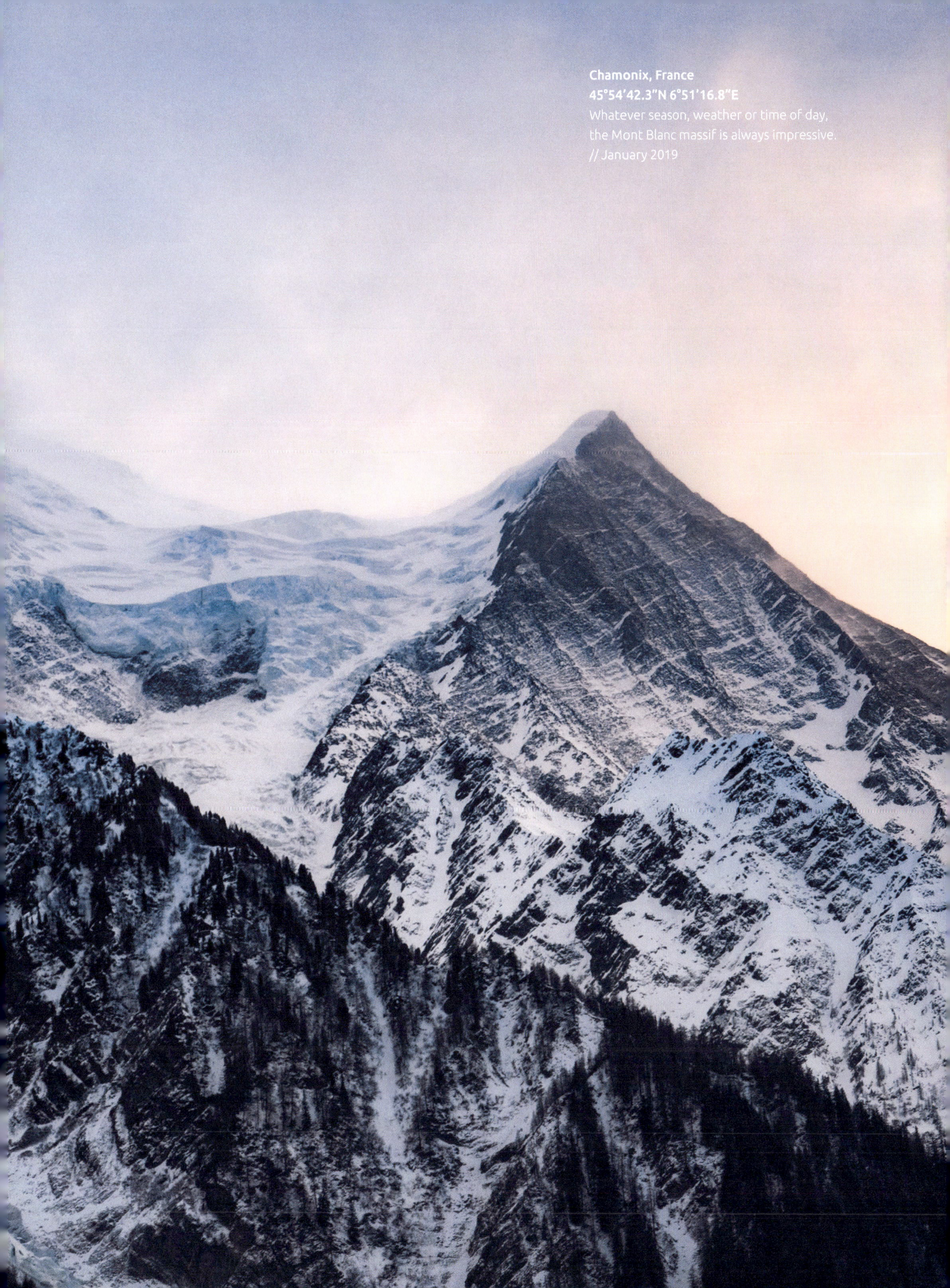
Chamonix, France
45°54'42.3"N 6°51'16.8"E
Whatever season, weather or time of day,
the Mont Blanc massif is always impressive.
// January 2019

Exploring the Southwest
Route and travel suggestions

Scenic regions and nature reserves

Cities and towns

Cultural experiences

Spectacular roads and scenic routes

○ Photo location

● Travel suggestion

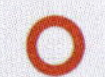 Photo page number

 Travel suggestion number

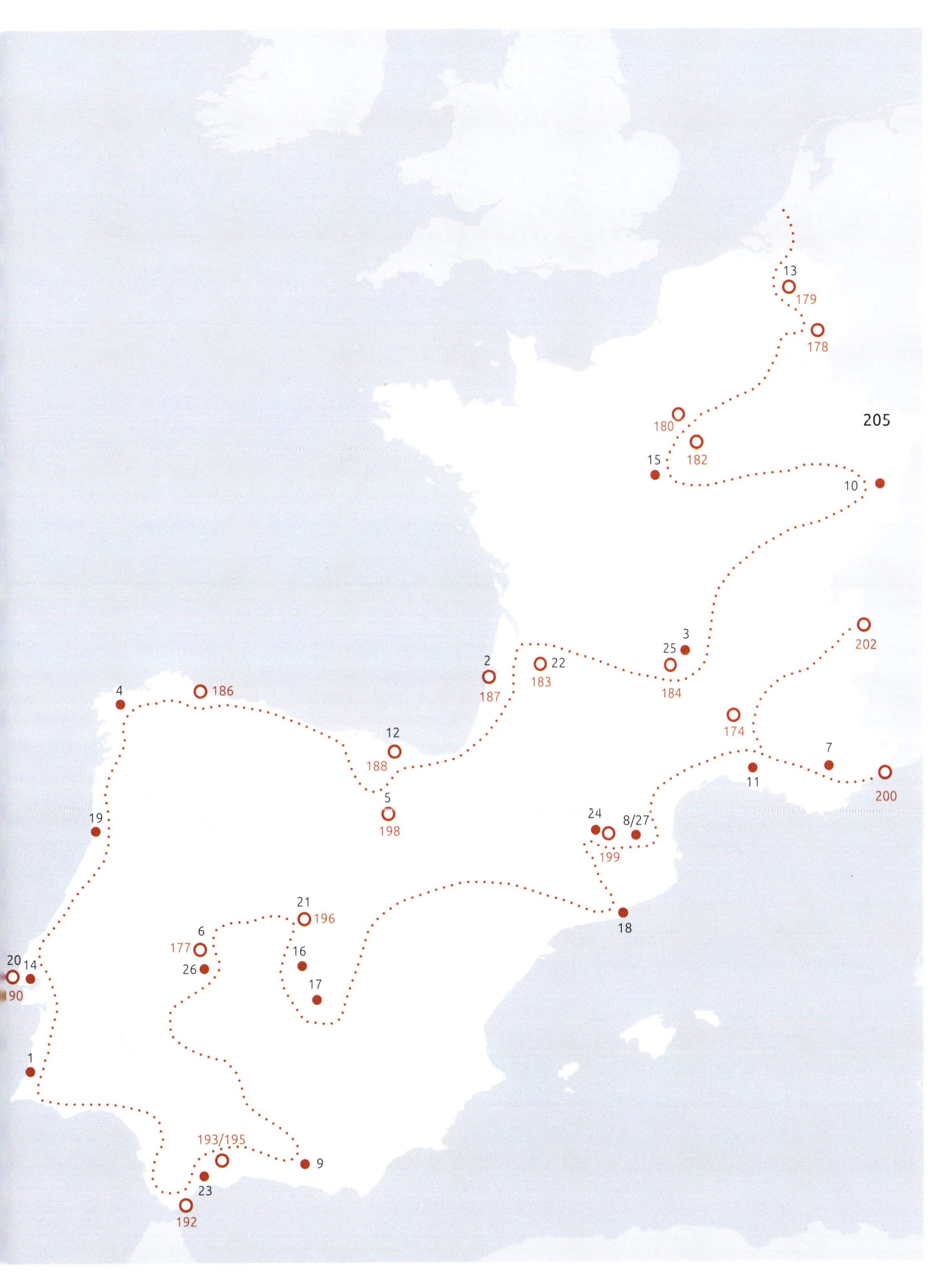

13
179
178
180
15
182
10
3
25
2
22
183
184
202
4
186
174
12
188
7
5
11
198
19
24
8/27
199
200
21
196
6
177
16
26
17
18
20
14
90
1
193/195
9
23
192

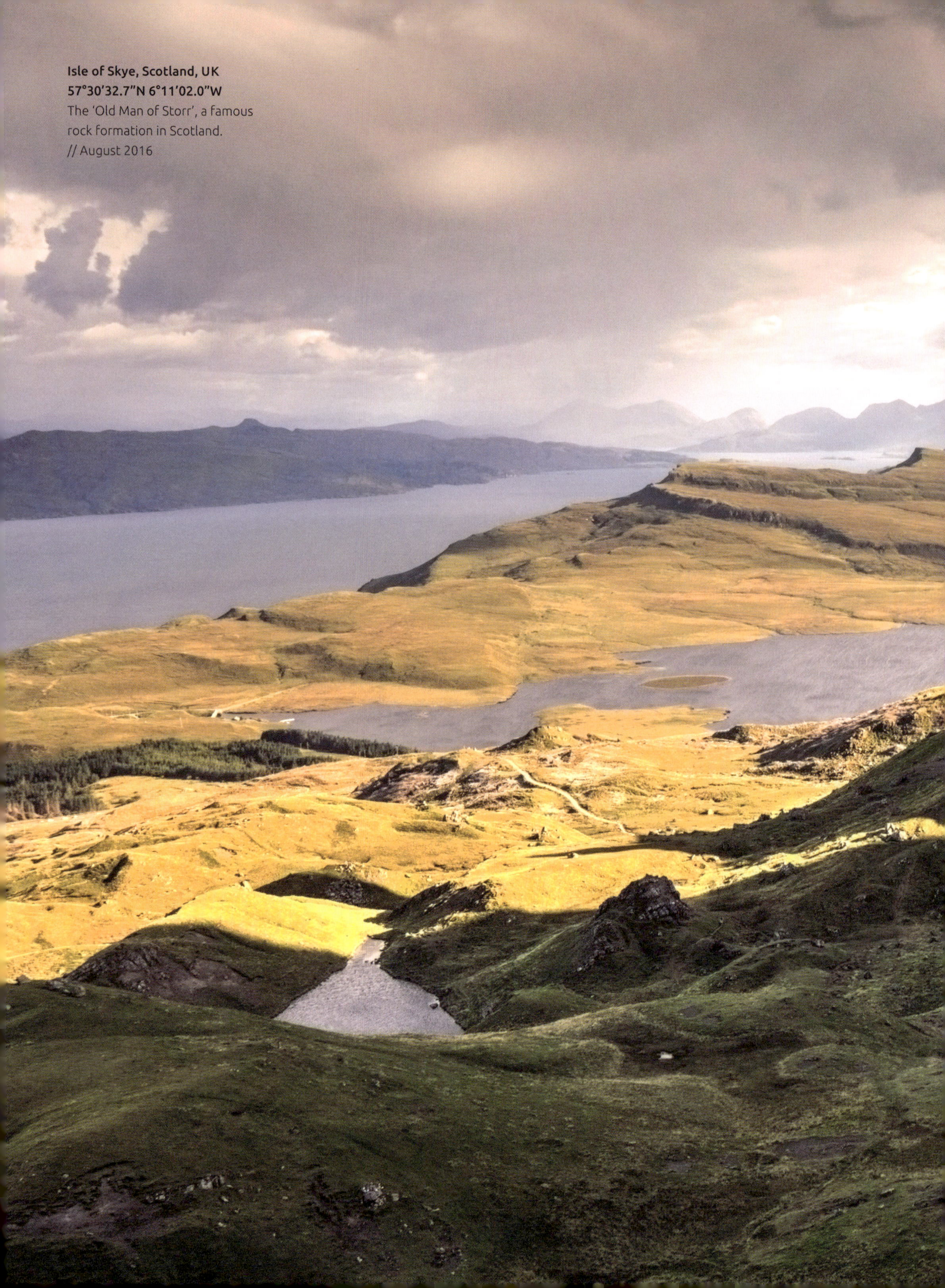

Isle of Skye, Scotland, UK
57°30'32.7"N 6°11'02.0"W
The 'Old Man of Storr', a famous
rock formation in Scotland.
// August 2016

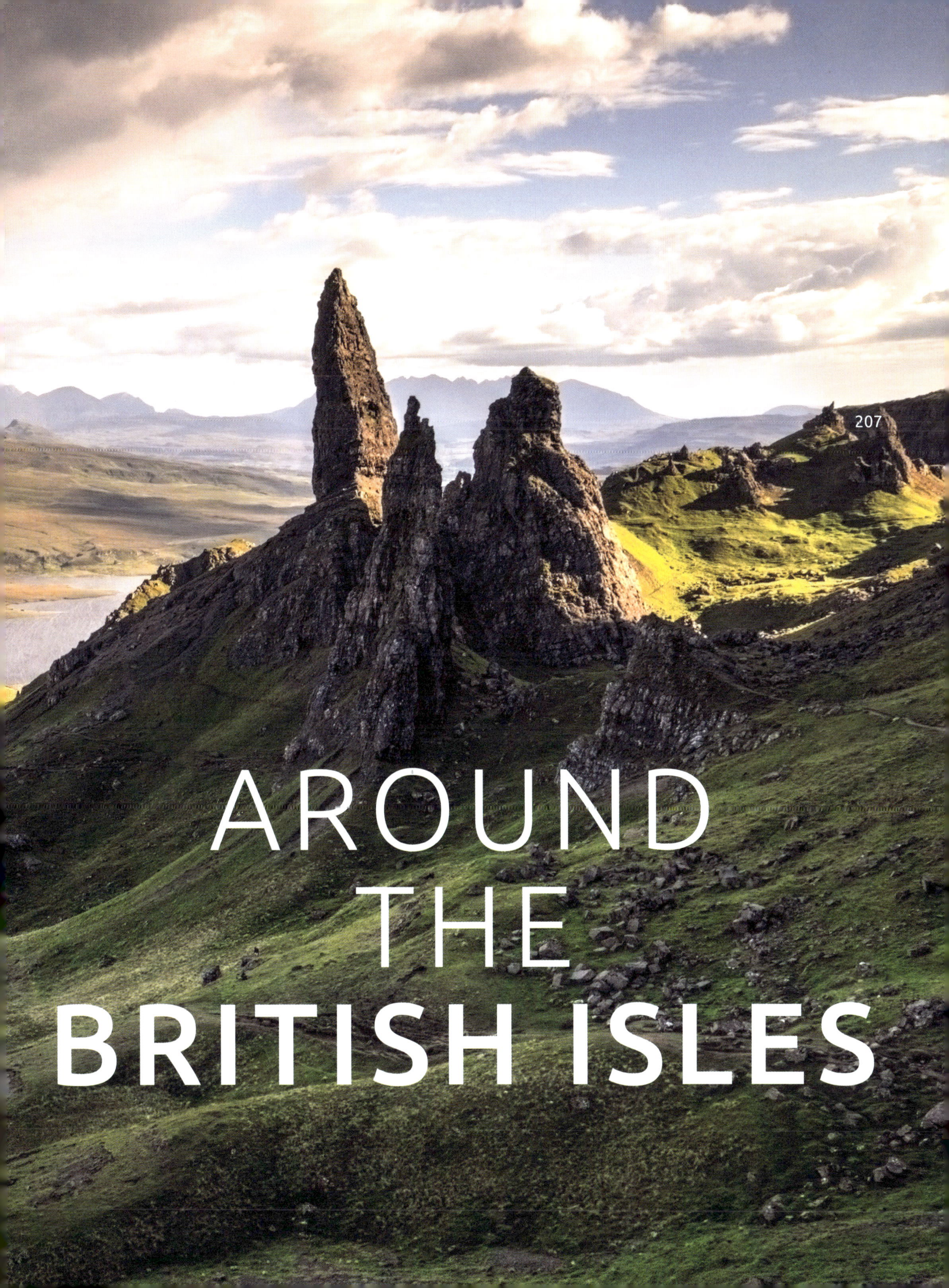

AROUND
THE
BRITISH ISLES

Around the British Isles

A ROAD TRIP around the British Isles guarantees many spectacular coastal view-points, picturesque towns and villages, winding narrow country roads with stone walls on either side, and usually several types of weather in one day. No news so far. But the British Isles do hold a fair number of surprises, too. For example, my favourite scenic route lies hidden in County Mayo in Ireland where you might not expect it. The R335 between Louisburgh in the north via Cregganbaun to Delphi in the south gets more exciting with every turn. After Cregganbaun you will probably want to stop the car every minute to enjoy the view and take yet another picture.

A little further to the south lies Connemara National Park, which offers panoramic hikes through mainly heathland and bogs.

Another surprise is Skomer, an island just off the coast of Wales, part of Pembrokeshire Coast National Park. It is home to a large colony of puffins and many other seabirds. This place is a true bird lover's paradise each spring. Seeing thousands of puffins hopping around with sand eel in their beaks is a wonderful spectacle that will stay in your memory forever.

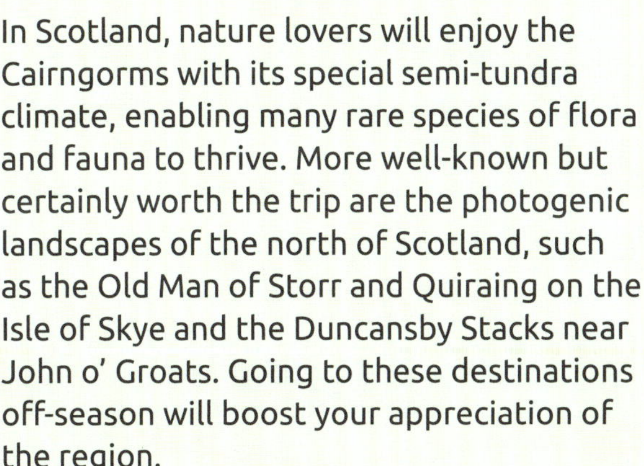

In Scotland, nature lovers will enjoy the Cairngorms with its special semi-tundra climate, enabling many rare species of flora and fauna to thrive. More well-known but certainly worth the trip are the photogenic landscapes of the north of Scotland, such as the Old Man of Storr and Quiraing on the Isle of Skye and the Duncansby Stacks near John o' Groats. Going to these destinations off-season will boost your appreciation of the region.

For me, there's no better place to visit in England than the North York Moors National Park. Colourful heather moorland and seaside towns and villages like Whitby and Robin Hood's Bay form a picturesque landscape. Together with the nearby Bempton Cliffs and the historic city of York, this area provides plenty of opportunities to experience England at its best.

'After Cregganbaun you will probably want to stop the car every minute to enjoy the view and take yet another picture.'

Fanad Head, Ireland
55°16'36.5"N 7°38'00.7"W
I tripped over a sheep fence in an attempt to catch the last rays of sunlight on this lighthouse in the far north of Ireland. I missed the shot at that time, but luckily for me the sun returned two hours later to take this picture.
// August 2016

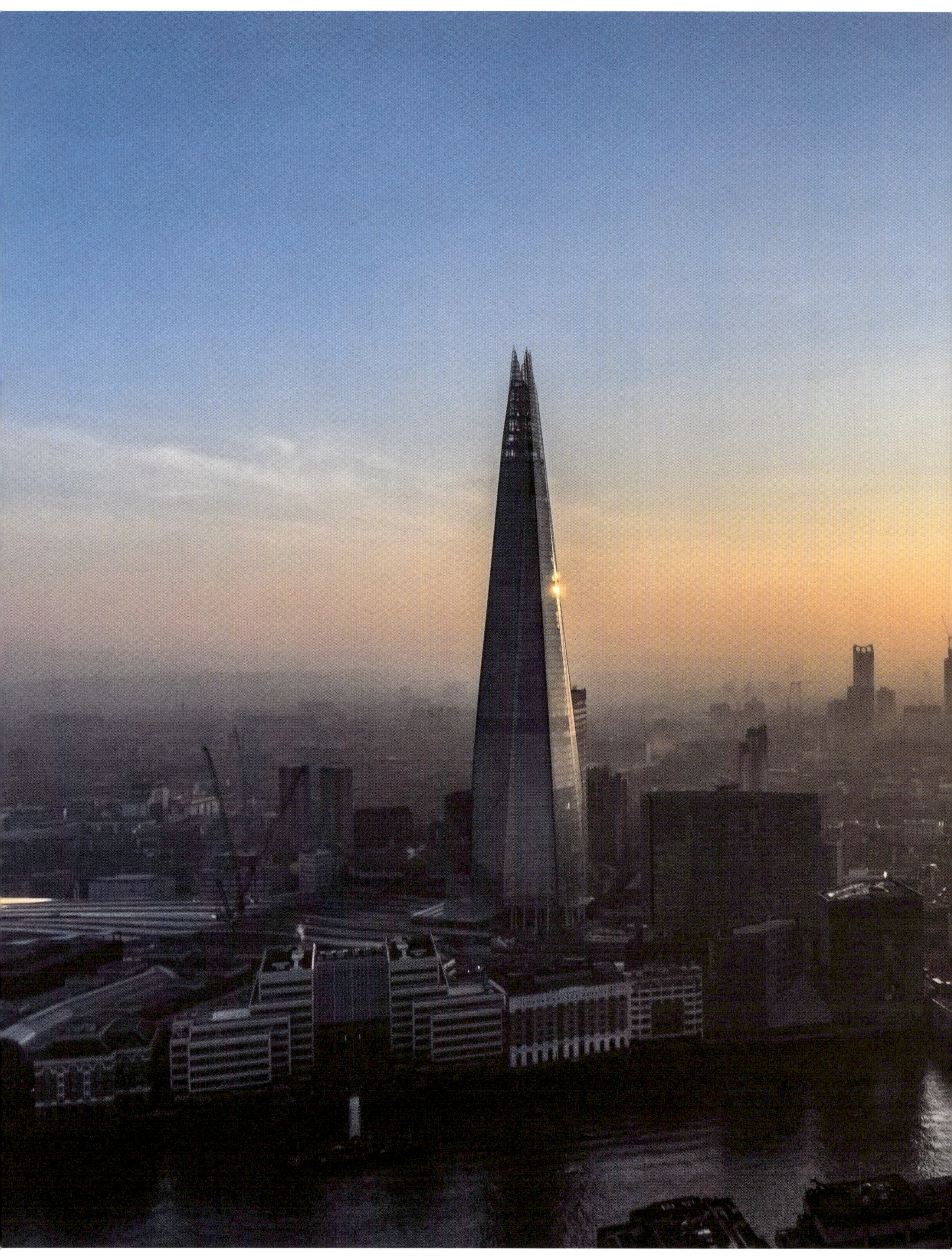

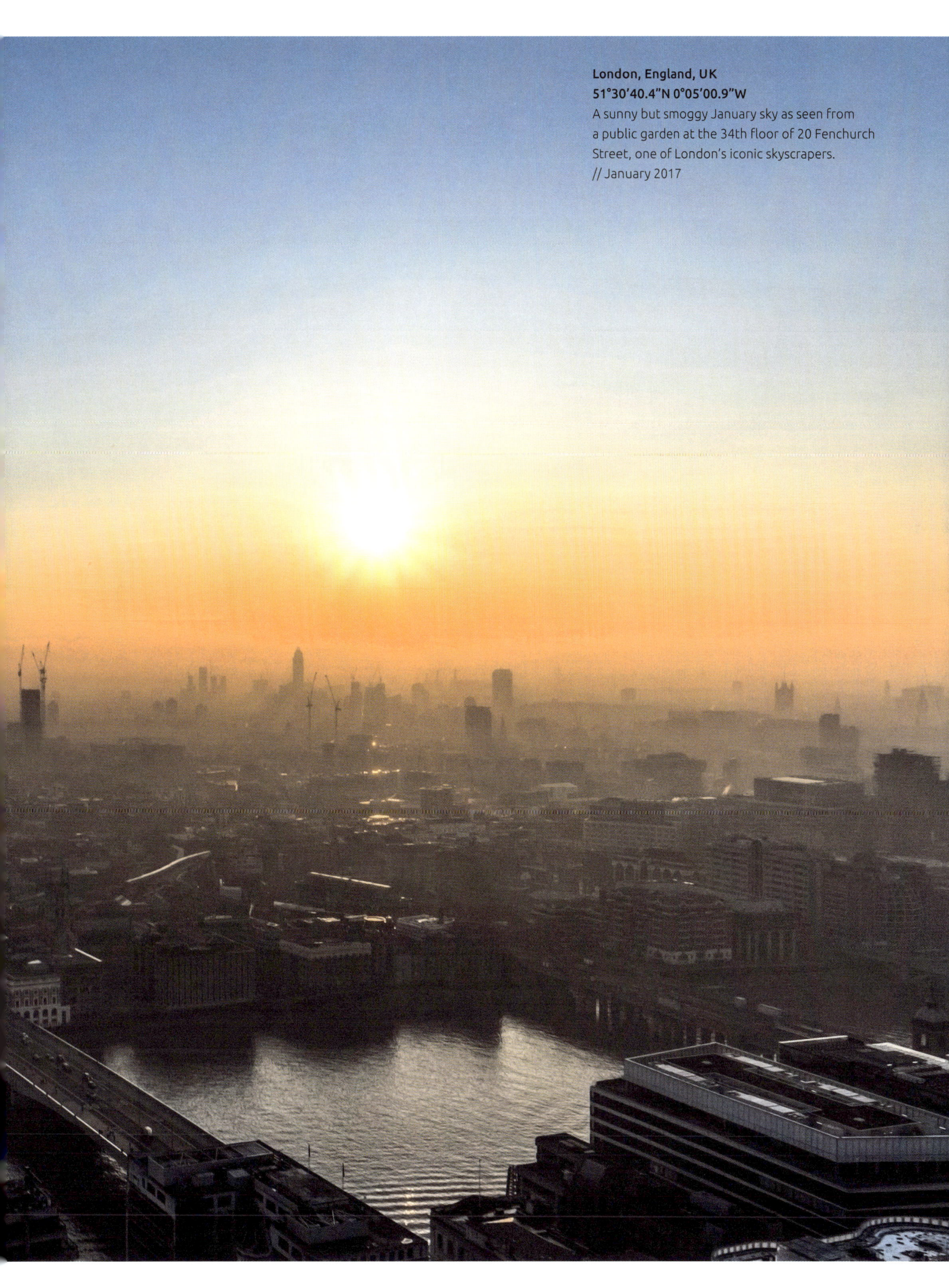
London, England, UK
51°30'40.4"N 0°05'00.9"W
A sunny but smoggy January sky as seen from
a public garden at the 34th floor of 20 Fenchurch
Street, one of London's iconic skyscrapers.
// January 2017

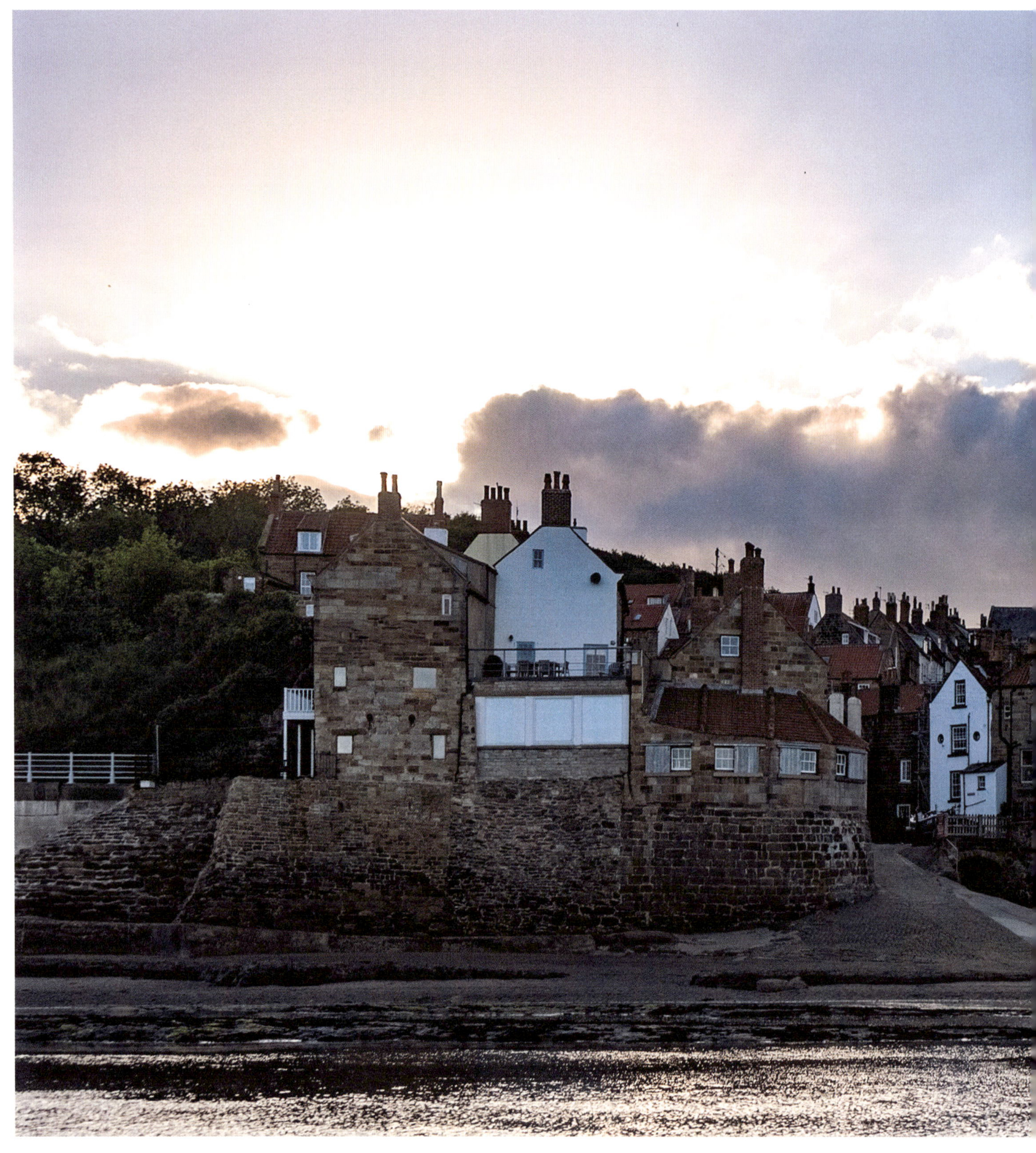

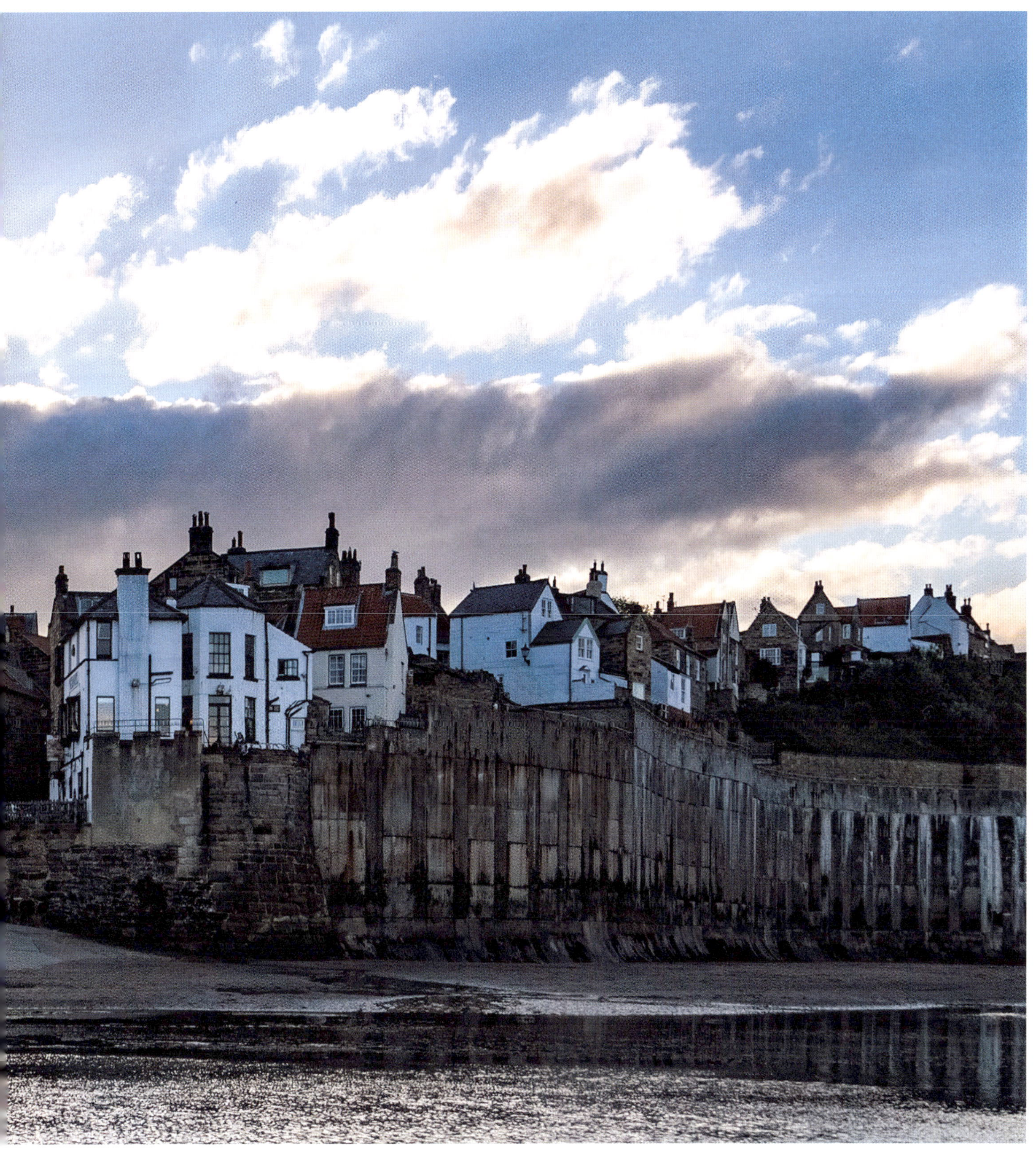

Robin Hood's Bay, England, UK
54°25'48.6"N 0°31'53.9"W
The picturesque seaside village of Robin Hood's Bay.
// May 2011

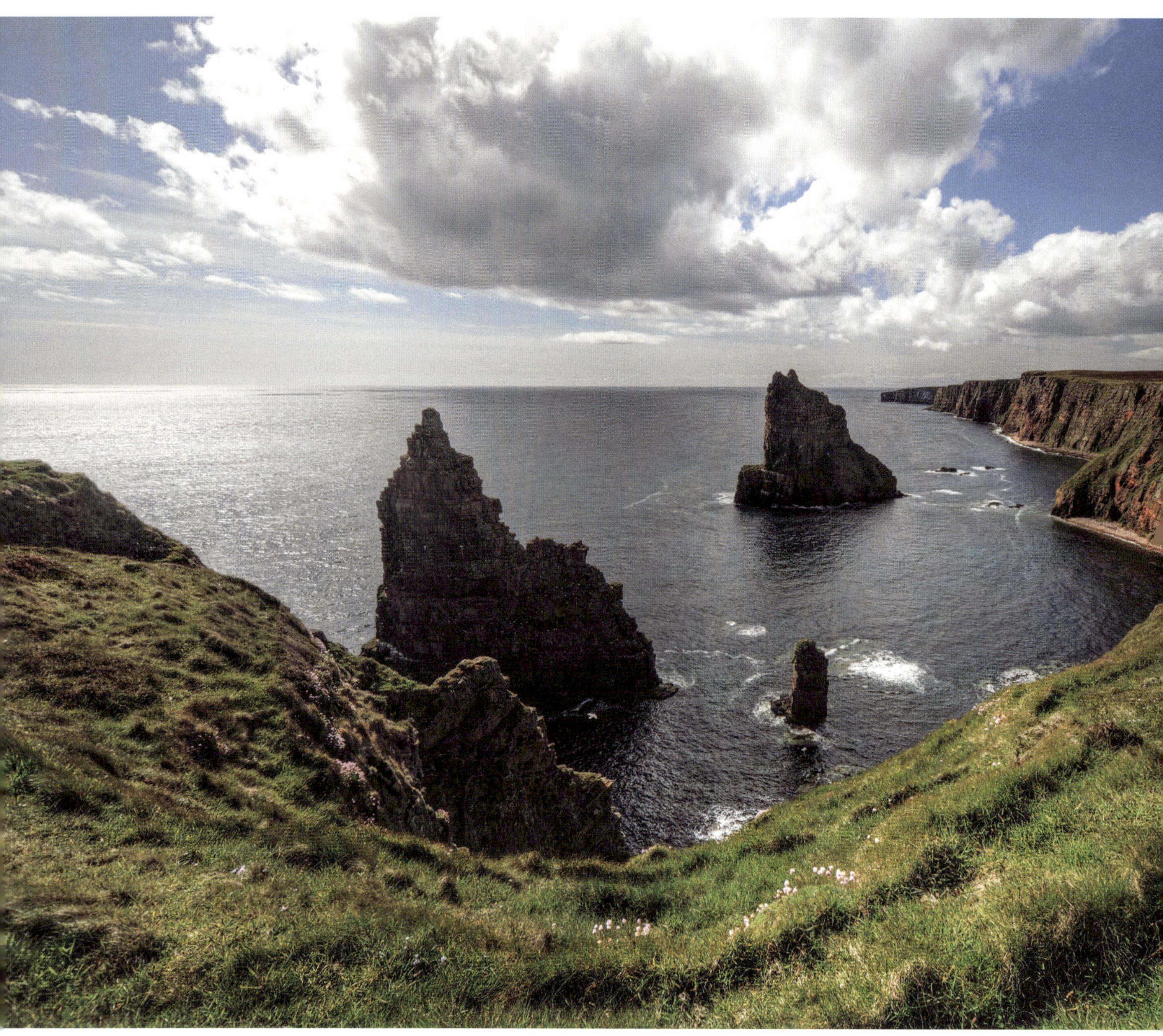

Duncansby Stacks, Scotland, UK
58°37'59.4"N 3°02'17.3"W
Thousands of birds inhabit these rocks near John o' Groats in the most northerly part of Britain. The Duncansby Stacks are impressive from every angle.
// May 2011

Glasgow, Scotland, UK
55°52'17.1"N 4°17'18.3"W
With its photogenic arches, colourful interior and atmospheric lighting after sunset, few buildings spark the imagination in quite the same way as the University of Glasgow.
// August 2016

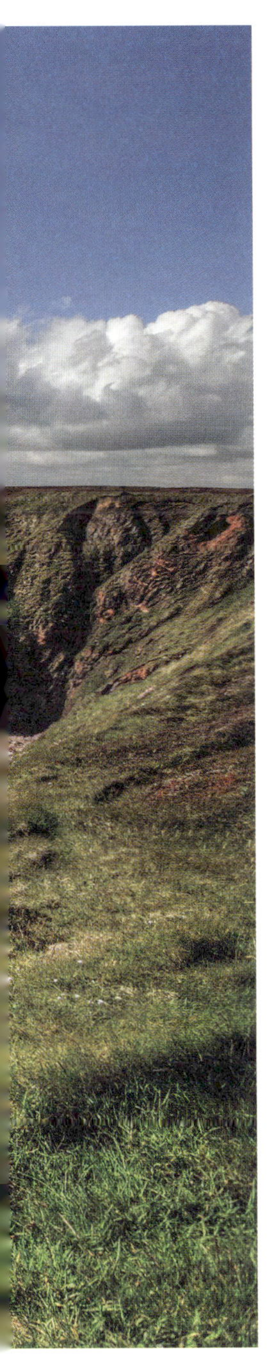
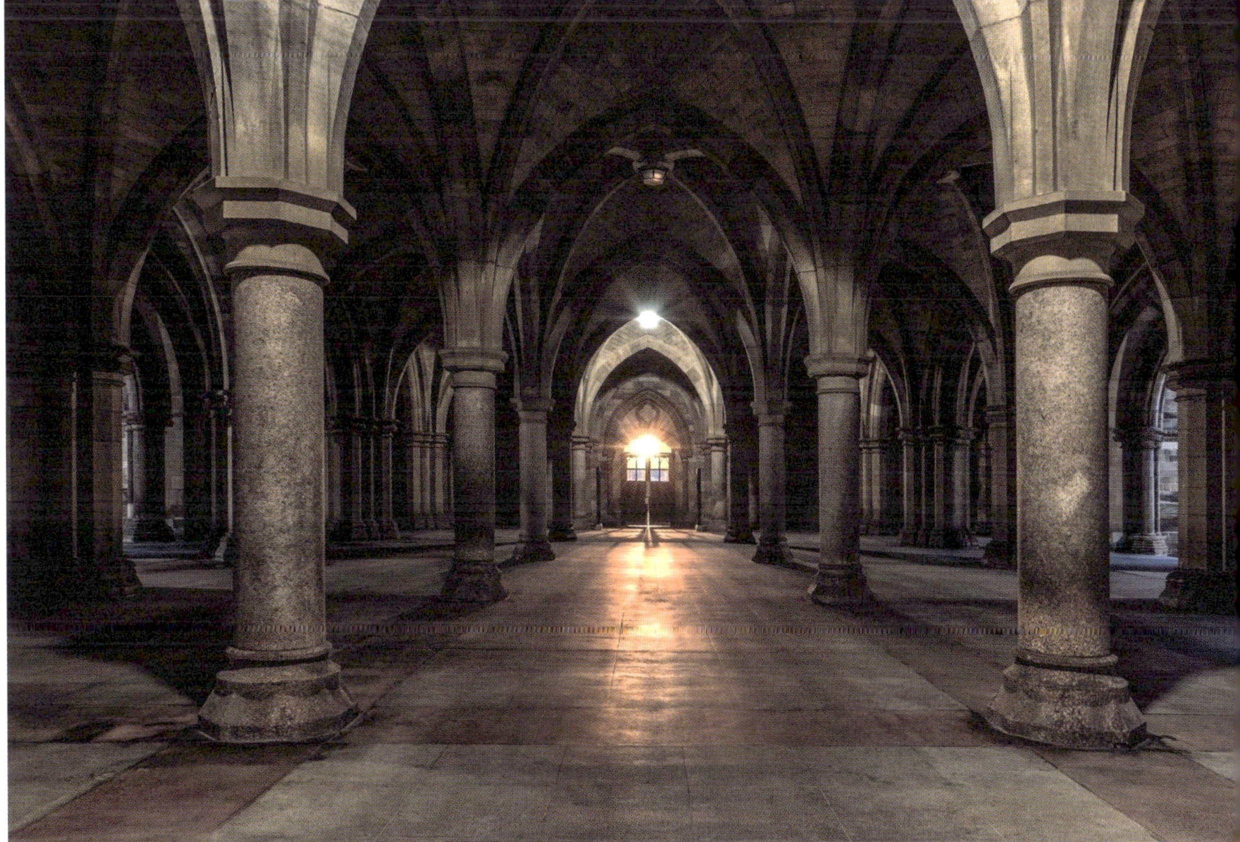

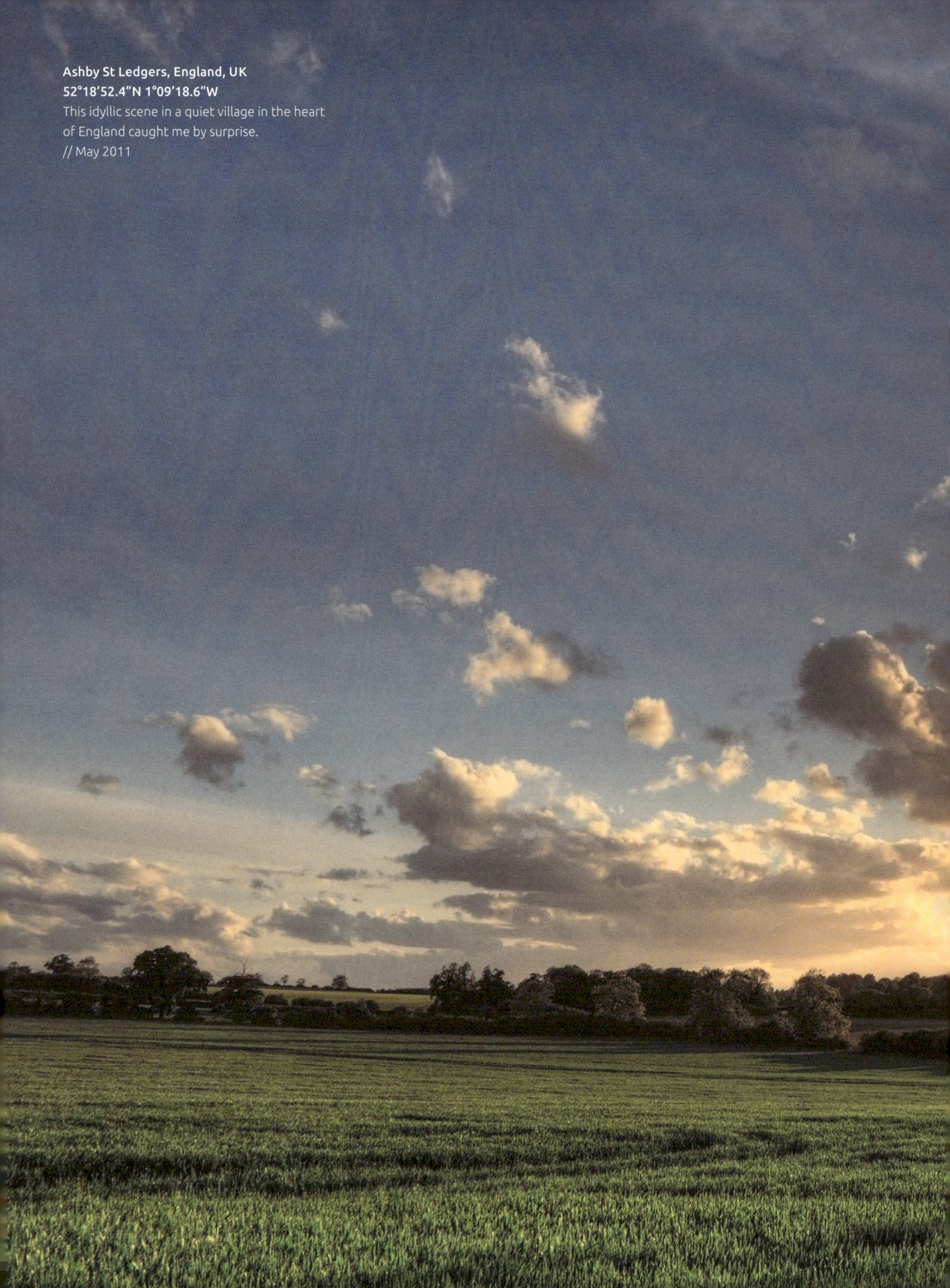

Ashby St Ledgers, England, UK
52°18'52.4"N 1°09'18.6"W
This idyllic scene in a quiet village in the heart
of England caught me by surprise.
// May 2011

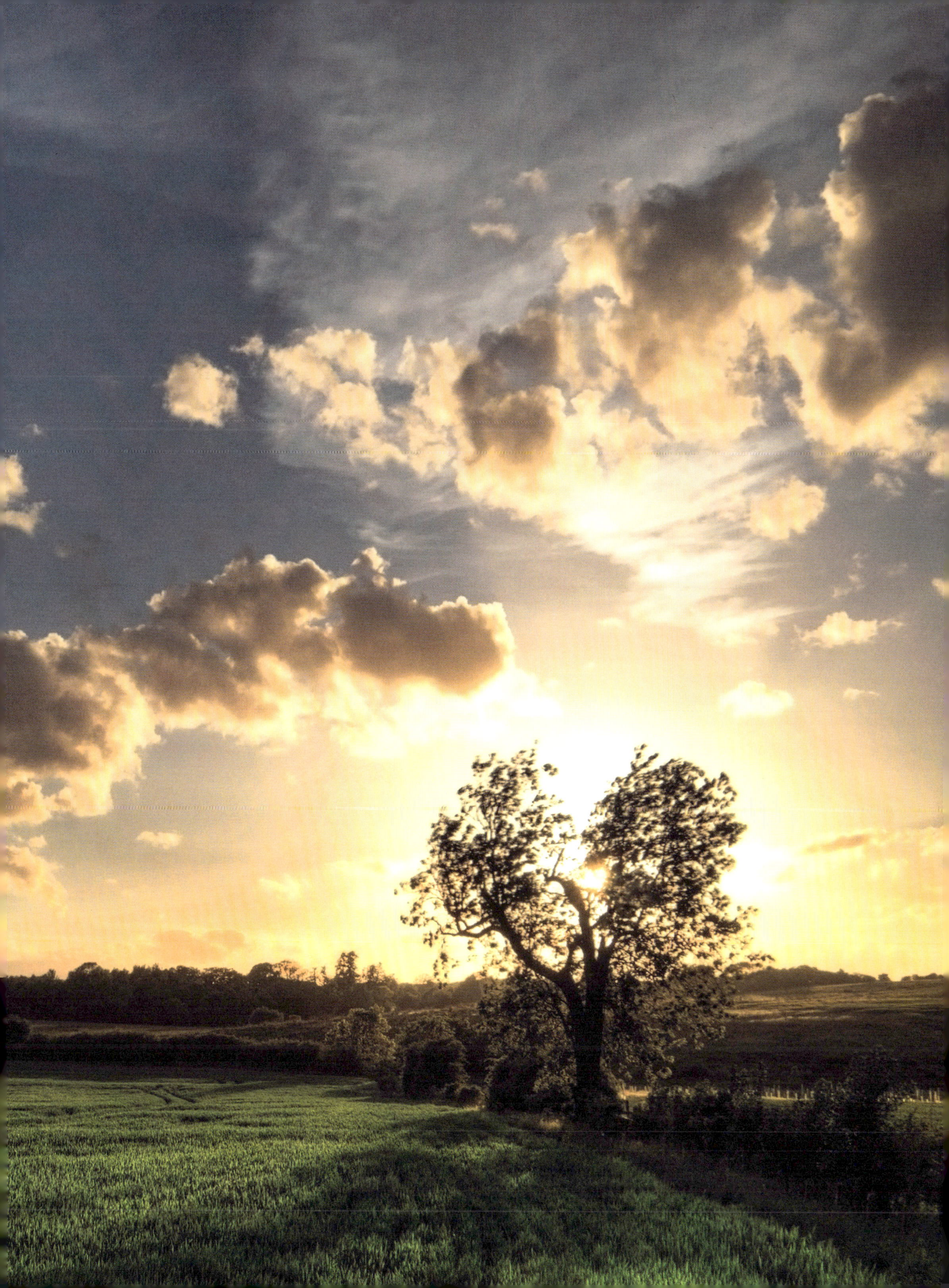

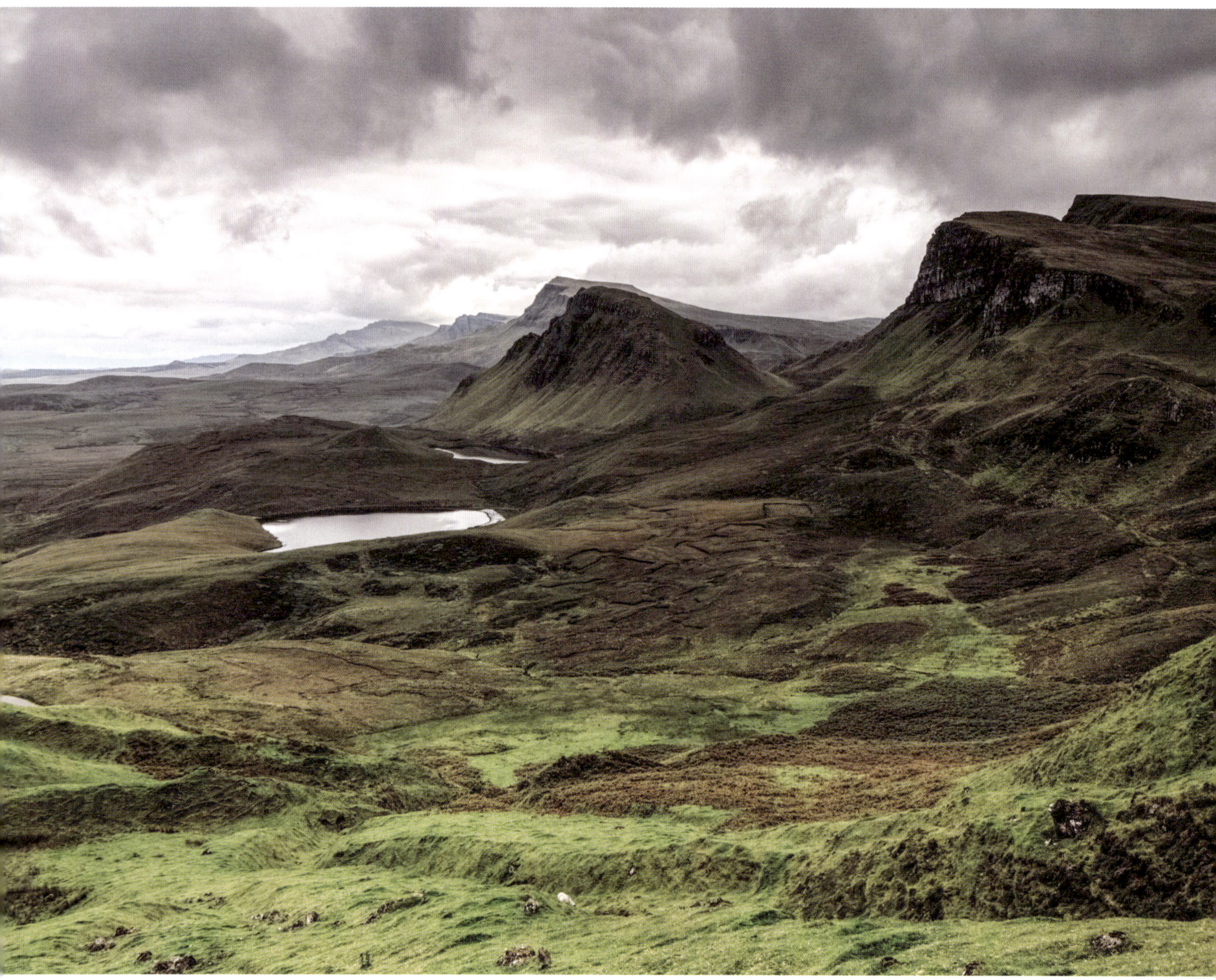

Quiraing, Isle of Skye, Scotland, UK
57°38'04.7"N 6°16'52.3"W
The rough and empty landscape of Quiraing
is one of the most remote regions of the Scottish
mainland. A narrow hiking trail takes you past
some very impressive views on the landscape
that has been formed by a series of landslides.
// August 2016

The Dark Hedges, Northern Ireland, UK
55°08'04.7"N 6°22'52.0"W
Once a well-kept secret, this charming lane
of beech trees is now a popular tourist attraction,
putting this little gem at risk of degradation.
// August 2016

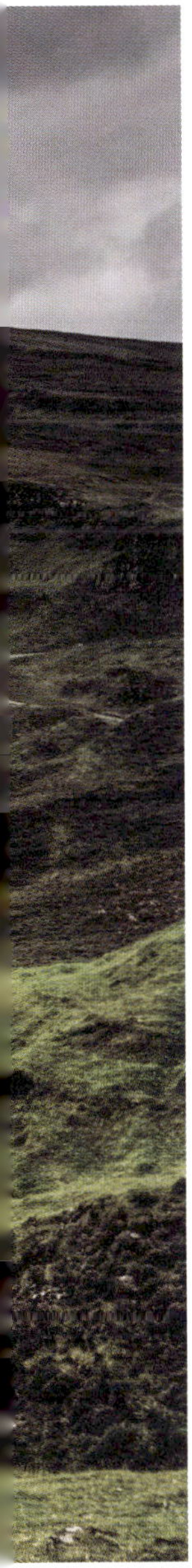

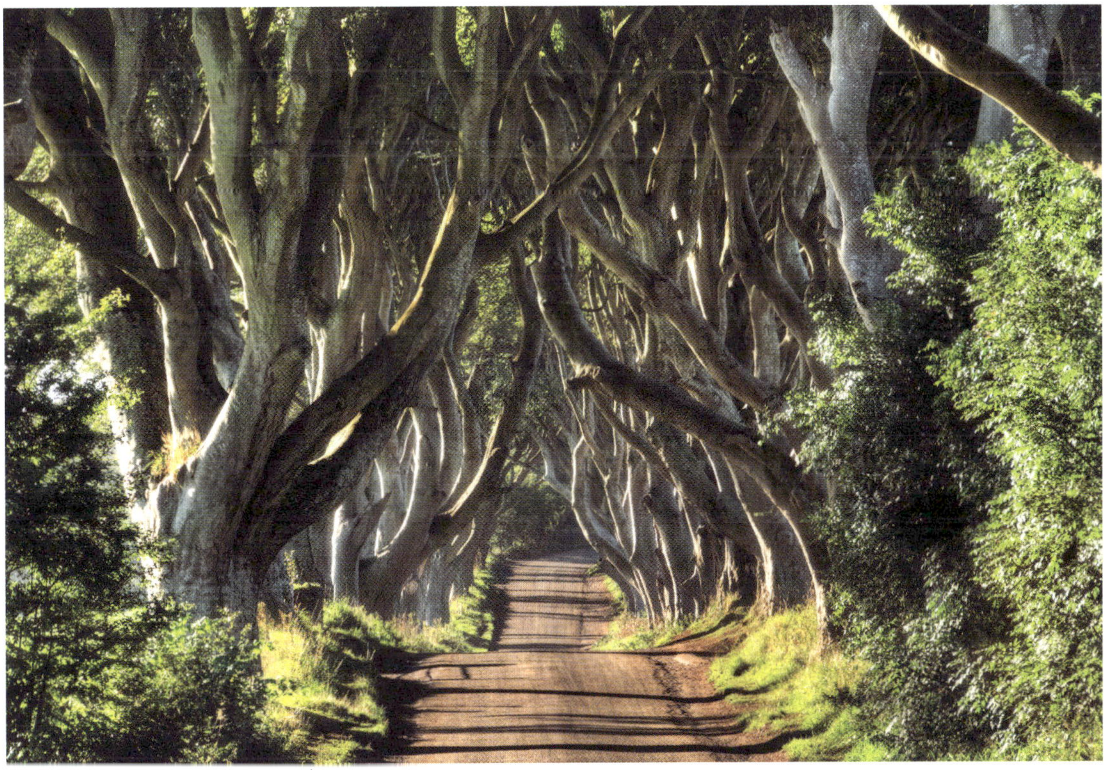

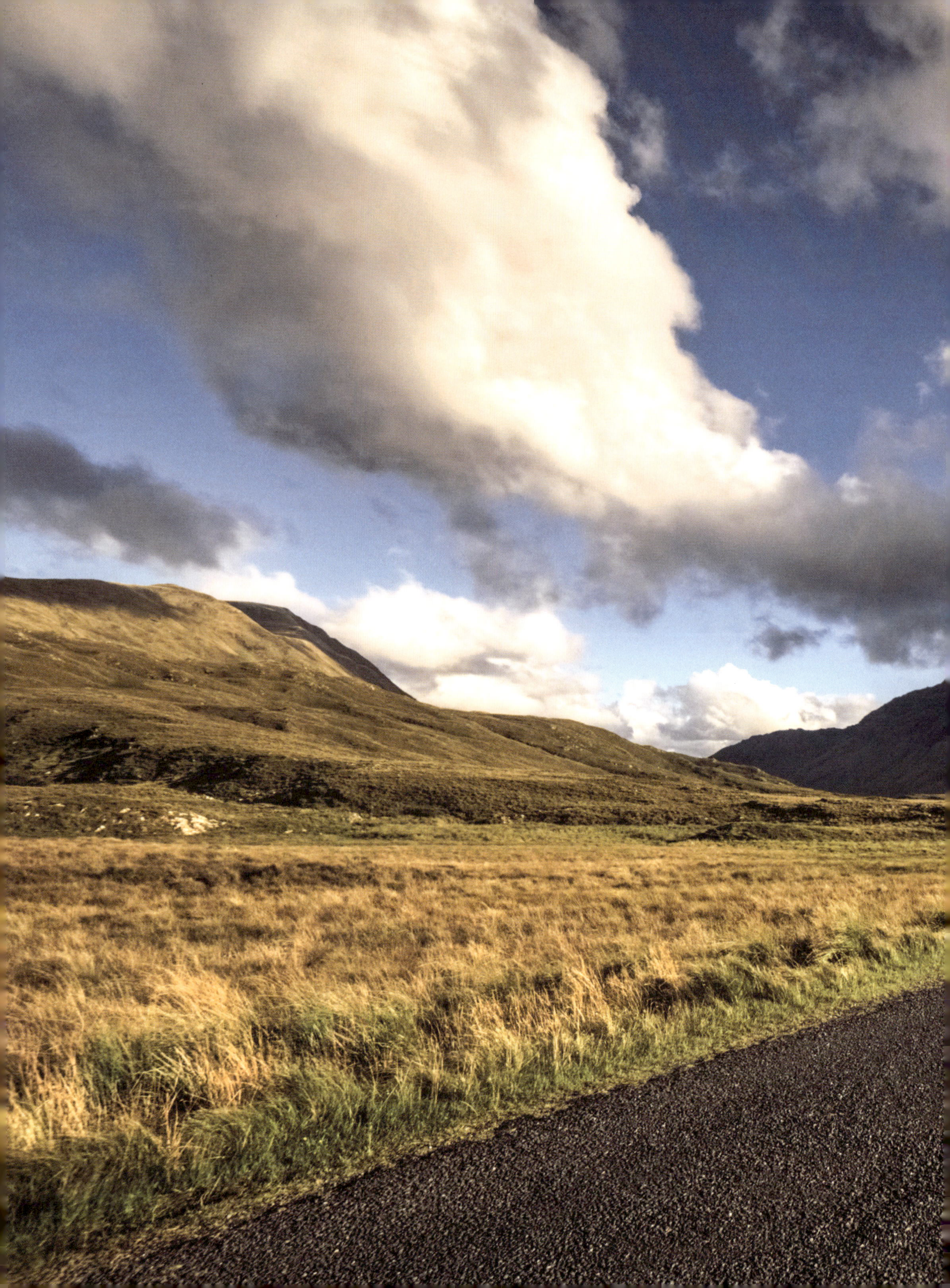

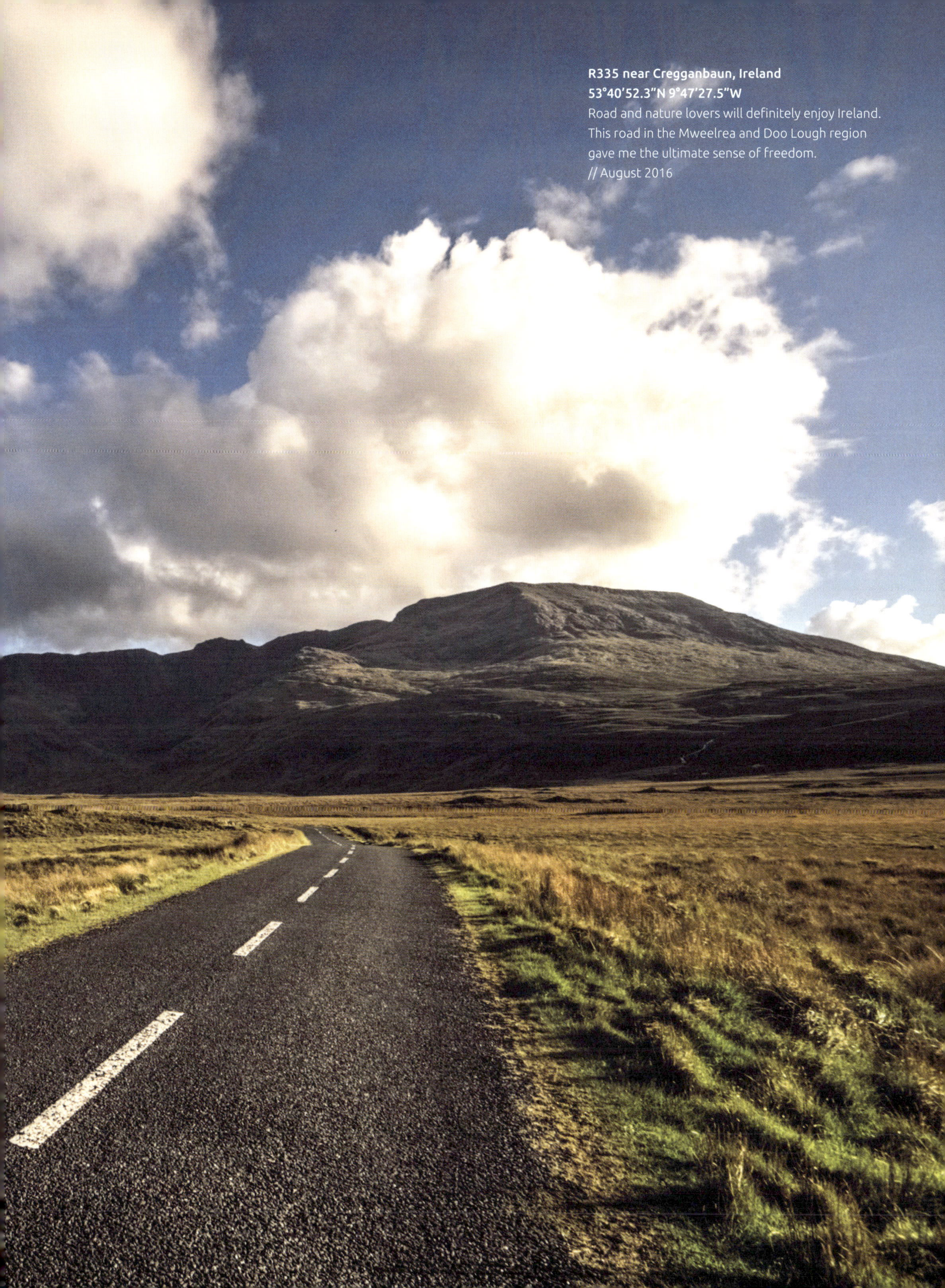
R335 near Cregganbaun, Ireland
53°40'52.3"N 9°47'27.5"W
Road and nature lovers will definitely enjoy Ireland.
This road in the Mweelrea and Doo Lough region
gave me the ultimate sense of freedom.
// August 2016

222

Skomer Island, Wales, UK
51°44'10.8"N 5°17'01.8"W
Skomer Island is a bird-photographer's heaven.
On this little island just off the Pembrokeshire
coast various types of birds are found, including
a large number of puffins.
// May 2011

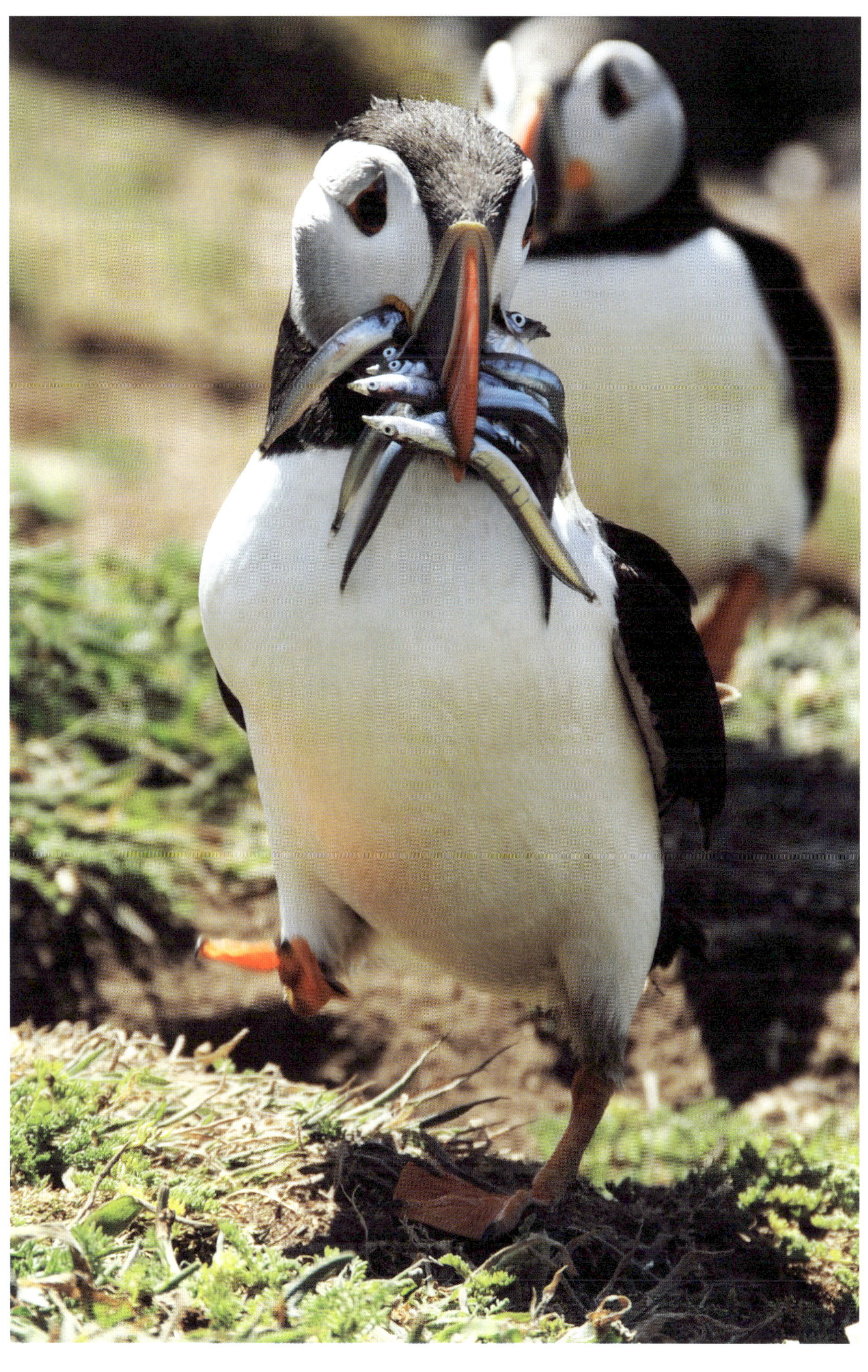

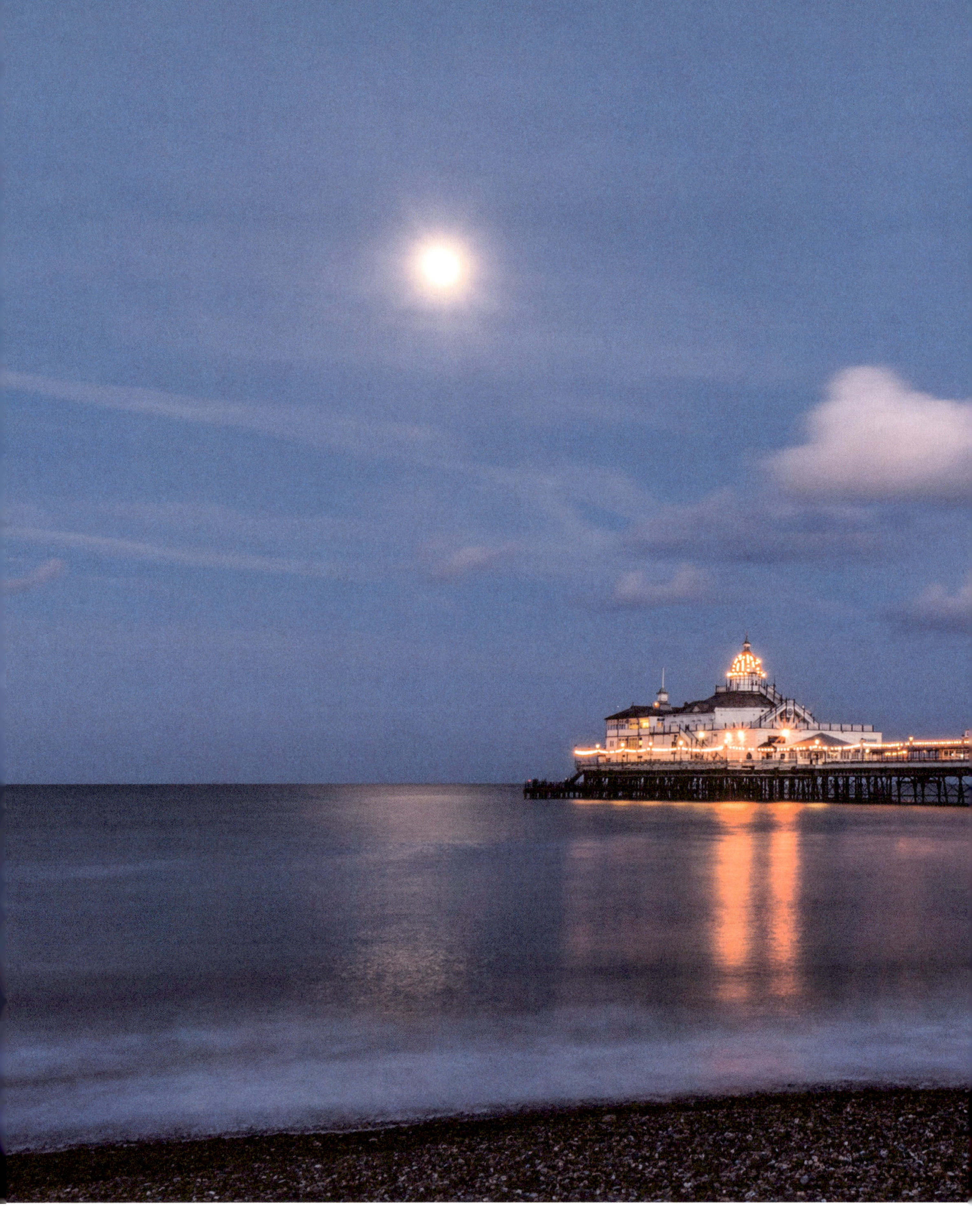

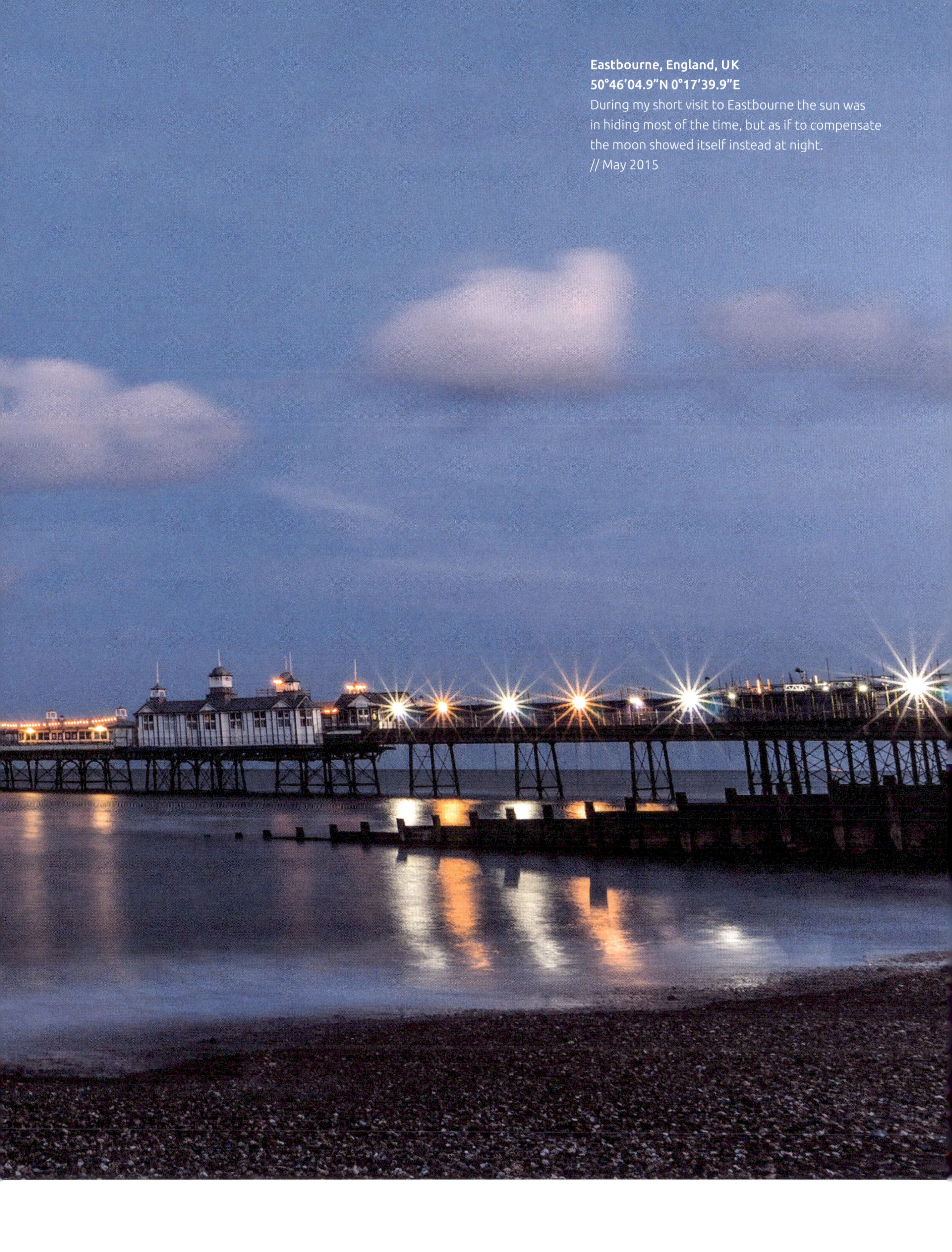

Eastbourne, England, UK
50°46'04.9"N 0°17'39.9"E
During my short visit to Eastbourne the sun was
in hiding most of the time, but as if to compensate
the moon showed itself instead at night.
// May 2015

Around the British Isles
Route and travel suggestions

Scenic regions and nature reserves
1   Bempton Cliffs, England // **UK**
2   Cairngorms, Scotland // **UK**
3   Connemara // **Ireland**
4   Duncansby Stacks, Scotland // **UK**
5   Isle of Skye, Scotland // **UK**
6   North York Moors, England // **UK**
7   Pembrokeshire Coast, Wales // **UK**

Cities and towns
8   Dingle // **Ireland**
9   Dublin // **Ireland**
10 Edinburgh, Scotland // **UK**
11 York, England // **UK**

Cultural experiences
12 Trinity College, Dublin // **Ireland**
13 University of Glasgow, Scotland // **UK**

Spectacular roads and scenic routes
14 A82 between Achallader and Glencoe, Scotland // **UK**
15 A836 & A838 between Thurso and Rhiconich, Scotland // **UK**
16 A855, Isle of Skye, Scotland // **UK**
17 R335 through Mweelrea and Doo Lough region // **Ireland**
18 Ring of Beara, County Cork/County Kerry // **Ireland**
19 Sky Road, County Galway // **Ireland**

○   Photo location
●   Travel suggestion
123 Photo page number
123 Travel suggestion number

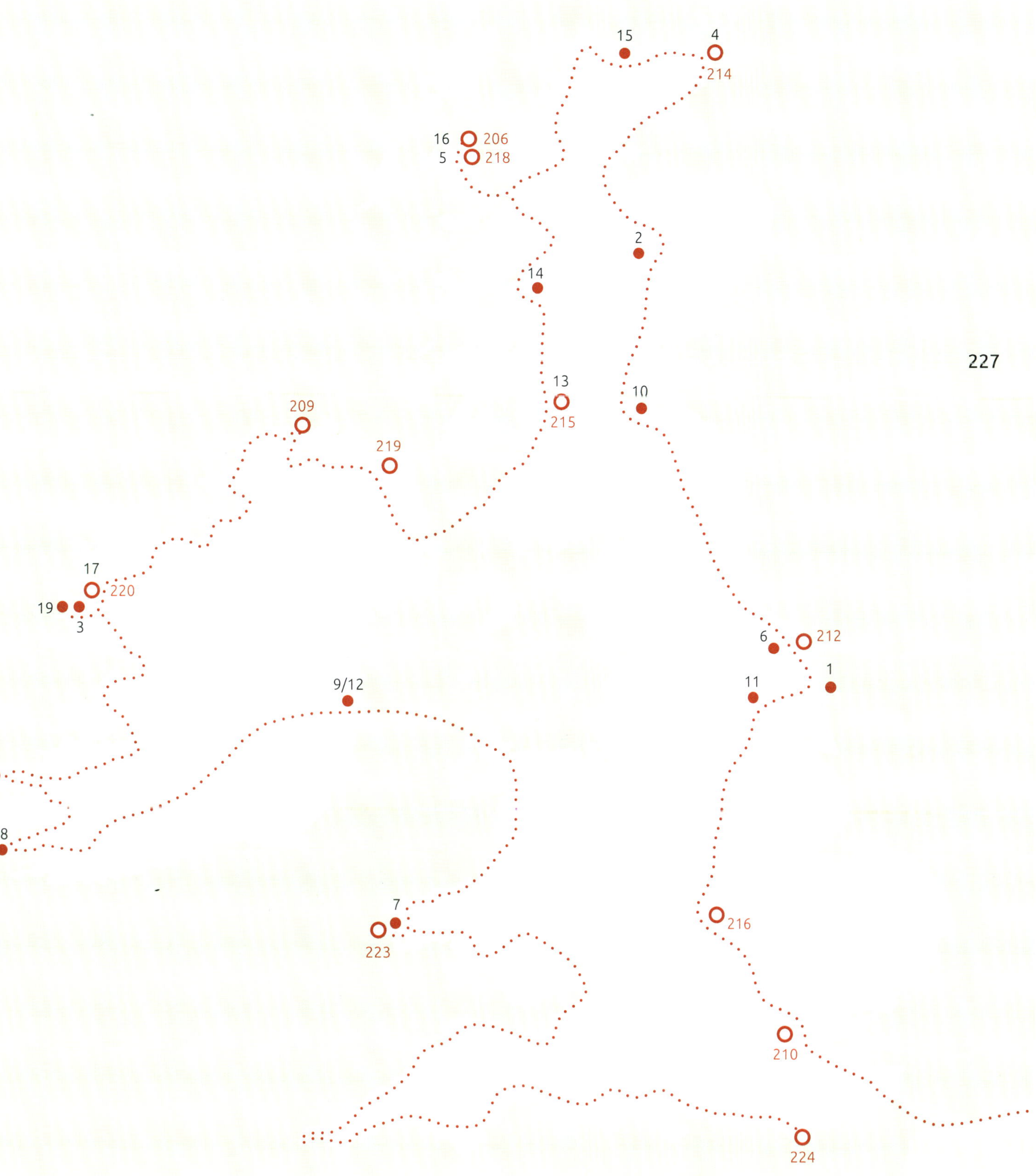

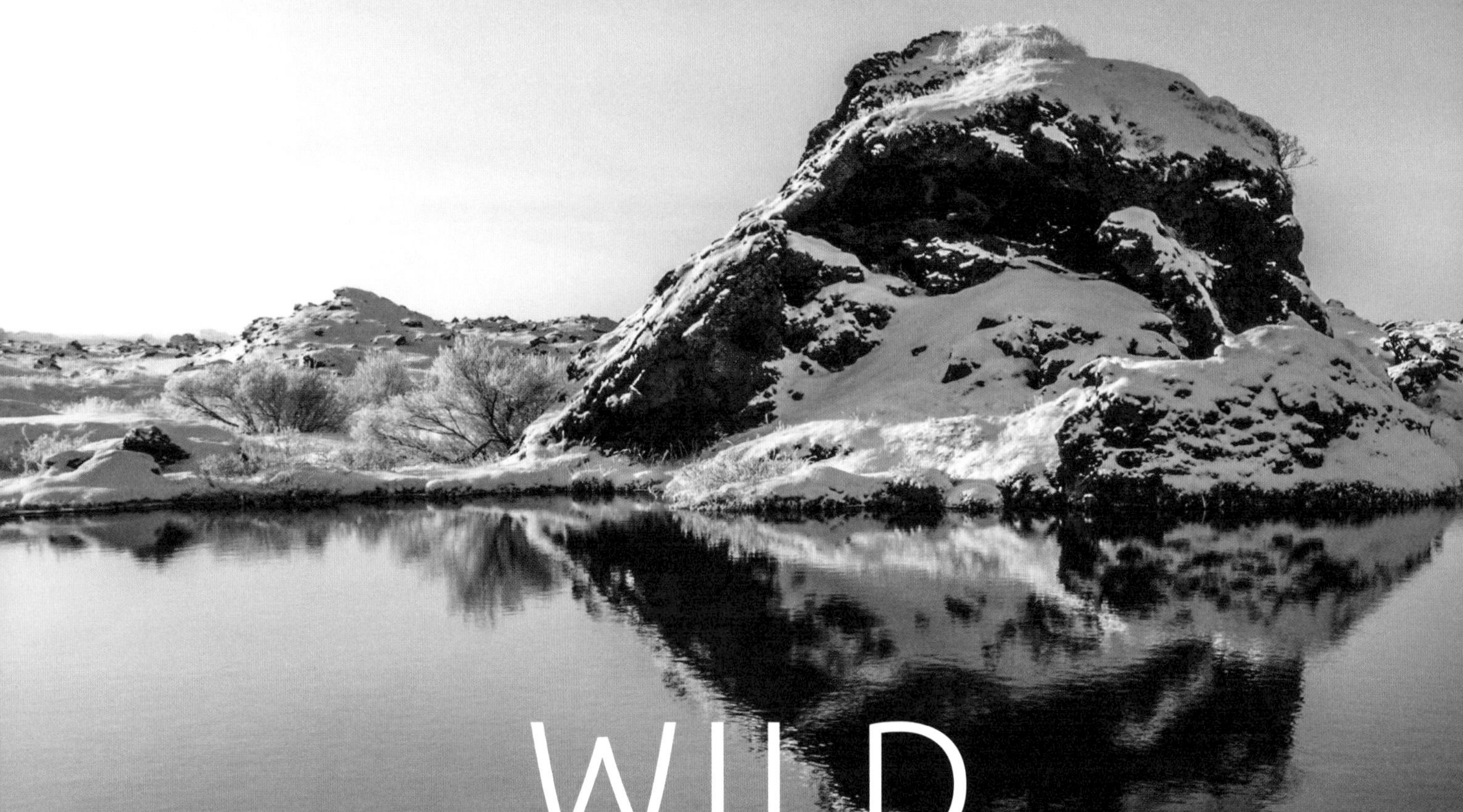

WILD
WINTER
SCAPES

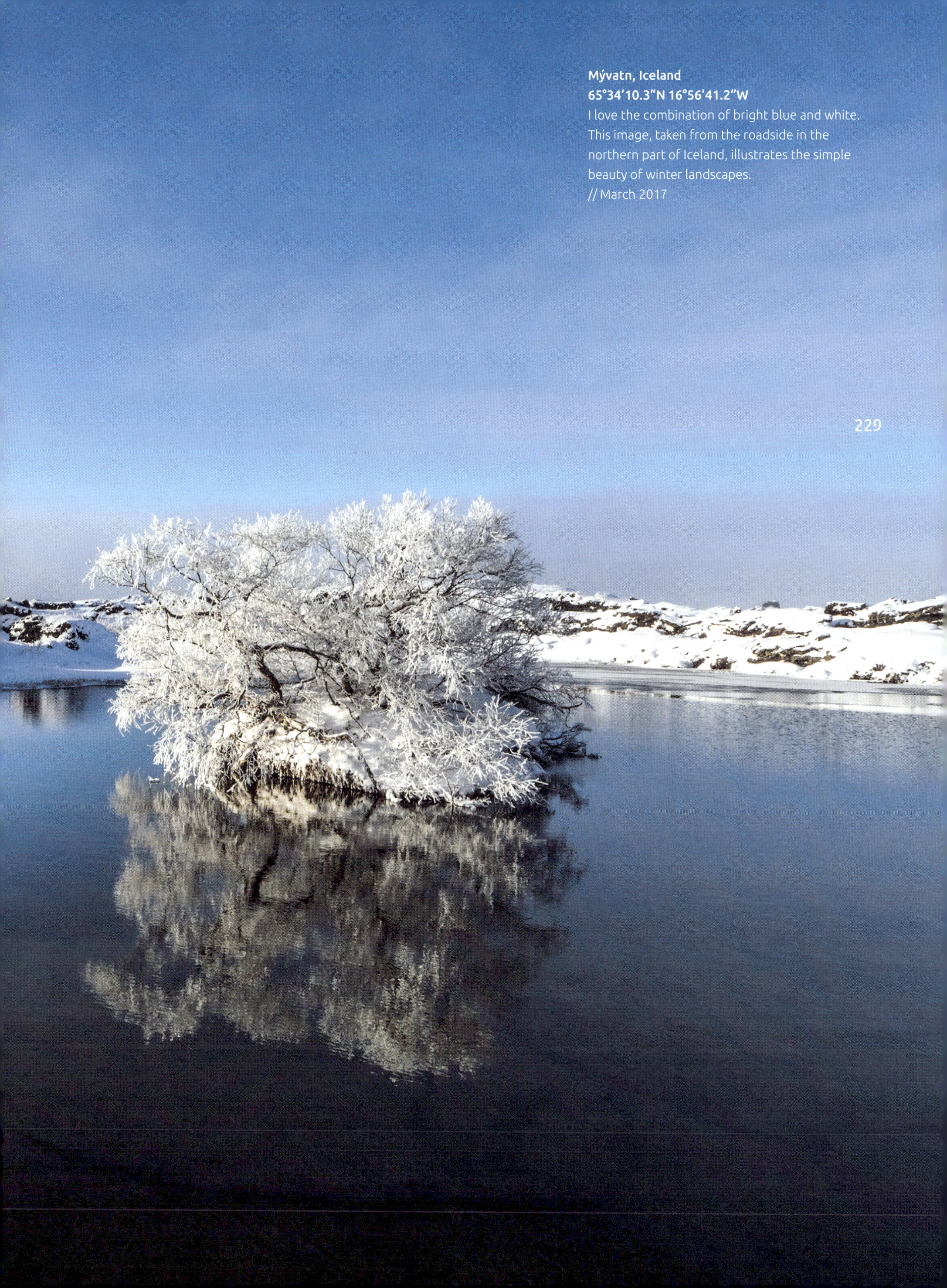

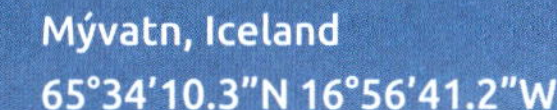

Mývatn, Iceland
65°34'10.3"N 16°56'41.2"W
I love the combination of bright blue and white.
This image, taken from the roadside in the
northern part of Iceland, illustrates the simple
beauty of winter landscapes.
// March 2017

'Thanks to its dramatic and varied landscapes, some say Snæfellsnes is like a miniature version of Iceland.'

ONLY ONE COUNTRY in Europe is so wild and remote that it cannot be merged into any of the other road trips in this book. Iceland, by many regarded as a landscape photographer's paradise, is an island of extremes. To add a touch more drama, I chose to go in winter instead of summer, which was probably the best decision of the entire road trip. I was treated to awe-inspiring aurora night skies (best seen from an outdoor hot tub), frozen waterfalls, endless snow fields and bright-blue ice caves. And, on the first day of the trip, a record amount of over half a metre of snow in Reykjavík that caught even the cool-headed Icelandic citizens off guard.

Europe has many beautiful landscapes. But the density of spectacular views on Iceland is absolutely astounding. At the top of my list is Snæfellsnes, a peninsula in the west of Iceland. Thanks to its dramatic and varied landscapes, some say it is like a miniature version of Iceland. The route around Snæfellsnes is one of the most remarkable roads you will ever drive.

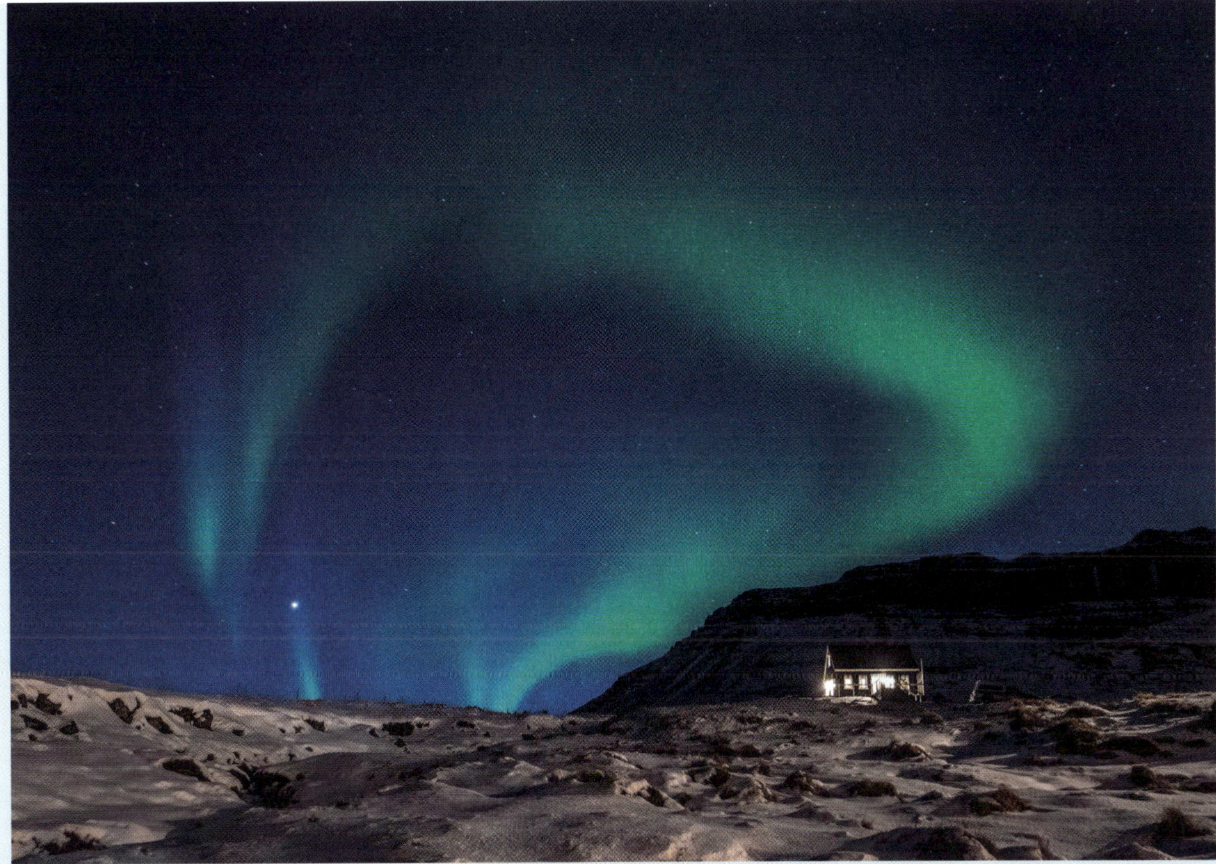

Next on my list of highlights is the northeast of Iceland. Up in the north you will come across many impressive sights on your way to and around Lake Mývatn, such as the Goðafoss waterfall, the Hverfjall tuff ring volcano, the Krafla caldera and the Hverir geothermal site. A little further north, the fishing town of Húsavík colours the rough landscape. And in the far northeast corner of Iceland, near the village of Raufarhöfn, a strange rock formation appears on the horizon. It looks prehistoric, so you may well be surprised to learn that this Arctic Henge is actually less than 25 years old and still under construction.

The third and last region in Iceland I would like to recommend is Mýrdalssandur, particularly the outwash plain around Hjörleifshöfði. Watching the rock statues standing in a sea of sand and pebbles, you lose any sense of scale, as is the case with many of the majestic natural monuments of Iceland.

Road 1, Western Iceland, Iceland
64°47'16.6"N 21°30'30.6"W
A wonderful aurora night sky, photographed just a few steps away from the hot tub in our hotel.
// February 2017

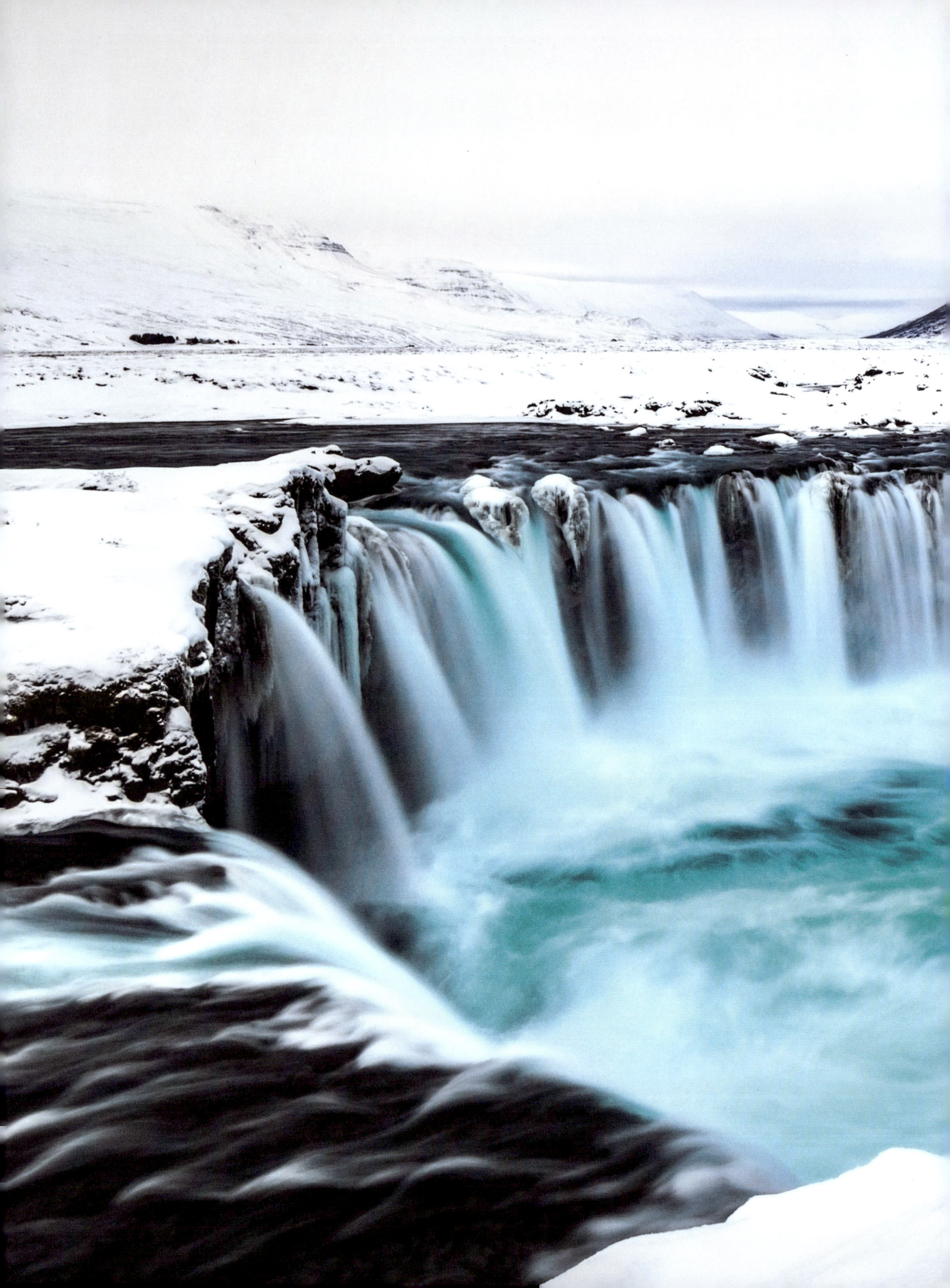

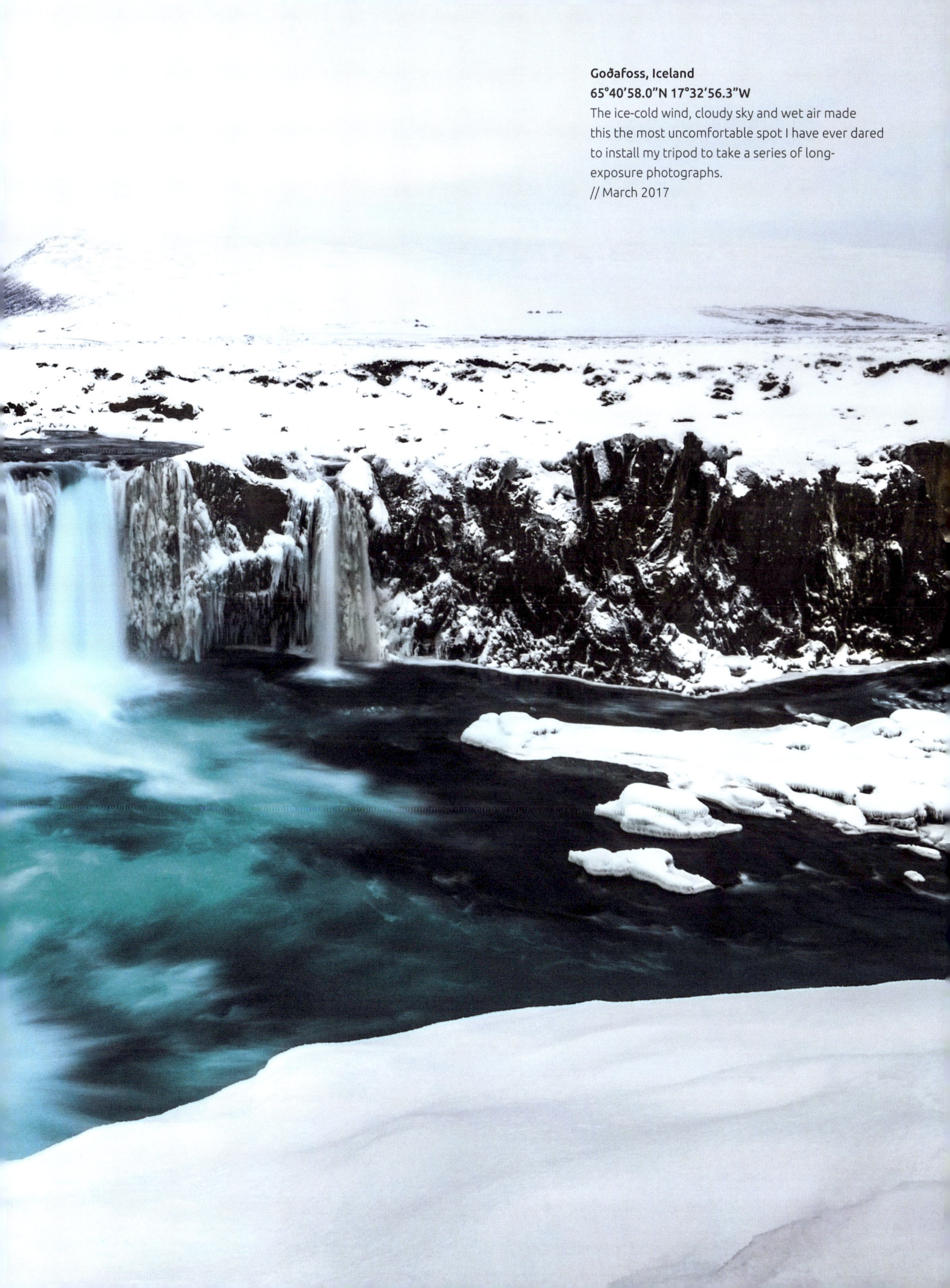

Goðafoss, Iceland
65°40′58.0″N 17°32′56.3″W
The ice-cold wind, cloudy sky and wet air made
this the most uncomfortable spot I have ever dared
to install my tripod to take a series of long-
exposure photographs.
// March 2017

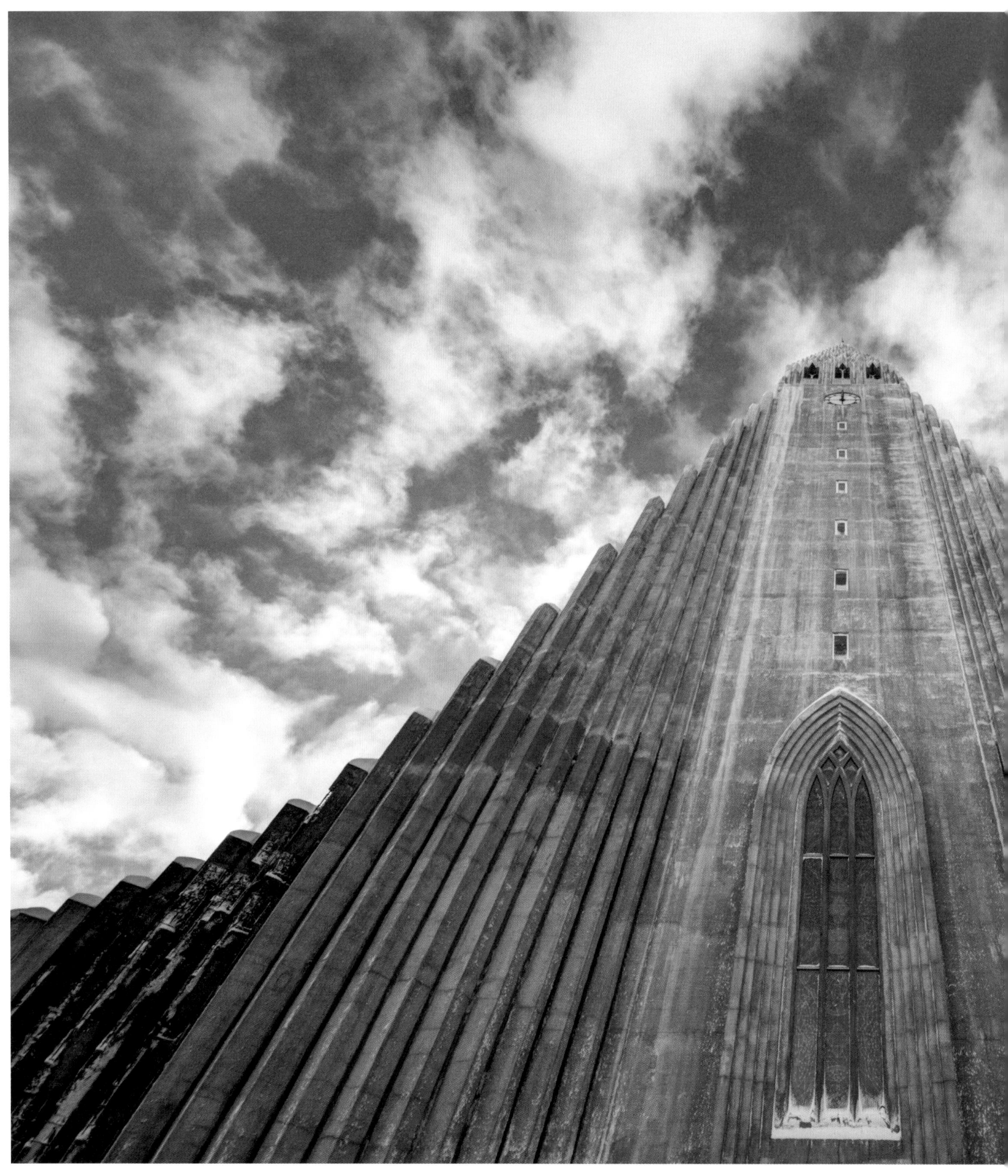

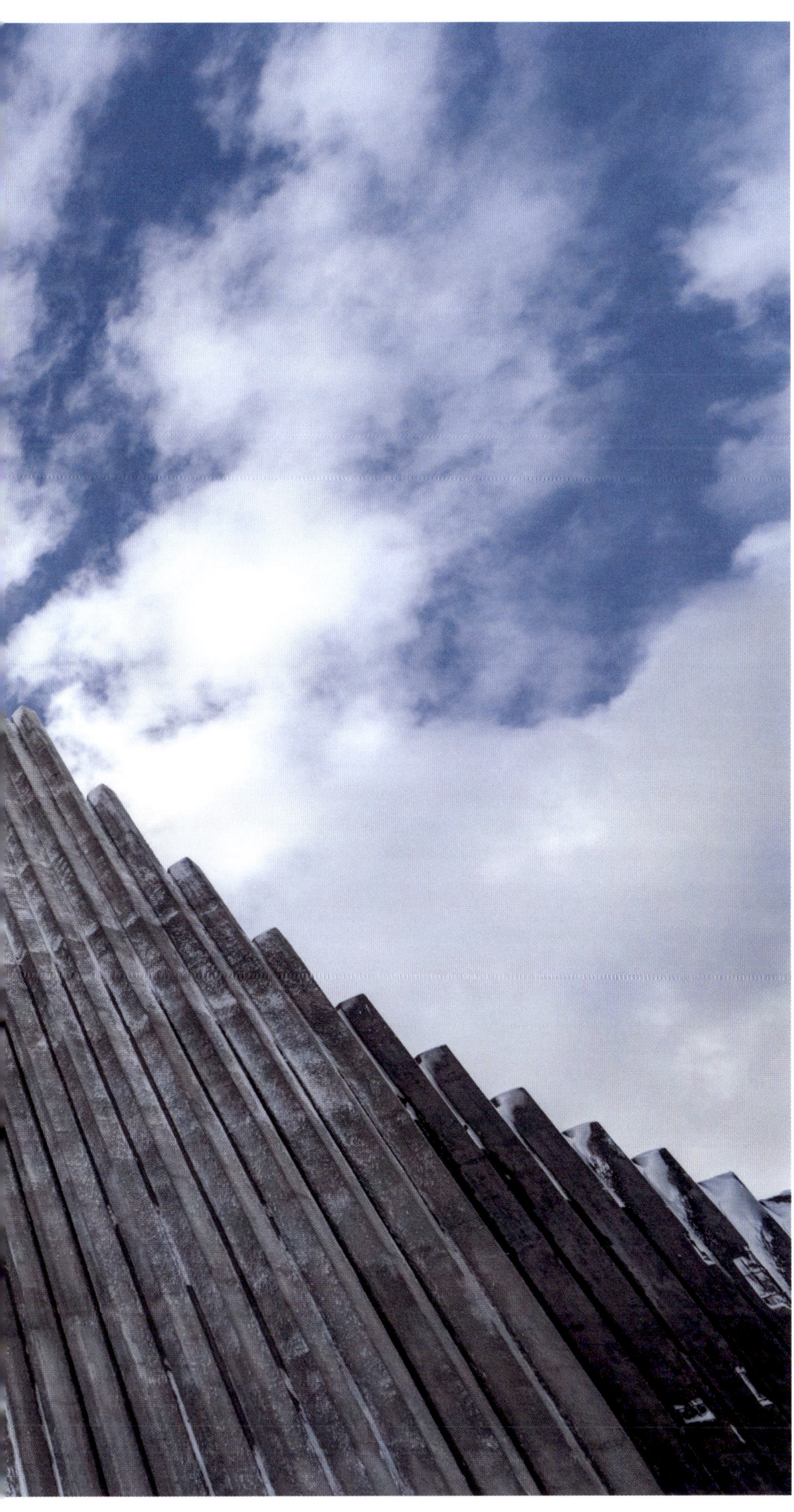

Reykjavík, Iceland
64°08'31.9"N 21°55'38.6"W
The façade of the iconic Hallgrimskirkja.
// February 2017

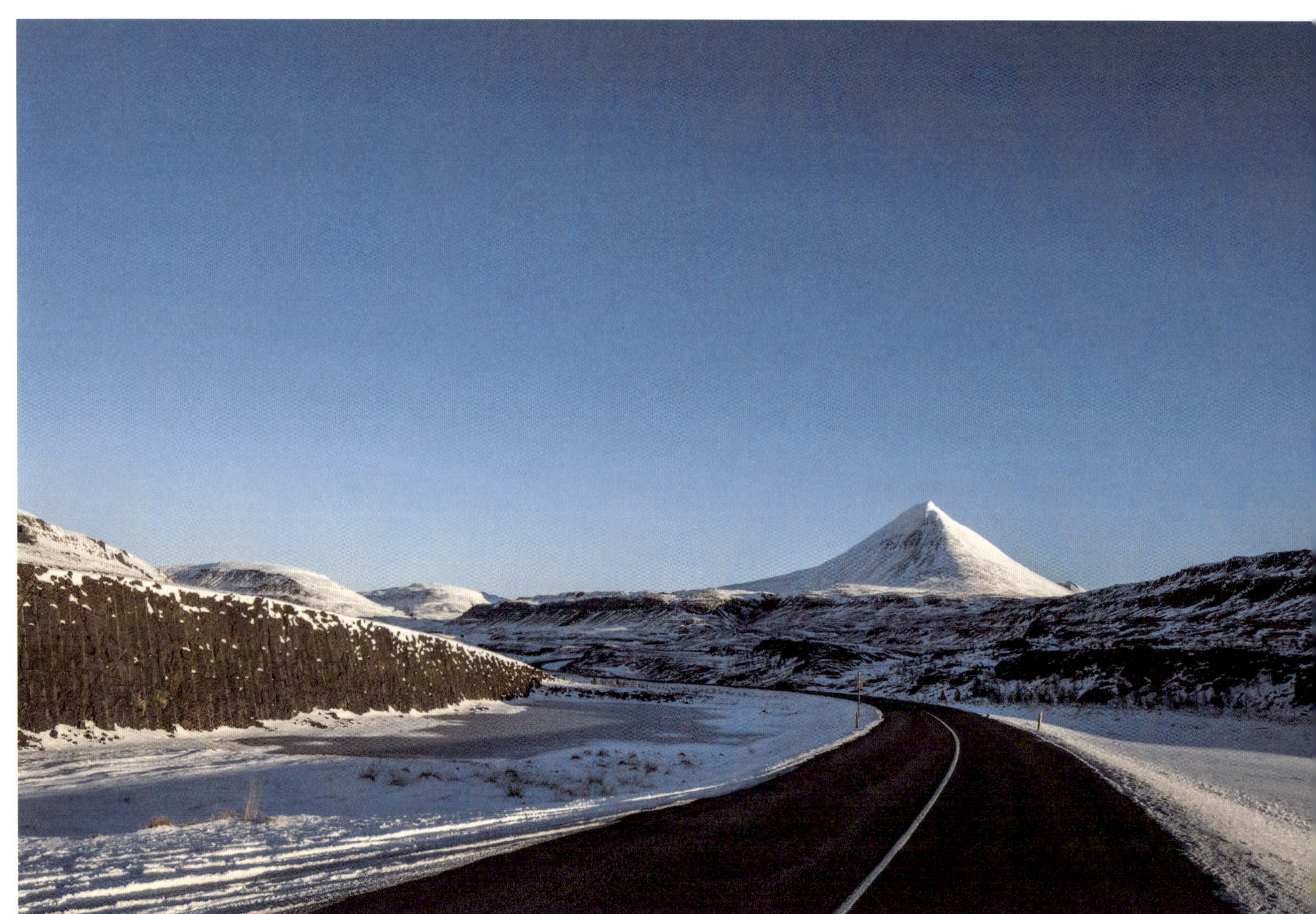

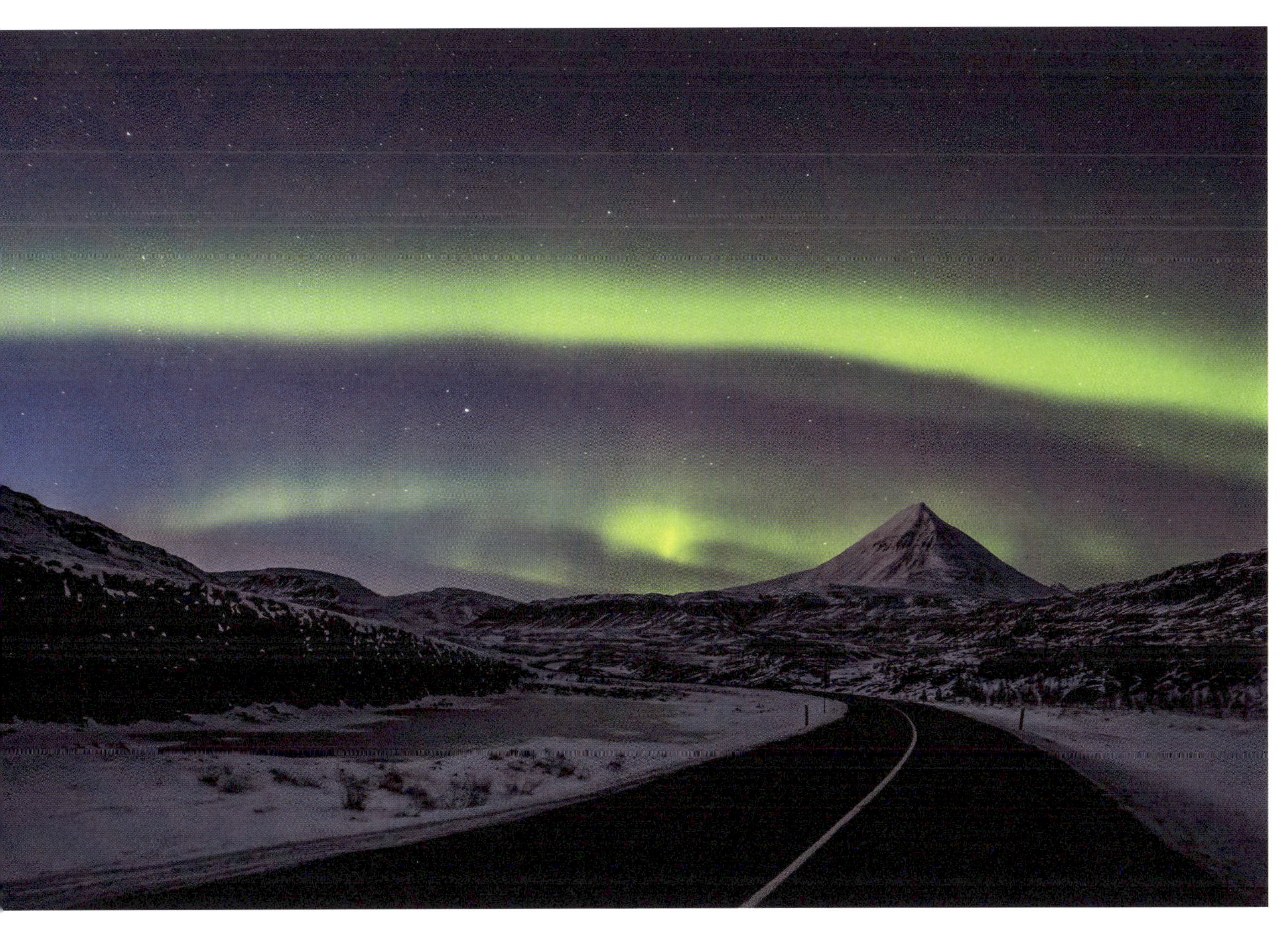

Road 60, Western Iceland, Iceland
64°48'23.9"N 21°28'21.4"W
On returning from a day trip to Snæfellsnes I saw
this beautiful aurora in the rear mirror. I stopped,
mounted my camera on a tripod and stood there
waiting for a long time, in the middle of the road,
watching the magical theatre of light. Next day
I came back to take the same picture by daylight.
A colourful contrast of day and night.
// February 2017

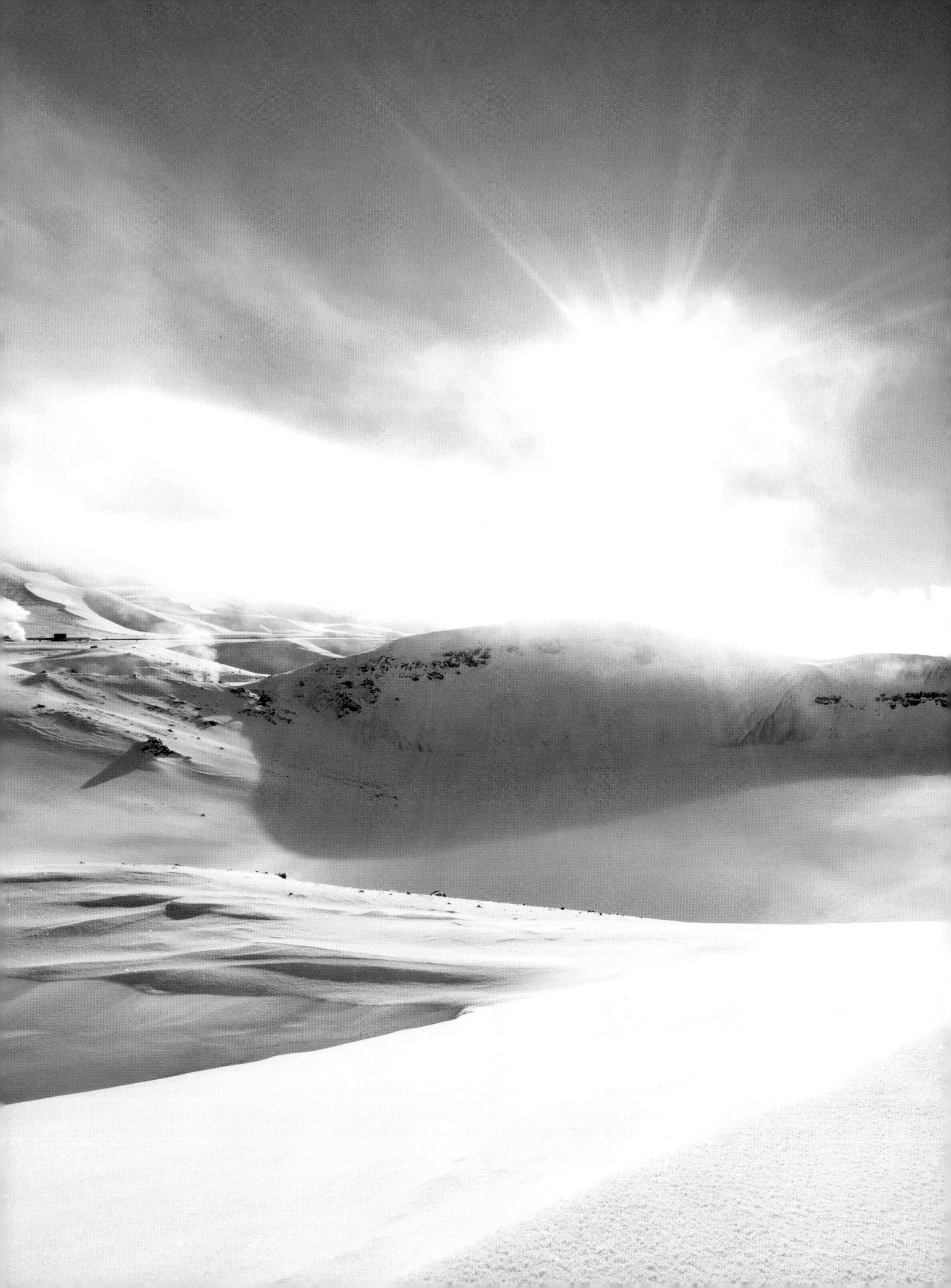

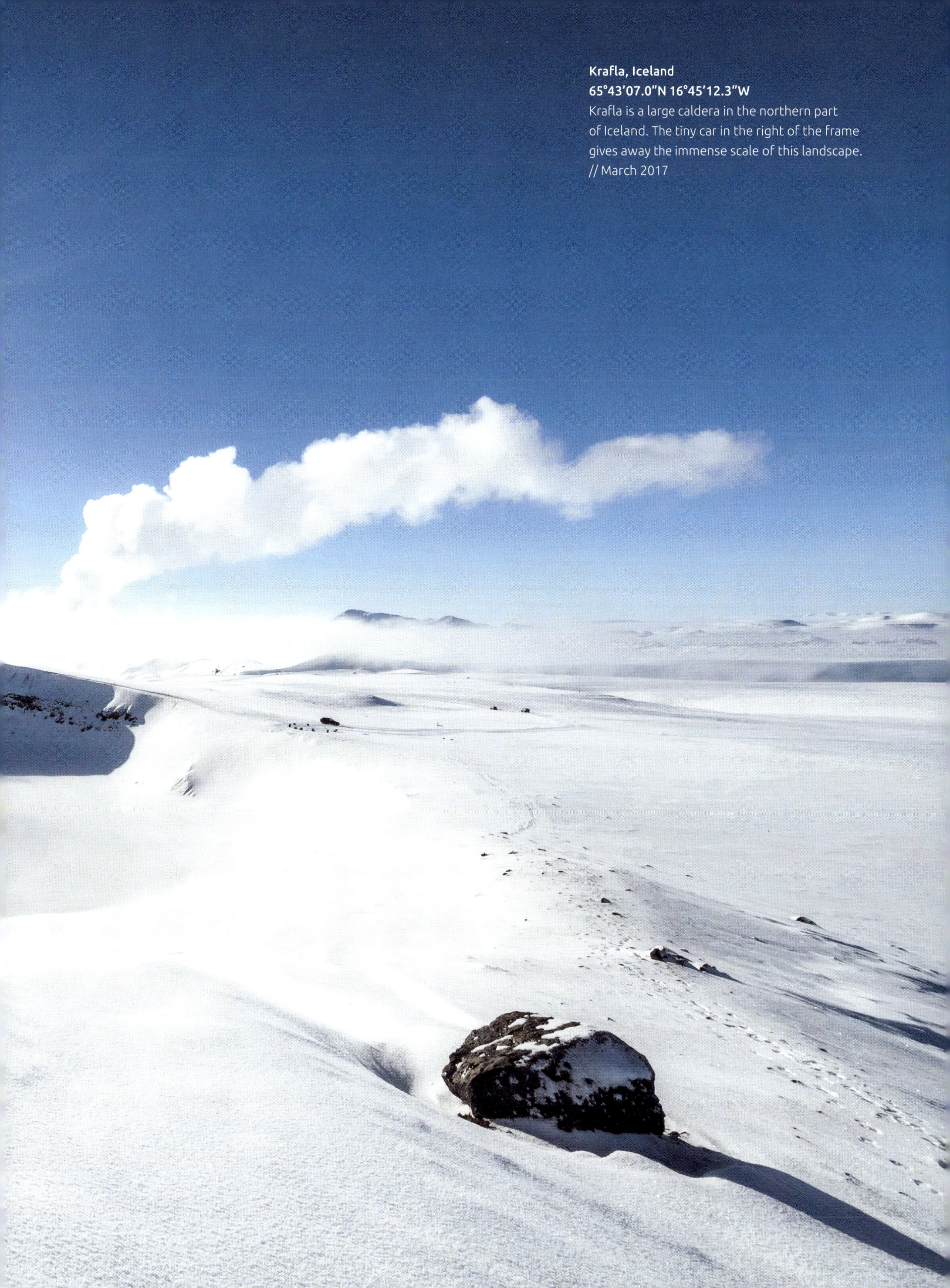

Krafla, Iceland
65°43'07.0"N 16°45'12.3"W
Krafla is a large caldera in the northern part
of Iceland. The tiny car in the right of the frame
gives away the immense scale of this landscape.
// March 2017

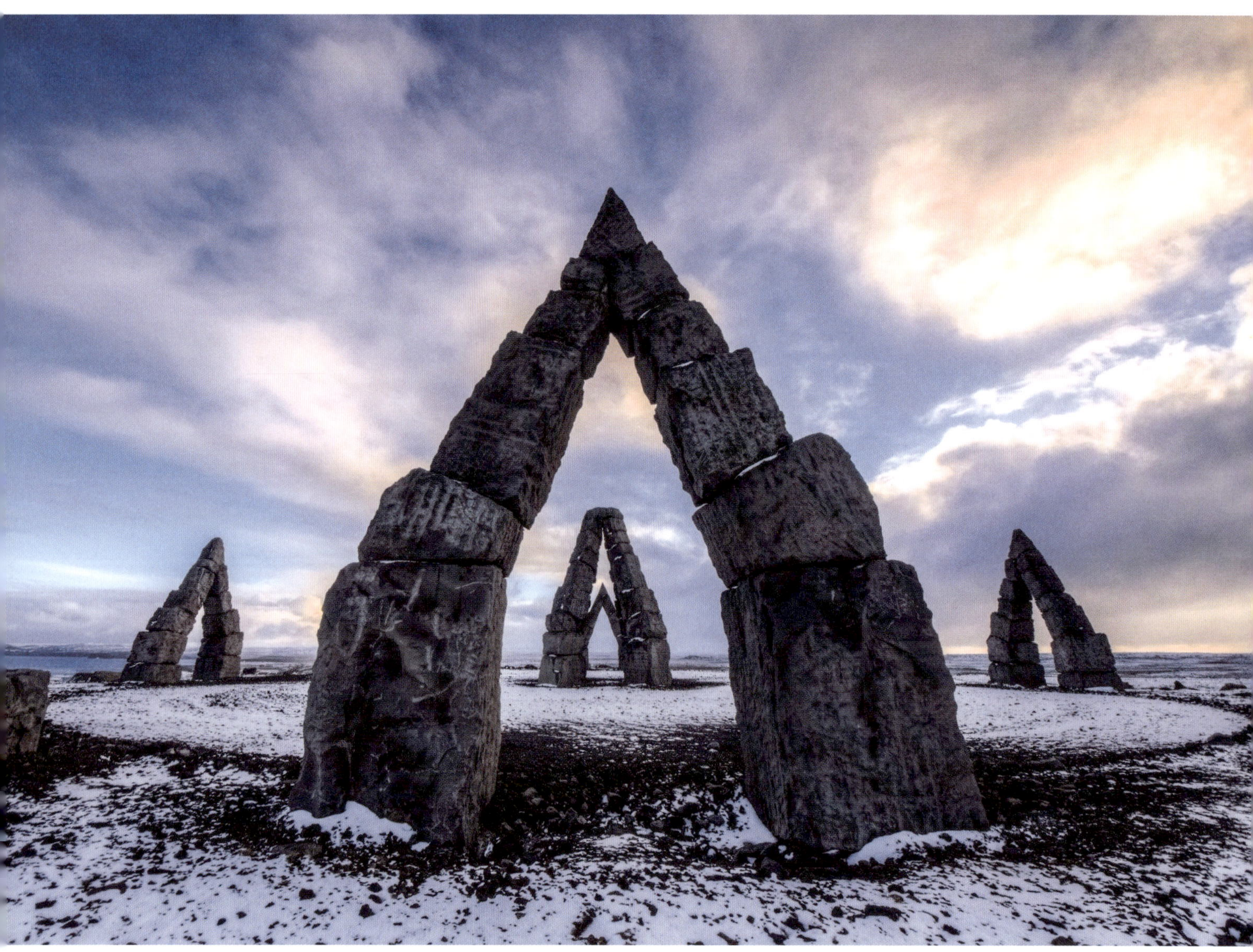

Raufarhöfn, Iceland
66°27'43.9"N 15°57'44.3"W
Heimskautsgerðið near Raufarhöfn in the northernmost tip of Iceland is a mystical place in a harsh
environment. This 'Arctic Henge' is just a couple
of kilometres away from the Arctic Circle.
// March 2017

Húsavík, Iceland
66°02'45.1"N 17°20'50.1"W
This friendly-looking town is where the first
settlement on Iceland took place. It is also the
whale watching capital due to frequent visits
by these magnificent mammals.
// March 2017

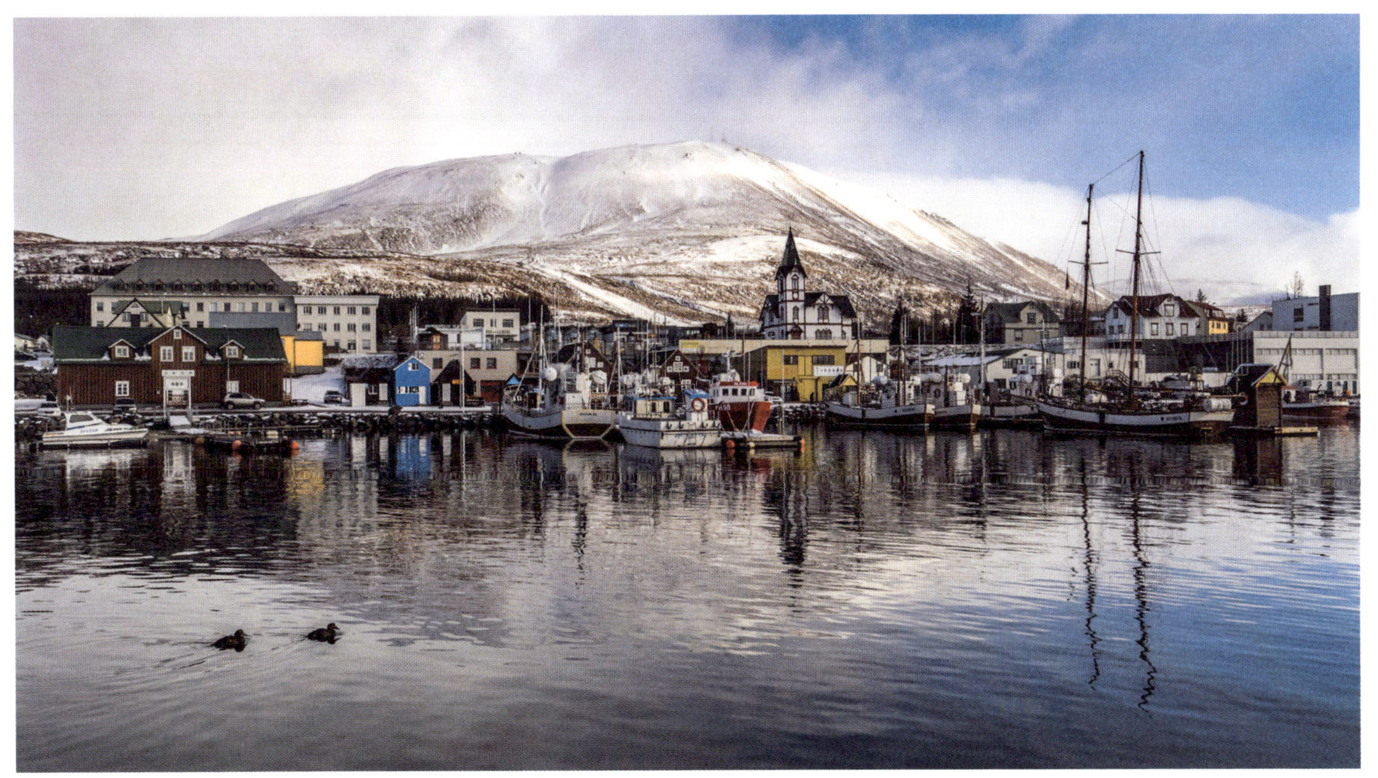

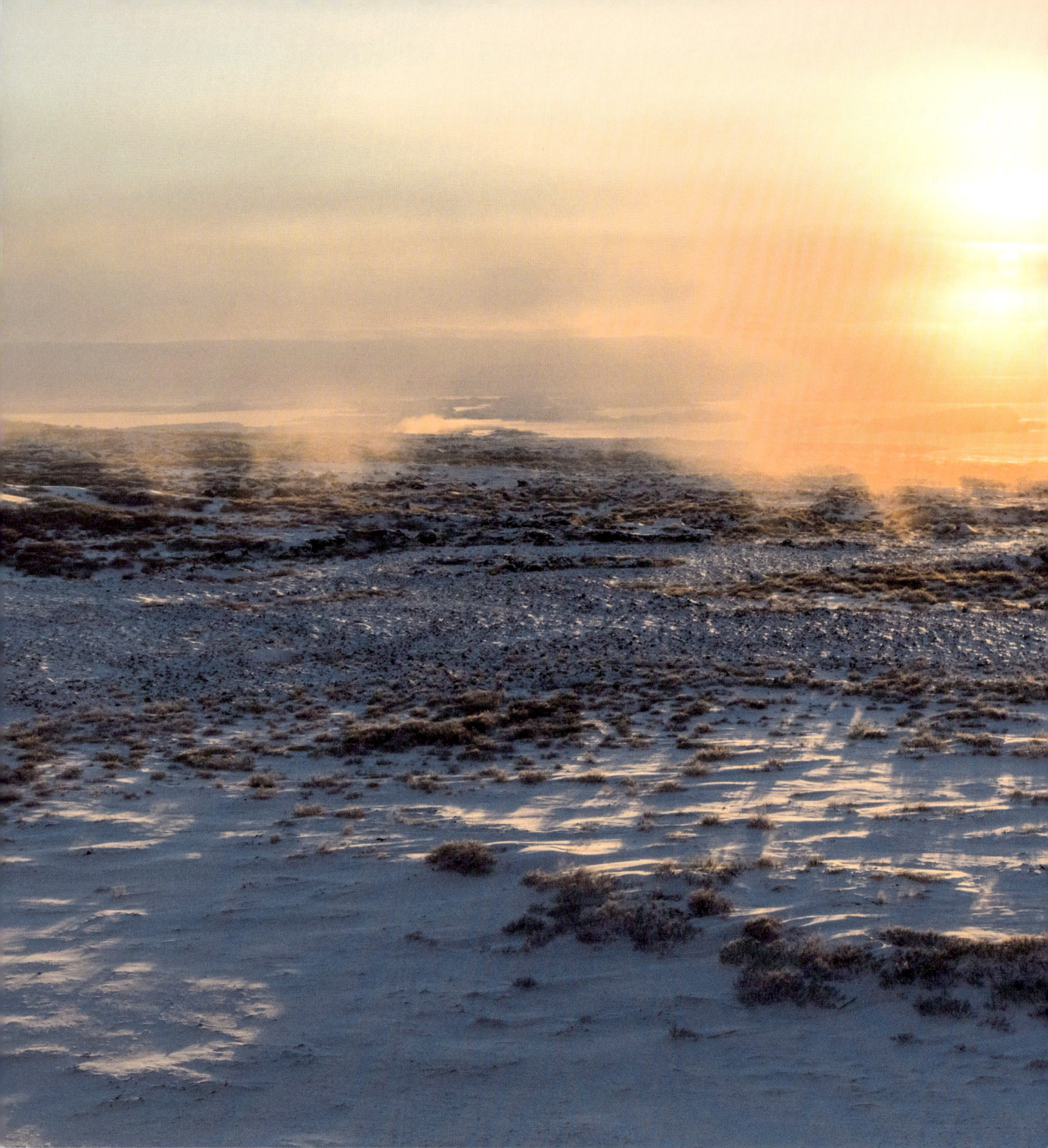

Hverfjall, Mývatn, Iceland
65°36'29.4"N 16°52'50.4"W
While standing on top of the explosion crater
Hverfjall, the sun starts hiding behind the fog,
covering Mývatn in a warm evening glow.
// March 2017

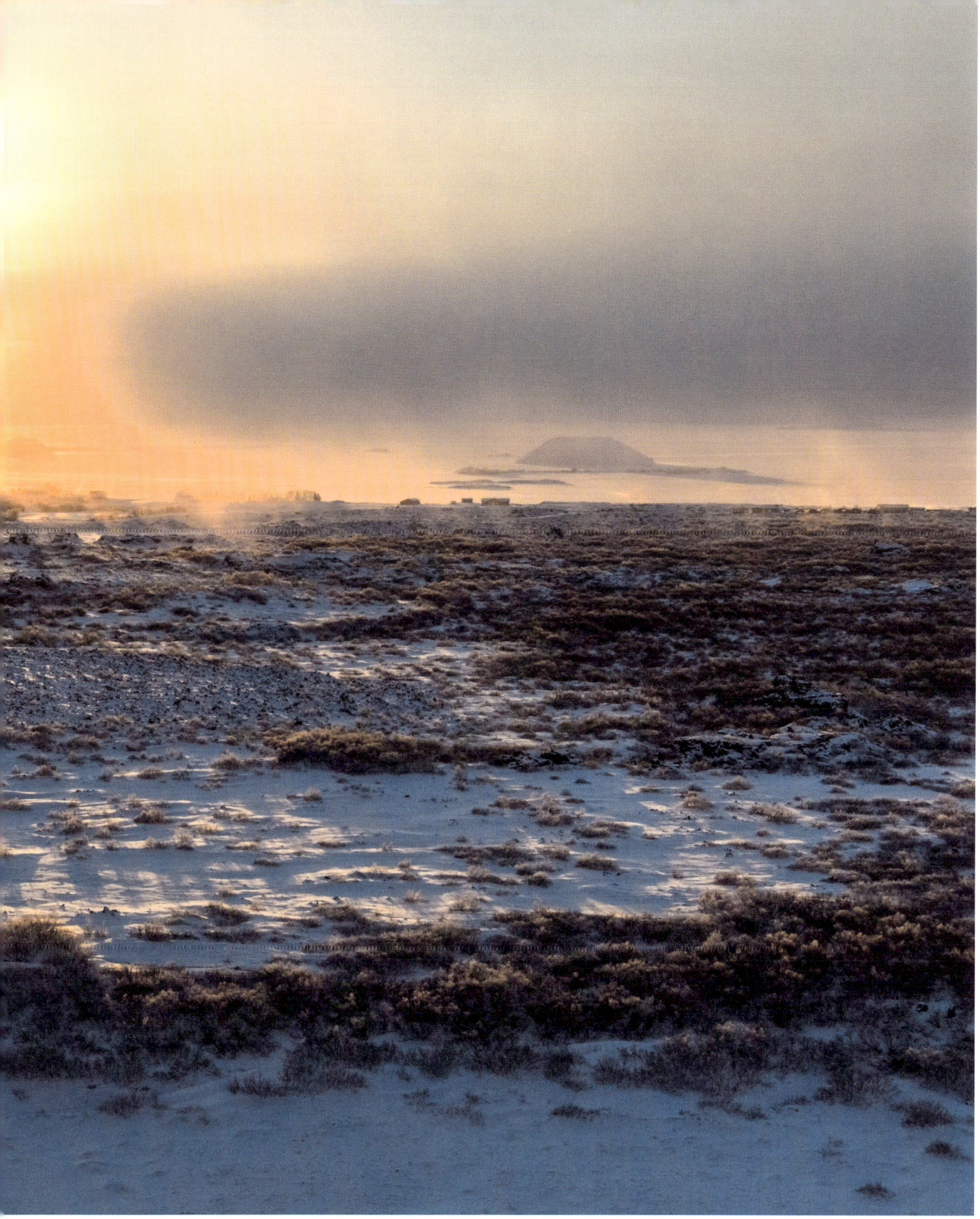

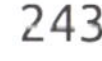

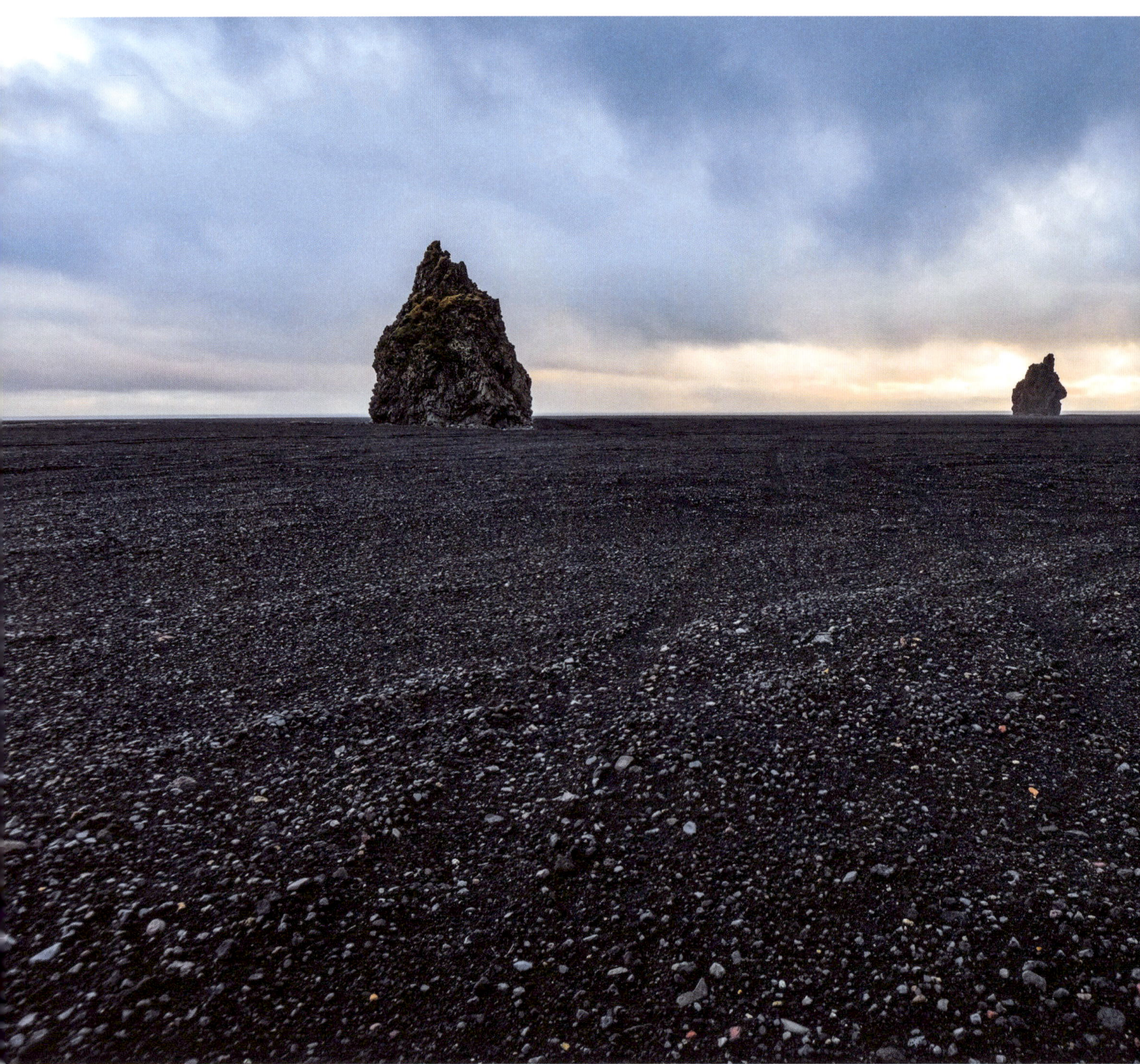

Mýrdalssandur, Iceland
63°24′48.4″N 18°44′36.5″W
Several volcanic eruptions of Iceland's Katla
volcano formed Mýrdalssandur, a large outwash
plain surrounding the inselberg Hjörleifshöfði.
A landscape where every sense of scale is lost.
// March 2017

Breiðamerkurjökull, Iceland
64°15′45.9″N 15°50′41.4″W
The location, shape, size and appearance of ice
caves on Iceland vary every year. Once discovered,
they are dream locations for photographers.
// March 2017

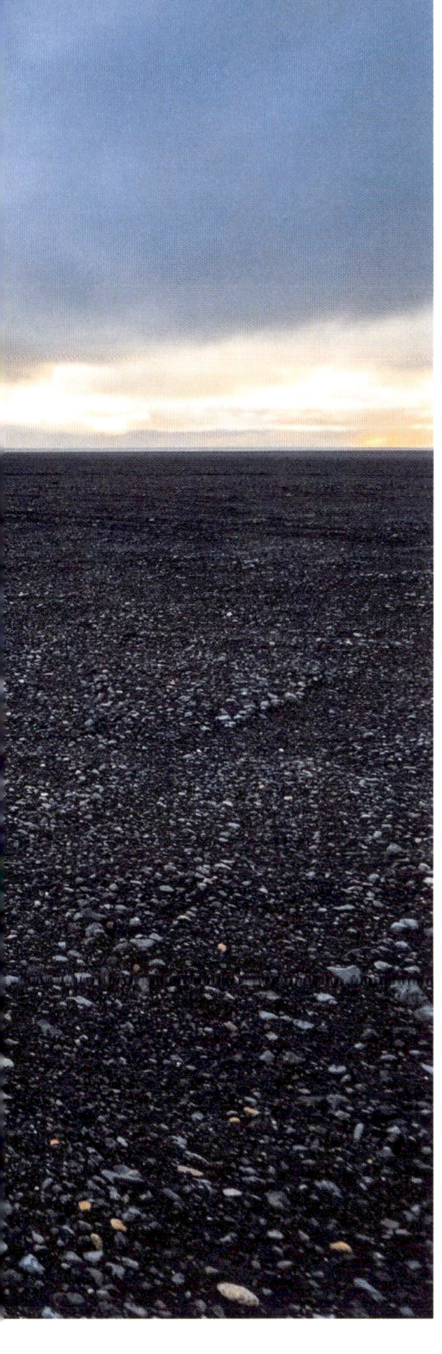

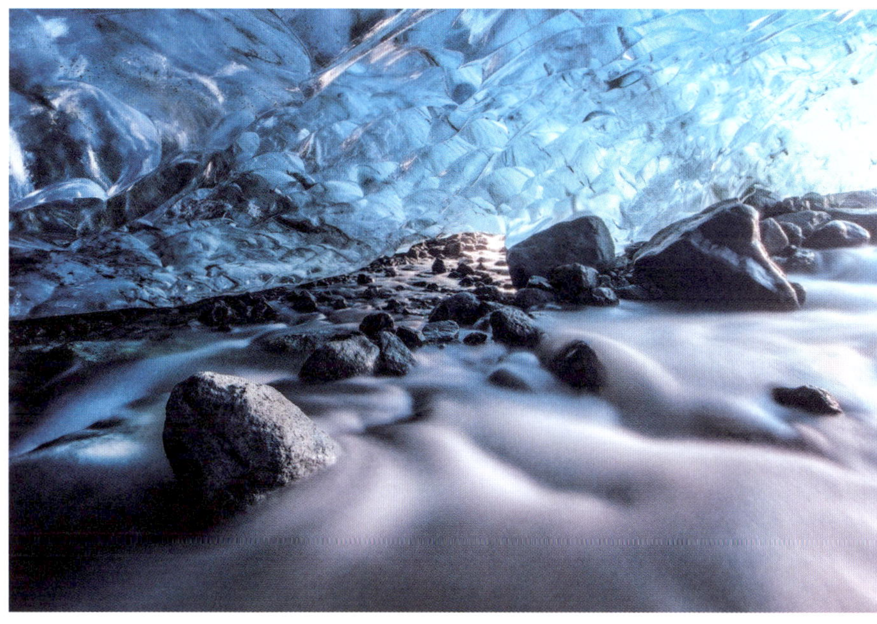

Wild Winterscapes
Route and travel suggestions

Scenic regions and nature reserves
1   Borgarfjörður
2   Dettifoss
3   Goðafoss
4   Hverfjall
5   Hverir
6   Krafla
7   Mýrdalssandur
8   Mývatn
9   Reynisfjara
10 Snæfellsnes

Cities and towns
11 Húsavík
12 Reykjavík

Cultural experiences
13 Hallgrimskirkja

Spectacular roads and scenic routes
14 Útnesvegur & Route 54, Snæfellsnes
15 Route 1 between Egilsstaðir and Reyðarfjörður

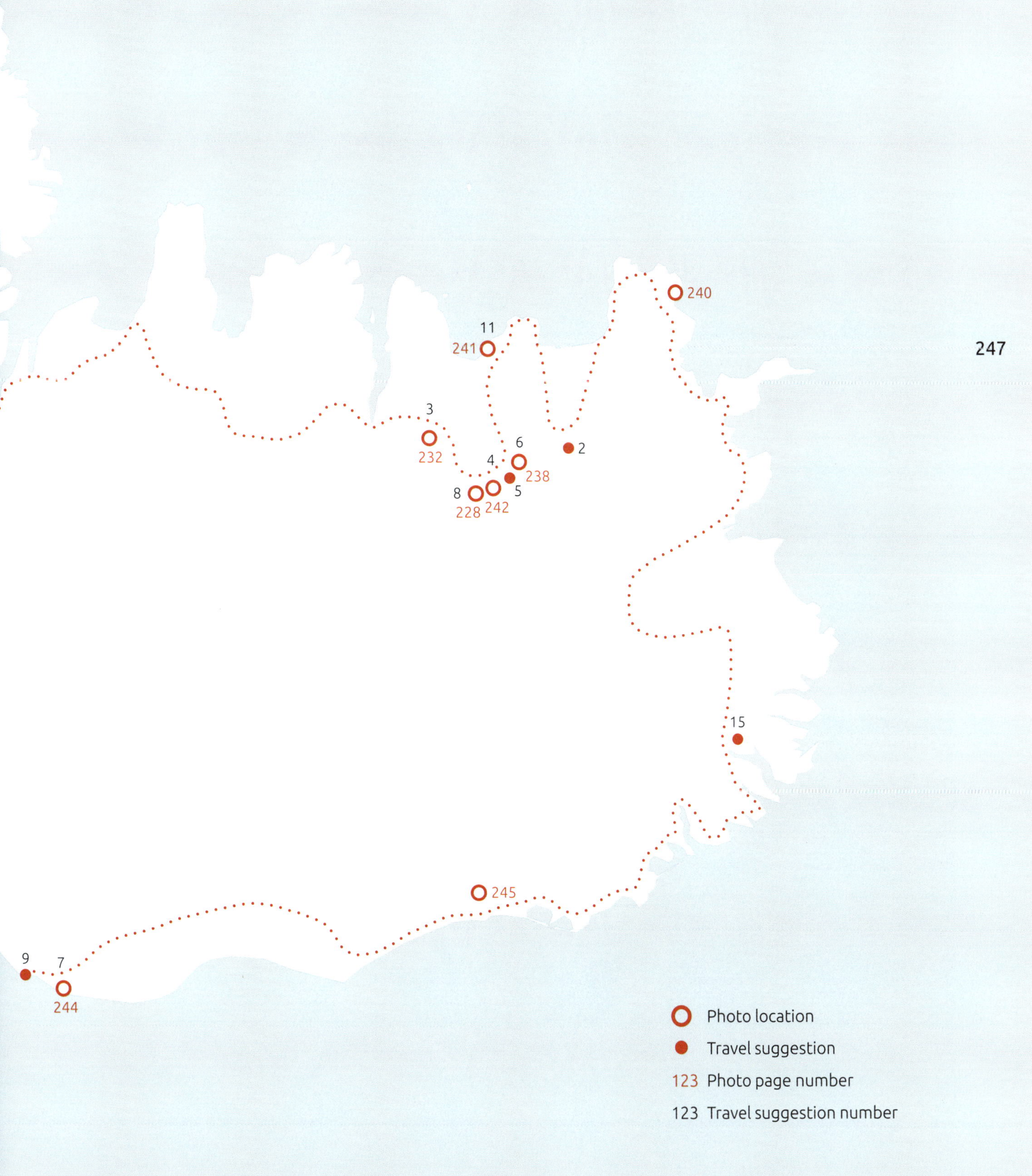

Photo location
Travel suggestion
123 Photo page number
123 Travel suggestion number

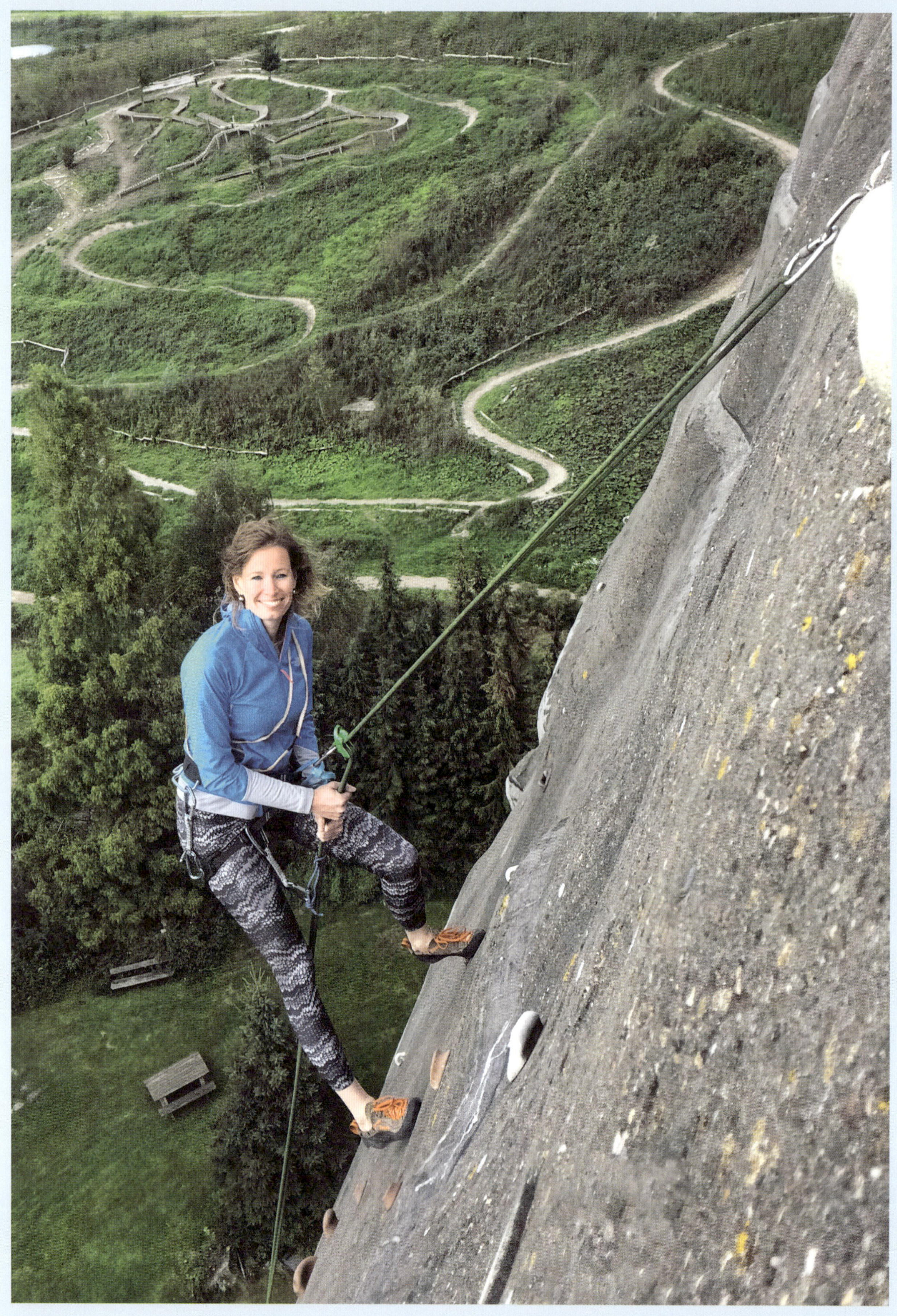

About

Sabine de Milliano

A DECADE AGO I would never have expected road trips to be so liberating, exhilarating and rewarding at the same time. This perception changed in May 2010 when I embarked on my first long road trip from the Netherlands to the North Cape. The stunning scenes and ultimate feeling of freedom while driving thousands of kilometres to the north fuelled my curiosity. It became an adventure, an ambition, a new way of exploration – both geographic and personal.

Many more travel adventures followed after this positive experience. First to the west, then to the south and later to the east. Trips grew increasingly ambitious over the years as the 'project' kept expanding towards the edges of our continent. In September 2014, while enjoying a beautiful sunset view on a remote gravel road somewhere in the heart of Belarus – a country full of positive surprises –

I reckoned all the other countries in Europe would also be worth exploring, photographing and sharing. And so it happened that a whole series of road trips and ultimately this book came to be, spanning over 100,000 kilometres throughout all the countries of Europe between 2010 and 2020.

Along the way, these road adventures led me to replace prejudice by open-minded interest. Fear of unknown places was conquered by a desire to push geographic boundaries and myself a little further, time and again. After all those experiences on the road I can now simply say that there is no place like the unknown.

Bergschenhoek, the Netherlands
51°58'38.0"N 4°32'09.9"E
Abseiling from the 35-metres tall 'Monte Cervino', my favourite Dutch climbing venue.
Photo by Ed van Aalst.
// September 2018

As a creative person with an engineering background, I love to combine art with technology. Photography provides that ideal combination.

I started photographing in 2005 and soon became a part-time event and commercial photographer during my studies at Delft University of Technology from 2006 to 2008. It was a perfect side job for me. Not only could I earn back the investment I made in my photographic equipment, it also offered me the opportunity to try out various photographic fields. From rocket launches to promotional shoots at the Faculty of Aerospace Engineering and from weddings to workshops, I was given the chance to do it all. These experiences have made me an all-round photographer, able to handle challenging lighting conditions and capture the unexpected on camera.

All images in this book have been made with Nikon DSLRs: first a D50 until 2011, then a D300s from 2011 to 2016, and finally a D500 from 2017 onwards. Although you need a good camera for photography, the right lenses, handling, composition and post-processing are even more important for the final image. Two technologies have contributed significantly to my style of imagery: High Dynamic Range (HDR) photography and wide-angle lenses.

In 2006, I first discovered HDR photography, a technique in which multiple exposures are blended together to capture the full spectrum of light in a scene. Through the years, I experimented a lot with HDR and have now developed my own style and image processing workflows to fully capture the beauty of the places I visit. Additionally, in 2009, I fell in love with the power of wide-angle lenses. Many of the photographs in this book are taken with Sigma lenses with a focal length range of 8-20 mm. They offer a wider perspective than we can see with the human eye and make it possible to create dramatic landscape panoramas in just one single frame.

It is my passion for photography that keeps me going when things get rough or uncomfortable. When I see the potential of an awe-inspiring landscape, I do not mind waiting a while in the pouring rain or freezing cold for the right conditions to show up. Sometimes I do silly things when I am in a hurry to capture a scene in the right light. For example, I once tripped while jumping over a sheep fence trying to chase the last rays of sun on the Fanad Head lighthouse. It must have been such a ridiculous spectacle – me going headfirst into the mud while trying (and managing) to save my camera equipment at the same time! Well, 'no pain, no gain', they say.

'After all those experiences on the road
I can now simply say that there is no place
like the unknown.'

When in cities, the best time to take pictures is usually when people are eating, drinking, shopping or relaxing after work. The light is at its best then, so that is when I go out to photograph a city. Usually I only have 2-3 hours to visit locations and take the pictures I have in mind. During this short window of opportunity, from roughly two hours before to one hour after sunset, I watch the city slowly transform into a play of light. People and cars rush by while I guard my tripod and camera, waiting for the shutter to close after a long exposure. It is a perfect opportunity to watch local people and sense the smell, sight and sound of the places I visit.

The 'blue hour' is even shorter: it is the twilight zone after sunset when the last rays of daylight paint the sky in different shades of blue, purple and orange. It is not yet fully dark, but the local lights are already turned on. This is my favourite time of day to photograph. Not only do I love the colours and interesting contrasts, but twilight also enables me to use long exposure times (typically from a few seconds up to a minute).

Long exposures tend to blend any moving matter into the surrounding environment. Market squares reveal their full shapes and colours as crowds largely disappear in the images. Chaotic flows of traffic turn into orderly rays of light. Rough rivers transform into smooth blankets of water. Photography can turn even the most hectic of scenes into a serene oasis of peace and quiet.

Nowadays, my photographic efforts are focused on travelling, landscapes and a little bit of urban exploration ('urbex'). Packed lightly with an 8-16 mm lens mounted on my D500, a tripod, a lens cleaning wipe and my laptop, I have everything I need to capture Europe's surprising scenery.

Photography is currently not my main occupation. These days I photograph exclusively during road trip adventures, day trips to cities and nature reserves, rock climbing activities and business trips. And yet, photography is indirectly a key factor in my working life as well. As an entrepreneur in the geographic data and satellite applications business, I enjoy beautiful images of the Earth taken from space every day.

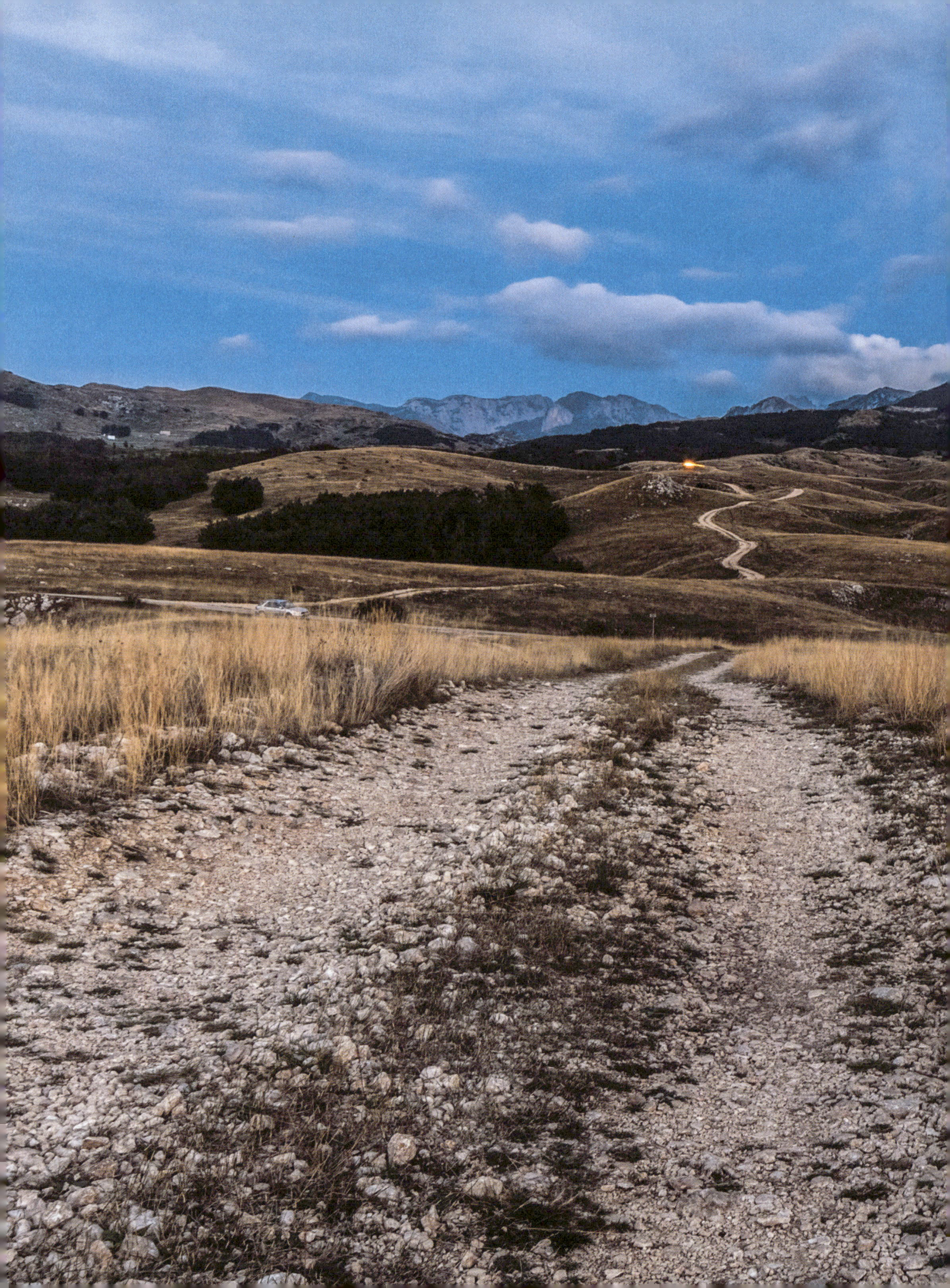

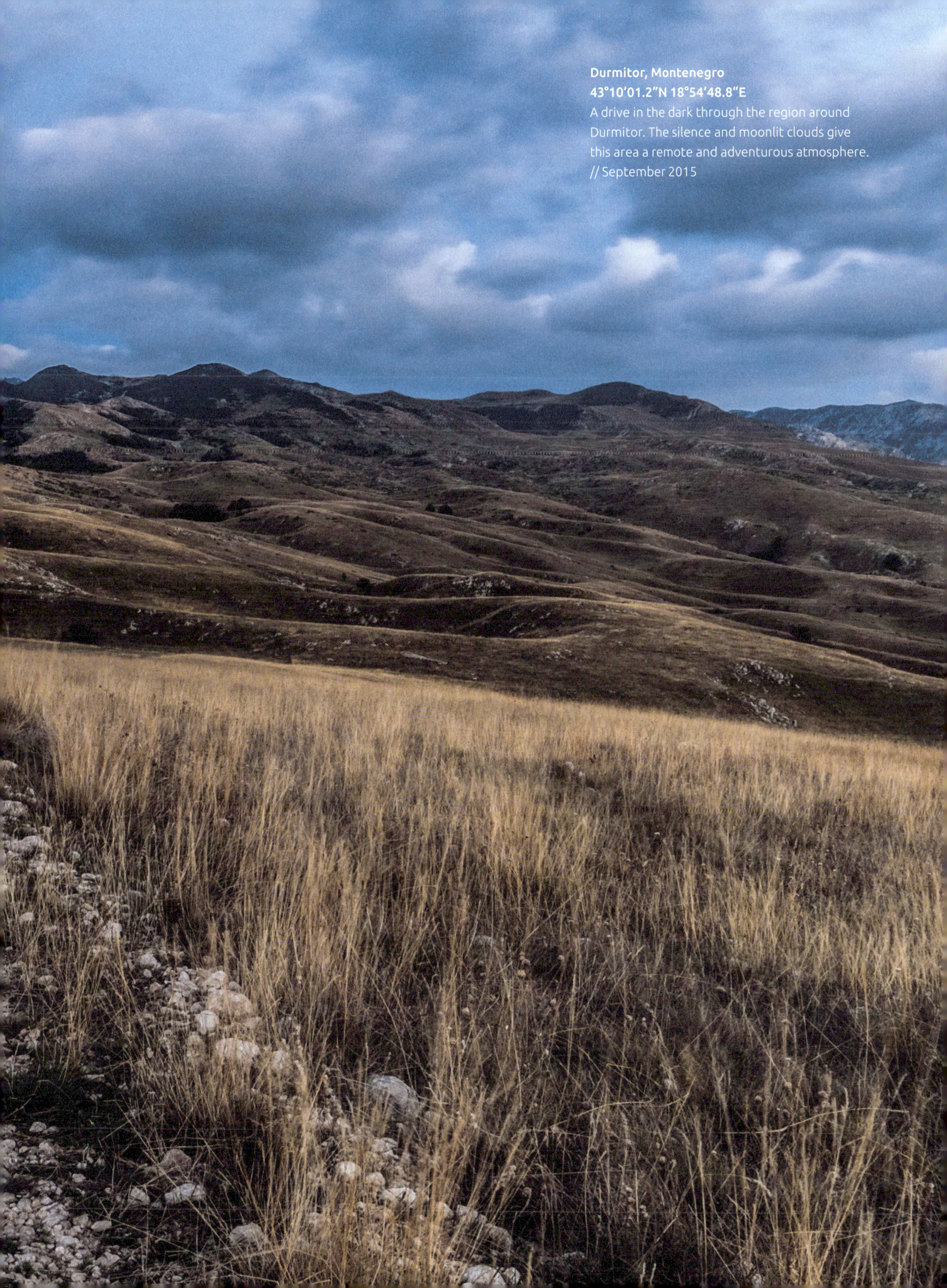

Durmitor, Montenegro
43°10'01.2"N 18°54'48.8"E
A drive in the dark through the region around
Durmitor. The silence and moonlit clouds give
this area a remote and adventurous atmosphere.
// September 2015

Acknowledgements

254

THIS BOOK WOULD NOT have been created without the unconditional love and support of Martijn, whose charming surname I use since a couple of years. Martijn, you have been the best travel companion imaginable. The challenging adventures we undertook together would have been very tricky if not impossible to complete on my own. I continue to admire your endless energy, practical mindset and impressive language skills – your knowledge of Russian has saved us a number of times and made many border crossings surprisingly smooth. I hope to enjoy many more adventures with you in the future.

Thank you Kees and Nel for inspiring me to go on that first epic road trip adventure to the North Cape. You allowed me to fully explore the world on my own from a very young age. From climbing the tall horse-chestnut trees back home to my first teen-age solo adventures abroad, those early days of exploration laid the foundation for my way of travelling and taught me that hard work and perseverance pay off.

Sass Queder, Switzerland
46°24'38.7"N 9°58'21.6"E
Enjoying the winter panorama on the summit of the Sass Queder at 3065 metres altitude.
Photo by Martijn de Milliano.
// February 2013

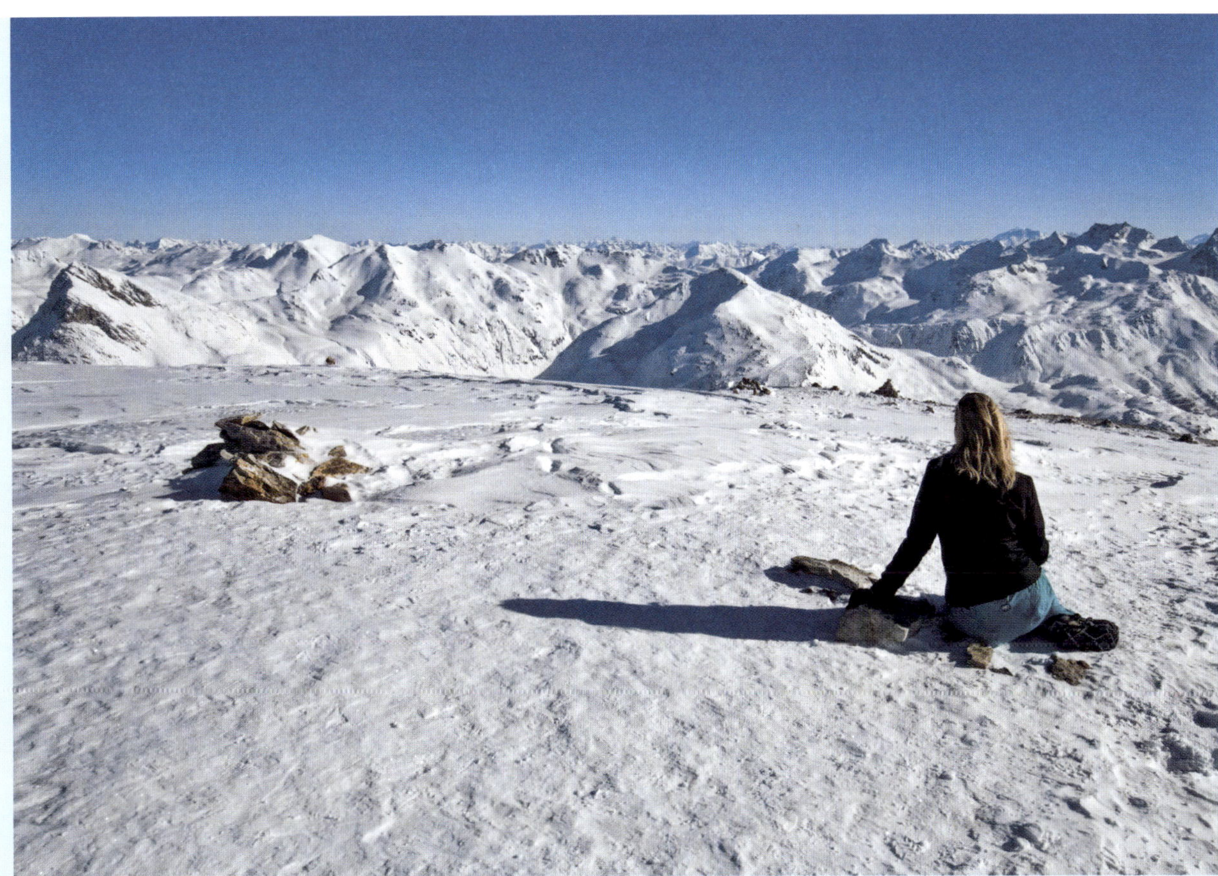

During my travels through Europe I encountered many challenging road conditions. From icy mountain roads to desert sands and from large potholes to muddy forest tracks, our faithful old Subaru Impreza conquered them all. Thanks Wim, Martien and Willem from former Auto Wiegel for your reliable maintenance work and proactive support before and during our road adventures – and for selling us this car in the first place. Although you even trained us in the basics of car mechanics so we could survive a breakdown in the middle of nowhere, we never had any major issues along the way and the odometer is now approaching half a million kilometres.

My thanks also go to friends and colleagues who have been close to me during the final years of this creative journey. Most of you have listened patiently to hours of 'book talk' and provided valuable feedback on the concept and the early pages of this book. In alphabetical order, thanks Douwe, Ed, Koen, Martin, Sven and Thijs for your support and friendship. You have all contributed in your own way. Long walks and talks outdoors, sharing great wines and good food, climbing rocks together, building businesses together. And every one of you has given me moral support when things got difficult. Your friendship means very much to me and I hope we will share many more memorable moments in the future.

Credits

© 2020
Uitgeverij Terra is part of Uitgeverij TerraLannoo bv
P.O. Box 23202
1100 DS Amsterdam // The Netherlands
info@terralannoo.nl
www.terra-publishing.com

terrapublishing
terrapublishing

Text & photography Sabine de Milliano // www.knalblauw.nl
Graphic design cover & inside Susan de Loor // www.kantoordeloor.nl
Proofreading Nick Gale // www.galecommunication.com & Hans Hoekman

First print // 2020

ISBN 978 90 8989 822 7
NUR 512 // 653

Photo cover
Jikurebi Lake, Georgia
41°32′46.1″N 45°21′51.6″E
Autumn light highlights the warm
colours of the remote fields and salt
lakes around Udabno.
// September 2015

Photo page 6
Lviv, Ukraine
49°50′19.1″N 24°01′56.1″E
Enjoying a traditional Lviv-style coffee
in Fixage Café Museum.
Photo by Martijn de Milliano.
// September 2014

Map projection
ETRS89-extended // LCC Europe
(EPSG:3034)

Explore more of Europe on
www.surprisingeurope.nl

*Discover many more
surprising scenes and
destinations in Europe
with this interactive map*

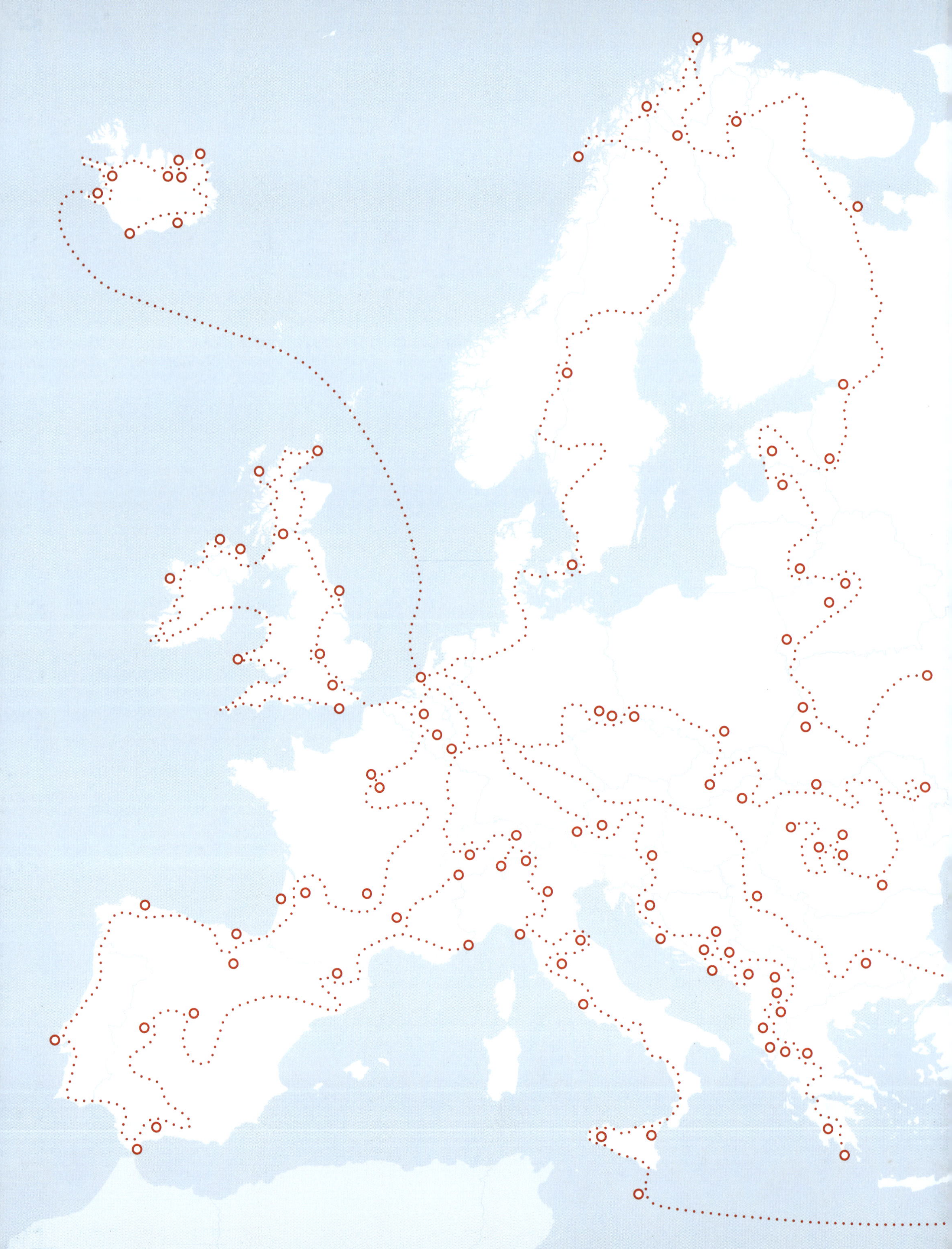